IMPROVING
INTERGROUP
RELATIONS

■

*We dedicate this book to the courageous
and creative pioneers who developed these
intergroup relations programs.*

IMPROVING INTERGROUP RELATIONS

■

WALTER G. STEPHAN
New Mexico State University

COOKIE WHITE STEPHAN
New Mexico State University

Sage Publications
International Educational and Professional Publisher
Thousand Oaks ■ London ■ New Delhi

For information:

Sage Publications, Inc.
2455 Teller Road
Thousand Oaks, California 91320
E-mail: order@sagepub.com

Sage Publications Ltd.
6 Bonhill Street
London EC2A 4PU
United Kingdom

Sage Publications India Pvt. Ltd.
M-32 Market
Greater Kailash I
New Delhi 110 048 India

Printed in the United States of America

Library of Congress Cataloging-in-Publication Data

Stephan, Walter G.
    Improving intergroup relations / by Walter G. Stephan & Cookie White Stephan.
        p.   cm.
    Includes bibliographical references and index.
    ISBN 0-7619-1023-4 (p)
    1. Group relations training. 2. Intergroup relations. 3. Group relations
training—United States. 4. Intergroup relations—United States. I. Stephan, Cookie
White. II. Title.
    HM1086 .S74 2001
    302'.14—dc21   2001000041

01   02   03   04   05   06   07   7   6   5   4   3   2   1

Acquiring Editor:	Jim Brace-Thompson
Editorial Assistant:	Karen Ehrmann
Production Editor:	Denise Santoyo
Editorial Assistant:	Kathryn Journey
Typesetter/Designer:	Tina Hill/Denyse Dunn
Indexer:	Teri Greenberg
Cover Designer:	Jane Quaney

CONTENTS

Preface   xiii

1. A Brief History of Intergroup Relations   1

Goals and Content of This Book   1

Historical Overview
of Intergroup Relations in the United States   3

What Lies Ahead   13

Conceptualizing Intergroup
Relations Training Programs   16

Summary   17

2. Intergroup Relations Theories and Concepts   19

Contact   20

A Revised Contact Theory   20
Using Contact to Improve Intergroup Relations   22
    Societal Factors   22
    Situational Factors   23
    Person Factors   24

Prejudice   25

Prejudice Defined   25
Old-Fashioned and Modern Prejudice   25
Modern Theories of Prejudice   26

Ambivalence-Amplification   26
Aversive Racism   27
Symbolic Racism   27
Compunction   27
Other Theories of Prejudice   27
Realistic Group Conflict   28
Integrated Threat   28
Social Dominance   28
Social Identity   28
Prejudice Reduction Processes   29
Making Value-Behavior Discrepancies Explicit   30
Reducing Threat   30
Increasing Perceptions of Similarity Among Groups   30
Creating Superordinate Groups   31
Decategorization by Emphasizing Multiple Identities   31
Reinforcing and Modeling Positive Behaviors   32
Modifying Associations Between Cognitions and Affect   32
Using Dissonance to Create Attitude Change   33
Creating Empathy   33
Correcting Misattributions   34

Stereotypes   35

Stereotypes Defined   35
Origins of Stereotypes   36
Stereotype Activation and Maintenance   37
Stereotyping Reduction Processes   38
Creating Superordinate Groups and Emphasizing
    Multiple Identities   38
Counteracting Expectancies   39
Using Self-Regulation   39
Correcting Misattributions   39
Differentiating the Outgroup   40

Discriminatory Behavior   40

The Theory of Reasoned Action   40
Changing Discriminatory Behavior   41
Modifying Attitudes About Outcomes and
    Altering Perceptions of Subjective Norms   41

Dimensions on Which These Psychological
Processes Differ 42

Summary 44

3. Multicultural Education Introduction 47

Goals of Multicultural Education 48

The Controversy Surrounding Multicultural Education 49

The Content and Techniques
of Multicultural Education 51

Studies of the Effects of Multicultural Education
Programs 55

Longer Programs 55
Short-Term Studies 59
Overall Evaluation of Research on Multicultural Education 61

Psychological Processes
Underlying Multicultural Education 63

Processes Employed in Segregated Settings 64
Processes Employed in Integrated Settings 66

Problems and Recommendations 68

Summary 73

4. Diversity Initiatives in the Workplace 75

Diversity Initiatives 77

Managing Diversity 78
Valuing Diversity 80
Diversity Training Programs 80
Types of Diversity Training Programs 82

Research on the Effectiveness of
Diversity Training Programs 85

Psychological Processes
Underlying Diversity Initiatives 90

Processes Related to Managing Diversity 90
Processes Related to Valuing Diversity 91
Diversity Training Programs 92

Problems and Recommendations 93

Resistance to Diversity Initiatives 93
Planning Diversity Initiatives 95
Training Issues 97
Evaluating Diversity Training Programs 99

Summary 100

5. Intergroup Dialogues **103**

Types of Intergroup Dialogues 104

Intergroup Dialogues in Educational Settings 104
Intergroup Dialogues in Community Settings 108
Problem-Solving Workshops 109

Research on the Effectiveness of Dialogue Groups 114

Psychological Processes Underlying Dialogue Groups 117

Problems and Recommendations 121

Summary 127

6. Intercultural Training Programs **129**

Designing Intercultural Training 133

What Are the Components of Intercultural Effectiveness? 133
Should Theory Guide Intercultural Training? 134
    Culture Theory 134
    Intergroup Anxiety 135

Intercultural Training Techniques 137

Lectures and Discussions 137
Language Training 139
The Cultural Sensitizer 140
Critical Incidents 143

Experiential Techniques   144
   Simulation Games   145
   Role-playing   146
   Cultural Simulations and In-Country Training
      Programs   147
   Other Experiential Techniques   148

Summary of Research Findings
on Intercultural Training Techniques   149

Psychological Processes
Underlying Intercultural Training   150

Problems and Recommendations   152

Summary   154

7. Cooperative Learning Groups   **155**

Major Cooperative Learning Programs   157

   The Slavin Techniques   158
   The Johnsons' Learning Together Technique   160
   The Jigsaw Classroom   162
   Group Investigation   163
   Complex Instruction   165

Summary of Research Findings for
Cooperative Learning Techniques   169

   Intergroup Relations Measures   169
   Personality and Social Skills Measures   170
   Intergroup Relations Findings: A Summary   170
   Achievement Measures   171
   A Focus on Racial and Ethnic Minorities   173

Psychological Processes
Underlying Cooperative Learning   174

Problems and Recommendations   177

Summary   178

8. Conflict Resolution Programs   181

Types of Conflict Resolution Programs   183

Community-Based Conflict Resolution Programs   *183*
   Mediation   183
   Third-Party Consultation   185
   The Town Meeting   186
   Conflict Containment   187
Conflict Resolution Programs in Organizational Settings   *187*
   Mediation   188
   Positive Bargaining Models   189
   Third-Party Consultation   190
School-Based Conflict Resolution Programs   *191*

Summary of Research Findings
on Conflict Resolution Programs   194

Research in Community and Organizational Settings   *195*
   Research on Mediation   195
   Research on Negotiation   195
   Research on Other Conflict Resolution Techniques
      in Community and Organizational Settings   196
School-Based Peer Mediation Programs   *197*

Psychological Processes
Underlying Conflict Resolution   199

Problems and Recommendations   201

Interethnic Conflict Resolution: Special Concerns   203

Summary   206

9. Moral and Values Education Programs   209

Major Approaches to Moral and Values Education   211

Caring Models of Antiprejudice   *212*
Facing History and Ourselves   *215*
Kohlberg's Just Community Concept   *217*
The Berkeley Model   *219*
Moral Discourse   *220*

Personality Development Programs   222
Interpersonal Sensitivity and Respect Programs   223
Values Clarification and Education Programs   224
Norm Transmission and Character Education Programs   226

Summary of Research Findings
on Moral and Values Education   228

Psychological Processes
Underlying Moral and Values Education   230

Problems and Recommendations   232

Summary   234

10. Evaluating Intergroup Relations Programs   **237**

Qualitative Techniques   238

Postprogram Surveys   239
Nonsystematic Observation   240
Focus Groups   242
Systematic Observation   243
Content Analyses   245

Quantitative Techniques   245

Pretest and Posttest   246
Posttest Only With Control Group   248
Pretest and Posttest With Control Group   250
Mediational Analyses   252
Statistical Analyses   253

Creating Measures   254

Unobtrusive Measures   258

Comparative Studies   259

Publication   259

Summary   260

11. Conclusions — 263

Programs to Improve Intergroup Relations — 263

Multicultural Education Programs — 264
Diversity Training Programs — 264
Intergroup Dialogues — 265
Intercultural Training Programs — 266
Cooperative Learning Groups — 266
Conflict Resolution Training — 267
Moral Education Programs — 267

Intergroup Relations Programs:
Assessment and Critique — 268

Psychological Processes
Underlying Intergroup Relations Programs — 271

Psychological Processes in Interactive Programs — 271
Psychological Processes in Didactic Programs — 275

Recommendations for Intergroup Relations Programs — 276

In the Beginning — 276
Program Contents — 277
Conducting Effective Programs — 278
Issues for Trainers — 279

Basic Design Issues — 280

Conclusion — 283

Resource Literature — 287

References — 291

Author Index — 321

Subject Index — 333

About the Authors — 345

PREFACE

A S WE BEGIN A NEW millennium, humankind is still plagued by intergroup conflict, racism, prejudice, stereotyping, and discrimination. To a greater or lesser extent, relations between groups are troubled in all societies. This book is the culmination of our years of interest in intergroup relations. When we wrote our last book, *Intergroup Relations* (Stephan & Stephan, 1996), we were able to report on only a relatively small number of programs that had been devised to improve intergroup relations. More programs existed at that time, but we were unaware of them. It was difficult to learn about them because few reports had been published on them, and they originated in a diverse range of disciplines including psychology, education, sociology, political science, and anthropology. Since that time, there has been an explosion of such programs and more published sources are available.

We can only estimate the number of intergroup relations programs that are currently being conducted, but it would probably be conservative to say that thousands of them are conducted every year in the United States and other countries. The questions we address in this book are, What approaches are being used to improve intergroup relations? and What do we know about their effectiveness? We have categorized these programs into specific types for purposes of exposition, but most of the programs we have examined are rather eclectic, drawing upon a wide range of specific techniques. Some of these techniques have been well researched, but most have not. The study of intergroup relations programs is still in its infancy. We hope that this book can help move the study of these programs forward so that eventually we will know what works and why.

We would like to add a note on nomenclature. We are well aware of the controversy surrounding the use of words such as Black and White because they can be taken to mean that the concept of race has some biological basis, which it does not. We do not endorse the racial connotations of these words, but we do recognize that race is a social construct of great importance in American society. Accordingly, we have chosen to employ these words despite this controversy, because they are the labels that Americans most commonly use to refer to these groups.

We have had help from a number of people, whom we would like to acknowledge. Our editor, Jim Brace-Thompson, has been supportive, encouraging, and insightful. The reviewers, including Jack Dovidio and Tom Pettigrew, provided us with invaluable reflections on our first draft of the book. And we thank our graduate students for their contributions to our own research, which we report in this book.

A BRIEF HISTORY OF INTERGROUP RELATIONS

1

IN THE SPRING OF 1991, a Black motorist named Rodney King was stopped by the Los Angeles police after a high-speed chase (Caproni & Finley, 1997). The officers later testified that King resisted their commands. Their response was to beat him with their nightsticks and kick him repeatedly. His face was fractured in 15 places and one of his legs was broken. The beating was videotaped by a bystander and resulted in two trials for four of the officers. In the first trial, an all-White jury acquitted the four officers, all of whom were White. Two of the officers were later convicted of violating King's civil rights in the second trial. When the verdict in the first trial was announced, it set off a riot in the Black neighborhoods of South Central Los Angeles. Forty deaths occurred, and 2,000 people were injured. A billion dollars in property was destroyed. In an interview after the riot, King asked, "Why can't we all just get along?"

Goals and Content of This Book

We believe that in an increasingly complex social world, people **must** learn to get along. This obvious and clear statement hides a mountain of complications. The history of relations between groups teaches us that people from different social groups have great difficulty getting along. Peaceful, productive relations involving mutual respect between groups do not come naturally; they require assistance. The recognition of this basic fact has led to the creation of a wide range of programs to improve intergroup relations among racial, ethnic, religious, cultural, and other types of groups.

This book analyzes these programs. We will describe each of the programs, evaluate the research that has been done on them, try to understand what makes them effective, and make recommendations for their improvement. We will also offer advice on how to evaluate intergroup relations programs.

This book was written for people who conduct intergroup relations programs in schools, businesses, communities, and with leaders of nations in an attempt to improve intergroup relations locally, nationally, or internationally. It was also designed for students of intergroup relations and those who teach them. In addition, it was intended to serve as a resource for anyone interested in techniques for improving intergroup relations, including researchers, academics, and policy makers.

Intergroup relations consist of attitudes and behaviors directed toward outgroup members. Outgroups are all the groups to which we do not belong. In this book, our primary focus is on racial, ethnic, religious, and cultural groups. However, it should be noted that the causes of negative attitudes based on race, ethnicity, religion, and culture are very similar to the causes of prejudice based on other social identities, such as social class, sex, disability status, and sexual orientation.

Prejudice and discrimination exist in individuals and societies. In this book, we focus on programs to address personal or individual-level prejudice and discrimination. By doing so, we do not mean to imply that societal-level or structural-level prejudice is unimportant. The racial prejudice and other types of bias that pervade societies and the institutions within them are powerful forces, in part because they are often unnoticed and unchallenged. Racial and other forms of inequality form a backdrop for the history of most societies. Initial inequalities become institutionalized, as powerful social groups attempt to maintain their power by defining the prevailing stratification system as just, right, and proper, in fact, as natural. Since all members of society are, to some degree, socialized to accept the norms of their society, these systems of inequality tend to be perpetuated. The entrenched nature of systems of inequality and the vested interests of powerful groups in their continuation make them extremely resistant to change.

For this reason, the most widely used intergroup relations training programs existing today have concentrated primarily on individuals, not social systems. They are specifically designed to change individuals' attitudes and behaviors. Most programs place less emphasis on directly challenging societal institutions that maintain group differences in wealth, power, and prestige. However, an underlying premise of these programs is that by changing the attitudes and behaviors of individuals, they will cause the institutions that control society to be transformed eventually because the individuals who work in them will themselves have been changed. In this book, we will be writing about the most common and intensively researched programs being conducted today.

In this first chapter, we discuss the origins of intergroup relations programs and preview the contents of the book. To appreciate the social context from which programs designed to improve intergroup relations emerged, we start with a brief historical overview of intergroup relations in the United States during the post–World War II era. We concentrate primarily on relations between Blacks and Whites because the history of prejudice and discrimination against Blacks and the ongoing difficulties in relations between these two groups led to the emergence of most of the intergroup relations programs examined in this book. The programs themselves have broader applications and have been used with a wide range of social groups.

Historical Overview of Intergroup Relations in the United States

The decade after the end of World War II was a period of great ferment in the social sciences in the United States. During this time, the foundations were laid for the theory and practice of programs to improve intergroup relations. The lead role was played by social scientists. One group of social scientists created what has come to be known as the *contact hypothesis,* which stipulated the conditions under which inter-group contact was believed to improve relations between groups (G. W. Allport, 1954; Harding, Kutner, Proshansky, & Chein, 1954; Watson, 1947; R. M. Williams Jr., 1947). The contact theorists believed that simply bringing groups into contact would not improve inter-group relations. Instead, they thought that in order to improve inter-group relations, contact among members of different groups should be cooperative, involve equal status and common goals, and take place with the support of relevant authority figures (Pettigrew, 1971).

Just after the war, one of the most famous of all studies of the ori-gins of prejudice was published. Titled *The Authoritarian Personality,* it delved into the flawed personalities of anti-Semitic and other highly prejudiced people (Adorno, Frenkel-Brunswik, Levinson, & Sandford, 1950). It held that people who follow the dictates of established author-ity and are rigid, hostile, conforming, and dependent are the most likely to be prejudiced. In 1954, Gordon Allport published *The Nature of Prejudice,* another landmark study of prejudice and its causes. Echoing the authors of *The Authoritarian Personality,* Allport, too, thought that the cognitive processing of prejudiced people differed from that of nonprejudiced people. He believed that prejudiced people think in terms of dichotomies (us versus them), make overgeneralizations about other groups (i.e., hold stereotypes), are intolerant of ambiguity, use differences as an excuse for rejecting others, and blame outgroups for their own problems. However, he also recognized that all people stereotype other groups to some extent and that conformity to the norms of a prejudiced society can sustain prejudice. Adorno and col-leagues (1950) and G. W. Allport (1954) were concerned with trying to understand openly expressed, blatant prejudice. In Chapter 2 we will show that as prejudice changed over time, the theories used to explain it also changed.

During the fifties, social scientists also played an important part in the *Brown v. Board of Education of Topeka* (1954) decision on school segre-gation. This decision played a crucial role in the origins of the civil rights movement. One of these social scientists was Kenneth Clark, a Black psychologist who had done research on the racial identification of Black children. In his testimony in one of the trials that led to the *Brown* (1954) decision, he stated,

> I have reached the conclusion from the examination of my own results
> and from an examination of the entire field that discrimination, preju-
> dice, and segregation have definitely negative effects on the personal-
> ity development of the Negro child. The essence of this detrimental
> effect is a confusion in the child's concept of his own self-esteem—
> basic feelings of inferiority, conflict, confusion in his self-image, resent-
> ment, hostility toward himself, and hostility toward Whites. (Kluger,
> 1976, p. 353)

In Clark's view, segregation led to low self-esteem among Black students, and it also caused prejudice. Although the studies on which
Clark's testimony were based have been criticized subsequently on
methodological grounds (Cross, 1991), they were of great historical importance. Social scientists also contributed an *amicus curiae* (friend of
the court) brief in the *Brown* (1954) case. This brief contained a version of
the contact hypothesis.

> Under certain circumstances desegregation . . . has been observed to
> lead to the emergence of more favorable attitudes and friendlier rela-
> tions between the races . . . There is less likelihood of unfriendly rela-
> tions when change is simultaneously introduced into all units of a
> social institution. . . . The available evidence also suggests the impor-
> tance of consistent and firm enforcement of the new policy by those in
> authority. It indicates also the importance of such factors as: the
> absence of competition . . . the possibility of contacts that permit indi-
> viduals to learn about one another as individuals, and the possibility
> of equivalence of positions and functions among all the participants.
> (F. H. Allport et al., 1953)

The impact of the testimony given by the social scientists in the *Brown*
(1954) trial can be seen in the words used by the court in its decision. It
read, in part,

> Does segregation of children in public schools solely on the basis of
> race, even though the physical facilities and other "tangible" factors
> may be equal, deprive children of the minority group of equal educa-
> tional opportunities? We believe that it does . . . to separate Negro

school children from others of similar age and qualifications, solely because of their race generates a feeling of inferiority as to their status in the community that may affect their hearts and minds in a way unlikely ever to be undone. . . . We conclude that in the field of public education the doctrine "separate but equal" has no place. Separate educational facilities are inherently unequal. (*Brown v. Board of Education*, 1954)

The *Brown* decision made school segregation illegal, but years passed before the decision began to be implemented.

During the first decade after the war, other events also occurred in American society that would shape intergroup relations in the upcoming years. In 1948, President Truman ordered the armed forces to be integrated. In 1950, Jackie Robinson became the first Black man to play in major league sports in the United States. These two events symbolized the movement of Blacks into jobs previously forbidden to them.

In 1955, Rosa Parks, a Black woman, boarded a city bus in Montgomery, Alabama, and took a seat in the fifth row alongside three other Blacks (J. Williams, 1987). The bus driver, James Blake, a White man, took notice of the Blacks in the fifth row and, as the bus filled, he asked them to move so a White man could sit down. He made this request because, by law, Blacks had to move to the back of the bus if it began to fill with Whites. The four Blacks did not move, and he said to them, "Y'all better make it light on yourself and let me have those seats." Three of the Blacks changed seats, but Rosa Parks refused to move, and Blake asked if she was going to stand, and she replied, "No, I am not." And then he said, "Well, if you don't stand up, I'm going to have to call the police and have you arrested." To which she responded, "You may do that." And he did. Her arrest touched off the Montgomery bus boycott, the first of the many civil rights protests to follow in such places as Birmingham, Greensboro, Nashville, Selma, Little Rock, Washington, D.C., and Memphis.

The bus boycott in Montgomery was led by Martin Luther King Jr., as were many other civil rights demonstrations. His approach was nonviolent, although the reactions of established authorities to these demonstrations was often anything but nonviolent. The nonviolent civil rights demonstrations were attempts to force concessions from local, state, and federal governments by exposing the moral bankruptcy of the laws that were used to discriminate against Blacks.

It took a decade of demonstrations and bloodshed before the Civil Rights Act (1964) was passed and the laws of the land finally began to reflect demands for equality in relations between the races. As a consequence of this Act of Congress, it became illegal to discriminate on the basis of "race, color, religion, or national origin." (Civil Rights Act, 1964). Also in 1964, Congress passed the Voting Rights Act in an attempt to eliminate discrimination at the ballot box. This act was one of the most successful of the civil rights legislative initiatives. In 1965, the Elementary and Secondary Education Act empowered the federal government to force schools to implement the *Brown* decision by withholding funds from school districts that were not in compliance with the law. More turmoil followed as schools in the South began to integrate.

An especially dramatic confrontation took place in 1963 at the University of Alabama. It pitted Governor George Wallace against the Justice Department, which was headed by Robert Kennedy, brother of President John F. Kennedy.

At the time, Wallace was well known for having said during his inauguration, "Segregation now! Segregation tomorrow! Segregation forever!" Wallace maintained that it was wrong for the courts "to force on people that which they don't want. . . . I will never submit voluntarily to any integration of any school system in Alabama . . . there is no time in my judgment when we will be ready for it—in my lifetime, at least" (Frady, 1968, p. 153). But Wallace could not stand against the tide of public opinion and the force of the federal government. The University of Alabama was integrated despite his opposition.

In 1963, over 700 civil rights demonstrations were held in the United States (Burstein, 1985). The protests were not confined to Blacks and Whites. The belief that change and social justice were possible spread to other minority groups. For instance, 1966 marked the beginning of a boycott of grapes led by United Farmworkers (UFW) union organizer Cesar Chávez. The Mexican American farmworkers represented by the UFW were paid extremely low wages and worked under some of the worst conditions in the country. The boycott was designed to focus attention on their working conditions. In 1973, a siege took place at Wounded Knee on the Pine River Indian Reservation that involved the Sioux Indians and the federal government (P. C. Smith & Warrior, 1996). The siege began because of a dispute concerning the tribal government that led to the occupation of the village of Wounded Knee by a group made up of traditional Sioux elders and young Sioux militants. The federal government responded to this occupation by surrounding the village. The siege lasted for two bitter months and brought the downtrodden state of Native Americans to the attention of the world.

The concept of affirmative action, as applied to minority groups, was ushered into existence by President Kennedy in 1961. Affirmative action was intended to give minorities equal opportunities to obtain jobs in the workplace. However, it was not until 1978 that the Equal Employment Opportunity Commission (EEOC) developed guidelines for the implementation of affirmative action. Affirmative action plans began to be mandated in the workplace in the 1980s.

Progress in civil rights was achieved slowly, and by the late 1960s and early 1970s, disillusionment and frustration started to set in. The frustration sometimes took the form of rioting. In 1965, the ghetto of Watts exploded in a riot that lasted 3 days and cost 34 lives, with 1,000 more injured and 4,000 arrests. There were riots in many other American cities in the 1960s including New York, Philadelphia, Chicago, Cleveland, Detroit, and Newark. In 1967 alone, there were 250 serious disturbances (Burstein, 1985).

In 1967, a year before his death at the hands of an assassin, Martin Luther King Jr. expressed his own disillusionment when he said,

> For years I labored with the idea of reforming the existing institutions of society, a little change here, a little change there . . . Now I feel differently. I think you've got to have a reconstruction of the entire society, a revolution of values. (Garrow, 1978, p. 562)

In 1968, a presidential commission that had been established to report on the state of race relations concluded that the United States was "moving toward two societies, one Black, one White—separate and unequal" (National Advisory Commission on Civil Disorders, 1968).

By the early 1970s, it was becoming apparent that school desegregation was going to be difficult to implement in the North because, unlike the South, school segregation there was not brought about by laws that created separate school systems. In the North, segregated schools were the result of residential housing patterns that often concentrated Blacks in central cities, which were surrounded by White suburbs. For this reason, extensive busing was required to desegregate the urban schools of the North. Due to the difficulties of desegregating Northern schools, the move toward desegregation began to falter and finally ground to a halt (Orfield & Eaton, 1996; W. G. Stephan, 1980; 1991).

The political will to enforce desegregation and other social programs created by previous Democrat administrations began to dissolve when the Republicans took power during the Nixon administration (1968-1973). The gradual demise of desegregation was facilitated by evidence from the social sciences suggesting that desegregation was not as effective in improving race relations in the short term as had been anticipated by social scientists (St. John, 1975; W. G. Stephan, 1978). For instance, W. G. Stephan (1978) concluded that in the short term, "desegregation generally does not reduce the prejudices of Whites toward Blacks . . . and desegregation leads to increases in Black prejudice toward Whites about as frequently as it leads to decreases" (p. 217). The evidence also suggested that in the short term, desegregation did not increase the self-esteem of Black students, and it had only limited effects on raising the achievement scores of Blacks (W. G. Stephan, 1986). It should be noted, however, that these pessimistic conclusions about the short-term effects of desegregation do not apply to the long-term effects of desegregation, which are generally more positive, but desegregation had to be in place for a number of years before this type of research could be done (W. G. Stephan & Stephan, 1996).

In the early 1970s, civil rights demonstrations began to decline, and by 1972, almost none were reported (Burstein, 1985). An era of public protest was coming to a close as Blacks became disenchanted with protest as a technique for creating social justice. At this time, when desegregation did not seem to be achieving the hoped-for goals, and the divide between Blacks and Whites still loomed large, the first programs to improve intergroup relations emerged. In one sense, these programs were social science's answer to the lack of progress that was being made in intergroup relations through the use of laws and government-sponsored programs. Prior to the mid 1970s, isolated studies had been done on brief intervention techniques, but no coordinated, full-scale programs to improve intergroup relations had been developed. This changed in the 1970s, when nearly all the programs we discuss were born.

Diversity training in the military and multicultural education in the schools was first developed in the 1970s. In the international arena, the first problem-solving workshops designed to improve international relations emerged during this decade, as did the initial intercultural relations training programs. Other programs that addressed intergroup relations issues less directly, such as cooperative learning groups, conflict resolution training, and moral education, were also developed during this decade. In general, these programs were designed to change the thoughts, feelings, and behaviors of individuals, although some were also explicitly concerned with creating changes in the institutions in which they were conducted (e.g., the schools, the military). All had the goal of changing society from the bottom up by changing the ways that people from different social groups related to one another. Although the majority of these programs originated in the United States, they have since spread to countries around the world.

The growing impetus in the social science community to devise programs to improve intergroup relations was accompanied by a curious phenomenon that was taking place in the domain of public opinion. On the one hand, public opinion polls taken from 1950 through the 1990s document a progressive increase in the number of Americans who regarded prejudice and discrimination as wrong (Kinder & Sanders, 1996; Pettigrew, 1979a; Schuman, Steeh, & Bobo, 1985). Americans were becoming increasingly opposed to racial discrimination, and their attitudes expressed that feeling. In fact, many Whites believed that discrimination was no longer a problem in the United States.

On the other hand, perhaps in part because of this belief, many Americans opposed the governmental policies that were being used to implement programs designed to eradicate discrimination. This objection was especially characteristic of Whites, many of whom opposed busing school children for desegregation purposes and affirmative action. As Kinder and Sanders (1996) wrote, "While White approval of the principles of equality and integration was steadily advancing over the last four decades, White support for the policies that might bring such principles to life was not" (p. 270). They report that in surveys taken between 1986 and 1992, only 30% of Whites supported quotas in college admissions, 35% supported school desegregation, and 46% supported government efforts to ensure equal employment opportunity. The corresponding figures for Blacks were 80%, 83%, and 90%.

These contradictory themes suggest that the nature of prejudice was itself changing. By the 1980s, most Americans no longer considered it appropriate to express prejudice openly. Prejudice was becoming more covert, and the people who harbored negative feelings toward other racial, ethnic, and religious groups were increasingly reluctant to express them in public. However, prejudice did not disappear. For example, a recent set of studies using a subtle technique for measuring prejudice shows that vast majority of Whites in the United States displayed a pro-White bias. Further, many were completely unaware of this bias (Greenwald, McGhee, & Schwartz, 1998). Thus, although prejudice has become less overt and less acceptable, it is still with us.

We should not overlook the real progress that was made in intergroup relations as a result of the civil rights movement (Hacker, 1992; J. M. Jones, 1997; Pettigrew, 1979a; Wilson, 1973). The incomes of Blacks and many other minority groups have increased relative to those of Whites. Blacks and other minorities can be found in a wider range of occupations than before the civil rights movement began. Changes in the voting rights laws have led to the increased participation of Blacks and other minorities in the electoral process, resulting in large gains in the proportion of Black elected officials. The education levels of Blacks and other minority groups increased as more Blacks and members of other minority groups completed high school and attended college. Overall, the living conditions of many Blacks and members of other minority groups improved.

At the same time, prejudice and discrimination have proven to be intractable enemies, far more so than the optimistic social scientists in the early post–World War II period could have imagined. Despite the progress that has been made, segregation in housing and schools is still widespread. Hate groups and hate crimes are increasingly a part of the daily headlines (according to the FBI, 7,755 hate crimes were committed in 1998). Hate sites abound on the Internet. Discrimination in the

TABLE 1.1   Changes in the Racial/Ethnic Composition of the U.S.
Population

	1990	2000	Percentage Change
White, non-Hispanic	188.32	196.66	4%
Black, non-Hispanic	29.30	33.48	14%
Hispanic	22.38	32.44	45%
Asian and Pacific Islander	7.00	10.50	50%
American Indian	1.98	2.05	14%

SOURCE: Salisbury, 2000.

American workplace is so prevalent that tens of thousands of complaints are registered every year by the EEOC. Income differentials between many racial and ethnic minorities and Whites and between
women and men are still substantial. A disproportionate percentage
of minority group members still live in poverty and suffer the consequences—illness, inadequate healthcare, poor housing, and inter-
rupted education (Cose, 1999; J. M. Jones, 1997). As Kinder and Sanders
(1996) conclude, the United States is still a nation divided by color.
And people of color make up an increasingly larger portion of the population (see Table 1.1). In other parts of the world, hatred and ethnic
violence have also continued to be an omnipresent problem.

In some respects, the need to address these issues is greater now
that ever before. America, like many other countries around the globe,
is clearly becoming more diverse. In 2005, the labor force in the United
States will consist of 73% Whites, 11.6% Blacks, 11.1% Latinos, and
4.3% Asian Americans and other groups (Bond & Pyle, 1998). Minority
groups are increasing in size faster than the majority group, as can be
seen in Table 1.1. As a result, by 2020, nearly half of the students in
American schools will be, according to estimates, persons of color
(Riche, 2000). Large numbers of immigrants continue to arrive in the
United States. Between 1990 and 1998, over 7.5 million people immi-
grated to the United States (Riche, 2000). Clearly, in the future, people

will have to work together and interact across group boundaries to a greater degree than ever before. In addition, contact across cultures will continue to increase as a result of the globalization of the world economy, migration, international exchanges, and tourism. Americans and people from all the countries of the world will have to learn to communicate effectively with one another. Standing in the way will be prejudice, stereotyping, and discrimination—the topics we turn to in the next chapter.

What Lies Ahead

In Chapter 2, we explore intergroup relations theory and concepts to better understand intergroup relations problems and their solutions. We begin the chapter with an analysis of contact theory and its relevance for designing programs to improve intergroup relations. We then address three concepts: prejudice, stereotyping, and discriminatory behavior. In the process, we examine social-psychological theories and concepts that explain the processes that underlie prejudice, stereotyping, and discrimination, as well as the ways in which these theories and concepts allow us to formulate approaches to changing prejudice, stereotypes, and discrimination.

Then, we analyze a variety of widely used intergroup relations techniques. We begin in Chapter 3 by analyzing multicultural-education programs, which are based on the idea that students of all groups need to learn about the history and culture of other racial, ethnic, cultural, and religious groups (Banks, 1973; J. H. Katz, 1975). These programs often attempt to present history from the perspective of minority groups, to counter the more traditional approach to history that emphasizes the perspective of the dominant group. One of the goals of these programs is to improve intergroup relations by helping students to acquire the knowledge, attitudes, and skills needed to participate in the social, civic, and cultural life of a diverse society (Banks, 1997).

In Chapter 4, our theme is diversity training programs. These programs were first created for use in the U.S. military (Landis, Day,

McGrew, Thomas, & Miller, 1976; Tansik & Driskill, 1977), but later diversity training and diversity initiatives became popular in civilian organizations. Diversity training typically attempts to increase the participants' awareness of dissimilarities among racial, ethnic, and cultural groups and to lead them to value these differences. These programs are usually relatively short and use both didactic (e.g., lectures and readings) and experiential (e.g., role-playing, simulation games) techniques.

Intergroup dialogues are the topic of Chapter 5. The first dialogue-based, problem-solving workshops emerged in the United States and England in the 1970s (Burton, 1974; Doob, 1974; Kelman, 1979; Kelman & Cohen, 1976) to help ameliorate long-standing, international disputes. More recently, intergroup dialogues have been used to help resolve disputes between racial and ethnic groups through the use of dialogue. In these techniques, members of disputing parties are brought together in a neutral setting. They discuss their dispute and its resolution with the help of trained facilitators. The goals are to analyze the dispute rationally and help the disputants take the perspective of the other group in the conflict.

In Chapter 6, intercultural relations training programs are reviewed. One impetus for the initial development of these programs was the difficulties that Peace Corp volunteers experienced in adapting to foreign cultures (Brislin & Pedersen, 1976). These training programs are designed to teach citizens of one country about the culture of another country and how to adapt to it. They also are used to familiarize citizens of a country about the cultures of people from their own country from whom they are dissimilar. Intercultural relations training programs employ an approach that includes didactic techniques, such as lectures, readings, and discussions, as well as experience-based techniques, such as role-playing and simulation games.

Chapter 7 explores the most popular cooperative learning techniques. Investigators in Colorado, Minnesota, Maryland, and Texas independently developed these programs for use in the schools (Aronson, Blaney, Stephan, Sikes, & Snapp, 1978; Blaney, Stephan, Rosenfield, Aronson, & Sikes, 1977; DeVries, Edwards, & Slavin, 1978; Johnson & Johnson, 1992a; Weigel, Wiser, & Cook, 1975). With these techniques, children from different racial and ethnic groups are brought together in small, cooperative, work groups to learn standard academic materials. These techniques rely on the contact between the students to improve relations between groups.

Intergroup conflict resolution techniques provide the theme for Chapter 8. Building on the pioneering theoretical and experimental work of Blake and Mouton (1984) and Sherif (1966), the early conflict resolution techniques often involved members of the two groups defining and reviewing a specific problem, developing and debating a range of solutions, evaluating potential solutions, and selecting a final solution. Initially, these techniques were used largely in work settings (Adlerfer, 1977; Burke, 1970; Fisher, 1976). Later, practitioners developed and implemented programs designed to resolve intergroup disputes in community and school settings (Fisher, 1990; Johnson & Johnson, 1996).

In Chapter 9, we examine our last technique, moral education training. In the late 1960s, Kohlberg published a stage theory of moral development in which he argued that children develop the capacity to reason morally through a series of stages (Kohlberg, 1969b). At the lowest stages, children's reasoning about morality is based on the consequences of behavior. Later, their reasoning begins to reflect the moral conventions of their society. If children attain higher levels of moral reasoning, they base their moral judgments on universal principles such as justice. By the early 1970s, the first *just community* schools based on this theory were created (Kohlberg, 1981). These schools not only taught moral reasoning but were also designed to create egalitarian, caring communities.

In Chapter 10, we argue that describing and evaluating intergroup relations training programs makes a valuable contribution to the theory and practice of intergroup relations programs. We also present a series of different types of evaluations, ranging from the nonrigorous and informal to very rigorous and formal.

In Chapter 11, we conclude the book by presenting an overall assessment of the programs that we have examined, and we make suggestions for the design of effective programs to improve intergroup relations. Then, we consider a number of issues that must be addressed in the creation of intergroup relations programs and look at the possible societal consequences of these programs.

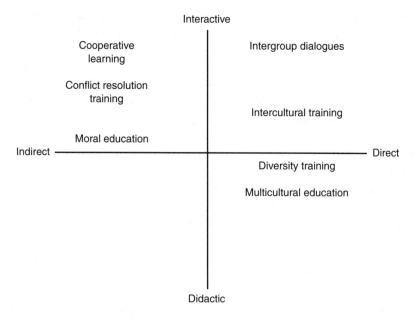

Figure 1.1. Intergroup Relations Programs

Conceptualizing Intergroup Relations Training Programs

The programs reviewed in this book vary on many dimensions. Some programs have the improvement of intergroup relations as the predominant focus, whereas others are designed to address these issues indirectly or were originally designed for other purposes and tend to improve intergroup relations as a by-product. Some programs take a didactic approach to intergroup relations training, whereas others are more interactively oriented. Didactic strategies consist of cognitive, verbal, and intellectual types of training relying on lectures, films, and other classroom-based means of instruction. Interactive procedures employ action-oriented and experience-based training. In Figure 1.1, we place the programs to be examined on these two dimensions, direct-indirect and didactic-interactive. We will use this conceptual framework to organize our presentation of these programs. The first two programs we will cover are multicultural education and diversity training, which are largely direct and didactic. Then, we will present intergroup dialogues and intercultural training, which are usually direct and interactive. The last three programs we will discuss, cooperative learning, conflict resolution training, and moral education programs, are more indirect.

We will follow the same general outline for each chapter. The chapters will begin with a general description of the programs and their goals. Examples of the content and techniques employed by the program will also be included. Research that has been done on the effectiveness of the programs will be covered in the next section, followed by a discussion of the psychological processes underlying the programs. Problems and issues associated with each program will be examined in the following section, and the chapter will end with recommendations for the implementation of these programs.

Summary

In this chapter, we have traced the history of intergroup relations in the post–World War II period in an attempt to show that programs designed to improve intergroup relations emerged from a particular historical context. These programs were first developed when the civil rights movement was drawing to a close after achieving important legislative successes and considerable improvements in the lives of minority group members in the United States. However, not all members of these groups benefited equally, and many were left behind. In addition, prejudice, stereotyping, and discrimination continued to flourish, albeit in altered form. Whites became less willing to express prejudice publicly, but they were not reluctant to express opposition to policies designed to benefit minority groups.

The major types of intergroup relations programs all had their origins in the 1970s during a period in which many members of minority groups were experiencing frustration and disillusionment at the rate of progress in improving civil rights. The programs addressed the issues involved in improving intergroup relations in different ways. Diversity training programs were designed to improve intergroup relations in the workplace by increasing awareness and appreciation of group differences. Multicultural education was designed to increase students' knowledge about outgroups. Problem-solving workshops that relied on intergroup dialogue were first created to resolve international disputes. Intercultural relations training was used to teach citizens of one culture about those of another culture. Cooperative learning programs were designed to improve intergroup interaction in the schools. Conflict resolution and mediation were initially developed in community and work settings but were later used extensively in the schools. Moral development programs attempted to increase levels of moral reasoning and create more just learning communities.

INTERGROUP RELATIONS THEORIES AND CONCEPTS 2

ALL INTERGROUP RELATIONS programs must confront a legacy of negative intergroup contacts as well as prejudice, stereotypes, and discrimination. In this chapter, we discuss these central concepts and examine how they can be addressed in intergroup relations programs. While exploring these concepts, we discuss social-psychological theories that explain the processes that underlie them, and we provide approaches to changing them.

Figure 2.1 shows the interrelationships among these four major concepts. Negative contact is a direct cause of stereotyping, prejudice, and discrimination. Stereotyping is a cause of prejudice, but prejudice also creates stereotypes. Prejudice and stereotyping are major causes of discriminatory behaviors. Thus, intergroup relations can be improved by creating conditions for positive contact and reducing prejudice, stereotyping, and discrimination. We address contact first.

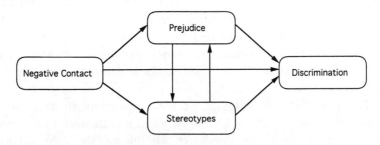

Figure 2.1. A Causal Model of Discrimination

Contact

Although we discussed the historical context of contact theory in Chapter 1, in this section we take a more comprehensive approach to the role of contact in intergroup relations.

> Prejudice (unless deeply rooted in the character structure of the individual) may be reduced by equal-status contact between majority and minority groups in the pursuit of common goals. The effect is greatly enhanced if this contact is sanctioned by institutional supports (i.e., by law, custom or local atmosphere), and if it is of the sort that leads to the perception of common interests and common humanity between the members of the two groups. (G. W. Allport, 1954, p. 267)

This classic statement of the contact hypothesis suggests that the necessary conditions for contact to improve intergroup relations are equal-status interactions, the pursuit of common goals, support by authority figures, and a perception of common interests and humanity. Other theorists have added a large number of additional features that affect the outcomes of contact (for reviews, see Pettigrew, 1971, 1986; 1998; W. G. Stephan, 1987; W. G. Stephan & Stephan, 1996). In fact, the list of such factors has grown so large that it has become necessary to reconceptualize the original contact theory.

A Revised Contact Theory

Four categories of factors affect the outcomes of intergroup contact: societal factors, situational factors, person factors, and mediating factors (W. G. Stephan & Stephan, 1996). In this approach, societal factors are thought to influence person factors and situational factors, which in turn influence individual cognitions and affect, and these mediating factors then influence the outcomes of contact (see Figure 2.2).

The societal factors that impact contact include the structure of the society, in particular, the degree to which it is organized into hierarchies based on power, race, gender, or religion, and the historical relations among the groups involved in the contact situation. They also

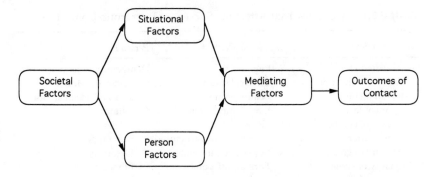

Figure 2.2. A Causal Model of the Contact Hypothesis

encompass the current relations among the groups, as well as the cultural backgrounds of the individuals in the contact situations. The situational factors include the setting in which the contact occurs, the nature of the interaction, and the type of tasks the participants perform. The person factors refer to the demographic characteristics of the individuals, their personality traits, and the attitudes and beliefs they bring to the contact situation. The impact of these factors is filtered through the cognitive and emotional responses of the individual participants. These responses are referred to as *mediating factors* because they intervene between events that occur before and during the contact and the outcomes of the contact. Some of the societal, situational, and personal factors relevant to the outcomes of intergroup contact are listed in Table 2.1.

Some theorists argue that intergroup contact has sequential effects that unfold over time: It first leads to liking for the individuals involved in the contact, creating interpersonal liking (Hewstone, 1996; Hewstone & Brown, 1986; Pettigrew, 1998). This process often involves decategorization or personalization, thinking of people as individuals rather than as members of a group. Next, contact generalizes to the group, creating intergroup liking in situations in which the group identity is salient. Contact can ultimately lead to the perception that individuals are part of an overarching group. This superordinate group perception results in deemphasized group differences. We will discuss techniques that promote recategorization and creating superordinate groups later in the chapter.

TABLE 2.1   Variables That Affect the Success of Intergroup Contact

Societal Context	Situational Context	Person Factors
Social structure	Setting	Demographic characteristics
Social stratification	Physical setting	Personality traits
Historical relations	Seating patterns	Task and social abilities
Prior contact	Nature of interaction	Cognitions
Degree of conflict	Goals	Beliefs
Current relations	Structured/unstructured	Stereotypes
Amount of contact	Superficial/intimate	Prejudice
Quality of contact	Formal/informal	Ethnocentrism
Degree of conflict	Positive/negative	Expectancies
Cultural background	Authority support	Values
Socialization practices	Equal/unequal status	Affect
Subjective culture	Equal/unequal power	Threat feelings
Social norms and roles	Cooperative/competitive	
	Short/long term	
	Task	
	Interpersonal/	
	task oriented	
	Success/failure	
	Program staff	
	Racial/ethnic	
	composition	

We now explore ways in which the factors in this model can be used to improve intergroup relations.

Using Contact to Improve Intergroup Relations

Societal Factors

In intergroup relations programs involving intergroup contact, contact theory suggests that the organizers should first consider the societal context in which the contact takes place. For instance, all social systems are stratified to some degree by class, race, and gender; these unfair systems of stratification breed high levels of hostility. Most intergroup relations programs try to create equal-status conditions within the training setting, because equal-status conditions improve intergroup perceptions (E. Aronson, Blaney, Stephan, Sikes, & Snapp,

1978; Weigel, Wiser, & Cook, 1975). If the participants are not equal on such demographic characteristics as social class, educational level, or age, it is particularly important to create equality within the contact situation. Equal status in the contact situation increases the chances that similarities between individuals from different groups will be noticed and perceived; similarity tends to reduce prejudice (McClendon, 1974). Making minority group members higher in status within the training setting can have particularly positive consequences for intergroup relations (Cohen & Lotan, 1997).

Situational Factors

Educators and trainers should also take situational factors into account. A wealth of research has suggested ways to create favorable conditions for contact. For example, research indicates that cooperating in racially or ethnically mixed groups improves intergroup relations (Johnson & Johnson, 1992a; Johnson, Johnson, & Maruyama, 1984; Miller & Harrington, 1992; Slavin, 1985, 1992; Worchel, 1986). Cooperation is most effective when the process is engaging and the cooperation leads to favorable outcomes (Blanchard, Adelman, & Cook, 1975). When mixed groups fail, outgroup members may be blamed for the failure (Blanchard et al., 1975; Burnstein & McCrae, 1962; Rosenfield, Stephan, & Lucker, 1981).

In addition, people should be assigned to cooperative groups in a way that does not make social categories salient (Miller, Brewer, & Edwards, 1985; Miller & Harrington, 1990a). Encouraging participants to focus on interpersonal relations leads to more favorable intergroup relations outcomes than encouraging a task focus (Rogers, 1982, cited in Brewer & Miller, 1988; Miller & Harrington, 1990a). However, the group identities of the participants must ultimately be made salient if the positive interpersonal effects resulting from intergroup contact are to generalize to outgroup members who are not a part of the training (Hewstone, 1996; Pettigrew, 1998). Balanced ratios of ingroup and outgroup members are also usually beneficial, at least in small-group settings (Gonzales, 1979; Miller & Davidson-Podgorny, 1987).

Furthermore, intergroup contact should be nonsuperficial and offer students the opportunity to get to know one another as individuals (Amir, 1976). In particular, attempts should be made to create conditions in which friendships can be developed (Pettigrew, 1998). Research indicates that forming intergroup friendships is a powerful factor in reducing prejudice (Blumberg & Roye, 1980; Hallinan & Teixeira, 1987).

Support by respected authority figures, such as community leaders, upper-level executives, administrators, teachers, and parents, enhances the effects of intergroup contact (Adlerfer, 1982; E. Aronson et al., 1978; Cohen, 1980; Slavin, 1985; R. W. Williams Jr., 1977). Authority figures can establish norms of civility, tolerance, and respect that can be promoted through the creation of policies and procedures as well as by directly rewarding such behaviors. In organizational settings, authority figures can also make it clear that people will not be allowed to violate others' rights with impunity. The greatest improvements in intergroup relations are likely to occur when the authority figures promote voluntary intergroup relationships (W. G. Stephan & Rosenfield, 1978; W. G. Stephan & Stephan, 1984). It may be difficult to improve intergroup relations when authorities impose the contact, because people may react negatively to a loss of control over their freedom of association.

Person Factors

Intergroup relations programs should also take the characteristics of the participants into consideration. The participants' affect toward and cognitions about the other group are especially important. Their age, sex, ethnicity or race, religion, and cultural background must also be carefully considered when designing programs that meet the participants' needs. The programs must be tailored to the resources, time, cognitive abilities, learning styles, and motivation of the participants. If possible, the program design process should include designers and trainers from every group of participants and every group who is the subject of training.

Contact theory is valuable because it provides information that can be directly applied to the creation of effective intergroup relations programs to reduce prejudice, stereotyping, and discrimination. It is also helpful in understanding why some programs are successful and others are not. Next, we examine prejudice, the second of our major intergroup relations concepts.

Prejudice

In this section, we define prejudice, explore changes in explanations for prejudice, and discuss a number of newer theories of prejudice. Then, we concentrate on using these and other social science theories and concepts to devise ways of reducing prejudice in intergroup relations programs.

Prejudice Defined

Prejudice may be defined as "negative attitudes toward social groups" (W. G. Stephan, 1985, p. 600). Prejudice occurs when individuals are prejudged and disliked based on their group membership. Traditionally, prejudice has been considered to have a tripartite structure consisting of attitudes, affect, and behavioral predispositions (Harding, Kutner, Proshansky, & Chein, 1954). Although these three components are typically consistent with one another, they are not always congruent. For example, an individual may hold prejudiced attitudes but behave in a nonprejudiced manner.

Old-Fashioned and Modern Prejudice

The oldest theories of prejudice, such as those of Adorno, Frenkel-Brunswik, Levinson, and Sanford (1950) and G. W. Allport (1954), argued that prejudice was deeply rooted in the flawed character structure of prejudiced people. Beginning in the 1960s and 1970s, sociocultural explanations for prejudice focused more on the discriminatory social structures pervading the United States and other societies (Duckett, 1992).

In the past, prejudice was often blatantly expressed and justified in terms of biologically based inferiority. As we noted in Chapter 1, however, public expressions of prejudice in the United States have became less acceptable in the post–civil rights era, and they have become markedly less common in public life. But we have also seen that— although Americans have become more reluctant to outwardly express prejudice, discrimination, hate speech, violations of civil rights, and everyday acts of intergroup aggression—hostility, bias, and avoidance continue to occur. In addition, opposition remains high to policies to redress the consequences of prejudice and discrimination.

This inconsistency between attitudes and behaviors regarding race and ethnicity, along with the current, less overt expression of prejudice, has led a number of American theorists and researchers to reformulate their understanding of the nature of prejudice in American society. Newer theories of racism view prejudice as stemming from an often covert set of contradictory attitudes and feelings. These newer theories were initially developed to explain White prejudice directed toward Blacks. However, all of them have now been applied to a wide variety of groups who suffer from prejudice and discrimination including women, the handicapped, older persons, lesbians, gay males, and other racial, ethnic, and nationality groups (Devine & Monteith, 1993; Glick & Fiske, 1996; Sears & Huddy, 1990; Sidanius & Pratto, 1999; Swim, Aiken, Hall, & Hunter, 1995; Tougas, Brown, Beaton, & Joly, 1995).

Modern Theories of Prejudice

As the famous Swedish sociologist Gunnar Myrdal (1944) noted, a contradiction has always existed in American society between the democratic and egalitarian values espoused in the United States Constitution and the inequalities, discrimination, and prejudice that exist in relations among racial, ethnic, and religious groups in the United States. These newer theories of prejudice take this fundamental contradiction into account. We briefly explain four such theories: ambivalence-amplification, aversive racism, symbolic racism, and compunction theories.

Ambivalence-Amplification

Ambivalence-amplification theory focuses on the ambivalence created by simultaneously experiencing incompatible feelings: sympathy for the suffering of members of disadvantaged outgroups and an aversion toward them (I. Katz, Wackenhut, & Hass, 1986). In situations in which the aversion overrides sympathy, negative attitudes and behaviors are directed toward outgroup members.

Aversive Racism

Aversive racism theory argues that the contradiction is between values and feelings (Gaertner & Dovidio, 1986). From this perspective, people experience unacknowledged negative affect towards minority groups but struggle to avoid having these feelings reflected in their behavior because they also hold egalitarian values and regard themselves as nonprejudiced. These feelings lead to anxiety and avoidance of outgroup members.

Symbolic Racism

Symbolic racism theory contends that prejudice consists of negative affect toward the outgroup in question plus the belief by those who exemplify symbolic racism that members of the other group violate some traditional values that they themselves hold dear, such as individualism and self-reliance (Sears, 1988). Symbolic racism theory suggests that this combination of factors leads to opposition to race-based social policies, such as affirmative action.

Compunction

Compunction theory maintains that many Whites have come to believe that prejudice is wrong and experience guilt or self-criticism (compunction) when they think or behave in ways that reflect negative stereotypes or prejudice (Devine, Monteith, Zuwerink, & Elliot, 1991; Zuwerink, Devine & Monteith, 1996). These theorists have shown that people can be trained to override negative feelings about outgroups.

Other Theories of Prejudice

In addition to theories that incorporate the idea of contradictory attitudes, beliefs, and feelings, other theories of the causes of prejudice are helpful in understanding how to structure intergroup relations programs. We will examine realistic group conflict, integrated threat, social dominance, and social identity theories.

Realistic Group Conflict

Realistic group conflict theory postulates that group antagonisms arise from competition for scarce resources, such as territory, wealth, or natural resources (LeVine & Campbell, 1972; Sherif, 1966). According to LeVine and Campbell (1972), "Real threat causes hostility to the source of the threat" (p. 30), and this animosity increases in a situation of declining resources. A perceived threat can be as important a source of prejudice as an actual threat, even though it may have no basis in reality.

Integrated Threat

Integrated threat theory asserts that four types of threat can lead to prejudice (W. G. Stephan & Stephan, 2000). Outgroups are disliked if they are perceived to pose realistic or value threats to the ingroup, if ingroup members are anxious about interacting with the outgroup because they expect negative outcomes from such interactions, or if negative stereotypes of outgroups are threatening. It is important to note that perceived threats are often unrealistic or exaggerated.

Social Dominance

Social dominance theory views prejudice as an outcome of belief systems that enable dominant groups to legitimize the power, privileges, and prestige they enjoy (Sidanius, 1993). Research supports the idea that people who have a more hierarchical conception of society tend to be more prejudiced (Sidanius & Pratto, 1999).

Social Identity

Social identity theorists believe that people favorably evaluate ingroups in an effort to maintain their own self-esteem (Abrams & Hogg, 1990; Tajfel & Turner, 1986). In the process of doing so, they often disparage outgroups. A similar idea is at the heart of the concept of ethnocentrism, "the view of things in which one's own group is at the center of everything, and all others are scaled or rated with

TABLE 2.2   Current Theories of the Causes of Prejudice

Theory	Cause
Modern racism theories	
Ambivalence-amplification	Incompatible positive and negative feelings
Aversive racism	Contradiction in values and feelings
Symbolic racism	Negative affect and perceived value differences
Compunction	Negative attitudes and guilt
Other theories	
Realistic group conflict	Perceived competition for scarce resources
Integrated threat	Threats involving resources, values, anxiety, stereotypes
Social dominance	Belief in ingroup superiority
Social identity	Ingroup enhancement

reference to it" (Sumner, 1906, p. 13). Ethnocentrism leads naturally to the assumption that the differences between groups in values, morals, and beliefs reflect negatively on outgroups.

These theories and their explanations for the causes of prejudice are listed in Table 2.2.

Prejudice Reduction Processes

Intergroup relations trainers can use the theories just discussed (and other, related theories and concepts) to help overcome prejudice. We will consider a number of processes that can be incorporated into intergroup relations programs, including making value-behavior discrepancies explicit, reducing threat, increasing perceptions of similarities among groups, creating superordinate groups, decategorization by emphasizing multiple identities, reinforcing and modeling positive behaviors, modifying associations between cognition and affect, using dissonance to create attitude change, creating empathy, and correcting misattributions. These remedies should be seen as complementary rather than competing approaches.

Making Value-Behavior Discrepancies Explicit

One of the common features of the modern theories of prejudice is the finding that egalitarianism is associated with low levels of prejudice (I. Katz, Wackenhut, & Hass, 1986). Studies have shown that because most Americans believe in equality, confronting them with the discrepancy between their beliefs in equality and their attitudes and behaviors toward minority group members leads to changes in these attitudes and behaviors (Grube, Mayton, & Ball-Rokeach, 1994; Monteith, 1993; Rokeach, 1971). Intergroup relations programs can also address other values relevant to positive intergroup relations and help people become aware of discrepancies between these values and their behaviors.

Reducing Threat

Integrated threat theory argues that feelings of threat are a cause of prejudice. Intergroup relations programs can reduce feelings of threat, and therefore prejudice, by providing more accurate information on group differences. They can also reduce threat by providing conditions for positive face-to-face interaction with outgroup members, so expectations for future interactions will no longer be as negative.

Increasing Perceptions of Similarity Among Groups

From the perspective of social identity theory, changing the belief that the outgroup differs from the ingroup in ways that are integral to self-identity should lead to reductions in prejudice. Considerable evidence indicates that increasing the perception of the similarity of others to the self increases liking for these others (Byrne, 1971; Rokeach, Smith, & Evans, 1960). Thus, in intergroup relations programs, information and experiences that erode the assumed dissimilarity between groups can potentially play a significant role in reducing prejudice and ethnocentrism.

Creating Superordinate Groups

Creating strong identification with overarching social categories provides another way to reduce prejudice stemming from issues of identity. Identifying with superordinate groups, such as the school, the organization, the community, the nation, or humankind, converts groups that had considered themselves to be ingroups and outgroups into a single group with a shared identity. In a classic study of intergroup relations, Sherif and his colleagues found that creating an emergency at a summer camp that forced contending groups of children to work together improved relations between these groups (Sherif, Harvey, White, Hood, & Sherif, 1961). Several laboratory studies have likewise demonstrated that creating superordinate groups reduces bias against outgroups (Gaertner, Mann, Dovidio, Murrell, & Pomare, 1990). When membership in superordinate groups, such as the school, the work organization, the community, or humanity itself, is salient, subgroup differences fade in importance.

Decategorization by Emphasizing Multiple Identities

In a third, identity-related technique for reducing prejudice, people are reminded of the multiple social categories to which they belong. Every person is simultaneously a member of many social categories, and these social categories overlap with those of others in a crisscrossing pattern. Not only are people members of racial and ethnic groups, but they also are simultaneously males and females; Protestants, Catholics, Jews, or Muslims; old, middle-aged, or young; firstborns or later-borns; talented in art or science; tennis players; and so forth. Research suggests that reminding people of the crosscutting groups to which they belong reduces prejudice (Commins & Lockwood, 1978; Hewstone, Islam, & Judd, 1993; Vanbeselaere, 1991). Individuals can also interact with members of outgroups to find areas of personal similarity (Brewer, 2000; Brewer & Miller, 1984). Although individuals may be divided from others by some social categories (e.g., race or ethnicity), they are united with them on other meaningful personal categories (e.g., similarity of attitudes, feelings, interests, abilities), which can be discovered through interpersonally focused interaction. It is difficult to dislike people with whom one shares important aspects of identity.

Reinforcing and Modeling
Positive Behaviors

Social learning theory highlights the role that reinforcements and modeling play in changing behavior and attitudes (Bandura, 1986). People who find interacting with outgroup members rewarding are likely to change their behavior and attitudes toward them. Rewarding people for nonprejudiced behaviors is one of the most powerful tools available to intergroup relations trainers. In a simple demonstration of this effect, it was found that reinforcing students for sitting next to a "new friend" in the school cafeteria increased the frequency with which students from different racial groups sat next to one another (Hauserman, Walen, & Behling, 1973). This increase in cross-racial interaction generalized to a free play period.

Likewise, the models to whom they are exposed influence people's behavior. When the behavior of a model leads to rewards, others imitate their actions. Some intergroup relations programs include leaders from a variety of groups who model behavior toward one another that they wish their trainees to learn.

Modifying Associations
Between Cognitions and Affect

Social learning theory also emphasizes the learned associations between objects and emotions, including associations between social groups and affective responses to them (Bandura, 1986). All too often, people have learned to link certain social groups with negative affect through socialization, exposure to the media, and direct experience. As a consequence, some outgroups are feared, disliked, and avoided. In intergroup relations programs, it is possible to modify the associations between outgroups and negative affect by providing people with positive experiences and information about outgroups.

Using Dissonance to Create Attitude Change

Dissonance theory argues that when people behave in ways that are inconsistent with their customary views of themselves, they become uncomfortable about this discrepancy (E. Aronson, 1997). This discomfort is labeled dissonance, and it can motivate people to change their former attitudes in order to maintain a consistent view of themselves. Thus, if people who are prejudiced, ethnocentric, or biased toward members of another group behave in positive ways toward members of this group, they will be motivated to change their previously prejudicial attitudes to be consistent with their current behavior. For instance, in one study, White students who voluntarily wrote an essay favoring a large increase in scholarship money for Blacks had more positive racial attitudes after writing the essay than they did before writing (Leippe & Eisenstadt, 1994; see also Gray & Ashmore, 1975). Dissonance can have powerful effects on attitudes in intergroup relations programs that use cooperation, role-playing, and simulation games to encourage people to behave in positive ways toward members of previously disliked groups.

Creating Empathy

Creating empathy in intergroup relations programs can also result in prejudice reduction. Research has demonstrated that empathizing with outgroup members can lead to decreased prejudice (Batson et al., 1997; W. G. Stephan & Finlay, 2000). When people empathize with outgroups, their empathic reactions can take two forms, the first of which is cognitive empathy. Individuals experience cognitive empathy when they take the role of another and view the world from that person's perspective. Cognitive empathy is promoted by acquiring knowledge about the outgroup, including their worldview and their practices, norms, and values. It may also help people to learn about the way the outgroup views the ingroup. Cognitive empathy can transform the previously unintelligible into the understandable, thereby reducing feelings of threat and uncertainty.

The second empathic reaction involves emotional empathy. In intergroup relations programs, emotional empathy consists primarily of compassion-related emotions that arise from a feeling of concern for the suffering of others. Experiencing emotional empathy is likely to lead to favorable changes in attitudes toward the outgroup. According to Batson and his colleagues (1997), emotional empathy causes people to value the welfare of the group, leading to more "positive beliefs about, feelings toward, and concern for the group" (p. 106). Finlay and Stephan (in press) suggest that emotional empathy can also lead to attitude change by undercutting the tendency to blame the victims of discrimination for the problems they suffer.

Reading information about the experiences of another group or listening to the members of an outgroup describe their experiences can create cognitive and emotional empathy for that group. Role-playing exercises may also arouse emotional empathy for outgroups. For example, in one study, third-grade students participated in a simulation game designed to create empathy for people who are the targets of discrimination (Weiner & Wright, 1973). The students were divided into two groups and asked to wear either orange or green armbands. The orange-banded children then experienced a day in which they were negatively stereotyped, discriminated against, and not praised by the teacher. The roles were reversed on a second day. The students exposed to this experience learned firsthand how it felt to experience arbitrary discrimination, and as a result, they became less prejudiced than a comparison group. These changes in attitude persisted over a 2-week period.

Correcting Misattributions

The tendency to misattribute the causes of the behavior of outgroup members is another cause of prejudice that can be addressed in intergroup relations training. Outgroup members tend to be blamed more for negative behaviors than ingroup members (Pettigrew, 1979b; W. G. Stephan, 1977). Correspondingly, ingroup members tend to be given more credit for positive behaviors than outgroup members. This bias in making attributions for the behavior of outgroup members is commonly referred to as the *ultimate attribution error,* and it can be directly addressed using intergroup relations training techniques (Pettigrew, 1979b). One such technique, the cultural sensitizer, is designed to help ingroup members make appropriate attributions for the behaviors of outgroup members. In a study using this approach, it was found that White officers and enlisted men who worked through a programmed learning book increased their knowledge of Black culture as well as their ability to think in complex, rather than oversimplified, ways about it (Landis et al., 1976).

From a focus on prejudice, we now move to an examination of stereotypes.

Stereotypes

We first define stereotypes and examine their origins. We then explore the ways stereotypes are activated and maintained. Finally, we consider ways of reducing stereotypes.

Stereotypes Defined

The basis of stereotyping is the categorization of people into groups. Stereotypes consist of the characteristics attributed to categories of people (for reviews of this literature, see Hamilton & Sherman, 1996; Hilton & von Hippel, 1996; Oakes, Haslam, & Turner, 1994). Unfortunately, stereotypes are all too often overgeneralized, inaccurate, and negative. Thus, members of majority groups tend to see members of minority groups as being all alike and possessing the same negative traits. The stereotypes of members of minority groups about the majority group and other minorities similarly reveal contempt and a failure to recognize diversity in outgroups. Regrettably, stereotypes are frequently used to dominate, disparage, or dehumanize members of outgroups. In particular, dominant groups use negative stereotypes to justify and maintain their power (Jost & Banaji, 1993).

Although most people think that stereotypes of outgroups consist of a fixed set of characteristics, research indicates that the characteristics associated with a given group vary as a function of the context and the frequency with which specific stereotyped characteristics have been applied to the group in the past (Oakes et al., 1994). For instance, different stereotypes of a group may be brought to mind on an athletic field than in a work setting.

One function of stereotypes is to create order out of the chaos of social reality. Stereotypes provide guidelines for social interaction and explanations for the behavior of others. When people attribute a set of characteristics to an outgroup, they then have a basis for expectations about their behaviors. People commonly base their own behavior toward outgroup members on stereotype-related expectancies. The members of the outgroup may react to being treated in this manner by acting in ways that confirm the initial expectancies, thus creating a self-fulfilling prophecy (Harris, Milich, Corbitt, Hoover, & Brady, 1992; Snyder, 1984, 1992; Snyder & Swann, 1978; Snyder, Tanke, & Berscheid, 1977; Word, Zanna, & Cooper, 1974). For instance, a Korean American who expects Latinos to dislike Koreans may act in such a cold or suspicious manner around them that Latinos respond in a similarly negative manner, thereby fulfilling the Korean's expectations.

Stereotypes serve another function by enabling ingroups to perceive that they are distinctive from outgroups, thus contributing to group identity. In the process of forming social categories, the differences between groups tend to be accentuated, and variability within the outgroup tends to be minimized. The perception of outgroups as homogeneous is most likely to occur for negative traits, and majority groups seem more prone to display this bias than do minority groups (Oakes et al., 1994).

Origins of Stereotypes

Stereotypes are partly a product of the history of relations between groups. A history of hostility produces negative stereotypes. The content of stereotypes also tends to reflect the current role and status of relations between the groups (LeVine & Campbell, 1972). Rich and poor people, urban and rural dwellers, management and labor, Latinos and Asian Americans, and men and women have views of one another that are shaped by their role relationships. Groups often do differ in beliefs, norms, and behaviors, but these differences are rarely evaluated neutrally. Instead, the traits possessed by the outgroup are evaluated negatively. When relations between groups involve conflict or disparities in status that are considered unjust, the stereotypes are particularly likely to be negative.

Stereotype Activation and Maintenance

The stereotypes learned through these processes are commonly activated automatically by observable features of other people, such as sex, race and ethnicity, age, physical handicaps, nationality, and social class. Social-compunction theory proposes that people in all societies are exposed to the prevailing racial, ethnic, religious, and cultural stereotypes during socialization (Devine, 1989; Devine et al., 1991). These stereotypes automatically come into play unless their influence is consciously overcome.

Stereotypes can also be activated consciously, for instance, when people call to mind the characteristics of another group. When group stereotypes are activated, either consciously or unconsciously, they typically lead to biased processing of information, and this bias is strongest for well-developed stereotypes, such as those about sex and race (Stangor & McMillan, 1992). Stereotypes are maintained in part by the tendency for people to better remember expectancy-confirming information about social groups than expectancy-disconfirming infor-mation (Fyock & Stangor, 1994; Stangor & McMillan, 1992). These biases affect the information that is noticed, remembered, stored in long-term memory, and recalled (Bodenhausen & Wyer, 1985; Stangor & McMillan, 1992). Another memory bias, *illusory correlation,* leads people to remember that members of minority groups have engaged in negative behaviors more frequently than they actually have (Hamilton & Rose, 1980).

People often explain the negative behaviors of outgroup members in terms of their internal traits. People fail to take situational causes of behaviors into consideration when they should, resulting in stronger negative stereotypes of outgroups than the evidence warrants (Schaller, Asp, Rosell, & Heim, 1996; Schaller & O'Brien, 1992). An example of this tendency is provided by the explanations people give for the fact that Blacks in the United States score lower then Whites on national tests. Many Whites attribute these findings to a lack of intelligence on the part of Blacks, failing to take into account such situational factors as biases in the tests, poor educational facilities, and a lack of exposure to relevant educational materials in their home environments because of poverty.

People sometimes avoid changing their stereotypes by subtyping. That is, they break a larger group down into smaller subcategories. For instance, when White people who stereotype Blacks as unintelligent are confronted with an obviously intelligent Black person, they may create a subcategory of *smart Blacks* to separate this person from other Blacks. Thus, subtyping preserves the stereotype of the larger group.

Stereotyping Reduction Processes

It is depressingly difficult to change stereotypes once they have been acquired. The evidence strongly suggests that it is easier to strengthen negative stereotypes than to weaken them. However, creating superordinate groups and emphasizing multiple identities, counteracting expectancies, using self-regulation, correcting misattributions, and differentiating the outgroup can reduce stereotyping.

Creating Superordinate Groups and Emphasizing Multiple Identities

It is possible to undercut the tendency to see the social world in terms of us versus them. Just as superordinate categories can be used to reduce prejudice, so, too, can they be used to undermine stereotyping. If superordinate groups are created that include members of both the ingroup and the outgroup, the tendency to view outgroup members as all alike and in negative terms is no longer functional. Most intergroup relations programs create superordinate groups that undermine this dichotomous thinking.

The tendency to see the world in terms of dichotomies can also be reduced by reminding people of other important sources of identity. Every person is simultaneously a member of many social categories, and these social categories overlap. Racial or ethnic categories may divide people, but other important categories, such as sex or religion, can unite them. Reminding people of the crosscutting groups to which they belong should reduce stereotyping (Commins & Lockwood, 1978; Dovidio, Kawakami, & Gaertner, 2000; Hewstone, Islam, & Judd, 1993; Vanbeselaere, 1991).

Counteracting Expectancies

The expectancies associated with stereotypes that lead to self-fulfilling prophecies can be actively counteracted. Members of the stereotyped group who are aware of others' negative expectations can successfully offset the expectancy after being trained to behave in disconfirming ways (Cohen & Roper, 1972). They are particularly likely to counteract the expectancy if they are certain that they do not possess the expected trait (Swann & Ely, 1984). The self-fulfilling effects of negative expectancies also tend to disappear when people want outgroup members to like them (Neuberg, 1996). In addition, when ingroup members are dependent on outgroup members, the chances that disconfirming evidence will be effectively processed are increased (Darley, Fleming, Hilton, & Swann, 1986).

Using Self-Regulation

Although stereotypes are often automatically activated, people can learn to put self-regulatory processes into effect so that triggering stereotypes evokes guilt (Monteith, Zuwerink, & Devine, 1994). If people are motivated to overcome stereotyping, these guilt feelings will lead to the suppression of stereotype-related behaviors (Montieth, 1993). Intergroup relations programs often take active steps to teach people to counteract stereotypes when activated.

Correcting Misattributions

Negative outgroup stereotypes can be weakened if people engage in conscious, thoughtful processing of expectancy-disconfirming information and then attribute the causes of the disconfirming behaviors to internal factors (Crocker, Hannah, & Weber, 1983). Internal attributions are most likely to be made if a number of different outgroup members engage in the disconfirming behavior, and it occurs frequently in a variety of settings (Mackie, Allison, Worth, & Asuncion, 1992; Rothbart & John, 1985; Weber & Crocker, 1983). It is also helpful if the people displaying the disconfirming behavior are otherwise seen as typical outgroup members (Rothbart & Lewis, 1988). Schaller and his colleagues (1996) have found that briefly training people in the logic of making statistically valid inferences also reduces their tendency to stereotype groups.

Differentiating the Outgroup

The tendency to subtype can be undercut by providing contact with a number of different outgroup members (Rothbart & John, 1985). Differentiation results when so many new categories are created that subtyping becomes impossible (Langer, 1989).

Thus far, we have focused on counteracting negative contact, prejudice, and stereotypes, but intergroup relations programs also have changing discriminatory behaviors as a goal. In the next section, we consider the theory of reasoned action, which is useful in understanding how to bring about changes in intergroup behavior.

Discriminatory Behavior

As we have noted, the causal relationship between prejudice and discrimination is imperfect. People who are prejudiced do not always discriminate against outgroup members, and people who are not prejudiced sometimes behave in discriminatory ways. The existence of social norms is one factor that influences whether or not prejudice leads to discrimination. Social norms that proscribe discrimination can lead prejudiced people to refrain from discrimination, whereas social norms that prescribe discrimination can lead people to behave in discriminatory ways even if they are not prejudiced.

The Theory of Reasoned Action

The theory of reasoned action captures the interplay between the role of attitudes such as prejudice and social norms as determinants of behavior (Fishbein & Azjen, 1975). According to this theory, people's intentions to behave are a function of their attitudes toward the act and their subjective norms. The relevant attitudes toward the act are twofold: beliefs about the value of the outcomes of the possible behavior and beliefs about the probability that these outcomes will occur. Subjective norms are the perceptions people have of the attitudes of others who are important to them. The effect of subjective norms on behavior is influenced by the degree to which people are motivated to comply with the wishes of these significant others.

To understand how the theory operates, imagine a White apartment manager who believes that turning away prospective Black tenants will lead to retaining his current White tenants and easily finding new tenants. He values both of these outcomes. He may also believe that he could be sued if he turns away Black applicants. If he is fairly certain of reaping the benefits of discriminating against Blacks but thinks the probability of being sued for discrimination is low, then he is likely to turn Black applicants away. He may also be influenced by his perceptions of what significant people in his life think he should do in these circumstances. His tenants and neighbors might be especially important reference groups in this instance. If he believes that his current tenants would prefer not to have Black tenants and he thinks other people in the neighborhood also support this decision, then discrimination is likely. The theory of reasoned action has proven to be useful in predicting a wide range of behaviors including intergroup behaviors.

Changing Discriminatory Behavior

Modifying Attitudes About Outcomes and Altering Perceptions of Subjective Norms

Using the theory of reasoned action, it is possible to change discriminatory behavior by modifying people's attitudes about the outcomes of discrimination and by altering their perceptions of relevant subjective norms. For example, in the workplace, it may be possible to establish clear norms regarding the inappropriateness of discriminatory behavior, harassment, and derogatory speech. In addition to creating sanctions for discriminatory behavior, businesses can also seek to create a climate that values diversity so that there is normative support for behavior that is antithetical to discrimination. Creating a positive climate for diversity thus has two effects relevant to the theory of reasoned action. First, it changes the perceptions of the outcomes of discrimination. If discrimination is negatively sanctioned, people's attitudes about the consequences of discrimination will be altered along with their perceptions of the probability of receiving these negative sanctions. Second, as norms valuing diversity take hold, subjective perceptions of what people believe significant others wish them to do will also change.

Intergroup relations programs can also change perceptions of the personal rewards and costs of discrimination and thereby alter beliefs about the perceived consequences of discrimination in other ways as well. For instance, it should be possible to increase people's perceptions of the costs of discrimination by asking them to empathize with the victims of discrimination. People may need to be made aware of the types of behaviors that are perceived to be harmful or discriminatory by members of other groups. This heightened awareness should reduce the incidence of discriminatory behaviors. They can also be helped to recognize that their reference groups, such as the other participants in the program, their friends, or coworkers, are opposed to discriminatory behavior. If intergroup relations programs encourage people to publicly state their intentions not to behave in discriminatory ways, these statements are likely to increase the chances that people will follow through on their commitments to change their behavior.

Dimensions on Which These Psychological Processes Differ

The psychological processes we reviewed that result in improving intergroup relations can be categorized on two dimensions: the degree to which they require active versus passive involvement by the participants, and the degree to which they involve changes in affect versus changes in cognitions. Figure 2.3 provides a schematic diagram locating the processes we have reviewed on these two dimensions. The processes that are predominantly affective and active include self-regulation, reinforcing positive intergroup behaviors, making value-behavior discrepancies explicit, and modifying associations between cognition and affect. Those processes that are predominantly cognitive

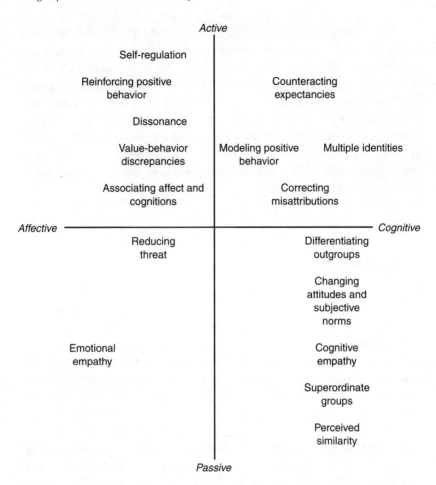

Figure 2.3. Processes Involved in Improving Intergroup Relations

and active consist of counteracting expectancies, modeling positive intergroup behaviors, correcting misattributions, and emphasizing multiple identities. Changing attitudes and subjective norms, differentiating the outgroup, creating cognitive empathy, creating superordinate groups, and increasing perceptions of similarity are predominantly cognitive and passive processes. The predominantly affective and passive processes include reducing threat and creating emotional empathy.

Most intergroup relations programs employ a variety of processes, although some rely primarily on processes of a single type (e.g., active, affective processes in dialogue groups, and passive, cognitive processes in diversity training). Many of the processes that are typically evoked passively could actually be evoked in a more active manner (e.g., acquiring information through experiential exercises, such as simulation games and role-playing, and differentiating the outgroup through intergroup contact). Selecting active means of employing these processes might well increase their effectiveness (Gudykunst, Hammer, & Wiseman, 1977).

Summary

In this chapter, we introduced a model suggesting that negative contact is a direct cause of prejudice and stereotyping, prejudice, and discrimination; stereotyping is a cause of prejudice but prejudice also creates stereotypes; and prejudice and stereotyping are the major antecedents of discriminatory behaviors. We then discussed these concepts and the ways intergroup relations programs can use these and other social science concepts and theories to improve intergroup relations.

A revised contact theory suggests that the outcomes of intergroup contact are affected by the societal context in which it occurs, the characteristics of the participants, and the characteristics of the contact situation itself. These factors can be used to ensure positive-contact conditions in intergroup relations programs.

Newer theories of prejudice, such as ambivalence-amplification, aversive racism, symbolic racism, and compunction theories, represent prejudice as stemming from an often covert set of contradictory attitudes and feelings. In addition, realistic group conflict theory argues that prejudice can stem from realistic threats. Integrated threat theory posits that prejudice derives from realistic or symbolic threats, stereotypes, and anxiety about interaction with outgroup members. According to social dominance theory, prejudice is an outcome of dominant groups' legitimization of their power, privileges, and prestige. Social identity theorists believe that prejudice can arise when an ingroup attempts to maintain a positive self-image by disparaging outgroups.

These theories suggest a number of remedies for prejudice including making value-behavior discrepancies explicit, reducing threat, increasing perceptions of ingroup-outgroup similarities, creating superordinate groups, emphasizing multiple identities, reinforcing and modeling positive behaviors, modifying associations between cognition and affect, using dissonance to create attitude change, creating empathy, and correcting misattributions about outgroup members.

Stereotypes are a product of cognitive and historical processes. They are commonly activated automatically by observable features of other people, and they serve such a wide range of functions that they are difficult to dislodge. However, creating superordinate groups and emphasizing multiple identities, counteracting expectancies, using self-regulation, correcting misattributions, and differentiating the outgroup can all help to reduce stereotyping.

According to the theory of reasoned action, the tendency to engage in discriminatory behavior is affected by people's attitudes toward the outcomes of the behavior and their perceptions of the attitudes of others toward the behavior. Increasing perceptions of the costs of discriminatory behavior while highlighting the rewards of nondiscriminatory behavior can decrease the incidence of discrimination, as can changing the perceptions of the beliefs of significant others concerning discrimination.

MULTICULTURAL EDUCATION INTRODUCTION 3

MULTICULTURAL EDUCATION is one of the most controversial and widely used techniques for improving intergroup relations. This controversy has arisen in part because there is no single definition of multicultural education, leading people to disagree about what it is and what should be included in multicultural education programs. Although the term is applied to a wide variety of programs, most programs share some common elements. All these programs can be classified as taking a direct approach (see Figure 1.1) to teaching students about the various racial, ethnic, cultural, and religious groups in their society. Some multicultural programs also focus on social stratification issues, particularly issues relating to the unequal distribution of resources and power in society (e.g., social class, the distribution of wealth across racial and ethnic groups). They usually include information on the history of the various groups as well as their cultural values and practices. In some cases, there is a celebratory element to multicultural education programs that involves learning about the food, dress, art, music, and dance of different ethnic, cultural, or religious groups. Multicultural education programs can also be classified as being largely didactic in nature (see Figure 1.1); that is, they are based on instructional approaches to education. However, to varying degrees, these programs also incorporate interactive exercises including role-playing, simulation games, group discussions, and other personally involving (experiential) exercises.

We begin our analysis of multicultural education with an examination of the goals of these programs. This section is followed by a review of the controversy that has surrounded multicultural education. We then discuss in more detail the content and techniques employed in multicultural education programs. A considerable number of empirical studies have evaluated the effects of long-term and short-term multicultural education programs, and these are analyzed next. The largely passive, cognitive, psychological processes involved in creating changes through multicultural education are examined in the following section. In the last section of the chapter, issues and problems associated with implementing multicultural education are analyzed, and recommendations for their solution are offered.

Goals of Multicultural Education

Multicultural education programs are designed to prepare students to function effectively in culturally diverse societies. Their approach is based on a clearly articulated set of values including equality of opportunity, justice, human dignity, respect for group differences, and pluralism [National Council for the Social Studies (NCSS) Task Force, 1992]. The first programs that were developed were primarily oriented toward assimilating students of color into the economic mainstream of society (Sleeter & Grant, 1987). In more recent years, as a result of changes in the cultural milieu, these programs have encouraged students of color to maintain their own cultural identities. The proponents of this approach now believe that education should not promote the ideology or values of any one group in society. They feel that the contributions of all racial, ethnic, cultural, and religious groups to their society should be acknowledged. Many multiculturalists believe that in order to promote the achievement of students from all types of backgrounds, the total school environment should reflect a multicultural focus. They argue that courses in many different subject areas can incorporate a multicultural orientation. Multiculturalists also feel that the administration of the school and the relations of teachers and administrators to parents and the community should incorporate a multicultural approach.

Banks (1997) has suggested that multicultural education programs have five basic goals. The first goal is to integrate multicultural curriculum into the school. The second goal involves providing students with an understanding that knowledge is culturally constructed and is influenced by race, ethnicity, and social class. The third goal concerns prejudice reduction and the improvement of intergroup relations. The fourth goal refers to the adoption of an equity-pedagogical approach, which stresses the need for cultural competence in teachers and sensitivity to such issues as ethnic-group differences in the learning styles and linguistic strengths of their students. The fifth goal is to restructure the entire school system to reflect changes along the preceding dimensions.

Almost all multicultural education programs occur in educational settings, and most are found in primary and secondary schools. Multicultural education programs are sometimes found in higher education as well, particularly in universities that educate teachers and counselors. In fact, almost 90% of all doctoral programs in counseling psychology require at least one course on multiculturalism (Ponterotto, 1996). The majority of multicultural education programs are offered in institutions in the United States, but multicultural education is also used in England, Canada, Australia, and other countries.

The Controversy Surrounding Multicultural Education

Conservative critics in the United States have argued that multicultural education undercuts traditional approaches to education that place a heavy emphasis on Western civilization (reviewed by Banks, 1993; and Sleeter, 1995). They believe that American education should stress Western culture, philosophy, literature, art, music, and science. They worry that multicultural education does not promote cultural cohesion and national identity and instead produces divisiveness. Because multicultural education does not promote the assimilation of minority groups into the mainstream of American life, they believe it will create a more fractious and less unified society. They regard it as detrimental for educational institutions to teach students about such issues as racism, sexism, and ethnocentrism. The critics are also concerned that because multicultural education stresses minority perspectives toward American history, it will lead to interpretations of the meaning of the American experience with which they disagree. They also believe that the time devoted to multicultural education will detract from learning basic skills.

Critics from the political left have a different set of criticisms of multicultural education, arguing that it fails to promote structural reform of racist, societal institutions (Banks, 1993; Sleeter, 1995). They argue that in some cases, multicultural education is used in all-White schools as a way of avoiding more fundamental changes, such as integrating the schools. They are particularly concerned that in all-minority and integrated schools, multicultural education functions to make minority groups more accepting of the status quo by increasing their self-esteem, promoting positive relations between groups, and creating strong ethnic identities. These opponents of multicultural education believe that schools reflect the same social inequalities that exist in the society at large and thus schools promote the status quo and foster the maintenance of existing social inequalities. They call for more fundamental reforms of the schools that would involve replacing authoritarian approaches to leadership and teaching with more egalitarian and democratic practices. They feel that multicultural education does not go far enough toward changing the social system. They want an explicit focus on the problems of capitalism, racism, and the unequal distribution of power and wealth. Thus, conservatives criticize multicultural education for challenging the social order too much, whereas members of the political left criticize it for not challenging the social order enough.

Proponents hold a still different view of multicultural education (Banks, 1993, 1997). They believe that multicultural education promotes social cohesion by fostering respect and acceptance among different groups. They think it redresses the imbalance of a curriculum that emphasizes Western civilization by presenting the contributions to society of a great number of different racial, ethnic, and religious groups as well as the contributions of women. Although they accept the fact that many groups choose to assimilate into society, they feel that members of all groups should have the option of maintaining a strong identity with their ethnic, cultural, and religious groups of origin. They believe that creating equal opportunities for all groups and promoting achievement for all students will eventually lead to changes in the structures of society that previously supported inequalities, promoted segregation in housing, and denied access to educational institutions and labor unions. The proponents also think that multicultural education furthers the learning of basic skills rather than taking time away from learning these skills. For example, Banks (1993) says, "A major assumption of multicultural education is that a curriculum consistent with the learning and motivational styles of ethnic youths, and that validates their cultures, identity, and worth will enhance their ability to master the basic skills" (pp. 62-63). The proponents also argue that multicultural education promotes the underlying principles of participatory democracy by fostering egalitarian relations between groups.

The Content and Techniques of Multicultural Education

Multicultural education programs vary enormously. At one end of the continuum, they may be narrowly focused and last only a few weeks, but at the opposite end of the continuum, they may permeate the entire curriculum from K-12th grade and beyond. Some programs rely on the use of textbooks and formal instructional materials, whereas others incorporate an array of more involving materials and procedures, including movies, videos, field trips, class visits by members of the groups being studied, group exercises, simulation games, and role-playing. An examination of exercises included in three multicultural curricula can be used to illustrate the variety of these techniques.

One lesson in the first curriculum addresses controversial issues in intergroup relations (Banks, 1988). Teachers ask their students to research the views of civil rights activists of the 1960s (e.g., Martin Luther King Jr., Stokely Carmichael, Julian Bond, Eldridge Cleaver) and then hold a "convention" in which they discuss the attitudes of these figures toward racial integration versus segregation. In another exercise, students finish a set of unfinished sentences (e.g., "A racist is a person who . . .") and then discuss their answers in small groups. A third exercise in this curriculum asks students to conduct surveys in their schools or communities to provide them with information on various aspects of intergroup relations.

The primary principles that guide the second curriculum are that prejudice and intergroup violence are preventable, intervention should start early, and empathy promotes respect (McLaughlin & Brilliant, 1997). Others are that students should learn to appreciate differences and work together cooperatively, and they should become socially responsible. The curriculum employs videos, readings, discussions, and interactive exercises. In one activity, students watch a video about a victim of a hate crime after reading about the impact of hate crimes on their victims. The students write down their reactions to the video and discuss these reactions. In another activity, the students are introduced to the concept of stereotyping and asked to work in small groups to identify movies, television shows, videos, or magazines that present stereotyped images of social groups. The teacher then facilitates a discussion about stereotyping that focuses on which groups are most subject to stereotyping in the media and the effects that stereotyping produces. As a part of this curriculum, the students also study the Holocaust and the civil rights movement. In a final activity, the students develop a community service project to help reduce prejudice. The class brainstorms ideas for the project and critically analyzes them. The students come to a consensus on what goals they want to accomplish. Next, they form project committees and list the steps necessary to carry out the project. The students are then asked to volunteer for the project of their choice and to help carry it out.

The American Jewish Committee has developed another curriculum. Their *Hands Across the Campus* curriculum has been widely adopted for use in high schools (Genet, 1999). It has three primary goals: to create appreciation for America's multicultural heritage; to foster better communication among students from diverse ethnic, religious, and racial groups; and to strengthen democratic process. Prejudice reduction is one of the central aims of this program. Students are

n to define terms (e.g., *values, prejudice, discrimination,*
itify their own personal values, explain the forces that
iderstand the way that majority groups have treated

minority groups, and learn how to reduce prejudice and discrimination. The core values taught in the curriculum are personal responsibility, respect for others, fairness, cooperation with others, appreciation of cultural diversity, and community involvement.

Teachers lead students through a series of lessons that involve responding to personal surveys or handouts, class discussions, reading about historical incidents, learning about cultural heroes, role-playing, and team learning. Lessons cover such diverse topics as Hammurabi's legal code from ancient Babylonia, leaders who rebelled against colonialism, women's rights leaders in different countries, heroes of the Holocaust, more recent heroes (e.g., Golda Meir, Nelson Mandela), American heroes (e.g., Pocahontas, Black students at Little Rock High School), the uses of propaganda to foster stereotypes, American ethnic groups (e.g., Inupiat), stopping hate crimes, and poverty. For example, in the lesson on the Black students at Little Rock High School, the teacher begins with a general discussion of school segregation and the details of the *Brown v. Board of Education of Topeka* (1954) Supreme Court decision. The students then read material about desegregating Little Rock High School in 1957. In particular, they read a number of quotes from the Black students who were ushered into the school by U.S. marshals. The students are asked to volunteer to play the roles of central players in these events and to report on the events from the perspective of these individuals (a reporter, the governor of Arkansas, the president of the United States, a Little Rock High School teacher, a segregationist, and a mother of a student). After the role-play, the students discuss the values displayed by the Black students in Little Rock and the importance and meaning of equality. As an assignment, the students are asked to write about whether or not they would have volunteered to be the students who ended school segregation in Little Rock.

The teachers employ a set of guidelines as a basis for discussing sensitive topics. For instance, it is suggested that they preview the topic, invite student cooperation and involvement, provide students with reflection time, give students an opportunity to express themselves, hold small- as well as large-group discussions, set rules for class discussion (e.g., no name calling, respect the opinions of others, no one has to participate), and allow students to evaluate the appropriateness of the lesson.

An ethnographic study of Heritage High (not the actual name) provides an example of the goals and implementation of a multicultural program (Jacob, 1995). Heritage High is an inner-city school in a Northeastern city. A wide array of groups is represented in the school including Blacks, Latinos, and immigrants from non-Latin countries, as well as Whites. In this school, the multicultural approach involved integrating "the history, literature, accomplishments, and perspectives of all groups into the formal curriculum" (p. 372) in an attempt to change the entire learning environment. The teachers and staff in this school wished to improve cultural understanding and competence, but they were also interested in getting the students to be more actively involved in confronting racial and ethnic inequalities.

The multicultural program was combined with the school's bilingual program on two floors of this five-floor school. English and history teachers revised their curricula to emphasize diversity, a global-issues course was created, and cooperative learning and critical thinking were incorporated into some classes. The students in this program also participated in a number of social activities designed to create a sense of community among them and to celebrate their racial, ethnic, and cultural origins. For instance, at the beginning of the school year, students interviewed other students in their homerooms and then introduced them to the entire class. The students decorated the halls with the art and cultural heroes of their groups. They also had talent shows, assemblies, academic forums, meals, dances, and extracurricular activities that were organized around racial, ethnic, and cultural themes.

According to Jacob (1995), the program changed the social climate of these two floors. Many of these changes were positive, but in his view, a few were not. The students commented that there was a "warm, comfortable feeling" in these classrooms. An informal survey suggested that there were a great number of cross-group friendships and many informal intergroup dialogues in these classes, as well as closer student-teacher bonds. He also reported a greater identification with the school. Nonetheless, there was still a degree of ethnic segregation, and there were complaints that one ethnic group dominated the school. Some teachers and students complained that the program highlighted differences rather than similarities among groups.

The effectiveness of multicultural education programs is examined in the next section.

Studies of the Effects of Multicultural Education Programs

The effects of multicultural education have been examined in a number of studies. We divide these studies into two types: Those that are relatively long term and have examined the effects of multicultural curricula, and those that are short term and have examined only components of multicultural education programs, such as the use of videos, simulations, and discussions of values.

Longer Programs

The ideal study of the effects of multicultural education would use a pretest and posttest design in which the same group of participants is examined before the program begins and then again after it is terminated. This study would also include a control group that was measured at the same two points in time but was not exposed to the program. In an ideal study, the participants would be assigned to the treatment and control groups randomly to ensure that the two groups are equivalent to one another at the beginning of the study. In practice, most studies of multicultural education use control groups that are comparable to the treatment group, but the participants are not randomly assigned to treatment and control groups. When multicultural education leads to statistically significant positive changes from pretest to posttest, but the control group does not change, that constitutes strong evidence that the program is successful. Nearly all the studies of multicultural education that we will review employed this type of design, although a few lacked a control group (Brown, Parham, & Yonker, 1996; Byington, Fischer, Walker, & Freedman, 1997; Grant & Grant, 1985; Washington, 1981).

Studies of the longer-term programs have targeted four populations: students in primary and secondary schools, graduate students in

TABLE 3.1   Studies of the Effects of Multicultural Education Programs

	Predominately Positive Effects	A Mixture of Positive and No Effects	No Effects	Predominantly Negative Effects
Long-Term Studies	13	9	2	2
Short-Term Studies	12	2	1	0

NOTE: The numbers indicate the number of studies showing each type of effect.

counseling, preservice teachers, and undergraduate students. We examine the effects of multicultural education programs on each population in turn, and we provide examples to illustrate each type of program.

We begin by reviewing studies done in primary and secondary schools. The majority of these studies (7 of 9) found that multicultural education had positive effects on measures of intergroup relations (Table 3.1). A few of these studies reported no effects, and one study reported negative effects (Aboud & Fenwick, 2000; Avery, Bird, Johnstone, Sullivan, & Thalhammer, 1992; Colca, Lowen, Colca, & Lord, 1982; Litcher & Johnson, 1969; Verma & Bagley, 1973, 1979; Wittig & Molina, 2000; Yawkey, 1973; Yawkey & Blackwell, 1974). One of the successful programs employed a multiethnic reader with White second-grade students (Litcher & Johnson, 1969). This program led to more favorable attitudes toward Blacks after 4 months of classes. A program that had no effects consisted of an 8-week language arts program that exposed White junior high school students to information about five racial and ethnic minority groups, using books, films, art, and guest speakers (Lessing & Clarke, 1976). This program had no effects on stereotyping. A program that had negative effects used mixed-race pairs of trained college students to provide eight sessions of training that lasted 1 hour each (Wittig & Molina, 2000). The program provided information on the history and contributions of various racial or ethnic groups, covered concepts related to racism, provided cultural awareness training, and emphasized respect for all groups. The participants in this study consisted of hundreds of middle school and high school students who represented a wide array of ethnic or racial groups. The program led to greater bias toward other racial groups, on a measure assessing willingness to interact with out-group members, and to a deterioration of the classroom interracial climate. The findings of this study suggest that minimally trained college students may not be effective as teachers of a multicultural education curriculum.

A number of studies have also been done with adults, most of them involving training in multicultural counseling or teacher education. Most counseling programs provide multicultural training because it is recognized that counselors need skills to deal with clients from different types of racial, ethnic, cultural, and religious backgrounds. Nearly all the studies done on this type of multicultural training (7 of 8) have found that multicultural programs have positive effects on intergroup relations (Brooks & Kahn, 1990; Brown et al., 1996; Byington et al., 1997; D'Andrea, Daniels, & Heck, 1991; Lefley, 1985; Parker, Moore, & Neimeyer, 1998; Van Soest, 1996; Wang, 1998). For instance, one study examined the effects of a 45-hour, multicultural course designed to provide counselors with an understanding of multicultural concepts, a knowledge of stereotyping and discrimination, and skills relevant to counseling minority group clients (D'Andrea et al., 1991). The course increased multicultural awareness and knowledge as well as counseling skills. Predominantly negative effects were found in a study of a social work course on oppression that emphasized the injustice of power differences and inequality and employed both didactic and experiential components (Van Soest, 1996). The course led to increases in beliefs that the world is just (that people deserve what they get and get what they deserve), which is the opposite of what was expected. The author speculates that receiving an intense lesson that the world is not a just place was so threatening that it led these predominantly White students (91%) to embrace more strongly than they had before a belief that the world is just.

Several studies have examined the effects of multicultural training on teachers. Like counselors, a great many teachers work in a diverse environment. In many schools of education, prospective teachers are required to take courses designed to teach them about the backgrounds of the students they may be teaching. Most of the studies of these courses (3 of 4) indicate that multicultural, teacher training programs improved intergroup relations, although one found no effects

(Grant & Grant, 1985; Hennington, 1981; Richards & Gamache, 1979; Washington, 1981). In one study with primarily positive effects, pre-service teachers were given 21 hours of instruction (Hennington, 1981). The attitudes of these teachers toward a variety of social groups became more positive as a result of this training, as did their knowledge of stereotyping and discrimination. The knowledge effects were still present 3 weeks later, but the attitude effects were not. A 1-week, teacher training workshop involving films, audiotapes, group activities, and curriculum development sessions had no effects on the multicultural attitudes of either White or Black teachers, perhaps because it was too short (Washington, 1981).

A final set of studies targeted undergraduate students. In these studies, too, the effects were predominantly positive (4 of 5), although one study reported that the program had no effects (Astin, 1993; J. H. Katz & Ivey, 1977; Neville & Furlong, 1994; Pascarella, Edison, Nora, Hagedorn, & Terenzini, 1996; B. Robinson & Bradley, 1997). Two of the studies are notable because they included multiple institutions. One large-scale study of 217 colleges and universities found that participating in cultural awareness workshops led to positive changes in cultural awareness and commitment to racial understanding, along with better undergraduate retention, better academic skills (e.g., critical thinking, writing ability), and more social activism (Astin, 1993). Similar positive effects were reported for participation in ethnic studies classes. As is true for many of the studies we have reviewed, the students in this study chose to take these cultural awareness classes, which may mean that they were predisposed to respond favorably to them. The other large-scale study involved 18 institutions and examined the effects of participating in racial or cultural awareness workshops (Pascarella et al., 1996). These workshops led students to be more open to diversity. The positive effects of participating in these workshops were greater for White than for non-White students.

The picture that emerges from these studies is that the outcomes of multicultural education programs were predominantly, but not uniformly, positive. Of the 30 studies we have just reviewed, 13 found predominantly positive effects, 9 found a mixture of positive effects and no effects, 4 found no effects, 2 found a mixture of positive and negative effects, and 2 found primarily negative effects on measures related to intergroup relations. One concern with evaluation studies is that only those with the most favorable results are published. For this reason, it is possible that the published studies present a more favorable picture of the outcomes of multicultural education than is actually the case.

In evaluating these studies, it is important to bear in mind that these programs were all unique, which makes it difficult to compare across studies. In addition, they employed different measures of intergroup relations. Many of these measures are not well established, and some may not have been valid. The use of weak measures may have led to inaccurate assessments of the effects of these programs in some cases. The programs were conducted in different regions of the country on samples that differed widely in age and other demographic characteristics, and these factors also may have influenced the results. Furthermore, the contexts in which these programs were conducted were very different from one another, and this, too, complicates the picture. At best, any conclusions formed on the basis of these studies must be regarded as tentative. With these reservations in mind, it appears that most multicultural education programs are achieving a degree of success, but many of them are not fully realizing the goals they were designed to achieve, and in a small number of cases, these programs actually lead to negative outcomes.

Short-Term Studies

In addition to the studies of relatively long-term effects of multicultural education programs, a number of studies have examined the short-term effects of components of multicultural programs. Most multicultural education programs include readings, films and videos, role-playing, and discussions. Short-term studies have been employed to examine the effects of these components of multicultural education programs. These studies indicate that the components of these programs typically have positive effects on intergroup attitudes and behaviors. Of the 15 studies of short-term programs (Table 3.1), 12 found predominantly positive effects, 2 found mixed effects, 1 found no effects, and none found negative effects (Aboud & Doyle, 1996; Barnard & Benn, 1988; Byrnes & Kiger, 1990; Culbertson, 1957; Gardiner, 1972; Gray & Ashmore, 1975; Hohn, 1973; Kehoe & Rogers, 1978; Leippe & Eisenstadt, 1994; Mitnick & McGinnies, 1958; Peak &

Morrison, 1958; Rokeach, 1971; Vrij, Van Schie, & Cherryman, 1996; Wade & Bernstein, 1991; Weiner & Wright, 1973).

Several of these studies are noteworthy. One study was patterned after a well-known elementary school demonstration invented by Jane Elliot to illustrate the effects of arbitrary discrimination. In this study, Byrnes and Kiger (1990) divided White college students into those with blue or brown eyes. During a 3-hour simulation game, brown-eyed students were allowed to discriminate against blue-eyed students in a variety of ways. The researchers found that this experience led to a greater willingness to act in nondiscriminatory ways but had no effects on racial attitudes. This study was criticized because of the distress it caused for the students who participated (A. Williams & Giles, 1992). The authors' response was that simulations, even those that cause distress, are justifiable if participants are informed beforehand of the general nature of the simulation and are thoroughly debriefed afterward—and as long as there is a reasonable expectation that the simulation will lead to greater compassion for others (Byrnes & Kiger, 1992).

When students engage in discussions in multicultural education programs, they often find that other students hold views about race and ethnicity that differ from theirs, and they are often led to examine inconsistencies in their own values. Experimental studies of this component of multicultural education programs suggest that it can lead to changes in prejudice. In a well-known study conducted by Rokeach (1971), White college students were exposed to the discrepancy between their beliefs in equality and their attitudes toward civil rights issues. Although this procedure did not lead to immediate attitude changes, 4 months and 16 months later, the students in the experimental condition had more positive attitudes toward civil rights than students in a control condition, who were not exposed to the procedure. Students in the experimental group were also more likely to join the National Association for the Advancement of Colored People (NAACP) and to enroll in ethnic studies classes than students in the control condition.

In some multicultural education programs, participants are taught skills that are relevant to interacting effectively with people who are from different racial or ethnic groups. In a short-term study that bears on this issue, Wade and Bernstein (1990) gave professional counselors (half Blacks and half Whites) 4 hours of training in techniques for interacting with Black women who were on welfare. The skills included articulating the clients' problems within a cultural framework and attending to the clients' values. Actual clients rated the trained counselors higher on empathy, expertness, and trustworthiness than an untrained control group of counselors. The clients were also more likely to return for subsequent sessions and were more satisfied with their counseling if the counselors had received the cultural sensitivity training. The attitudes and behaviors of a control group did not change. This study is important because it shows that the clients themselves perceived differences between trained and untrained counselors.

In comparing the outcomes of short-term programs with those of the longer term studies (Table 3.1), it is tempting to conclude that the shorter term programs were more successful, but this probably is not the correct interpretation. The shorter term programs suffer from demand characteristics—the implicit demand that participants feel to report that the intervention had positive effects—because the pretest and the posttest measures are so close together in time. The short-term programs are also very specific, and the measures designed to assess their effects tend to be very precise, which means that it is possible to detect small changes in attitudes. The longer term programs are more diffuse in nature, often combining multiple techniques, and the measures used may not be the most sensitive ones available. Thus, it is likely that the generally positive outcomes of the short-term programs somewhat overstate their effectiveness.

Overall Evaluation of Research on Multicultural Education

Multicultural education is one of the most frequently used techniques for improving intergroup relations. Its widespread use is due in part to the ease with which multicultural materials can be adopted in language arts, social science, and history classes in primary and secondary schools. Extensive resources now exist for the teaching of multicultural education. Thousands of articles have been written about multicultural education. It has been the subject of debate in the media as well as in educational circles.

The limited number of studies we have reviewed indicate that multicultural education generally has favorable effects on intergroup relations and rarely has negative effects. These studies have both strengths and weaknesses. On the positive side, they included a variety of age groups and formats for presenting multicultural curricula. Most of these studies employed strong designs that included pretests and posttests with both treatment and control groups. These studies used a number of different types of measures to assess the effects of multicultural education on intergroup relations. Based on these studies, we can tentatively conclude that multicultural education leads to changes in attitudes, knowledge of other groups, and behavior and that many of these changes endure for some period of time.

On the negative side, few of the studies examined programs that are as comprehensive as most multicultural programs in place today, and none of them lasted longer than half a school year. The majority have examined the effects of multicultural education on only White students. Only a small number of the longer studies (6) have included Blacks, and they show mixed results at best. Even fewer studies have examined the effects of multicultural education on other minority groups. It is possible that multicultural education has different effects on Whites and members of minority groups, but until further research is done, it will be impossible to tell. None of the studies has investigated the long-term effects of multicultural education on such factors as choice of integrated housing, working in integrated environments, choice of friends, voting patterns, racial and ethnic attitudes, or participation in organizations devoted to improving intergroup relations. Finally, too many programs are being conducted with no evaluation at all.

Overall, the results of these studies do provide considerable support for the effectiveness of multicultural education programs, but there are many gaps in our knowledge. One of the most common findings in these studies is a mixture of positive effects and no effects. Clearly, there is room for improvement in the implementation of many of these programs.

Multicultural education programs are typically a complex amalgam of techniques, including written materials, discussions, films and videos, experiential exercises, and celebratory features. Some of the research we have reviewed indicates that the components of multicultural education can have a positive impact on intergroup relations. However, we do not know which of these components is the most influential, and we do not know which components of multicultural education are most effective for students of different ages or from different ethnic or racial groups or social-class backgrounds. Until more research is done, multicultural educators may be wasting time on components of these programs that are not effective or do not work with certain groups. Little improvement in the practice of multicultural education can occur without more thorough evaluation of the programs that are in place.

Studies that did not obtain positive results are often more valuable than those that do obtain positive effects. We need to learn what does not work just as surely as we need to learn what does work. When a study reports increases in tolerance but no changes in attitudes (Avery et al., 1992), we need to know why the program had no effects on attitudes. Similarly, when a study reports a program that is effective for some groups (Whites and Black males), but not for others (Black females), as a study by Verma and Bagley (1973) did, we need to understand why this occurred. Similarly, when a program actually backfires and produces greater intolerance, as a tolerance education program did for students who were low in self-esteem, high in authoritarianism, and reported feeling threatened by other groups (Avery et al., 1992), then we want to know what could be changed in the program to reach these students also. One of the best ways to improve multicultural education programs is to refine them based on an understanding of what their weaknesses are. Another way that these programs can be strengthened is by understanding what makes them successful. It is to this topic that we turn now.

Psychological Processes Underlying Multicultural Education

The psychological processes that influence the impact of multicultural education consist primarily of passive, cognitive processes because the program itself places so much emphasis on didactic approaches to teaching (Figure 2.3). The psychological processes that can come into play depend, to some extent, on contextual factors, particularly on whether or not the school is segregated or integrated.

Processes Employed in Segregated Settings

In segregated settings, a variety of relatively passive, cognitively oriented processes are employed including overcoming ignorance of and anxiety about other groups, learning humanitarian values that promote intergroup relations, creating superordinate groups, and stressing cross-cutting identities and cognitive empathy. Programs in segregated educational settings cannot employ intergroup contact and must depend for their success on written materials, supplemented by films, videos, and a limited range of experiential exercises. In these contexts, the ways in which other groups are portrayed are likely to be crucial to their success.

Information about other groups attacks one of the main causes of prejudice—ignorance (W. G. Stephan & Stephan, 1984). In the absence of knowledge about other groups, people are apprehensive about interacting with them, and they tend to rely on stereotypes when interacting with them. Information about other groups can also lead to greater understanding and acceptance of these groups. The information in multicultural materials puts a human face on outgroups that may have been previously viewed in a stereotypical and dehumanized way. This information can diffuse anxiety about interacting with members of these groups by providing students with an understanding of the norms, beliefs, and values of other groups. In addition, accurate information about outgroups can undercut unrealistic fears and unfounded concerns about value differences. In addition, learning about other groups can counteract the tendency to make unfavorable attributions for their behaviors. Multicultural materials accomplish these goals by presenting information on group differences in norms, beliefs, and values in a positive light.

Multicultural programs emphasize the values of justice, equality, and tolerance implicitly or explicitly by presenting information about many different groups in an even-handed manner. Acquiring or strengthening these humanitarian values in multicultural education programs can help students guide their own behavior in ways that result in less stereotyping, prejudice, and discrimination. Research by Devine and her colleagues (Devine, 1995) indicates that students who believe that prejudice is wrong can learn to regulate their own cognitions in order to suppress the expression of any negative stereotypes they may possess. In a like manner, students who believe in justice, equality, and tolerance may learn to regulate their behavior. Programs that emphasize respect for other groups establish a norm that can come to pervade the social climate of the school and help to foster favorable intergroup relations.

Multicultural programs that stress the common humanity of all groups reduce prejudice by de-emphasizing racial, ethnic, and religious group boundaries and creating a larger, superordinate identity that incorporates all students. The superordinate group might be the community, the nation, or even humanity itself. Creating superordinate identities can offset the potentially divisive effects of presenting group differences. Ample evidence indicates that emphasizing superordinate identities can reduce prejudice among groups (Dovidio, Kawakami, & Gaertner, 2000; Gaertner, Dovidio, Nier, Ward, & Banker, 1999). Another factor that has been shown to reduce prejudice in laboratory studies is emphasizing cross-cutting identities. All people have multiple identities relating to sex, age, social class, birth order, and eye color, as well as religion, racial, ethnic, and cultural groups. By showing students that they are similar to other students in some respects but different in others, the impact of any one type of difference can be diluted.

Multicultural educational materials are often designed to present the history of various groups from the perspective of members of those groups. By presenting history and attitudes toward current social issues (e.g., affirmative action) from the perspective of minority groups, multicultural educational programs may capitalize on empathic processes. Research indicates that empathy for the experiences of minority group members can reduce prejudice (Batson et al., 1997; Gray & Ashmore, 1975; W. G. Stephan & Finlay, 2000). Reading about the experiences of others while identifying with them can create an empathic response in the reader that leads to valuing the welfare of these people and viewing them more favorably.

Empathizing with the discrimination suffered by minority groups may arouse feelings of injustice (Finlay & Stephan, 2000). Feelings of injustice can counteract prejudice, particularly if the prejudice is based on beliefs in a just world (Lerner, 1980). People who believe that the world is just and that others receive what they deserve tend to blame the suffering of minority group members on negative traits they believe this group possesses. They then derogate the group because of the negative traits they have attributed to them. However, reading about suffering and discrimination may lead people to reappraise their assumptions concerning victim blame, and they may come to believe that the victims of prejudice and discrimination do not deserve to be treated so unjustly. If the victims do not deserve to be mistreated, it is unreasonable to hold negative attitudes toward them.

In addition to providing students with information about other groups and their experiences, most multicultural programs incorporate a variety of experiential exercises that can be used in segregated settings. Some exercises, such as the blue-eyes/brown-eyes simulation game, provide students with a sense of what it is like to be the target of discrimination. The changes in attitudes and behaviors brought about by these exercises probably occur through the creation of empathy for the victims of discrimination. These exercises are likely to be even more powerful than simply reading about discrimination and the suffering it causes.

Processes Employed in Integrated Settings

In integrated settings, processes associated with intergroup contact can be employed, and experiential exercises requiring multiple groups can be used. We will discuss processes involved in intergroup contact, as well as counteracting stereotypes, creating attitude change through dissonance, and celebrating diversity.

In integrated settings, the variables included in the contact hypothesis come into play. To the extent that multicultural education promotes intergroup contact that is cooperative, based on equal status, positive, individualized, and supported by authority figures, it should improve relations between groups (G. W. Allport, 1954). Discussions and experiential exercises can play a crucial role in creating optimal contact in integrated settings. In Chapter 7, we will discuss the potentially positive effects of using small, mixed groups that work together cooperatively to learn academic materials, and in Chapter 5, we discuss the beneficial effects of using intergroup dialogues. Both of these techniques can be used in settings in which multicultural education programs are being implemented. Role-playing exercises and written materials designed to create empathy for outgroup members can also be employed in integrated settings with the added advantage that experiences during these exercises can be discussed later with members of the other groups.

Integrated settings provide more opportunities for students to unlearn their stereotypes than do segregated settings. Exercises can be used that provide students with individualized experiences with a number of different outgroup members. These experiences can lead to a more differentiated perception of the groups as a whole and thus undermine stereotyping. Multicultural programs can also create the type of environment that leads to cross-ethnic friendships, and research indicates that having friends from another racial or ethnic group is associated with reductions in prejudice (Blumberg & Roye, 1980; Hallinan & Teixeira, 1987).

Highly involving exercises are the most likely to have an impact on prejudice (McGregor, 1993; W. G. Stephan & Stephan, 1984). For instance, arguing in favor of greater rights for minorities or for other counter-attitudinal positions leads to attitude change by invoking the process of cognitive dissonance. When students come to agree with arguments that run counter to their previously held attitudes, they experience a sense of discomfort (dissonance). They can eliminate this discomfort by changing their former attitudes to be consistent with the views for which they have just argued (Gray & Ashmore, 1975). Simply presenting counterarguments in written materials is not as involving and is unlikely to have the same beneficial effects on attitude change.

It is easier to introduce the celebratory aspects of multicultural education (a day or week devoted to celebrating particular racial, ethnic, or cultural groups) in integrated than in segregated settings because members of different groups are present. Although the use of celebratory events is controversial, because they are thought to be too superficial to have beneficial effects on intergroup relations, celebratory events often do present racial, ethnic, cultural, and religious outgroups in a positive light. Associating positive affect with previously disliked groups can start the process of changing students' feelings about these groups. Eating delicious foods found in the cuisine of other cultures, learning new dances and songs, hearing presentations of music, and viewing interesting art created by other groups can all generate positive affect that becomes linked to these groups. Celebratory events are most likely to be beneficial when they are part of comprehensive multicultural programs.

Problems and Recommendations

Creating highly effective, multicultural education programs is a daunting task. For instance, some of the goals of these programs can potentially conflict with others. These programs may well promote positive identity with racial, ethnic, cultural, and religious ingroups, but in doing so, they run the risk of creating bias against outgroups. Teaching people to favor their ingroups but also to accept and respect outgroups is a tall order, because it runs against a deeply ingrained tendency to disparage outgroups in order to make comparisons that cast the ingroup in a favorable light (Tajfel, 1978, 1981, 1982). Multicultural education programs can inadvertently feed into this process of making favorable comparisons to outgroups by providing information on group differences. However, multiculturalists in Canada argue that creating strong ingroup identification lays the foundation for accepting outgroups, and there is evidence that this does occur (J. W. Berry, 1993). For instance, Aboud and Doyle (1993) found that most White and Black Canadian 7-year-olds did not display a bias in favor of the ingroup even though they clearly identified themselves with their ingroups. Teachers play an important role in determining whether strong ingroup identities increase or decrease prejudice. If teachers are fair, impartial, and respectful in their treatment of all groups, it should be less likely that ingroup pride will lead to disparaging outgroups.

Group differences in values, norms, and practices must be handled with particular care, because the danger of heightening ethnocentrism is high. One problem with presenting differences between groups is that perceived dissimilarity can cause prejudice (Byrne, 1971). Great care must be taken to present differences in a nonevaluative manner or to highlight the beneficial aspects of the differences presented. It is particularly important to present information on group differences in ways that are not threatening, because feelings of threat can easily lead to prejudice (W. G. Stephan & Stephan, 2000). When group differences in values are presented, many students assume that the values of their own group are good, natural, and moral, whereas groups with different values must be bad, unnatural, and immoral. The values held by the other group are often perceived to be a threat to the ingroup. However, if the benefits of these values for the people who hold them are also presented, the tendency to reject people who possess these values can be counteracted.

When multicultural educational materials describe racial, ethnic, or cultural group values, norms, and practices, they run the risk of stereotyping these groups. These materials are not usually written to reflect the complex array of members of different racial, ethnic, cultural, or religious groups, but they probably should be, if changing stereotypes is a goal of such programs. Research on stereotypes indicates that they can be most successfully undermined with multiple examples of counterstereotypical behaviors that are engaged in by different members of the other group in different settings (Rothbart & John, 1985). Multicultural readers could present this type of information, but in many cases they do not. Multicultural readers often emphasize the accomplishments of the most successful or prominent members of these groups. This positive information may not generalize to the group as a whole and may simply lead to subtyping these people as exceptions to the rule.

A common dilemma that multicultural education programs must confront is how to deal with group differences in the development of identity. A number of theorists have suggested that minority and majority group members in the United States go through a somewhat different set of stages in the development of their racial or ethnic identities. For instance, Ponterotto and Pedersen (1993) argue that many minority group students initially identify with the White majority, but then they break with this identity and come to strongly identify with their own groups, often rejecting the Whites at this stage. Cross (1995) has suggested that some Black students even adopt an oppositional identity in which they reject everything associated with the dominant group. Following this stage, minority group members may then go on to a stage in which they adopt a more balanced view. Ethnic identity at this stage is secure, and prejudice toward other groups is attenuated.

For members of the majority group, Ponterotto and Pedersen (1993) argue that initially, there is an unquestioning acceptance of the stereotypes of minority groups, but as they begin to examine their own cultural values, they may experience some confusion over their identities and guilt over White racism. This leads many White students to adhere to nonracist values, but others retreat into White culture and feel fear and anger toward minority groups. If they achieve the highest stages of identity development, Whites become more flexible and open in their intergroup relations. It is not clear that all children go through these stages, and it may be impossible to categorize some students using these stages.

The goal of multicultural education programs is to facilitate movement toward the highest stages of ethnic identity proposed by these models. However, the theories of ethnic identity development indicate that educators in multicultural education programs may have to deal with some potentially complex issues concerning identity. Teachers must be aware that their students may be in different stages of ethnic identity development. Both majority and minority students may be especially resistant to attempts to change their attitudes at certain stages. In addition, it appears that there are group differences in the manner in which racial and ethnic identity develops. Thus, teachers in integrated schools must face the problem that students from different groups in their classes will be going through different experiences as their identities develop. For instance, with young children, Black students may be in a stage in which they accept Whites, but many Whites may be in a stage in which they reject Blacks. Teachers should try to determine the stages of racial or ethnic identity of their students, and they should choose the techniques that are best suited to the mix of stages in their classrooms.

Another complex problem in multicultural education revolves around exercises that elicit deeply felt emotions or bring out conflict between groups. Many teachers are not trained to help students cope with these emotionally explosive situations, and thus there is a risk that some students may emerge from these exercises more angry, resentful, or prejudiced than when they began. This issue is closely tied to another factor that influences the outcomes of multicultural education: the age of the participants. Multicultural materials and exercises must be suited to the cognitive, social, and emotional development of the students. Young students may not be equipped to handle the emotional turmoil created by an open consideration of racism, stereotyping, ethnocentrism, and prejudice in discussion with members of other groups. They may also not have developed the cognitive maturity to analyze and understand these concepts. Techniques that rely on empathy may also have to await the development of cognitive skills in perspective taking and perhaps moral reasoning as well. There is also a greater risk of creating stereotypes with younger students, because they may not have formed impressions of other groups on their own. To avoid creating stereotypes, students can be provided with individualized interaction with outgroup members and information on a wide range of different outgroup members. This type of information should lead to differentiated perceptions of outgroups.

Older students are in a better position, in terms of both their emotional and cognitive maturity, to openly discuss the more sensitive issues related to relations with outgroup members. Their greater capacities to monitor their behaviors, analyze the implications of their actions, and have insight into themselves make it possible to use techniques that emphasize the acquisition of skills in regulating their behaviors and suppressing tendencies to stereotype others or discriminate against them.

Teachers play a critical role in multicultural education. To be maximally effective, teachers need to be well trained in a variety of skills related to teaching multicultural education. Not only must they be educated in the content area of multicultural education, but they also need to acquire skills in dealing with intergroup interactions, including facilitating discussions of emotion-laden topics and handling conflicts in productive ways. The vast majority of teachers in the United States are White [87%, according to Ordovensky (1992)], and they need to become aware of the subtle nature of the implicit biases and privileges that are a product of their membership in the majority group.

Teachers are responsible for enforcing classroom and school rules. It is important that these rules be egalitarian and that they are enforced in a fair and impartial manner. By their own conduct and their interactions with students, teachers can help to create a climate of tolerance, respect, and acceptance of differences. Teachers obviously serve as role

models for students, so they must take great care to display in their
own behavior the same egalitarian values they wish their students to
adopt. Thus, the role of teachers in multicultural education is complex.
In evaluating students and implementing school and classroom rules,
they must disregard social categories, such as race, ethnicity, cultural
background, religion, and sex and treat all students fairly and impar-
tially. However, in relating to their students and in teaching them, they
must be sensitive to group differences and learning styles.

Teachers of multicultural education should be very clear about the
goals they are attempting to achieve. Multicultural education programs have varied goals. Some multicultural education programs are
targeted at particular groups and aim to facilitate their ability to function effectively in mainstream society. Other programs are directed at
maintaining racial, ethnic, or cultural identity. Still others are oriented
primarily toward improving intergroup relations. Some programs aim
to improve all students' abilities to achieve, and others are designed to
combat social inequality (Sleeter & Grant, 1987). Unless teachers have
a clear sense of what specific goals they are attempting to achieve,
multicultural education runs the risk of being so diffuse as to achieve
little or nothing.

Teachers must also tailor programs for their particular context.
They may wish to emphasize the social groups from which their students are drawn. They may also want to take into consideration the
prior relations among these groups in the community. There is likely to
be some value in integrating current issues in the community into their
presentations.

In his book *Choosing Democracy,* Campbell (1996) uses the case of
Maria Delgado to illustrate the important role that teachers play in
multicultural education. Mrs. Delgado teaches high school in Texas.
Her presence alone indicates to her students that Mexican Americans
can go to college. In this and other ways, she serves as a role model for
her students. She was trained as a counselor, so she is particularly
adept at being a sensitive and concerned listener. She tries to establish
personal relations with her students, and she attempts to create a supportive environment in which her students can express their concerns.
The students perceive her as a person who understands their problems
and conflicts. She is particularly able to provide culturally sensitive sup-

port to her Latino students, and she is involved in her community. Mrs. Delgado furnishes an example of why it is important that the teaching staff reflect the ethnic, racial, religious, and cultural background of the students.

Summary

Multicultural education programs are widely used in primary and secondary educational institutions. To a lesser degree, they are also found in institutions of higher education. They are oriented toward preparing students to function effectively in multicultural societies. They accomplish this goal through a variety of didactic techniques including readings, discussions, simulation games, videos and movies, as well as celebratory activities. Most programs present information on the history and practices of different racial, ethnic, cultural, and religious groups—often from the perspective of members of these groups. Many programs also explicitly include information on topics such as racism, sexism, prejudice, stereotyping, discrimination, and ethnocentrism.

Studies of multicultural education have found that it generally has positive effects on intergroup relations, although studies of some programs have found no effects. Short-term studies of components of multicultural education programs, such as simulation games, videos, and discussions of values are also generally supportive of the positive effects of multicultural education. In general, too few studies of the effects of multicultural education have been done, and unfortunately, there appear to be no studies of long-term societal effects of comprehensive multicultural education programs.

An analysis of the contents of multicultural education programs suggests that they have beneficial effects as a result of reducing ignorance about outgroups, fostering humanitarian values, creating superordinate groups and cross-cutting identities, arousing cognitive empathy, promoting intergroup contact under favorable conditions, counteracting stereotypes, causing dissonance concerning discrepancies between cognition and behavior, and associating positive experiences with outgroup members. When implementing multicultural education programs, it is recommended that teachers focus on creating strong ingroup identities without fostering rejection of outgroups, present group differences in a positive way, deal with students at different stages of ethnic identity, present age-appropriate materials, and serve as models for the behaviors they wish their student to learn.

DIVERSITY INITIATIVES IN THE WORKPLACE

4

M ANAGING DIVERSITY HAS become big business in the American workplace. As the workplace becomes more diverse, businesses in the United States and around the world have come to recognize the necessity of training management and labor to work effectively across racial, ethnic, religious, age, sex, and cultural boundaries. It is estimated that by 2005, only 38% of the U.S. workforce will consist of White males (Bond & Pyle, 1998).

Let there be no doubt, intergroup relations problems abound in American businesses. Every year, thousands of complaints of discrimination are filed with the Equal Employment Opportunity Commission (EEOC), and hundreds of lawsuits are initiated against American businesses. In 1997, there were 36,419 resolutions of race-based discrimination charges tallied by the EEOC, up from 28,914 in 1991. Similarly, there were 32,836 cases of sex-based discrimination resolved in 1997 compared to 18,817 in 1991 (Flynn, 1998). A "glass ceiling" prevents minority group members and women from reaching the upper levels of management (Dominguez, 1992; Stroh, Brett, & Reilly, 1992). And every day, in ways that are not so blatant, women and members of racial and ethnic minority groups suffer from resentment, hostility, harassment, and discrimination at the hands of their coworkers. Often, they are simply ignored or avoided by members of the majority group. An example of the subtle forms of discrimination faced by minorities in the workplace is presented by a study conducted by Howitt and Owusu-Bempah (1990) in England. They sent letters of inquiry to organizations from applicants seeking positions. The letter writer used either the last name Croft or the last name Kumari as a way of indicating race. The investigators wished to determine if this simple difference in the racial association of the name of the applicant would affect how he was treated. It did. The replies to the Croft letter were rated as more encouraging than the replies to the Kumari letter and, when the reply said there were no positions, Croft received more suggestions of other organizations to approach than did Kumari.

The costs of poor intergroup relations in the workplace are tangible and substantial. They lead to lowered productivity, poor communication, and conflict (Ellis & Sonnenfield, 1994). They also cost companies money to defend and settle lawsuits. In 1992, Shoney paid $105 million to compensate victims of racial discrimination after a lawsuit was filed and, in 1997, Texaco agreed to pay $176 million to its Black employees as a result of a lawsuit (Lindsay, 1998). In 2000, the federal government agreed to pay $508 million to women who had been discriminated against at the Voice of America (the radio station that transmits American programming abroad). One study found that corporations that had been found guilty of discrimination suffered an immediate loss in the value of their stocks on the stock market (Wright, Ferris, Hiller, & Kroll, 1995). Correspondingly, winning an award for their affirmative action plans led to immediate increases in stock values.

Costs are also associated with replacing women and other minority group workers who quit because they are dissatisfied with their jobs. Cox (1993) reports that women expressed a much higher probability of leaving their present jobs than men. The reasons they listed for wanting to leave were lack of career opportunities and dissatisfaction with their rates of progress. Largely due to these types of problems, Corning Glass found that racial-minority group members and women had turnover rates that were twice as high as those of White males (Cox, 1993). In addition, workers in environments with hostile intergroup relations suffer from stress and the physical by-products of stress that lead to lowered commitment, absenteeism, sick leave, accidents, and expenses for the treatment of physical and mental health problems. Discrimination against minority groups is costly in another way. It leads to an inefficient use of human resources by not taking advantage of people's skills, simply due to their race, ethnicity, culture, religion, or sex.

Diversity initiatives were created to deal with the special problems of intergroup relations in the workplace. The failure to address these issues can impose heavy costs on the organizations themselves as well as create human costs through prejudice, stereotyping, harassment, and discrimination. Most of the programs we cover in this book are for children and young adults whose stereotypes, attitudes, beliefs, and behaviors are still in their formative stages. Organizations face a greater challenge in seeking to improve intergroup relations through diversity programs because adults are more resistant to change than young people. In addition, to effectively create a positive climate for diversity, the organizations themselves must change in fundamental ways. In the business world, the primary concern is the bottom line, which can make business organizations more resistant to change than other types of organizations (e.g., educational institutions). Businesses are concerned that costly changes will undermine their profitability. And yet, as the advocates of diversity programs would argue, the refusal to change may be even more damaging.

We will begin this chapter by covering the basic types of diversity initiatives, after which we will discuss the limited research that has been done on diversity training. We follow this discussion with an analysis of processes that may be responsible for bringing about improvements in intergroup relations when these programs are employed. In the concluding sections of the chapter, we present some problems associated with diversity initiatives and make recommendations for the implementation of diversity programs.

Diversity Initiatives

In the world of business, a distinction is made between managing diversity and valuing diversity (Henderson, 1994). *Managing diversity* usually refers to changing facets of organizational structure, policies, and practices of the organization. The purpose of attempts to manage diversity is to create equality in the workplace and to ensure the fairness of the practices used in the workplace. *Valuing diversity* is concerned more with changing individual attitudes and behaviors. Valuing diversity is reflected in the stated values of the organization as well as in the availability of diversity training programs. Obviously, managing diversity and valuing diversity must be intertwined if either is to be successful.

Managing Diversity

The ultimate goal of diversity management is to change the institutions themselves from the inside out so that they provide true equality of opportunity. The aspects of the organizational structure that are relevant to managing diversity include the racial and ethnic composition of management as well as those at other levels of the hierarchy, promotion and recruitment procedures, the rewards the organization offers and the basis for those rewards, communication patterns across and within levels of the organization, and grievance procedures. Organizations have a wide range of specific tools at their disposal to manage diversity (Cox, 1993). Among them are an emphasis on affirmative action in recruitment and promotion and the use of success in fostering diversity as an explicit component of performance evaluations. For instance, BostonBank Corporation rates the diversity competence of its employees. The scale runs from "not effective," meaning that the employee has difficulty dealing with people from different cultures and discourages people from different cultural backgrounds from participating in the work environment, to "role models," who create work environments in which diverse styles are welcome and encourage the development of diversity (Digh, 1998). Motorola holds managers accountable for developing and retaining women and other minorities (Digh, 1998). A survey of *Fortune* 500 companies by the Society for Human Resource Management indicated that 42% tie compensation or performance ratings to diversity efforts (Digh, 1998).

Organizations can also sponsor advisory and support groups based on group identity, design benefits packages that are suited to diverse groups (e.g., daycare, flextime, a choice of health care packages), and create greater flexibility in the prevailing social norms of the organization. In addition, organizations can ensure minority representation on key internal committees and create career development programs for minorities.

The Allstate Insurance company provides an example of a company with a comprehensive plan to manage diversity (Wah, 1999). Allstate tries to create a multiethnic workforce by recruiting from traditional Black colleges and from universities in Puerto Rico. In their recruitment efforts, they use the fact that they have been named in surveys as one of the best corporations for Latino workers. Thus, they use their success in creating diversity to promote further diversity. Their goal is to have the multiethnic nature of their clientele reflected in their workforce. New employees are given a pamphlet stating the company's expectations. Wah reports that the pamphlet says that employees are expected to exhibit no bias and to foster dignity and respect and that the company will promote an environment that is inclusive. When considering prospects for promotion, multiethnic lists of candidates are examined. For managers, 25% of merit pay is determined by diversity efforts. Allstate also conducts community outreach programs that are related to diversity, such as giving awards to outstanding Black citizens who have helped build stronger communities. The company tracks its success in achieving diversity goals through a twice-yearly survey.

The people who favor diversity management in organizations assume that diversity confers a competitive advantage. Its proponents argue that it can lead to better decision making, increased creativity, and more successful marketing and recruitment, in addition to avoiding the costs of poor diversity management (Cox, 1993). As Gottfredson (1992) notes, "Women and minorities bring different perspectives, new ways of doing things, and special knowledge about important markets" (p. 283). Many employers express a concern that the education their employees have received has trained them in job skills only, not in working together effectively. People who favor workplace diversity argue that women and minorities are typically more collectivist (group oriented) than men in their attitudes toward work and interpersonal relations. Thus, they often bring to the workplace greater interpersonal skills than White males, who tend to be more individualistic in orientation. These interpersonal skills can enhance productivity when collaboration, cohesion, and teamwork are important. Although these arguments are obviously plausible, very little direct evidence supports them, and likewise, little evidence refutes them. One exception is a survey of the 500 companies included in the Standard and Poor's index (Dass & Parker, 1999). This survey found that the top 100 firms in terms of their equal employment histories for women and other minorities had annualized returns of 18.3%, whereas the worst 100 firms had annualized returns of 7.9%. Although results such as these cannot prove that diversity efforts increase profitability, because there are other potential explanations for them (e.g., these companies probably treat all their employees better), they are consistent with the idea that diversity management is valuable.

Valuing Diversity

The goal of valuing diversity is to create a more positive intergroup relations climate by articulating the values of the corporation and offering diversity training programs that are specifically designed to improve intergroup relations. In this chapter, our primary focus will be on diversity training programs because they are the most widely used, but many companies also offer other types of programs to improve intergroup relations. For example, companies that value diversity might offer conflict resolution training, language instruction, and mentoring programs that provide minority group members with the skills and contacts to move up in the organization. Proctor and Gamble has a unique mentoring program in which junior-level women are assigned to senior-level male managers, not to learn from them but to teach them how their attitudes and behaviors and the unspoken norms and practices of the company have a negative impact on women (White, 1999).

Diversity Training Programs

The goal of diversity training programs is to increase awareness of racial, ethnic, and cultural differences and help managers and employees to value these differences (Hollister, Day, & Jesaitis, 1993). The programs are intended to make racial and ethnic minorities and women feel appreciated (Gottfredson, 1992). Some programs aim to provide participants with cultural and historical information relevant to understanding the implications of diversity in the workplace (Plummer, 1998). Other programs are designed to provide participants with skills for interacting with members of other groups and to open dialogue between groups (Plummer, 1998). For example, Digital Equipment Corporation conducts 2-day training programs designed to train participants to understand the dynamics of group differences (B. A. Walker & Hanson, 1992). This corporation also sponsors core groups (small, ongoing, dialogue groups) that deal with issues of intergroup relations. These core groups were created to counteract stereotypes, explore and understand differences, build relationships across group lines, and increase feelings of personal empowerment.

In terms of the dimensions we have used to categorize intergroup relations programs (Figure 1.1), diversity training programs take a very direct approach to confronting intergroup relations issues, and they do so by employing a mix of didactic and interactive approaches. The specific techniques employed are common to many other intergroup relations programs and include lectures and discussions as well as videos, role-playing, simulation games, and other experiential exercises. For example, board games are sometimes used to raise awareness of diversity topics and stimulate dialogue (Gunsch, 1993). One of these games involves players rolling dice and moving game pieces around a board that looks like a race track. When the players land on squares of a given color, they draw cards. Some of the cards require them to answer multiple-choice questions, such as, "Latinos place the highest value on (A) achievement, (B) money, (C) being on time, or (D) respect for elders." The answer is D, according to the manufacturer, who cites references supporting this answer. Other cards ask participants to share personal information, ask for information from other players, respond to diversity-related dilemmas, or respond to questions that may reveal stereotypes or biased attitudes. Players win play coins for correct answers and making progress on the board. Facilitators help the players process their experiences during and after the game. The premise for using games is that they are an enjoyable, nonthreatening way for participants to learn about and discuss diversity issues.

Types of Diversity Training Programs

Some diversity training programs are thoroughly grounded in theory, whereas others consist of a pragmatically selected set of techniques. An example of a theory-based program is the multicultural, diversity competence approach to training (Garcia, 1995). The theoretical underpinnings of this approach are anthropological, based on the idea that culture is at the heart of group differences. Culture includes knowledge, beliefs, art, morals, customs, and habits. It is dynamic and constantly evolving and influences the ongoing processes of social interaction. The goals of the training are to help the participants become more culture minded by expanding their awareness of the role of culture in social interaction and to train participants to use interpersonal skills based on cultural understanding.

Participants are introduced to the aspects of culture and are taught, through simulations and discussions, how they influence social interaction. For example, to introduce participants to the social processes involved in communication, differences in nonverbal communication styles might be examined. Participants would be asked to interact with another person while systematically altering some component of their communication style (e.g., stand three inches closer than you normally would, use more gestures than you normally would). The discussion of this exercise would focus on personal communication styles, the origins of these communication styles, and practical implications of differences in these styles of communication. In an illustration of the multilevel aspects of culture, participants might be asked to write down examples of their own personal culture, the culture of different subgroups in their society (e.g., Blacks, Latinos), the mainstream culture in their society, and the culture of their organization. In other exercises, case histories concerning barriers to communication (e.g., language, stereotypes, judgments) would be discussed, and participants would practice interacting, using a set of rules that focuses on mutual respect and open inquiry (e.g., listen to understand, paraphrase what you hear, express your own views). Cultural simulations that address resolving conflict, as well as analyses of case studies of problems related to diversity within their own organizations, might also be employed. Practitioners who conduct diversity training programs believe organizations that truly value diversity will prosper and be more productive and will provide their workers with more satisfying lives.

An example of a pragmatic diversity training program that derives from many sources is a short training program developed by the National MultiCultural Institute (Nile, 1994). The program is designed to give participants insights into their personal cultural perspectives, increase their sense of cultural identity, create a greater understanding of culture-based misunderstandings and issues of power, and provide participants with knowledge and skills that they can put into action in the workplace. The general approach involves describing an upcoming activity to participants, having the participants engage in the activity, processing what occurred during the activity, analyzing the dynamics of the activity, generalizing what was learned from the activity, and applying this learning. After the training group establishes norms for social interaction (e.g., being open, not blaming, maintaining confidentiality, taking personal risks), the group might discuss such topics as the value of cultural diversity, stereotyping, sexual harassment in the workplace, and organizational culture. In preparation for these discussions, the group would do sets of exercises, such as sharing personal histories and memories of being different (e.g., due to race, sex, or class), analyzing group labeling as an aspect of organizational culture, and discussing personal experiences within the organization. They might do skits illustrating subtle racial and gender insensitivities and also engage in collective action planning.

For example, one exercise is designed to highlight issues involved in stereotyping. In preparation, panelists write down five facts about themselves that do not provide clues to their group identities (race, ethnicity, gender, etc.). This information is then posted, and the remaining members of the group are divided into small groups that have the task of deciding which set of responses describes each panelist. Next, the panelists indicate which set of facts applies to them, and the whole group discusses the process of trying to fit the facts to the panelists. The facilitator helps the participants to see how difficult it is to match people to the facts of their lives simply by looking at them. At the end of the training program, the participants engage in a closure activity in which they come together as a group and summarize what they have learned.

Another pragmatically based training program has been developed by Hemphill and Haines (1997). In response to the growing criticism of diversity training programs focused on changing the knowledge and attitudes of White males, they developed a program that emphasizes skills training. Their approach emphasizes appropriate workplace behaviors and standards that transcend group membership. They do this, in part, through teaching participants about the communication process, particularly about effective listening. The participants are expected to learn to control their own potentially unacceptable behaviors by challenging their own perceptions, breaking bad habits, managing negative emotions, and reframing negative thoughts. Participants also learn conflict management skills, such as not blaming, manipulating, or coercing the other person but instead taking responsibility for their own behaviors, paying attention to the other person, emphasizing areas of agreement, and seeking solutions that benefit both parties. The goal is to "teach employees the skills to work together effectively regardless of their differences" (Hemphill & Haines, 1997, p. 67).

In practice, managing diversity and valuing diversity are combined in organizations and are presented in a variety of different ways. For some organizations, little effort is put into managing diversity, and valuing diversity means bringing in outside teams of consultants to provide short-term training programs. But for other corporations, diversity issues are considered to be so important that a division within the corporation may be solely devoted to them. For instance, Xerox Corporation has a well-developed internal program that includes both diversity management and valuing diversity (Sessa, 1992). Their diversity training programs employ videotaped scenarios, role-playing, and skills training to help individuals interact across group lines. Minority group members are recruited into career paths that lead to higher management positions. Caucus groups for Blacks, Latinos, and women discuss diversity issues. Managers at Xerox are evaluated in part on their performance in achieving affirmative action and balanced workforce goals.

Research on diversity training programs provides mixed evidence of their success, as we see in the next section.

Research on the Effectiveness of Diversity Training Programs

Unfortunately, only a small number of studies have been done on the effects of diversity initiatives. We were able to locate only six studies of diversity training programs. We will review them in the order in which they were conducted.

The first study of a diversity training program was done on a Southwestern military base in 1977 (Tansik & Driskill, 1977). The program involved 20 hours of instruction in race relations and was designed to train supervisors from all racial and ethnic groups and both sexes. It employed cases studies and role-playing as well as some lectures. Participants were randomly assigned to the training and control groups. The training group was measured at 2-week intervals for 12 weeks after the end of the program. The program initially produced only small changes in attitudes toward a variety of racial and ethnic groups. However, these attitudes generally became more favorable over time. By the 5th week after the training, the attitudes toward most outgroups were significantly more positive in the training group than in a control group. At the 6th week, a gradual downward trend appeared that ultimately led, at the 12th week, to more negative attitudes in the training group than in the control group toward some outgroups. These complex results suggest that the training took some time to take hold but that these gains were then lost over time.

An interesting study employing modeling of appropriate relations between supervisors and employees was done in South Africa (Sorcher & Spence, 1982). It used random assignment to condition and measured both employees and supervisors before and after the program. During the 10-week program, White supervisors and Black employees watched videotapes of effective relations in the workplace and then role-played similar situations while being reinforced for the acquisition of effective behaviors. The eight videotaped situations for supervisors included "How to Correct Unacceptable Work Habits," whereas the eight videotapes for employees included "How to Respond to Constructive Criticism." There were no changes in attitudes for either supervisors or employees immediately after the training. Analyses of structured interviews revealed nonsignificant positive changes in attitudes 6 weeks after the training. A posttest done 20 weeks after training indicated that the attitudes of each group toward the other had become significantly more positive. These results suggest that the managers and employees initially had difficulty implementing what they had learned, but they became more successful at doing so over time.

A study by Dunnette and Motowildo (1982) examined the effects of a 3-day workshop designed to reduce the incidence of sexist attitudes and behaviors in a large corporation. The workshop consisted of small-group discussions, readings, seminars, and videos. The participants responded to questionnaires about their attitudes, were rated by their supervisors, and their performances on a simulated role-playing exercise were evaluated. Pretest and posttest comparisons were made between participants who had received the training and people who had not yet received the training. For male participants, there were few positive effects of the program. Just 5 of 36 comparisons were significant, and among these 3 were positive and 2 were negative. For female participants, 11 of 36 comparisons were significant and all represented positive changes. Thus, the awareness training program had relatively little impact on the attitudes or behavior of men, but it did have some positive effects on women.

Adlerfer (1992) examined the diversity management and valuing-diversity programs at the fictitiously named XYZ corporation. Interventions were designed to redress power distribution problems within the corporation (managing diversity) and to increase the understanding of race relations within management (valuing diversity). An upward-mobility program was created to identify and train promising minority group employees for management positions. Personnel committees charged with evaluating candidates for promotion were carefully balanced with respect to race, ethnicity, and gender. A 3-day, race relations competence workshop was created for managers. It consisted of lectures, role-playing, and other experiential group activities.

Employment records maintained by the corporation indicate a steady increase in the number of minority group members and women who joined the ranks of management over the years. Evaluations of the workshops indicate that more than 80% of the participants felt that the workshops helped race relations in the organization, but significantly more Blacks (95%) than Whites (83%) felt this way. More of the Black (86%) than the White (62%) participants felt they had benefited personally from the workshops. Also, more White (18% of males, 9% of females) than Black participants (8% of the males and none of the females) felt that the workshops hurt race relations in the organization. Thus, the efforts of XYZ corporation to manage diversity met with considerable success. However, it appears that the diversity training program was less successful with members of the dominant group, and a sizable number of participants from this group actually felt the training was detrimental.

In a study of a short-term, diversity training program, a questionnaire was given to participants after a 1-day seminar that involved viewing videos and discussing them (Ellis & Sonnenfield, 1994). The videos dramatized incidents involving culturally insensitive behaviors between Whites and members of other groups. The majority of the participants (59%) regarded the seminars as worthwhile, but 31% felt that the seminars had a negative impact on some employees. More than 20% of the participants thought the seminar actually reinforced ethnic and gender stereotypes.

Another group of investigators examined the effectiveness of a diversity training program in the Federal Aviation Administration (Tan, Morris, & Romero, 1996). The training involved case scenarios, simulations, videos, and discussions. The 3-day workshop had 13 components. Pre- and postworkshop comparisons indicated that the workshops increased knowledge of diversity issues and barriers to change as well as sensitizing participants to the effects of stereotypes and prejudice in the workplace and to ways of preventing them.

Hanover and Cellar (1998) employed a pretest and posttest design, including a control group, to study the effects of diversity training on a group of predominantly White (95%) managers of a large corporation. The goals of the workshop were to underscore the importance of diversity in the workplace, understand cultural biases, heighten awareness of behavior that detracts from productivity, and reinforce skills related to managing a diverse workforce. The diversity workshop included videos, role-playing, examination of diversity practices, and action planning. It led to increases on a variety of measures of diversity practices, such as encouraging open discussions of group differences and discouraging comments that perpetuate stereotypes. After the training, the trained group also rated diversity-related management practices as more important than they had before the training.

Unfortunately, the small number of these studies and their mixed results make it impossible to draw any strong conclusions about the effects of diversity training programs. Although several of these programs reported considerable success in changing attitudes (Hanover & Cellar, 1998; Sorcher & Spence, 1982; Tan et al., 1996), others obtained both positive and negative effects (Adlerfer, 1992; Dunnette & Motowildo, 1982; Ellis & Sonnenfield, 1994) or were ultimately unsuccessful in improving intergroup relations (Tansik & Driskill, 1977). In addition to these studies of specific programs, there is a study that surveyed practitioners concerning the effects of diversity training programs. This survey echoes the mixed effects of the studies we have just reviewed.

The study was a survey of human resource managers in organizations that examined perceived success and the factors related to the perceived success of diversity training programs (Rynes & Rosen, 1995). The programs that were investigated rarely lasted for more than 3 days. These managers reported that 33% of the programs were considered to be largely successful, whereas 18% were considered to be largely unsuccessful. Not surprisingly, the programs were most likely to be perceived as successful in organizations that already valued and supported diversity. However, it was also found that programs requiring mandatory attendance by managers were thought to be more successful than voluntary programs—at least from the perspective of the human resource managers overseeing these programs. Perhaps mandatory programs were perceived to be more successful because they included the people who most needed the training but who would avoid voluntary programs, and because managers recognized the limitations of preaching to the choir. Unfortunately, this study was not designed to provide evidence on whether or not these programs actually had the intended impact on managers reluctant to take them.

Finally, there is an interesting qualitative study that examined a videotape widely used in diversity training programs (Layng, 1998). This video uses vignettes to communicate diversity problems and their solutions. The researcher found that they were quite successful in presenting images of diversity in the workplace. However, in attempting to counteract old stereotypes, sometimes they inadvertently introduced new ones. For instance, one vignette attacks the stereotypes of Asians as being technically proficient but winds up replacing this stereotype with one suggesting that Asians do not like to talk about themselves. The videos present two types of White male managers, those who create difficulties because they are indifferent or feel threatened and those who avoid problems because they are sensitive and value diversity. According to Layng, the problem with focusing so much attention on the incompetence of White male managers is that the very group the videos seek to reach may tune out the message because they feel they are being blamed and negatively stereotyped. Another issue Layng raises is the idea that all the communication problems result from the presence of women and minority group members in the workplace, thereby suggesting that diversity creates problems. Layng concludes that "the main implication of the video series is that diversity may be devalued by the viewers" (p. 264). Whether or not this conclusion is warranted, her analysis indicates how difficult it is for even well-meaning trainers to construct materials that effectively serve their intended purpose. And if such carefully constructed materials fail to achieve their goals, how much greater is the risk that less carefully developed materials will be effective?

Every year, thousands of diversity training programs are conducted in the United States and other countries, yet almost none of them is evaluated. The result is that we have no idea whether or not these programs are successful or are an enormous waste of time and effort. Clearly, more research is needed on the outcomes of diversity training programs and the processes involved in bringing about beneficial changes in these programs. When diversity initiatives are successful, what processes might be responsible for bringing about these positive outcomes? We turn to these processes in the next section.

Psychological Processes
Underlying Diversity Initiatives

The problems faced by diversity trainers are greater than those faced by trainers, educators, and facilitators implementing other intergroup relations programs because they deal with adults in organizations that have established norms and practices. They often have limited time in which to bring about changes, and the training they provide must frequently address legal issues (e.g., harassment) as well as intergroup relations issues. Moreover, in many cases there is resistance to these types of programs. We will divide into two sections our discussion of the psychological processes that come into play in business organizations. The first covers processes related to managing diversity, and the second covers processes related to valuing diversity.

Processes Related to Managing Diversity

Changing the structure and practices of business organizations can bring about changes in behavior through incentives and the creation of new procedures and norms. One of the strongest lessons of dissonance theory is that behavior change leads to attitude change. When managers find themselves implementing policies in recruitment, hiring, promotion, and evaluation that promote fairness in the treatment of women and other minorities, they can justify these behaviors by valuing women and other minority group members more. Dissonance based on behavior change is typically most effective when the behavior changes are perceived as voluntary. Thus, dissonance-related attitude changes on diversity issues are most likely to occur if the changes are introduced on the basis of democratic, consensus-based decision making involving both management and labor. If management and labor can agree on the importance of diversity-related initiatives, this agreement can also help to forge a superordinate identification with the organization itself, and this consensus may contribute to an improved climate supporting diversity.

Business organizations provide an excellent example of the manner in which making structural changes can create more positive attitudes and behavior. According to the theory of reasoned action (Fishbein & Ajzen, 1975), two of the most important determinants of behavior are perceptions of the subjective norms (attitudes) held by significant others and individuals' own attitudes toward the behavior. Structural changes create a normative climate that communicates approval of positive intergroup relations, thereby influencing subjective norms concerning intergroup relations. Employees will come to believe that management supports favorable intergroup relations. For instance, when organizational rewards (e.g., positive performance evaluations, promotions) are contingent on fulfilling diversity goals, this clearly communicates the organization's support for egalitarian intergroup relations. People are much more likely to be open to the acquisition of new skills for relating to people from other groups if they think that learning these skills will have a beneficial effect on their prospects for promotion.

Managing diversity also involves the implementation of practices that create negative sanctions for discriminatory behavior. Such sanctions influence individuals' attitudes toward discrimination by making the consequences clear. For instance, one common facet of managing diversity is creating and publicizing rules that proscribe statements and conduct that contain derogatory racial, ethnic, sexual, religious, or cultural content (Paskoff, 1996). These rules not only reinforce the institution's commitment to diversity, but they also lead people to believe that behavior that undermines positive intergroup relations will be punished.

Processes Related to Valuing Diversity

One way in which top management demonstrates its commitment to valuing diversity is ensuring that the organization's mission statement strongly endorses diversity. Statements by the major authority figures in an organization set the tone for the organization and help to support a normative culture that favors diversity. People in all societies are socialized to obey authority and conform to social norms. This tendency to conform to the dictates of authority can have either negative or positive effects on subordinates, depending on the content of those dictates. For instance, several studies have shown that when students role-play the job of manager and are given a rationale for discrimination (e.g., we wish to keep our marketing teams as homogeneous as possible), they are biased in evaluating the credentials of minority group members (Brief et al., 1997). Correspondingly, it can be anticipated that if those in authority advocate equality and fairness, employees will conform to these rules (Hitt & Keats, 1984). Thus, diversity initiatives become self-sustaining when the leaders of the organization support diversity in word and deed and this support is reflected in the normative culture of the organization.

Creating a positive climate for diversity also helps to foster the kinds of favorable conditions specified in the contact hypothesis (G. W. Allport, 1954) as leading to improved intergroup relations (e.g., cooperative, individualized, equal status). If conflicts and misunderstandings are reduced, the resulting positive interactions should be rewarding for managers and employees alike, and these rewards should help to sustain changes in attitudes and behaviors.

Diversity Training Programs

The most widely used technique for valuing diversity is the implementation of diversity training programs. These programs tend to emphasize passive processes that are primarily cognitive in nature (Figure 2.3). However, some programs also utilize some active and affective processes. To the extent that diversity training programs are successful, it is likely to be due to some of the same processes we have cited for related programs. Diversity training programs that employ videos, discussions, role-playing, and simulation games can have an impact on knowledge about, and understanding of, other groups by providing historical information as well as information on group differences in values, behaviors, norms, and beliefs. People may also gain insights into the origins of their own biases and become motivated to learn to regulate their own behavior so their biases do not influence their behaviors. Diversity training programs may also help to dispel stereotypes by providing participants with direct experiences that contradict their stereotypes and by providing information that is inconsistent with the participants' stereotypes. When role-playing is used, empathy for members of outgroups should be created, and this empathy can also lead to positive changes in attitudes and behavior.

However, the impact of these processes may be diminished in diversity training programs because adults have well-established attitudes and behaviors that are difficult to modify. Their stereotypes are based on a lifetime of experience and exposure to the mass media. Their attitudes may be so entrenched that they react with defensiveness and avoidance to information that might create change. If they feel that they and their ingroup are being blamed or attacked, it may blunt the impact of attempts to create empathy for the experiences of members of other groups.

Unless the changes that are brought about by diversity training are accompanied by a continued emphasis on diversity issues and a commitment by management to change in the organization and its reward system, diversity training is unlikely to have long-term effects on intergroup relations.

Problems and Recommendations

In this section, we will consider resistance to diversity initiatives, planning diversity initiatives, issues relevant to trainers, and evaluating diversity training programs.

Resistance to Diversity Initiatives

Diversity training often meets with more resistance than do other types of intergroup relations programs. Both the participants and the organizations to which they belong may resist diversity training. Participation in diversity training is often mandatory, which may undercut its popularity and its effectiveness but also ensures that the people who need it most will be exposed to it. Diversity training programs attempt to change people's attitudes and behavior. Many people experience change as threatening, leading to feelings of anxiety, resentment, and hostility. In addition, members of the majority group may feel threatened by diversity initiatives because they are concerned that their jobs may be at stake (Kossek & Zonia, 1993). When minority group members are included in diversity training programs, they are sometimes concerned that the training will focus on them and place them in the uncomfortable position of having to act as spokespersons for their group or ask them to divulge personal and often painful information. The programs themselves are sometimes seen as superficial and condescending, and if not done properly, they may arouse more negative affect and intergroup conflict than existed prior to their use.

There are also barriers to change within most organizations. The traditional structure of many American organizations can make it difficult to implement programs designed to value diversity. Traditional organizations tend to have a hierarchical structure that favors communication from the top down. The upper levels of these hierarchies are currently dominated by White males. Procedures tend to be standardized as much as possible in the name of efficiency. Conformity to the norms and rules is rewarded (Hollister, Day, & Jesaitis, 1993). In addition, recruitment and promotion are often based on selecting people who will fit in and maintain homogeneity within organizational subunits (Bond & Pyle, 1998). The informal practices and communication networks of many organizations keep women and minorities on the outside and create a climate that is not welcoming to diversity (Bond & Pyle, 1998). Women and other minority group members have less access to the informal networks that lead to promotion and are often more uncomfortable about expressing dissatisfaction than White males. Also, members of minority groups are often treated as tokens who are hired and promoted to present a facade of diversity. All these factors make traditional organizations inhospitable to minority group members. They also lead these organizations to resist change, especially diversity initiatives. Furthermore, the racial or ethnic and gender composition of the management of these organizations is often seen by those in management as a zero-sum game: If more minority group members and women move into positions of top management, fewer White males will occupy these positions. Thus, organizational resistance to change in the status quo through diversity management and valuing diversity is fundamental. The origin of this resistance in the unequal treatment of minorities is one reason that diversity initiatives are so necessary in business organizations.

Diversity trainers must to be prepared to counteract resistance to training and barriers to change within the organization. In general, the more traditional the organization, the stronger the resistance to change is likely to be. The resistance to diversity training is well illustrated in this quote from an executive who was asked to send his managers to a diversity training workshop:

> They don't need a program in which they sit around talking about their experiences with discrimination or what it's like to be a victim. I don't care what's politically correct: I'm not in the business of dealing with social issues. The people in my division have jobs to do, and this touchy-feely diversity stuff doesn't help us do our jobs. I'm not wasting my people's time trying to change the way they "feel" about people who are different from them. If there's a problem, just tell us what you want us to do. Don't waste our time with this diversity stuff. (Paskoff, 1996, p. 43)

Managers who hold attitudes such as these are unlikely to be convinced by arguments based on social responsibility, but arguments based on the practical utility of diversity training in terms of improving recruitment, retention, and productivity are likely to be more convincing.

Most diversity training programs in the United States are oriented toward changing White males. Although there is no doubt that many White males need such training, having only White males participate in training programs runs the risk of not providing them with experiences with a diverse set of people during the training itself, because members of minority groups are not included (Lindsay, 1998). Restricting training to White males also ignores the problems that minority group members and women may have in interacting with White males and the problems that different minority groups may have working with one another. In a related vein, most diversity training programs are designed for management, but this focus omits the levels of organizations in which the most intergroup contact typically occurs. Other employees of the organization also need diversity training. Thus, in order to be optimally effective, diversity training programs should include both majority and minority group members, and they should train employees from all levels of the organization.

Planning Diversity Initiatives

Before undertaking any diversity initiatives, organizations should conduct a "cultural audit" as a basis for formulating a plan to address diversity issues (Cox, 1993; S. E. Jackson, 1992; Kincaid & Horner, 1997; Lindsay, 1998). That is, they should conduct an analysis of the organizational climate, the history of the organization and its current practices, and the need for new policies. The usefulness of such cultural audits can be illustrated by examining the results of IBM's cultural audit. In their assessment of their own corporate culture, IBM found that its recruitment and reward policies strongly emphasized individualistic values. After determining that these values contradicted the diversity objectives of the organization, IBM restructured its policies and procedures to place greater emphasis on collaborative values (Lindsay, 1998).

A well-thought-out, comprehensive plan to undertake diversity initiatives is much more likely to prove successful than a hastily concocted plan that is a reaction to external or internal events. A diversity plan will probably meet with a more positive reception if management and labor have collaborated on its development. The plan should have clear objectives. Among the possible objectives are attracting and maintaining a qualified workforce, facilitating teamwork, fulfilling social responsibilities, creating synergy between geographically dispersed units, generating broader input into decisions, and fitting the organization to its markets (S. E. Jackson, 1992). The plan should also specify which diversity issues will be addressed and what programs will be implemented to address them. One reason to establish objectives is that progress toward them can be measured.

Any diversity plan that is developed should take into consideration the organizational climate in which it will be introduced. Organizational cultures that stress assimilation to the organization's norms and procedures and are relatively autocratic need to be approached differently from organizational cultures that have a more pluralistic and democratic culture. Once a set of initiatives has been identified, top management should vocally and visibly support it (Cox, 1993; Ellis & Sonnenfield, 1994; Rynes & Rosen, 1995). Some thought should also be given to possible resistance to the initiatives and how to deal with this resistance.

Diversity training programs should be one part of a comprehensive set of initiatives to address diversity issues. Diversity training programs are more likely to be successful if they are proactive rather than remedial. That is, the programs should be oriented toward the future, not the past. According to Mobley and Payne (cited in Henderson, 1994), diversity trainers should avoid being seen as pushing the agenda of a particular minority group. The training teams should themselves be diverse. One of the dangers of providing information about group differences in values, norms, and behaviors is that this information may itself create stereotypes. To counteract this problem, differences within racial, ethnic, religious, and cultural groups should be emphasized, and the similarities between the groups should be highlighted (Gottfredson, 1992). Diversity training should also be tailored to suit the particular groups represented in the organization.

Training Issues

In addition to providing training aimed at changing attitudes, stereotypes, and behavior, diversity trainers must be prepared to deal with a host of other issues. In many cases, the trainers must also help participants to understand the legal issues associated with affirmative action, harassment, and discrimination. In addition, the trainers need to be prepared to deal with conflict between groups and cope with the resentment of dominant group members toward change as well as the negative reactions of minority group members to the slow pace of change. They also need the skills to avoid the appearance of favoritism and to present diversity policies in a way that is acceptable to members of all groups (Rynes & Rosen, 1995).

Perhaps even more than in other types of intergroup relations training, diversity training should include elements of skills training (Hemphill & Haines, 1997). As one human resources manager at Hewlett-Packard noted, "There's a need for skills building, to help people use their awareness of diversity in the workplace" (Caudron, 1993, p. 55). The most important skills involve learning to interact effectively with people from a variety of racial, ethnic, religious, and cultural backgrounds. A pragmatic reason to focus special attention on relationship skills is that employers are legally responsible for the conduct of their employees. The behaviors that lead to the creation of a hostile work environment and to harassment and discrimination must all be replaced by behaviors that are more tolerant and accepting of diversity.

Diversity trainers must also face the dilemma of deciding how inclusive the materials for the training program will be. They may elect to focus on women and other minority groups as many programs do, but they could also include a number of other groups that play an important role in the workplace including religious groups, gays and lesbians, handicapped workers, immigrants, and older workers. The more inclusive the program, the broader the range of substantive issues that must be covered, and less time is devoted to any one group, but not covering a broad range of groups risks leaving people feeling left out.

Diversity trainers must pay careful attention to the racial, ethnic, and religious composition of the people who are being trained as well as the history of intergroup relations in each particular workplace setting. In designing their programs, trainers also may need to consider the age of the employees, their status within the organization, and the strength of their racial or ethnic identities.

Diversity trainers need to decide on the degree to which they wish to change the prevailing organizational culture. Traditional American organizations prize individualism and related values including self-reliance, competitiveness, and a certain type of aggressive ambition. A related set of implicit organizational values may also need to be challenged. Management practices in most organizations are expected to be impersonal, objective, and rational. Communication styles are expected to be clear and direct. And traditional organizations value managers who are tough-minded. These values are not compatible with the more collectivist values of many minority groups who are more likely to emphasize the importance of interdependence and a concern for the welfare of others (Maier, 1997; Prasad, 1997). In confronting this divergence of values, trainers have several different options. They can attempt to change these implicit values, they can discuss these differences so that members of both the majority and minority groups are aware of these issues, or they can ignore these value differences.

The foregoing discussion suggests that diversity trainers need to be thoroughly prepared for this role. However, they often do not receive extensive formal education in conducting diversity training. Currently, there are no licensing requirements for becoming a diversity trainer. The problem this lack of requirements creates is that many people who are unqualified to conduct diversity training do so. Thorough preparation for the role of diversity trainer is particularly important because the chances of doing harm to participants and the organizations in which they work seem quite high. Fortunately, specific programs designed to educate people to become trainers are beginning to appear in graduate schools, and certificate programs are now available in diversity training, but this effort has only just begun (Plummer, 1998).

It appears that most diversity training programs are too short to be effective. The majority of diversity training programs last 1 day or less (Rynes & Rosen, 1995). There is a great need for long-term training in business organizations in order to deal with the complexity of the issues involved. Diversity issues should be incorporated into all the training programs offered by an organization. In fact, addressing diversity issues should be an ongoing and integral part of the entire organization.

Evaluating Diversity Training Programs

In general, diversity trainers do not publish systematic evaluations of the effects of their efforts. There appear to be several reasons that there are so few such studies. Many diversity trainers are private consultants who do not wish to share their techniques with other professionals. In addition, the majority of diversity trainers are not trained in the techniques for doing evaluation research. Furthermore, evaluation research takes time and requires money, which undercuts the profits of private practitioners and requires additional resources from practitioners who are employed within organizations. Another reason that such studies are not conducted is that some types of evaluations take time away from the job and thus may be resisted by organizations due to the cost in lost labor. It also seems likely that evaluations are not conducted because the practitioners are concerned about what the results will be. Lynch (1997) quotes one researcher as saying, "People are afraid to find out that these programs don't work" (p. 196). A legitimate concern among practitioners may be that if the programs are shown to be unsuccessful, they will be terminated. The counterargument is that the only way to create successful programs is to determine, through systematic research, what techniques are successful with what populations in which contexts.

Summary

Diversity initiatives are becoming an accepted part of doing business in the United States and elsewhere around the globe. The costs of not confronting diversity issues can be high and include lowered productivity, conflict, lawsuits, and wasting valuable talent. Approaches to improving diversity in the workplace take two primary forms: managing diversity and valuing diversity. Managing diversity is principally concerned with altering the structure and functioning of organizations through increases in the representation of women, minorities, and other groups at all levels of the organization and with changes in policies and procedures to promote equality and fairness. Attempts to manage diversity influence recruitment, promotion, systems of rewards and benefits, and procedures for handling grievances. It appears there are many benefits of implementing diversity initiatives including increased productivity, better interpersonal and work relations on the job, and an increased capacity to function in diverse markets.

Valuing diversity is more concerned with changing the attitudes, feelings, and behaviors of individual managers and employees in order to increase their awareness and sensitivity to diversity issues. Attempts to value diversity take the form of creating mentoring programs, conflict resolution training, and diversity training. Diversity training programs are designed to increase awareness of racial, ethnic, religious, cultural, and sex differences and to provide people with the skills to put this knowledge to practical use. They typically employ videos, lectures, discussions, role-playing, simulations, and other experiential techniques. Diversity training frequently meets with resistance when it is mandatory, creates fear and resentment among those from the majority group, and places minority group members in the uncomfortable position of being the focus of attention. Some diversity programs are theory based, but most are a pragmatically assembled set of interrelated exercises.

Research on diversity training programs is in its infancy. The few studies that have been done indicate that it can be successful in changing attitudes and behaviors but may not always live up to its potential.

When attempts to manage diversity are successful, it is probably because they change the normative culture of the organization in ways that promote changes in the perception of subjective norms and attitudes toward egalitarian behavior. Managing diversity may also bring dissonance processes into play. Valuing diversity can influence attitudes and behavior by capitalizing on people's tendencies to conform to the dictates of authority figures. Valuing diversity may also foster conditions for favorable intergroup contact. Diversity training programs provide knowledge about other groups that can overcome prejudice and stereotyping, and they help to create self-insights that lead people to regulate their intergroup behavior.

Diversity training programs must confront a number of issues and problems. Organizations resist changes in their well-established policies and procedures, and adults have ingrained attitudes and behaviors that are difficult to modify. These organizations have often emphasized training White males too much and training women and minority group members too little. Before conducting diversity training programs, it is suggested that the trainers do a cultural audit to determine the needs of the organization. Diversity trainers must themselves be well trained because diversity training is so complex. Diversity trainers must decide the degree to which they wish to stress legal issues and social-skills training. They must decide how inclusive the training materials will be and the degree to which they wish to challenge the prevailing organizational culture. It is suggested that diversity training programs should be longer in duration and should be only part of a comprehensive plan to manage and value diversity. Diversity trainers are encouraged to evaluate their programs.

INTERGROUP DIALOGUES **5**

USING INTERGROUP DIALOGUES to improve relations between groups is probably as old as language itself, but the systemic use of intergroup dialogues as a technique for improving intergroup relations is a relatively recent invention. Their use is now becoming increasingly widespread in educational, community, and international settings. These dialogues are meant to foster an understanding of issues of contention between groups and create a commitment to address these issues. Intergroup dialogues are not merely talk. They involve facilitated discussions in which people are encouraged to listen carefully to one another and, in the process, "to correctly understand the values and beliefs that inform another's worldview" (Dubois & Hutson, 1997, p. 12). This is serious talk that is expected to lead to social action. In terms of the dimensions referred to in Figure 1.1, these programs are among the most direct and interactive of all the programs we will discuss.

In this chapter, we present three types of dialogue programs that have been developed to improve intergroup relations, and we examine the limited research that has been done on the effectiveness of intergroup dialogues. In addition, we review why dialogue programs work, highlighting psychodynamic processes, processes involved in intergroup contact and the roles of self-disclosure, empathy, dissonance, and anxiety reduction. We end by offering some suggestions for their implementation.

Types of Intergroup Dialogues

Dialogue groups have been used in educational settings, in community settings, and in the context of protracted international disputes. In the following section, we review each type of dialogue group.

Intergroup Dialogues in Educational Settings

In educational settings, dialogue groups are generally small, involving 10 to 20 students (Nagda, Zuniga, & Sevig, 1995). Typically, the students are drawn equally from two groups that have a history of conflict. These groups may be racial or ethnic groups (Blacks and Whites, Asian Americans and Latinos), but they might also be based on distinctions such as sex, sexual orientation, or religion. The dialogue groups meet under the direction of trained facilitators whose task is to guide the discussions and help the participants adhere to norms that are conducive to a productive exchange of views. The topics covered typically include current issues of central concern to both groups, group differences, and problems such as prejudice, stereotyping, and discrimination as well as their origins and effects. The participants are encouraged to voice their own concerns and feelings. The groups are often assigned readings, but they also engage in experiential exercises, role-plays, simulation games, and other structured exercises (Nagda et al., 1999).

A unique feature of these groups is that verbal conflicts and disagreements are not discouraged. Among the practitioners employing this approach, it is widely believed that openly addressing conflict in creative ways can be constructive, provided that rules for civil discourse prevail during the discussion of such issues. It is believed that participants benefit from an opportunity to express deeply felt emotions and opinions regarding central issues of contention between groups and that the members of the other group need to hear these concerns expressed in an open and honest way. In the process, people come to value the opinions and welfare of people who differ from them and they learn about the common values that are shared among groups. In successful dialogues, members of the other group are no longer perceived as adversaries. The participants are often encouraged to become aware of the ways in which social institutions have shaped their individual views. As the groups evolve, issues of identity inevitably arise and become the subject of group discussion. Toward the end of their existence, most dialogue groups turn to issues of social action and attempt to build coalitions to work on issues related to social justice.

In some dialogue groups in educational settings, the facilitators are trained peers of the participants (i.e., other students). The premise for using peer facilitators is that the presence of authority figures often inhibits open and honest expressions of opinions and experiences. Peer facilitators also provide role models with whom participants can readily identify. The guidelines that facilitators use to create civil and productive discourse include emphasizing to the participants that they should be honest and open with one another and that they should display respect for one another and be nonjudgmental. They are instructed that to disagree with the opinions of others is permissible, but they should disagree with the ideas without attacking the people who hold them. The differences between dialogue and debate are often discussed during the initial meetings of the group. Dialogue attempts to arrive at a mutual understanding and does not involve an attempt to win over the other side, as in a debate. The facilitator's intent is to create a safe environment in which participants feel free to express themselves. For this reason, the participants are told to treat the dialogues as confidential communications.

The role of the facilitator includes clarifying issues, providing information, mediating conflicts, and relating the interactions among the group members to larger theoretical or conceptual issues. When student facilitators are employed, they are usually trained in separate courses. This training helps them to become aware of their own communication and conflict styles, provides them with knowledge about intergroup dynamics and social justice, and teaches them to listen and provide feedback during dialogues (Nagda et al., 1995). When peer facilitators conduct dialogue groups, they are supervised by trained, professional personnel.

The intergroup dialogue program at the University of Michigan provides an example of a well-established dialogue program conducted in an educational setting. This program for lower-division undergraduate students consists of a semester-long class devoted entirely to intergroup dialogue. The goals of this program are to develop an awareness of social groups in the context of privilege and oppression; explore similarities and differences between groups; develop intergroup communication skills; explore the origins of intergroup beliefs, attitudes, and behavior; challenge misinformation and biases; and work toward social change (Zuniga & Sevig, 1997).

There are four stages in this program. In the first stage, the classes are devoted to learning the norms for dialogue and acquiring basic skills in communication. Students discuss their hopes and fears for the course and learn about such issues as creating a safe communication environment. They are encouraged to challenge assumptions with which they are comfortable. The students also are asked to begin keeping a journal of their thoughts and experiences concerning intergroup relations. Here is a quote from one student expressing her fears about the dialogue class.

> I worried that I would be squelched—as Whites think they can do to us in the classroom. I was concerned that we would be under represented and hence silenced—as we are in the classroom. I was mortally afraid that I would leave every session angry with issues unresolved—as I do from my other classrooms. (Zuniga, Scalera, Nagda, & Sevig, 1997)

In the second stage, the groups deal with issues of identity, especially multiple identities (e.g., the fact that people often identify with their ethnic group, religion, and sex), and the role of socialization in creating individual and group identities. They also learn about intergroup relations concepts (e.g., ethnocentrism, prejudice, stereotyping) and begin to communicate across group lines about similarities and differences in socialization into their groups. In addition, the students begin to identify group differences that lead to intergroup conflict. In this stage, the students are encouraged to make the dialogues concerning group differences more personal by relating experiences in their own lives to their group identities. In the following quote, a White student discusses a transition point in the dialogue and how she personally responded to it.

> [In one of the early exercises] we seemed inhibited to say things that make us look racist or ignorant. One man, though, was the exception.

> From that class on I began to be totally honest with myself and others. I talked more directly about my experiences. I wasn't scared any more of sounding a certain way. Another thing that helped was knowing that (a woman of color) wanted the White people to express their feelings. It was a huge relief and allowed me to be honest with myself and therefore helped me learn more about myself and others. (Zuniga, Nagda, Sevig, Vasquez, & Dey, 1998)

In the third stage, the dialogue groups turn to broader issues of social justice. These classes link the students' experiences to social institutions such as the family and educational, religious, legal, political, and economic institutions. The focus here is often on the creation of power and privilege through these social institutions. Case studies, videos, and readings are used during this phase of the course. These materials provide historical, statistical, and other information that is used as a basis for discussing specific issues. Conflicts often emerge during these discussions as participants consider the roles that their identity groups have played as victims and perpetrators. The students are invited to critically analyze the personal and institutional factors that lead to different perceptions of issues of contention. Here is one student's reactions to a class during this section of the course.

> It had never occurred to me how much this university alienated Blacks. Before I came to this group it used to upset me the degree to which Black people tend to keep to themselves on this campus but in reality it is not different from what my family did in choosing a place to live. They didn't want to have to think about being Jewish all the time. In the same way, Black people don't want to have to feel different all the time. (Zuniga et al., 1998)

In stage four, students are encouraged to build alliances across group lines in order to challenge prevailing social inequalities. The students are asked to consider realistic, achievable ways of continuing their own personal growth and moving from personal growth to practical actions. The students then write final papers that address what they have learned, the challenges they faced, rewards they experienced, their responses to conflict and the interaction in the group, the alliances they were or were not able to build, and the influence they believe the dialogue will have on their futures. Here is one student's reactions at the end of the program.

> In order for me to be an ally to White women, I need to be willing to help them get in touch with frustrations they might have about racism. I need to get over the belief that White women could never know the full horror of brute racism or the oppression that I have faced. I need to understand that White women have also faced oppression. We all need to understand that the world is here, so welcome and explore it. (Zuniga et al., 1998)

Intergroup Dialogues in Community Settings

Community-based dialogues are similar to those in educational settings in most respects, but they differ in some important ways. They tend to include a broader range of participants, they are mostly based on race and ethnicity, usually involving Blacks and Whites, and they often arise in response to specific local issues or crises (Du Bois & Hutson, 1997). Also, most community dialogue groups do not meet as frequently as do groups in educational settings, and in community dialogues there tends to be a strong stress on collective action or problem solving as an outcome. Approaches to solving community problems are expected to emerge from the dialogues as the participants gain a greater understanding of one another. Community dialogue groups are usually supported by local institutions such as religious or philanthropic organizations.

Community dialogues are also similar to dialogues in educational settings in a number of ways. Participants are invited to air their grievances, but attention is also paid to the underlying causes of such grievances. There is also an emphasis on openness, honesty, fairness, respect, and being reasonable. The confidentiality of the participants' comments is also emphasized.

One of the most widely used approaches to community dialogues has been developed by the Study Circles Resource Center (SCRC) (McCoy, Emigh, Leighninger, & Barratt, 1999). This organization promotes community dialogues to advance deliberative democracy and improve the quality of life in the United States. Study circles are used not only for intergroup relations but also to promote discussion of other political and social issues. Study circles usually have 5 to 15 participants who meet 3 to 6 times to discuss a specific issue or set of issues. They are participatory discussions in which people are provided with an opportunity to get to know the other participants before they proceed to substantive discussions of the issues. The discussions are facilitated by trained individuals (often those trained by SCRC). They strive to discover common ground and promote collaborative approaches to solving local problems. They often evolve over a series of successive meetings in which more and more members of the community become involved. The participants come to feel a sense of ownership concerning the issues at hand, and they learn they can express disagreements without feeling threatened. New approaches to solving the problem and new working alliances are expected to emerge from study circles. People wishing to implement study circles are provided with step-by-step materials to help them build a central organizing group; recruit sponsors, trainers, and participants; advertise the program; conduct the program; and follow up on the program.

Dialogue is key to the conduct of study circles. The members of SCRC regard dialogue as a collaborative exercise in which participants seek common ground by listening in order to understand one another. Participants are expected to be open to change and willing to introspect concerning their own positions. As in most dialogues, group conflict is considered to be positive because it reveals underlying assumptions and interests, brings out diverse views, deepens people's understanding of the problem, and generates more options for action.

Problem-Solving Workshops

Problem-solving groups are different from other dialogue groups because they are primarily focused on addressing a protracted conflict between two groups. They have most often been used in attempts to resolve international disputes of long standing. Problem-solving workshops evolved out of a long tradition of applied human relations training (Fisher, 1990). Some of these approaches to training were designed for industrial settings (D. R. S. Blake & Mouton, 1984), some—like sensitivity training groups—were designed to improve interpersonal skills (Lippitt, 1949), and some were designed to improve intergroup relations (Levinson, 1954). As they evolved, these techniques began to be applied to intractable international conflicts (Burton, 1974; Doob, 1974; Kelman & Cohen, 1986). A wide variety of international conflicts have been approached using problem-solving workshops, including relations between the Jews and Palestinians in the Middle East, the Turkish and Greek Cypriots, the Catholics and Protestants in Northern Ireland, the French and English Canadians in Quebec, the Tibetans and Chinese, and the Ethiopians and Somalians in the Horn of Africa.

Problem-solving groups usually consist of a relatively small number of select individuals who are brought together by the organizers of the workshop. In some instances, these workshops are created because an intergroup crisis has arisen, but more commonly they are created to help resolve long-standing conflicts. The participants are typically chosen because they hold positions of influence in their societies or groups (e.g., government advisors, journalists, business leaders, scholars). They are usually brought together on neutral ground and their discussions are facilitated by trained personnel. The workshops are generally very intensive and relatively short, rarely lasting more than a week or two, although there are examples of groups that have met over extended periods of time (Hubbard, 1997). The facilitators set the ground rules, establish the agenda, and intervene to move the dialogue forward. They attempt to be neutral with respect to taking sides in the dispute. They need to be credible to both parties as well as impartial in their treatment of both groups. The facilitators are selected to be well versed in the dynamics of group interaction, the nature of attitude change, and the complexity of intergroup conflict and its resolution. Ideally, they are very knowledgeable concerning the dispute at hand and committed to just and peaceful solutions to the dispute. One of the goals of the facilitators is to create a nonthreatening environment in which open communication can occur.

Ground rules for social interaction are established at the outset. The groups are expected to approach the conflict in an analytical manner. Participants are encouraged to try to understand the perspective of members of the other group and to examine the impact of their group on the other group. The participants often discuss "how each side views itself and understands its own actions, how it perceives its adversary and explains its behavior, how it projects the future of the conflict, and what it conceives as elements of changeability" (Kelman & Cohen, 1986, p. 335). When these ground rules are established, they have an impact on the dynamics of the group. For instance, one participant reported that she found the meetings exciting

> Because you had people who were . . . serious about wanting to understand another's point of view and who did have that basic underlying commitment to the self-determination of the other and, therefore, I think it was a lot easier to share some negative things with each other without destroying the fabric of the group. (Hubbard, 1997, p. 269)

The facilitators help the participants to see the ways in which communication processes within the group mirror aspects of the larger conflict between the groups (Hubbard, 1997). For instance, the same stereotypes and attributions are applied to outgroup members in the dialogue group that characterize relations between the larger groups that are in conflict. Legalistic arguments and accusatory diatribes are discouraged, but participants are encouraged to express their own emotional responses to the conflict. Participants are expected to go beyond the particulars of the dispute to deal with fundamental issues of identity, needs, values, and interests. It is hoped that the parties to the dispute will move to the view that the conflict itself is a joint problem to be solved. Creative approaches to resolving the conflict are expected to emerge from these dialogues. It is anticipated that these creative approaches will be fed back to policy makers by the participants. The dialogues themselves are usually relatively unstructured, but on occasion, the participants are asked to undertake specific, more structured activities. The workshops themselves are not designed to resolve the conflicts—that is, they are not meant to replace formal negotiations. Instead, the goal is to feed new ideas into the conflict resolution process in an effort to create win-win solutions in which both sides achieve some, if not all, of their goals.

One of the most successful examples of the use of intergroup workshops has taken place with respect to the conflict between the Israeli Jews and the Palestinians. We will discuss two types of workshops that have been used to help resolve conflict between these two groups. The first involves a series of problem-solving workshops between Israeli and Palestinian leaders that has taken place over several decades (Kelman, 1997, 1999; Kelman & Cohen, 1986). The second involves a program that brings Israeli Jewish and Arab students together for dialogues (Bargal & Bar, 1992, 1994).

The problem-solving workshops involve politically influential Israelis and Palestinians including leading political figures, military officers, government officials, and prominent journalists and scholars. These workshops are led by panels of social scientists who are knowledgeable in Middle Eastern affairs. The workshops are held in neutral settings under academic auspices. These workshop groups are quite small, usually involving only 3 to 6 individuals from each side, along with 2 to 4 facilitators. Strict rules of confidentiality encourage the participants to be open and forthcoming. No record is kept of the discussions. Equality between the two sides within the workshop is carefully maintained. The goals of these workshops are to engage in joint problem solving to identify steps that can be taken toward mutual assurance regarding issues of security and to develop a shared vision of a desirable future.

The participants listen to one another as they articulate their concerns, needs, fears, hopes, priorities, and constraints. Issues of mutual distrust invariably arise, memories of events of symbolic significance are evoked, resentments and recriminations (e.g., racism, terrorism) are exchanged, and concerns about annihilation are expressed. In the initial phases of each workshop, the two sides tend to view the conflict as a zero-sum game in which any gain for the other side comes at a loss to their side. Each group is viewed by the other as a threat to its existence. As the workshops progress, considerable time is spent exploring ways of accommodating the other group's identity needs while maintaining the identity of their own group. Eventually, the workshops lead to a more open, noncommittal exploration of options available for the future relationship between the two sides.

The dialogues between the two groups create a more humanized and differentiated view of the other side, and they contribute to the creation of a new political discourse that addresses the concerns of the other side. The dialogue groups also discuss solutions to contentious political issues such as Israeli settlements on the West Bank (in territory claimed by the Palestinians) and problems associated with Palestinian refugees living in other countries. These discussions have resulted in substantial inputs into the official negotiations between the two groups in efforts to achieve a peaceful settlement to their conflict.

A quite different application of the problem-solving workshop approach takes place at Neve Shalom/Wahat al Salam (these are Hebrew and Arabic names for the same community) in Israel (Bargal & Bar, 1992). In this community, Jews and Arabs live and work side by side, giving conflict management workshops that last 3 days to Jewish and Arab youths aged 16 to 17. Thousands of participants have passed through this program since its inception in 1970. Mixed Arab and Jewish groups of 10 to 13 young people hold dialogues that are facilitated by an Arab and a Jewish trainer. Before arriving at Neve Shalom/ Wahat al Salam, the students go through several preparatory sessions in which they are informed of the nature of the workshops, provided with an awareness of basic issues that will arise, and prepared to deal with emotional aspects of examining their attitudes and behaviors and confronting their fears (Bargal & Bar, 1992).

In the workshops, the participants engage in dialogues and structured exercises. They spend all their free time in mixed groups. Initially, the participants present their expectations and fantasies regarding the group. Later, cultural differences are discussed, prejudice and stereotypes are analyzed, political aspects of self-identity are raised, and the Arab-Israeli conflict is examined. During these dialogues, attempts are made to correct faulty perceptions and beliefs. The facilitators try to maintain an atmosphere of mutual trust and respect. In the final sessions, the students are prepared to return to their families, schools, and communities. The students often find the experience painful, as they confront their own faulty beliefs and come to see how difficult the problems will be to resolve. But they also report finding the dialogues enlightening and rewarding. After the dialogues end, the students engage in a series of follow-up experiences over the course of the next year. These activities are designed to strengthen the attitude and belief changes that have taken place during the workshops.

Are dialogue groups effective in improving intergroup relations? We examine the rather limited literature on this question next.

Research on the
Effectiveness of Dialogue Groups

There have been empirical studies of both the dialogues involving Israeli Jews and Arabs and the dialogue groups conducted at the University of Michigan. Studies of the effects of the Neve Shalom/Wahat al Salam program have been done in which participants were compared to nonparticipants in a pretest and posttest design (Bargal & Bar, 1992). The data suggest that the program was generally more successful with each succeeding year, but there were clearly years when the program was not successful in changing attitudes. A study of a related program in Israel obtained similarly mixed results (Hertz-Lazarowitz, Kuppermintz, & Lang, 1998). This program involved mutual school visits by Jewish and Arab students in Israel. These meetings focused on understanding culture and customs, reducing stereotypes, and issues of identity. Although the meetings were designed to create mutual liking and increase empathy and understanding, pretest and posttest comparisons indicated that very few positive effects and some negative effects occurred among participants in the program when compared to nonparticipants. The mixed outcomes of these programs are a reminder of just how difficult it is to improve relations between groups that have a history of protracted conflict.

Several studies have examined the effects of the dialogue program at the University of Michigan that was described earlier. In one of these studies, the effects of the dialogue program on understanding structural aspects of the political system, economy, and social life that create intergroup inequalities were examined (Lopez, Gurin, & Nagda, 1998, Study 1). The students taking this course were predominantly White, but a significant number were students of color (28%). The students who took the course displayed a greater understanding of the role that structural factors play in causing racial and ethnic inequality than did students in a matched control group. A second study by the investigators employed a pretest/posttest design and replicated the results of the first study. In addition, it was found that the students cited more structural causes when explaining poverty, and they believed that structural changes would be needed to overcome inequality to a greater extent than they did at the beginning of the course. Correlational analyses indicated that the more involved the students were in the content and exercises in the course, the more their beliefs about the causes of inequality changed.

Another study of the Michigan program used a pretest and posttest design with a matched control group and measured students' attitudes 3 years after the course was taken (Gurin, Peng, Lopez, & Nagda, 1999). White students who had participated in the program perceived greater commonality in values and interests with people of color as a result of the program. They also reported greater support for affirmative action policies and were more likely to believe that conflict can have beneficial outcomes as a result of the program. Students of color who participated in the program perceived that there was less racial divisiveness, supported affirmative action more, and believed in the beneficial effects of conflict more. Students of color who had participated in the program also had more positive interactions with Whites as a result of the program. Although some measures showed no effects of the program, overall, the program had predominantly positive effects on intergroup relations a full 3 years after the students participated in it. This study appears to be unique in all the literature on the effects of intergroup relations programs. No other study has examined the impact of such programs over so long a period of time.

In addition to these empirical studies, a small number of qualitative studies of dialogue groups help shed light on what occurs during these groups (Schoem & Stevenson, 1990; Zuniga & Sevig, 1997). One of these studies argues that the University of Michigan program has four primary effects (Zuniga & Sevig, 1997). First, it challenges misconceptions, biases, and stereotypes. For example, the authors cite one White participant who reported,

> My original stereotypes were that the people of color would be easily set off by a comment that a White person would make, and would become hostile to every White person in the group. I thought the people of color would just sit and talk about oppression. The dialogue experience made me rethink my stereotypes. (Zuniga & Sevig, 1997, p. 24)

Second, dialogue groups help participants develop more complex ways of thinking about intergroup relations, as illustrated in the following quote from a Latina participant.

> I was surprised to see some of us disagreeing with each other. I had made the assumption that people who are in the same social identity group also shared the same thoughts but I was soon proven wrong. Members of the other group also disagreed with each other. That also surprised me because I went into the dialogue thinking that Black people always agree with each other. (Zuniga & Sevig, 1997, p. 25)

Third, dialogues lead students to take a more positive approach to conflict. As one White participant said,

> Before this dialogue I had tended to avoid conflict, and think that conflict only led to anger and hate. However, now I realize this is not the case. Through our discussions, which did contain conflict, issues were brought out into the open and could no longer be ignored in the name of comfort. Yes, at times I have felt uncomfortable, just as I had initially feared, but that discomfort also resulted in learning and increased understanding and awareness. (Zuniga & Sevig, 1997, p. 25)

Fourth, participants in dialogues become more motivated to take actions that address issues of social justice. Here is a comment addressing this issue from a Latina participant: "Even though the twelve of us in the group, alone, cannot make the changes that are needed, we have definitely learned how to bond and work together to make a difference" (Zuniga & Sevig, 1997, p. 26).

These types of qualitative studies give an indication of what occurs during dialogue groups, but they cannot tell us how much change actually occurred or whether similar changes might have occurred even in the absence of dialogue groups, perhaps as a result of other courses the students are taking or of their experiences in the dorms in which they live.

The value of dialogue groups is difficult to assess. Some are so new that they have not yet been extensively investigated (dialogues in educational and community settings). Others have been used in applied settings (problem-solving dialogues) in which their effects are difficult to measure. Nonetheless, they appear to be a potentially powerful technique for improving intergroup relations, in part because the level of personal engagement is so much higher than in most other techniques.

Clearly, much more research is needed. This research will need to examine both the outcomes of dialogue groups and the reasons that these groups have these outcomes. At the moment, we can only speculate on the processes by which dialogue groups lead to positive outcomes, and we do this in the next section.

Psychological Processes Underlying Dialogue Groups

The psychological processes elicited in dialogue groups are likely to be a complementary mixture of affective and cognitive processes but with a heavier emphasis on affective processes. As befits the interactive nature of dialogue groups, these processes tend to be primarily active ones (Figure 2.3), including those involved in intergroup contact, self-disclosure, dissonance, and creating value-behavior discrepancies. Even the processes that we have categorized as passive and cognitive are likely to occur in a more emotionally involving, active manner in dialogue groups. These processes include promoting empathy, humanizing outgroups, creating superordinate groups, reducing anxiety and uncertainty, and changing attitudes and subjective norms concerning intergroup relations.

Most dialogue groups optimize the conditions of intergroup contact (G. W. Allport, 1954; W. G. Stephan & Stephan, 1996). The participants are of equal status, the interaction is generally cooperative, the participants have a common goal, the interactions are personalized, and the interactions are supported by the authority figures in the situation. For these reasons alone, they should improve intergroup relations among the participants.

More than most other techniques, dialogue groups provide opportunities for self-disclosure. Self-disclosure often leads to liking because it creates an atmosphere of trust and is usually reciprocal (Derlega,

Metts, Petronio, & Margulis, 1993). In the process of self-disclosure, people take risks and are generally responded to with acceptance and support by others in their own group and in the outgroup. Thus, self-disclosure commonly increases self-esteem and can enhance ingroup identity. In the context of intergroup dialogues, enhancing ingroup identity can lead to an acceptance of the identity aspirations of the outgroup, because both groups are encouraged to express their identification with their own group and accept the identity of others.

Dissonance processes may also operate in dialogue groups and lead to improvements in intergroup relations. Dissonance occurs when people engage in behaviors that are discrepant from their self-conceptions (E. Aronson, 1997). Participants in intergroup dialogues often engage in behaviors that are disapproved of by members of their own group and that are in direct conflict with their own prior beliefs. The close interpersonal relations and growing concern for the welfare of the other group must often be justified against a backdrop of prior contradictory behaviors and beliefs. One solution to this dilemma is to reduce the dissonance by changing one's attitudes to be consistent with the behaviors that have emerged in the group. In addition, confronting feelings of guilt, one's own mistaken beliefs and assumptions about the other group, and overcoming one's fears can all be distressing.

Dissonance theorists also argue that people feel compelled to justify such expenditures of effort, and the easiest way to do so is to regard the behaviors and the cause as having been worth the effort—a process called effort justification. Thus, participation in dialogue groups can lead to positive changes in attitude toward the groups involved as a way of justifying the distress caused by the experience. This is not an argument to increase the amount of distress that participants experience in order to increase attitude change through effort justification, but it does mean that the distress that often occurs during dialogue groups may serve a useful function.

Many dialogue groups discuss issues of egalitarianism and fairness. Such discussions may lead to reductions in expressions of prejudice. According to study by Monteith and Walters (1998), even individuals who are high in prejudice commonly hold egalitarian values. The study found that when highly prejudiced individuals define egalitarianism as equality of opportunity, they feel morally obligated to temper their expressions of prejudice. This study suggests that if dialogue groups lead group members to think of egalitarianism in terms of equality of opportunity, it could lead even highly prejudiced people to be more reluctant to express their biased attitudes. The dialogues may also evoke guilt feelings among participants over the discrepancies between their personal values and their actual behavior (Monteith, Zuwerink, & Devine, 1994). If so, they may reduce their expressions of prejudice, stereotypes, and discrimination to reduce their feelings of guilt.

Learning about members of the other group in a dialogue context seems likely to elicit both cognitive and emotional empathy (Davis, 1994; W. G. Stephan & Finlay, 2000). Most dialogue groups have the explicit goal of encouraging members of each group to understand the perspective of the other group. Seeing a conflict from the perspective of members of the outgroup is likely to reduce the distance between the groups by creating a greater understanding of the beliefs, values, motives, and behaviors of the outgroup. The ethnocentric view that one's group is the center of everything is necessarily challenged by an empathic understanding of the views of another group.

Emotional empathy for the suffering of members of the outgroup can lead to experiencing the same emotions as members of the group including feelings of anger and injustice. These feelings in turn may lead to a sense of guilt or responsibility by association with the ingroup members who have perpetrated these injustices. Ingroup members may also react with compassion to hearing about the suffering of outgroup members, leading to a greater concern for their welfare. Dialogue groups are particularly likely to evoke empathic processes because participants so often present personal narratives in these groups. The use of first-person descriptions by individuals who are familiar to the listener increases the likelihood that identification with the speaker will occur, and empathic processes will be set in motion. Listening to narratives is much more compelling than reading information about the suffering of members of outgroups in a reading assignment.

In dialogue groups that concern protracted conflicts, the dialogues serve to humanize members of the opposing groups. In some cases, members of these groups have had almost no contact with members of the other group, and the enmity between them has led to the creation of dehumanized images of the nature of the other group and its members. Negative stereotypes, negative attributions, and caricatures of members of the other group are invalidated during the dialogues. Dialogue groups create a social climate in which members of each group can learn about the diversity and humanity of the other group. Dialogues often provide an experience that is similar in some ways to insight-oriented therapies. The individual participants come to learn that their preconceived images are inaccurate and that members of the other group share a common humanity with them even if they do not necessarily share all the same values and beliefs. They learn to understand aspects of the other group and themselves that their own biases had prevented them from seeing.

Dialogue groups lend themselves naturally to the creation of superordinate groups (Gaertner, Dovidio, Nier, Ward, & Banker, 1999). In the process of dialoging, attachments to other group members evolve, and some of these attachments cross group boundaries. As the groups work together to come to consensus on proposed actions, they strengthen their bonds to one another and forge an identity as a group. These interactions generate positive attitudes toward the individual outgroup members who are participating in the group, and these attitudes may then generalize to the group as a whole. To the extent that the interactions in the group are interpersonally oriented and positive, generalization to the group as a whole should increase (Desforges et al., 1991; Miller & Harrington, 1990a).

According to anxiety and uncertainty management theory (AUM), people often enter into intergroup interaction uncertain of how to behave and anxious about the outcomes (Gudykunst, 1995). People often do not know how to predict the behavior of outgroup members, and they find the behavior of outgroup members difficult to explain. Uncertainty and anxiety undercut people's abilities to communicate effectively, and they can create prejudice and lead to a reliance on stereotypes. Initially, dialogue groups are likely to be characterized by high levels of uncertainty and anxiety, but the dialogues may well undercut uncertainty and anxiety as members of opposing groups become accustomed to one another and learn to interact effectively on the basis of the rules that prevail in these groups.

In AUM theory, it is argued that anxiety and uncertainty can be reduced by attraction to outgroup members, positive contact with outgroup members, interdependence with outgroup members, perceptions of similarity to outgroup members, and empathy—among other factors. Dialogue groups provide an opportunity for all these factors to operate. Dialogue groups also provide the participants with opportunities to acquire skills in interacting across group boundaries. Reduced anxiety and uncertainty along with improved intergroup relations skills should lead to improvement in intergroup communication and attitudes in future interactions.

To the extent that dialogue groups lead to social action, they may do so through processes outlined in theories that relate thoughts to behavior, such as the theory of reasoned action (Fishbein & Ajzen, 1975; Trafimow, 1998). In this theory, it is argued that behavior and the intentions on which they are based are influenced by people's attitudes toward the behaviors and their perceptions of how individuals who are important to them would feel about their engaging in these behaviors. Dialogue groups may promote social action by leading people to adopt different attitudes toward the value of engaging in these behaviors, but, perhaps more important, they may provide people with a new reference group of significant others who approve of engaging in social action. Thus, the perceived rewards for engaging in behaviors that promote social justice may be enhanced by the dialogue process. Research on this theory also indicates that when people state their behavioral intentions, they are more likely to carry through with them than when they merely mentally consider their intentions (Sheeran & Orbell, 1999). When dialogue groups discuss social action, people publicly commit themselves to taking action, which increases the chances that they will do so (Lewin, 1947). Dialogue groups may also lead people to be more confident that they can carry out their intentions to engage in social action, and research indicates that such perceptions enhance the chances that attitudes will lead to behaviors (Ajzen, 1988).

Problems and Recommendations

Dialogue groups present many unique problems. In discussing them, we focus first on formulating clear goals; then we examine issues relating to training, group process issues, and group differences in status and cultural background. We also explore issues associated with the guidelines for participation, the settings for the dialogues, the duration of the dialogues, the social groups for which this technique is most suited, and making the transition from talk to action.

One issue that dialogue trainers must confront is specifying the goals of their particular type of dialogue group. Some programs have well-defined goals, but others do not. For instance, Kelman (1990) has written that he expects participants in problem-solving workshops to have acquired four types of knowledge. They should have (a) learned that there are people on the other side to whom they can talk and that there is something to talk about; (b) gained insight into the perspectives, concerns, priorities, and needs of the other party; (c) become aware of changes that have taken place in members of the other group; and (d) become aware of changes that can be made to help resolve the conflict. Clear goals provide direction for all the efforts that go into dialogue groups, and they make it possible to assess the effectiveness of dialogue groups in achieving these outcomes.

It is important to have well-trained facilitators who are skilled in managing conflict and insightful with respect to the dynamics of intergroup relations and group identity (McCoy et al., 1996; Nagda et al., 1995; Zuniga et al. 1998). In academic dialogue groups, the peer facilitators typically receive a full semester of training and then meet regularly with their mentors when they are facilitating groups. The facilitators of international dialogues typically have extensive training in conflict resolution along with an extensive knowledge of the conflict itself. The training that facilitators receive should equip them to deal with the deep emotional responses that some participants will experience during the dialogues. Dialogue facilitators also should be taught to recognize and cope with group process issues (Volkan, 1998) and issues related to status (Abu-Nimer, 1999).

Volkan (1998) has identified a number of psychodynamic issues that pose problems in dialogue groups. Griesbach (1999) has done an interesting qualitative study of these issues. She interviewed nine practitioners concerning their experiences in intergroup dialogues. A few illustrations will demonstrate the role some of these issues play in dialogues. For instance, in the "echo phenomenon," events outside the group echo in the dialogues and need to be addressed or they will create unacknowledged tensions within the group. Here is an example of an echo phenomenon in a dialogue between pro- and anti-abortion advocates. The external event was the shooting of an abortion doctor.

> The leaders choose not to deal with it, not to create a space for conversation about the doctor. Big mistake. The echoes—you've got to pay attention to them. So they paid for it. People were distracted. It was brought up in the beginning and you could see the tension in the room, and it wasn't addressed or talked about. . . . The people that were the most tense were the quietest and the most uninvolved in the process. It wasn't until the break about three quarters of the way through that we [the supervisors] gave the facilitators some feedback. We said you have to at least acknowledge that it has come up. And acknowledge that there will be a place to talk about it or people will not be free of the preoccupation. So they announced that the next meeting would be spent discussing the doctor and it just freed the process right up. (Griesbach, 1999, p. 18)

Another common problem in dialogue groups is a kind of competition that develops to present the traumas one's own group has experienced and the past glories it has achieved. Here is an example of how this problem was dealt with in a dialogue group involving Greeks and Turks in Cyprus.

> We put a piece of masking tape down the middle of the floor, and we mark it off in decades. We say, okay Greeks on one side, and Turks on the other. Here's pieces of paper, and marking pens and string. For every piece of paper you want to put down there, put the date, put the event that was meaningful for you in your history, . . . and attach it by string to the decade. . . . We get a map on the floor of the two different histories. And then everyone walks down the line looking right and left, realizing that there are two sets of histories here. You have very deep conversations. (Griesbach, 1999, p. 21)

A third issue is labeled the *accordion,* and involves the group approaching, then avoiding, an issue repeatedly. Here is an example.

The group is unconsciously doing this dance, this accordion around
wanting to bridge to the other side and wanting to remain separate
from the other side. . . . It feels like the people in the workshops that I
am facilitating are eager to find a common bond because it feels better.
It is safe and secure, and we can feel good about ourselves. At the same
time we are terrified to have too much of a common bond because then
we are not distinct, we are not separate ethnicities. (Griesbach, 1999,
p. 23)

Other issues described by Volkan (1998) include one group project-
ing its own wishes on the other group concerning how they should
think, and the existence of hidden transcripts or motives. Not all these
processes will arise in every group, but cataloging them is helpful to
facilitators and researchers who are seeking to understand the dialogue
process. The existence of such psychodynamic issues in dialogue
groups clearly distinguishes dialogue groups from other intergroup relations techniques that rely on didactic approaches or structured exercises. Only in dialogue groups are these types of issues likely to emerge.
Coping effectively with them has the potential to lead to a deeper understanding of the problems that exist between the groups.

After analyzing Neve Shalom/Wahat al Salam and other dialogue
programs for Arabs and Israelis, Abu-Nimer (1999) discussed a number of problems that arise in conflict resolution workshops that would
seem to be relevant to a variety of different types of dialogue programs, especially those involving differences in status between the
two groups. Dominant groups are often reluctant to interact with
members of minority groups on an equal-status basis or even to participate in dialogues at all. Members of the dominant group may also be
reluctant to learn about the culture of the other group. The most difficult issues tend to be avoided, especially by members of the dominant
group. Also, the programs may weaken the identity of members of the
minority group. To avoid this last problem, at Neve Shalom/Wahat al
Salam members of the two groups meet separately beforehand to create a sense of ingroup cohesiveness (Bargal & Bar, 1992).

Abu-Nimer (1999) also argues that dialogues should not be used as
a substitute for action. He believes they run the risk of making the status quo more acceptable to the participants rather than prompting
them to take social action. With groups that are in political conflict,

support from authorities in both communities is crucial to success but is often lacking. He feels that cultural differences are much more important in dialogue groups than is generally recognized. Differences in communication styles, respect for authority, the roles of women and men, and the relative importance of the individual and the group all affect interactions in dialogue groups. To overcome these problems, he recommends that (a) dialogue programs be designed to empower both groups, (b) they stress equality both within and outside of this setting, (c) conflicts between the two groups be faced openly, and (d) the programs emphasize differences as well as similarities.

The guidelines for participation (e.g., adopting an analytical approach, taking the perspective of the other side, confidentiality) are one of the most critical elements of dialogue programs. They should be presented with considerable care. The content of the guidelines will vary depending on the type of dialogue group, the nature of the groups and their prior conflicts, and the goals of the dialogue, but the need for clear guidelines is a constant.

The setting in which the dialogues occur is also quite important in dialogue groups. Bargal and Bar (1992) refer to the setting of Neve Shalom/Wahat al Salam as a cultural island because the village is a geographically distinct entity away from the home communities of the participants. Isolation from distractions and pressures from other members of their identity groups is likely to make the dialogues more productive. One of the reasons that the 1993 dialogues between the Palestinians and Israelis that led to the Oslo Accords were successful is that these groups met in Norway, far from the Middle East.

The duration of dialogue groups is another important issue that practitioners must face. Many dialogue groups are relatively brief, meeting only three or four times. It is very probable that groups of short duration are limited in their effectiveness. If at all possible, dialogue groups should meet over an extended period of time because it is simply impossible to work through the complex issues involved in a protracted conflict in a short period of time.

It is not clear how old the participants must be before they can profit from dialogues. Dialogues depend for their success on the analytical capacities of the participants, which suggests that they may not be suitable for very young people. They also bring out strong emotions (e.g., fear, anger, hostility, pain) and involve open conflict. These aspects of dialogue groups may also contraindicate using them with young children, who may have difficulty dealing with their emotions. In addition, young children may not be able to follow the guidelines for effective interaction during conflict. Even with adults, instances are likely in which people have negative experiences that they feel are not being addressed in the group. Facilitators need to be aware of these types of problems because they can undermine the success of the group. One trainer provided us with a concrete warning about this problem when he paraphrased a comment made by a participant in a dialogue group: "Before I talked to them, I knew I hated them, but I didn't know why. Now that I have talked to them, I understand better why I hate them" (Gabriel Saloman, personal communication, November 8, 1999).

It is possible that dialogue groups will be more effective between certain types of groups than others. In particular, dialogues involving people from groups that prize harmony and avoid conflicts (as most collectivist cultures do) may find it difficult to engage in dialogue with members of groups that are more comfortable with confrontation, conflict, and direct communication styles (as are those in most individualistic cultures). Facilitators with a firm grasp of the cultural differences between the groups that are involved in the dialogue are more likely to be able to bridge these types of gaps than are facilitators who lack this type of cultural understanding.

All dialogue groups are action oriented, although some focus on action more explicitly than others do. For instance, in problem-solving groups at the community and international levels, the goal is to develop new solutions to the problems between the groups, whereas in academic dialogue groups, social action emerges during the terminal phases of the dialogue process. One of the greatest challenges to dialogue groups is making the transition from talk to action effectively. It may help to get participants to publicly commit themselves to taking action. The actions should be concrete and have a high probability of payoff. The initial actions should be relatively small in scale to increase the chances of success. It also appears to be important to monitor whether or not the actions are taken and to modify them and suggest new actions as time goes along (Marc Goldstein, personal communication, October 7, 1999).

Summary

Dialogue groups are becoming increasingly popular as a technique for improving intergroup relations partly because they can be used in such a wide range of settings. They have been used in academic and community settings as well as for resolving protracted international conflicts. They involve the simplest and most natural of all social relations, verbal communication, although it is verbal communication under very special conditions. Trained facilitators, employing clear sets of guidelines for interaction, conduct dialogues. The groups tend to be small, and they often meet on neutral ground. They discuss current problems as well as issues of identity, and they allow participants to convey their own experiences and express emotions concerning the topics under discussion. They aim to transform not only the individuals involved but also relations between the groups with respect to issues of mutual concern. They would appear to be more likely to promote social action than most other techniques because this is an explicit goal of these programs.

Research on their effectiveness is limited, but what research exists suggests that they have positive effects on attitudes, and they may increase the participants' understanding of the other group and themselves. They appear to have these beneficial effects because they maximize the conditions of contact specified in contact theory. They also provide opportunities for the participants to self-disclose, and this, too, may have a beneficial impact on attitudes and self-understanding. They may elicit dissonance concerning past attitudes and behavior and reveal discrepancies between the values people hold and their behavior toward other groups. They promote empathy for other groups and can humanize other groups. They provide opportunities to create superordinate groups and may decrease anxiety about interacting with outgroup members. Because they also facilitate attitude change and the emergence of new subjective norms, they can also alter behavior.

In sum, intergroup dialogues are a very promising, but not yet well-validated, technique for improving intergroup relations—one that is likely to see increasing use in the future.

INTERCULTURAL TRAINING PROGRAMS   6

W HEN PEOPLE OF DIFFERENT cultures interact, they often misunderstand one another and come into conflict. Programs designed to help people learn about, and adapt to, other cultures
constitute a valuable technique for improving intercultural relations.
These programs also constitute a useful method of enhancing intergroup relations within multicultural societies. They can be used to
train those who interact with immigrants and a variety of racial, ethnic, and religious groups within a multicultural society.

Just as individuals commonly misinterpret the values and behaviors of people from other cultures, so, too, do they misinterpret the values and behaviors of many individuals from within their own,
multicultural society. People from other cultures are stereotyped and
feared and become the objects of biased attributions. Similarly, members of many racial, ethnic, and religious groups from a given culture
are also stereotyped and feared and become the objects of misattributions. Furthermore, racism is often a strong component of difficulties in intergroup interactions both within and between cultures.
Finally, in all societies, *ethnocentrism*—judging another culture by the
standards of one's own society—is a by-product of socialization into
that society. People are taught the norms, values, behaviors, and beliefs of their own culture, and they think of these as being normal and
correct. Within a multicultural society, contacts between groups that
have differing norms, values, beliefs, and behaviors can lead people to
believe that these differing views are deviant and wrong.

In this introduction to intercultural training programs, we discuss the need for intercultural training, explain the goals of intercultural training programs and the types of people for whom they are designed, explore the characteristics of intercultural training programs, and distinguish the types and methods of training.

All individuals need intercultural understanding skills. Social, political, economic, and technological changes have led to the creation of a global community. Increased travel, international business, and international migration have greatly expanded face-to-face intercultural communication. It is unusual for individuals to escape intercultural contact, even if they rarely venture beyond their own neighborhoods. It also seems unlikely that with increasing migration and diversity, individuals in any society in the 21st century could thrive despite intergroup biases and misunderstandings.

Without intercultural training, people who have intercultural experiences frequently find they are marred by interpersonal and intergroup difficulties that are commonly referred to as culture shock. The need for cross-cultural training programs is exemplified by the failure rate of individuals who attempt to adapt to life in another culture. For example, the failure rate of U. S. business expatriates has been estimated at between 16% and 50% (Bhagat & Prien, 1996). Not surprisingly, intercultural adaptation decreases as differences between the home and foreign culture increase. Intercultural training enhances people's enjoyment of their intercultural experience and the benefits they derive from it and results in more positive relations among the individuals from both cultures (Brislin & Yoshida, 1994a). It also helps people achieve the goals of their intercultural interactions and reduces the stress of intercultural interaction.

Similarly, intergroup experiences within a diverse culture can also result in interpersonal and intergroup difficulties that mirror culture shock, with resulting difficulties in business, social, school, social service, and health care settings. Intergroup training based on intercultural techniques could increase the success of intergroup contact with groups within a diverse, multicultural society and reduce the problems associated with intergroup contact.

Not surprisingly, within a single culture, people from the dominant racial or ethnic group are most in need of intergroup training. The groups with less wealth, power, and prestige must understand the culture and behavior of the more dominant group in order to survive in a system that was not created with their group and its norms and values at the center. More dominant groups need to understand the culture and behaviors of less dominant groups, but their greater wealth, power, and prestige often obscures the waste of talent and the failures of understanding that their lack of knowledge creates (Feagin & Vera, 1995). People from less dominant groups pay closer attention to the dominant groups' perspectives and to the details of particular situations, whereas dominant group members are likely to be less attentive to groups lower in dominance and to situational variations in the behaviors of these groups (Devine, Evett, & Vasquez-Suson, 1996; Frable, Blackstone, & Scherbaum, 1990).

Intercultural training programs are intended to alleviate the problems of intercultural misunderstandings, stereotyping, biased attributions, and fear. They accomplish this task by improving interpersonal relations skills, increasing understanding of the other group, and boosting the accuracy of perceptions of the other group (Brislin & Yoshida, 1994a). These are precisely the skills needed to improve intergroup relations within a culture. The consequence of the changes brought about by this type of training within a multicultural society should be enhanced intergroup relations within the society, resulting in increased satisfaction with intergroup experiences.

The premise of all intercultural training techniques is that the differences between cultures are the primary causes of misunderstandings and conflicts. For this reason, information on group differences is included in intercultural training programs. This explanation of differences is a delicate matter. Group differences must be presented in a nonevaluative manner, so preexisting stereotypes and prejudices will not be reinforced. Thus, in intercultural training, the cultural reasons for the existence of the differences are often provided. Including information regarding similarities among the lives and goals of all peoples is also important in overcoming racial prejudice, stereotyping, ethnocentrism, and misattributions regarding behaviors. In practice, most training programs combine information regarding both differences and similarities. Likewise, differences between groups are the chief bases of misperceptions and disagreements within multicultural societies. As in intercultural training, the focus of intergroup training should be on nonevaluative presentations of group differences along with discussions of the many similarities among groups.

Intercultural training programs are most often used to train individuals who are leaving their home culture for an extended stay in another society. Cross-cultural training programs have been designed for a number of audiences including international students, refugees, overseas technical-assistance advisers, and businesspeople. In addition, cross-cultural training programs have been created for tourists seeking intercultural understanding, personnel officers and managers in businesses with employees from multiple countries, diplomats, and other government employees (Brislin & Yoshida, 1994a). Their application to intergroup relations within a multicultural society is less well known. Intergroup training programs have been designed for work, school, health care, and social service settings within culturally diverse societies. Intercultural training techniques could be used even more extensively in these and other intergroup settings.

In Chapter 2, we characterized intercultural training programs as falling in the direct-interactive quadrant (Figure 2.3). These programs are direct because they specifically address intercultural relations. We categorized them as interactive, even though some intercultural training exercises are didactic, because most intercultural training programs include training situations and exercises that require the participants' active involvement. Certainly, the best of these training programs includes many interactive components.

Two general types of intercultural training exist. Intercultural training can be culture specific, focused on understanding a particular culture, or cultural general, centered on a general understanding of the differences in goals, attitudes, values, and beliefs among cultures (Gudykunst, Guzley, & Hammer, 1996). The parallel types for intergroup training are programs concentrated on a particular racial, ethnic, or religious group within the society versus those focused on a variety of groups within a multicultural society.

Intercultural training can be accomplished by two general methods, *experiential* and *didactic,* which have some similarities to the interactive-passive distinction we have used in this book. Experiential training consists of action-oriented and experience-based training focused on problem solving, values, and emotions. Didactic training consists of cognitive, verbal, and intellectual types of training relying on lectures, films, discussions, and other classroom-based means of instruction (Gudykunst et al., 1996; R. Harrison & Hopkins, 1967). Although four approaches to intercultural training are thus possible (experiential, culture specific; experiential, culture general; didactic, culture specific; didactic, cultural general), in practice, most programs include both experiential and didactic components, and most culture-specific training also includes culture-general information (Milhouse, 1996; Paige & Martin, 1996).

We continue our exploration of intercultural training programs by considering two important issues—the components of intercultural effectiveness and the use of theory as a guide to training. Then, we discuss a number of widely used intercultural training techniques. Next, we summarize the research findings for intercultural training programs and detail the psychological processes that underlie their effects. Because the types of training are varied, the psychological processes also range across the active-passive and cognitive-affective domains. Finally, we explore problems regarding, and recommendations for, the implementation of intercultural training programs.

Designing Intercultural Training

Experts designing intercultural training programs must start with the question of what skills they should teach. They must also decide if their programs are to be guided by theory. We discuss these issues in turn.

What Are the Components of Intercultural Effectiveness?

Intercultural training techniques are designed to increase intercultural effectiveness. What skills are required for intercultural effectiveness? Hammer, Gudykunst, and Wiseman (1978) argued that intercultural effectiveness requires three general abilities: the ability to manage psychological stress, to effectively communicate, and to establish interpersonal relations. These abilities should also lead to effectiveness in interaction with groups from within a multicultural society.

More specific traits have been suggested for intercultural effectiveness in specific settings. For instance, Cui and Awa (1992) found five dimensions of intercultural effectiveness in organizational settings: (a) personality traits, such as patience, empathy, flexibility, and tolerance; (b) interpersonal skills, such as the ability to establish and maintain relationships; (c) the ability to initiate conversations with strangers, and language abilities; (d) social interaction skills, such as an understanding of the economic and political systems, showing respect, and behaving appropriately; and (e) managerial ability, such as motivation, creativity, and success in the home country as well as cultural empathy (as expressed in understanding the culture and its working style), tolerance for ambiguity and uncertainty, awareness of cultural differences, and the ability to be nonjudgmental. These traits and abilities should be similarly successful in multicultural work settings.

Should Theory Guide Intercultural Training?

Many intercultural experts argue that intercultural training should be based on theories designed to understand and explain the type of interactions for which the training is designed (Bhawuk & Triandis, 1996; Gudykunst et al., 1996). If the goal of training is cultural adaptation, training should be based on theories of cultural adjustment; if the goal is multicultural communication in the workplace, training should be based on a theory of intercultural communication effectiveness.

Culture Theory

Theories about major dimensions of cultural differences provide an explanation for the underlying causes of behaviors. Using culture theory allows interventions to be based on the most relevant cultural characteristics. According to Bhawuk and Triandis (1996), one can become a novice in intercultural expertise by going through some formal, intercultural training program that discusses cultural differences or by extended experience in another culture. However, one can become an expert only through the acquisition of culture theory, so that knowledge about cultural differences can be organized and understood through broad explanatory concepts.

Bhawuk and Triandis (1996) believe that the concepts of individualism and collectivism provide an important theoretical basis for intercultural training. They advocate that training be based on individualism and collectivism because these concepts predict a considerable amount of daily social behavior and explain such processes as cultural distance, self-concept, and perceptions of the ingroup versus the outgroup (Bhawuk & Triandis, 1996). Individualism and collectivism have several defining characteristics (Triandis, 1995). Individualistic cultures create individuals with independent selves; individuals with independent selves have goals independent from those of their ingroups; they emphasize attitudes; and they stress rationality. By contrast, collectivist cultures produce individuals with interdependent selves; individuals with interdependent selves have goals compatible with those of their ingroups; they emphasize norms; and they focus on relatedness. Individualists focus on their own needs and wants, define themselves as individuals, and seek self-actualization, whereas collectivists subordinate their needs to those of the ingroup, define themselves in terms of the ingroup, and seek ingroup acceptance. Intercultural training for individuals moving from an individualistic society to a collectivist one, or for those moving from a collectivist to an individualistic society, can be organized around the study of this extremely important difference, "the most important world view that differentiates cultures" (Triandis, 1994). Because many ethnic minorities and immigrants to the United States have cultures that are more collectivist than that of the individualistic Anglo American majority (Condon, 1997; Grossman, 1995; Haynes & Gebreyesus, 1992; Kitano & Daniels, 1995; Malloy & Malloy, 1998), individualism-collectivism may also provide a good foundation for intergroup training.

Intergroup Anxiety

Another type of intercultural theory is based on the idea that fear or anxiety provides the basis for culture shock and difficulties of intercultural adaptation, as well as problems in understanding immigrants and cultural outgroups within a culture (Gudykunst, 1988; 1993; 1995; C. W. Stephan & Stephan 1992; W. G. Stephan & Stephan,

1985, 1996; W. G. Stephan, Stephan, & Gudykunst, 1999). When individuals interact with others different from themselves, they experience anxiety about possible negative consequences of the interaction. People fear negative psychological consequences (e.g., confusion, frustration, feeling incompetent), negative behavioral consequences (e.g., being exploited, harmed), negative evaluations by outgroup members (e.g., being rejected or ridiculed), and negative evaluations by ingroup members (e.g., rejection, being identified with outgroup members). Unfortunately, intergroup anxiety is associated with prejudice against others different from oneself (C. W. Stephan & Stephan, 1992; W. G. Stephan & Stephan, 1989). Dislike of the host culture and its members is obviously a predictor of poor intercultural adaptation and intercultural ineffectiveness. In a multicultural society, intergroup anxiety has been shown to be a predictor of prejudice toward members of other cultures (C. W. Stephan & Stephan, 1992; W. G. Stephan, Diaz-Loving, & Duran, 2000), immigrant groups (W. G. Stephan, Ybarra, & Bachman, 1999; W. G. Stephan, Ybarra, Martinez, Schwarzwald, & Tur-Kaspa, 1998), and racial and ethnic groups (W. G. Stephan & Stephan, 1989).

Gudykunst's model of intergroup communication argues that managing anxiety and uncertainty are the primary tasks necessary for effective intercultural and intergroup adaptation (Gudykunst, 1988, 1993, 1995). A training program designed with this theoretical model would be based on techniques to help trainees understand that they can manage anxiety and uncertainty, and techniques to help them do so (Gudykunst et al., 1996). Such training might initially involve experiential exercises to evoke anxiety and uncertainty, followed by discussions of these exercises that focus on the influence of anxiety and uncertainty on behavior. This introduction might be followed by techniques to manage anxiety and practice in doing so through role-playing and simulations. Techniques to manage uncertainty, such as learning to make accurate predictions about people's behaviors using cultural similarities and differences, and practice in uncertainty management would also be included. Anxiety and uncertainty might also be reduced by learning about the major dimensions of cultural variability; practicing interaction with members from the foreign culture, the immigrant group, or the cultural outgroup; and gaining practical information regarding aspects of the foreign or immigrant culture or the cultural group.

We now consider the major intercultural training techniques currently being used.

Intercultural Training Techniques

Here, we explore a number of widely used intercultural training techniques including lectures and discussions, language training, cultural sensitizers, critical incidents, and experiential techniques, such as simulation games, role-playing, and cultural simulations (Gudykunst et al., 1996). All these techniques have been adapted to learning about cultural groups from within a multicultural society.

Lectures and Discussions

Virtually all intercultural training programs include some didactic-based material, relying on lecture and discussion techniques. Characteristics of the foreign culture may be presented along with a discussion of the home culture's influences on the trainees' behaviors. Major cultural differences are often discussed, as are the concepts of ethnocentrism, stereotyping, and culture shock. Frequently, orientations to the history, religion, economics, politics, and values of the culture and its people are introduced through lectures and discussions. Readings about general problems and the particular culture are typically used to supplement such lectures and discussions. Trainees may also be asked to conduct their own library research. Experts and consultants may be interviewed, and discussions with old hands (people from the home culture with long experience in the foreign culture) may take place. Case studies illustrating cultural differences and adaptive and maladaptive responses may be read and analyzed. Short scenarios illustrating cultural misunderstandings may be read and discussed as well. Each of these didactic techniques can be readily applied to intergroup settings, with racial, ethnic, or religious groups rather than cultures as the focus of learning. Accurate information about the various groups within a multicultural society is often as sparse as information about people from other cultures, and so didactic training is also a valuable tool in intergroup training within a multicultural society.

Here is an example of scenario applied to an intergroup setting. It concerns a misunderstanding in a store between two people who are acquainted, an Anglo American customer and a Latino employee (Storti, 1994, p.16):

> Roberto: Miss Thomas! How nice to see you.
> Miss Thomas: How are you, Roberto?
> Roberto: Fine, fine, thank you. What can I get for you?
> Miss Thomas: Well, to start with, I'd like half a dozen eggs.
> Roberto: Yes.
> Miss Thomas: And then I'd like a half-pound of butter.
> Roberto: Yes. Ah, Octavio! Good to see you. Como estas?
> Octavio: Bien, gracias. And you?
> Roberto: Bien. How can I help you?
> Octavio: I need some bananas.
> Roberto: Of course. Rosita! Como estas? I haven't seen you in a long time. How is that little boy of yours?
> Rosita: He's very well.
> Roberto: What can I do for you?
> Miss Thomas: Roberto, I thought you were helping me.
> Roberto: But I am helping you, Miss Thomas.

The ensuing discussion would almost certainly focus on the fact that Miss Thomas and Roberto are operating on two different conceptions of time. In Miss Thomas's monochronic culture, tasks are completed one at a time, people's needs are attended to in turn, and individuals try to follow precise schedules. Roberto is operating on polychronic time, which is typical of many Latin cultures and can be found among some Latino peoples in the United States. In Roberto's orientation toward time, several transactions can be conducted simultaneously because actions occur in a less linear, more dynamic time frame. Thus, Miss Thomas falsely attributes inattention and disrespect to Roberto when he is only trying to be inclusive and helpful to everyone. A trainer would probably also focus the discussion on the ways in which misunderstandings based on differing conceptions of propriety are often misattributed to negative personal characteristics of the people involved.

Lectures and discussions are effective means of conveying cultural information. In fact, lectures have been shown to be more effective than experiential techniques in conveying specific and unfamiliar knowledge (Brislin & Pedersen, 1976).

Language Training

Language training is an important tool for intercultural adaptation, and language skills are invaluable in easing intercultural adjustment. Language training is common prior to some types of intercultural experiences (e.g., for students or government workers planning long stays in the country) but is widely ignored by or unavailable to other types of individuals (e.g., businesspeople, U. S. military personnel). The lack of language training puts the individual at a serious disadvantage with respect to enjoyment, benefits, intercultural relations, goal attainment, and level of stress in intercultural interaction. Language training alone, however, runs the risk of creating only "fluent fools," people who speak the native tongue but have no understanding of the culture, so language training needs to be accompanied by cultural learning (Brislin & Yoshida, 1994a). Language fluency tends to be viewed by natives as equivalent to cultural competency, so cultural mistakes made by foreigners who are fluent in the language are sometimes thought to be the result of intended arrogance or disrespect. Lectures and readings regarding nonverbal communication are important, but frequently ignored, elements of language training programs.

Language training is typically overlooked within a culture, with resulting disadvantages to the citizens of multicultural societies. Language training would greatly assist many individuals in social, business, education, social service, and health care settings, particularly when accompanied by cultural training. Even within a multicultural society, nonverbal-communication training would be beneficial in many instances.

The Cultural Sensitizer

One widely used technique, the cultural sensitizer, teaches individuals about cultural differences using a programmed learning approach (Cushner & Landis, 1996; Triandis, 1972). This approach involves the analysis of specific instances of intercultural misunderstanding or conflict in order to teach the subjective culture of the other group. *Subjective culture* is the term used for aspects of culture such as norms, values, and beliefs that are often unquestioningly accepted by members of that group but typically remain hidden from outsiders. Subjective culture also includes the implicit worldview of the group. The purpose of cultural sensitizers is to make this implicit worldview explicit.

This purpose is accomplished by teaching trainees to make the same attributions for a cultural outgroup member's behavior as do members of that culture. This goal is achieved by giving trainees information regarding the culturally based reasons for the behaviors exhibited by members of the other culture. Ignorance of the subjective culture of another country often leads individuals to wrongly interpret a situation in terms of the subjective culture of their own country. Attributional training is intended to remedy these misattributions. Differences between two cultures in the use of personal space, gift giving, and helping norms provide examples of topics that might be the focus of items in a cultural sensitizer.

The typical sensitizer consists of a programmed learning workbook of 75 to 100 incidents in which members of one culture are likely to misunderstand members of another culture because the incident has different meanings in the two cultures. The learner is asked to read each incident and choose among several attributions explaining the outgroup member's behavior. Correct answers are followed by explanations regarding aspects of the host subjective culture that make the attribution correct. Incorrect answers are followed by explanations as to why the attribution is incorrect, and then the learner is asked to select another answer. The learner continues to make attributions until the correct one has been selected.

Cultural sensitizers can be of three types. Most are culture specific, designed to present information regarding a specific culture (e.g., to teach Americans about Vietnamese culture). Cultural sensitizers can also be culture general. Such sensitizers include information about a variety of different cultures and are intended to show individuals how their perceptions, attitudes, and behaviors are influenced by their own cultures. One culture-general sensitizer uses 18 themes of cultural misunderstanding found across a variety of cultures (Brislin, Cushner, Cherrie, & Yong, 1986). A culture-general sensitizer designed to improve intergroup relations would contain items about a variety of cultural groups from within a multicultural society. Finally, cultural sensitizers can be of a culture theory type, based on a theoretical model of the differences between cultures. For example, one culture theory sensitizer is based on explaining the differences in behaviors between individuals in individualistic and collectivist cultures (Bhawuk, 1998). Since many of the cultural groups in the United States are more collectivist than the individualistic, Anglo American majority (Grossman, 1995; Haynes & Gebreyesus, 1992; Kitano & Daniels, 1995; Malloy & Malloy, 1998), a culture theory sensitizer has a place in intergroup relations training as well.

Here is an example of a culture-specific cultural sensitizer item from the Thai American Cultural Sensitizer (Brislin & Pedersen, 1976). Items such as this are commonly used in industry to train individuals for assignments in Thailand. The first page would contain the following situation, question, and response options:

One day a Thai administrator of middle academic rank kept two of his assistants waiting about an hour for an appointment. The assistants, although very angry, did not show it while they waited. When the administrator walked in at last, he acted as if he were not late. He made no apology or explanation. After he was settled in his office, he called his assistants in and they all began working on the business for which the administrator had set the meeting.

If you had [observed the incident] . . . reported in this passage, which one of the following would you say describes the chief significance of the behavior of the people involved?

1. The Thai assistants were extremely skillful at concealing their true feelings.
2. The Thai administrator obviously was unaware of the fact that he was an hour late for the appointment.

3. In Thailand, subordinates are required to be polite to their superiors, no matter what happens, nor what their rank may be.

4. Clearly, since no one commented on it, the behavior indicated nothing of any unusual significance to any of the Thais.

The next four pages would contain the answer options, as follows:

You selected 1: The Thai assistants were extremely skillful at concealing their true feelings.

This is not entirely correct. It is quite characteristic of Thais to try to appear reserved under any circumstances. If the assistants were extremely skillful at concealing their true feelings, would you know that you weren't seeing their true feelings? . . .

You selected 2: The Thai administrator obviously was unaware of the fact that he was an hour late for the appointment.

A very poor choice. While the administrator acted as if he were unaware of his tardiness after observing the hour's wait, don't you suspect that perhaps he was acting? . . .

You selected 3: In Thailand, subordinates are required to be polite to their superiors, no matter what happens, nor what their rank may be.

Very good. You are utilizing the information in the episodes to the fullest extent. To some extent their "deference to the boss" may be observed almost anywhere in the world, but you are far more likely to find it carried to a higher degree in Thailand than in the United States. There were certain clues to help you select 3: the assistants' concealed feelings, the administrator's failure to apologize, the fact that no one mentioned the tardiness, and the subsequent keeping of the appointment which the administrator had set. . . .

You selected 4: Clearly, since no one commented on it, the behavior indicated nothing of any unusual significance to any of the Thais.

This is completely wrong. While the behavior reported in the passage does not seem so significant for the Thais in this relationship as it might be to Americans, why was nothing said about the tardiness? And why were the assistants "very angry" although they "did not show it"? . . . (Brislin & Pedersen, 1976, pp. 90-93)

A number of studies indicate that culture-specific sensitizers lead to improved understanding of other cultures (e.g., Landis, Brislin, & Hulgus, 1985; Landis, Day, McGrew, Thomas, & Miller, 1976; O'Brien & Plooij, 1977; Weldon, Carston, Rissman, Slobodin, & Triandis, 1975). O'Brien & Plooij (1977) found programmed learning to have more powerful effects than solely didactic training or no training. Studies of the culture-general sensitizer (e.g., Cushner, 1989) and the culture theory sensitizer based on the concepts of individualism and collectivism (Bhawuk, 1998) have also documented their effectiveness. In one study, the culture theory sensitizer based on individualism and collectivism was found to be more effective than both a culture-general sensitizer and a culture-specific sensitizer designed to teach people the subjective culture of Japan, as measured by behavioral intentions and cross-cultural sensitivity (Bhawuk, 1998). However, attributional techniques such as the cultural sensitizer have been criticized for their lack of experiential learning and their emphasis on the most dramatic misunderstandings that are likely to occur (Furnham & Bochner, 1986).

Critical Incidents

Subjective and objective culture can also be taught through the use of critical incidents. In a typical critical incident, a misunderstanding takes place between members of two different groups. In others, a person from one group acts inappropriately in interaction with a person from another group or people have differing ideas about what is appropriate. The trainees read the incident, discuss what the misunderstanding or differing value is, and come to a consensus about what an appropriate response would have been.

Here is an example of a critical incident involving potentially different value judgments that is generally applicable to any minority group in many cultures (H. Holmes & Guild, 1971):

> I am president of the local school association, in a district whose residents are mostly poor and members (like me) of a minority group. Many of these people want our school to have teachers from the same minority group, because they are afraid our culture will be overcome by the ways of the majority. The city education officials who administer our district insist that it is they who must select teachers for us, for

fear that the quality of education will fall. I have decided to accept this view, because good education is the hope of our people.

After reading this incident, trainees would individually make a judgment about whether they agree or disagree with the decision and give a brief justification for their assessment. They would then meet in small groups with other trainees and compare their judgments. The trainer would emphasize that there is no right answer. However, the trainees would be asked to discuss the issue until they arrived at a group consensus. They would also be asked to find a mutually agreed-on reason for their group decision and to give an acceptable substitute action to rectify the problem, if appropriate. In the discussion, issues of group identity, group autonomy, bureaucracy, and universal standards would probably arise.

When used in the programmed-learning format, critical incidents have been shown to be effective in teaching cultural knowledge (e.g., Landis et al., 1976; Landis et al., 1985; O'Brien & Plooij, 1977; Weldon et al., 1975). Critical incidents are also used in other formats, and experienced trainers rely on them heavily. For example, they can be used as the basis of scripted, role-playing exercises (Brislin & Yoshida, 1994b).

Experiential Techniques

Experiential techniques are among the most powerful of intercultural training tools (Goldstein & Smith, 1999; Gudykunst, Hammer, & Wiseman, 1977; Landis et al., 1985). These techniques can be either culture specific or culture general and can last from a few hours to a week or more. In these techniques, individuals are invited to confront a world different from their own and attempt to act appropriately and perform assigned tasks. Experiential techniques include simulation games, role-playing, and living in a simulated version of the culture to be adopted or in-country training programs (programs conducted while participants are living in a country not their own). All these experiential techniques apply as well to learning about racial, ethnic, and religious groups within a multicultural society as they do to learning about other cultures.

Simulation Games

The goal of simulation games is to give trainees experience with a simulated culture in which the norms, values, and behaviors of their own culture are misleading and inappropriate for successful functioning. Simulation games provide a safe situation in which to learn about how one reacts to new norms, as well as to practice what one has learned and become somewhat comfortable with these new behaviors (Fowler, 1994). It is also important for individuals living in a multicultural society to understand that their own values, norms, and behaviors are not appropriate in all settings within their society.

Barnga provides an example of a simulation game that provides experience with norms different from one's own (Thiagarajan & Steinwachs, 1990). Barnga is a card game that is played nonverbally. Players have a set time to learn the written rules, and then the rules are taken away, and no talking or writing of any kind is allowed. High- and low-scoring players change tables after every few hands of cards. The situation creates differing norms by providing each table of players with slightly a different set of rules for playing the game (e.g., ace is high, ace is low; spades are trumps, there is no trump suit). The situation is analogous to using one's own cultural rules in a foreign culture with different rules. Some players figure out the source of the problems and some do not, but all must negotiate the differing sets of rules in order to continue playing the game.

Many trainers believe simulation games are among the most effective intercultural training techniques (Fowler, 1994), but little formal research has documented their effectiveness. *BAFA BAFA*, a cultural simulation game in which trainees are divided into two hypothetical cultures and must interact with members of the other culture, is the most researched simulation game (see Bruschke, Gartner, & Seiter, 1993, for a review of this literature). Most data on the topic are impressionistic and suggest positive benefits of participation (Jacobs & Baum, 1987; Nieswand, 1986). Some empirical studies have also shown favorable results but are themselves limited in scope (Dunn & Wozniak, 1976; Thomas, Moore, & Sams, 1980). The most comprehensive studies have obtained a range of results varying from positive (Pruegger & Rogers, 1994), through no differences compared to groups without this training (M. W. Jackson, 1979), to mixed positive and negative results (Bredemeir, Bernstein, & Oxman, 1982; Bruschke et al., 1993). In one study of college students in communication courses, students who had studied culture for one half-semester and had participated in *BAFA BAFA* were motivated to do better in class but were more ethnocentric than students who had studied the culture only didactically and others who had not yet begun culture studies (Bruschke et al., 1993). Clearly, more research is needed to determine whether the optimistic expectations concerning the effects of simulation games are warranted.

Role-playing

Role-playing common situations that are likely to be encountered in a foreign culture is a common way of giving trainees experience with new norms, values, and behaviors about which they have only read. Role-playing is also used to reinforce new cultural learning regarding appropriate responses in a particular situation (Weeks, Pedersen, & Brislin, 1982).

Often, 2 to 6 trainees engage in role-playing while others make observations regarding the cultural differences represented and the ensuing problems in the interaction. The actors are usually given a general statement regarding the situation and the point of view of the character to be portrayed, and they are asked to improvise an interaction. The role-play may also be scripted. The role behaviors are intended to be logical and include conflicting ends or incompatible means in regards to achieving a common goal. The role-play is then followed by the observers' comments and a discussion of the ways in which such situations can be avoided or worked out.

Here is an example of a scripted role-play that could be used to train secondary school and college teachers who work with Arab immigrants (Storti, 1994, p. 15):

Ms. Anderson: Hassan was looking at your paper.
Abdullah: He was?
Ms. Anderson: Yes. He copied some of your answers.
Abdullah: Perhaps he didn't know the answers.
Ms. Anderson: I'm sure he didn't.
Abdullah: Then it's lucky he was sitting next to me.

The discussion among the teachers would probably focus on the differing views of copying answers on an exam in the United States and many Arab school settings. Whereas the American teacher perceived an act of cheating, the Arab student perceived a situation in which he could help a friend the way any friend would. The trainees might be encouraged to discuss the fact that cooperation and avoiding shame are key values in more traditional Arab cultures, and that self-reliance is not a key Arab value in these cultures.

An unscripted, role-play situation could be created from the non-verbal communication of Native American and Anglo American people in the United States. In some Native American cultures, people show respect for others by averting their eyes when they speak to them (Greenbaum & Greenbaum, 1983). Among Anglo American people, not looking others in the eye—particularly superiors—is viewed as insolent. Trainees could be given a situation, for example a Native American student speaking with an Anglo American teacher, and be told to role-play the following: As the Anglo American teacher becomes more and more upset that the student will not look at her, the Native American student continues to look away but obviously becomes increasingly uncomfortable. The discussion here would almost certainly focus on cultural differences in nonverbal behaviors but might also include ways people are unknowingly influenced by the norms of their own cultural group and their cultural ethnocentrism in assuming that all people share their own norms.

Role-playing has been shown to be an effective technique both alone (Goldman, 1992) and in combination with other experiential techniques (Gudykunst et al., 1977; J. K. Harrison, 1992; Landis et al., 1985). For instance, Goldman (1992) used two role-plays to teach Japanese employees bound for graduate school in the United States how to interact with Americans. The transcripts show that the Japanese managers became both less ethnocentric and more willing to express personal opinions during the course of this role-playing.

Cultural Simulations and In-Country Training Programs

Cultural simulations are elaborate one-day to several-week experiences in a setting designed to replicate the host culture as closely as possible. Simulations promote learning in the affective and behavioral realms and are relatively high-risk types of training, because they involve trainees in unfamiliar and emotionally involving tasks (Paige & Martin, 1996). For example, Trifonovitch (1977) trained American educators and their families bound for Micronesia during a 2- to 3-week period in which trainees lived in remote conditions very much like those in Micronesia. Trainees interacted with the Micronesian staff, who behaved in a culturally Micronesian manner and who, for several days, did not reveal their knowledge of the English language. One day of the training was spent living in true Micronesian fashion, without electricity and running water, with most of the trainees' day necessarily consisting of hauling water, gathering and fishing for food, and then preparing it over an open fire. This day in particular helped to dispel the trainees' views of Micronesians as lazy.

Because cultural simulations are costly and, inevitably, not as culturally rich and authentic as actual cultural experience, agencies such as the Peace Corps have replaced cultural simulation training with in-country training programs (Brislin & Pedersen, 1976). A form of intergroup relations training that parallels in-country training is spending time in a subculture of a multicultural society (e.g., working on an American Indian reservation or in an Appalachian mountain community) or in an immigrant community within a large city.

Other Experiential Techniques

A number of other experiential techniques are commonly used, including cultural observations; deriving cultural lessons from the proverbs of a racial, ethnic, or religious group; cultural treasure hunts in which individuals are given a list of items to be found in the racial, ethnic, or religious group (e.g., items related to religion, food, decoration) and are asked to learn about how the item is used. Trainees can also rewrite statements from their own culture or ingroup to be appropriate in the racial, ethnic, or religious group being studied (e.g., making an individualistic bold request or demand appropriate for a collectivist context) and can interact, guided by facilitators, with individuals from different cultures or racial, ethnic, or religious groups.

Summary of Research Findings on Intercultural Training Techniques

Reviews of the literature have found that intercultural training programs are generally successful in improving relationship skills and accuracy of intergroup perceptions. One review of the effectiveness of intercultural training indicates that of the studies employing untrained comparison groups, all of the 7 studies using intercultural training to improve adjustment to a new culture reported success (Black & Mendenhall, 1990). In addition, all 14 attempting to produce more accurate perceptions of the other culture succeeded, and all 10 using intercultural training to improve relationship skills relevant to intercultural relations reported success. The effective techniques included simulation games, role-playing, exercises that presented information about the other culture, case studies, and interactions with individuals from the other culture (Bhawuk, 1990; Brislin, Landis, & Brandt, 1983; Cushner & Landis, 1996; Gudykunst & Hammer, 1983). Studies of the effects of intercultural training techniques applied only to the intergroup relations sphere have shown similarly positive results (e.g., Landis et al., 1985; McGregor, 1993; Wade & Bernstein, 1991; Weldon et al., 1975).

Comparisons among the specific techniques have sometimes been made. Generally, experiential training (Goldman, 1992; Gudykunst et al., 1977; Landis et al., 1985) and programmed learning (O'Brien & Plooij, 1977) have been shown to be more effective than strictly didactic training. Other studies have shown theory-based techniques to be more effective than non-theory-based techniques (Bhawuk, 1998). However, some comparisons of techniques have shown few differences among them (Earley, 1987; Gannon & Poon, 1997; Pruegger & Rogers, 1994). More research needs to be conducted on these issues before definite conclusions can be drawn regarding the relative effectiveness of these techniques.

Some researchers are critical of the conclusion that intercultural training is generally effective (Kealey & Protheroe, 1996). These criticisms are based on the fact that the effects of practical information are typically assumed to be positive but remain unmeasured, and the influence of area-studies training involving the history, culture, economy, and politics of the country on cross-cultural adaptation is typically not tested. Also, the data on the effects of training in cultural-awareness and intercultural-effectiveness skills are usually not based on behavioral measures but on self-reports. Reviews of multiple studies of intercultural effectiveness are marred because they do not take into consideration the low quality of the effectiveness measures or the methodological problems with the studies (Kealey & Protheroe, 1996). The reported success rates for short-term training are particularly suspect, because changing attitudes and increasing awareness appears to be a long-term process (Gudykunst et al., 1996). These constitute very serious criticisms, particularly because the research data suggest that some of the most popular techniques may be less effective than the users believe them to be. Obviously, considerably more research needs to be conducted on these techniques, and this research should include control groups, attitudinal and behavioral measures, and information on the reliability and validity of measures.

Psychological Processes Underlying Intercultural Training

The psychological processes that underlie intercultural training range across the active-passive and affective-cognitive dimensions (see Figure 2.3). These processes include reducing cultural ignorance, reducing anxiety, creating empathy, increasing perceived similarities, decreasing perceived symbolic and realistic threats, correcting misattributions, reducing value-behavior discrepancies, increasing self-regulation, and modeling and reinforcing positive behaviors.

Ignorance of people's culture is one cause of prejudice and discrimination, and didactic intercultural programs are designed to reduce ignorance by providing cultural information (W. G. Stephan & Stephan, 1984). Unique among intergroup relations training programs, the information is focused largely on intergroup differences. Because these differences are presented in a nonevaluative way, the trainees should avoid negative reactions to the dissimilarities about which they learn.

We have seen that some theorists believe intercultural training should be based on culture theory, which offers explanations for cultural differences that discuss important underlying dimensions of cultural variability. These theoretical explanations can be included in didactic training, and their use should make cultural differences seem more intelligible and thus more acceptable.

Other theorists recommend basing intercultural training programs on anxiety reduction. Information about the dissimilarities among groups should decrease anxiety about appropriate ways of interacting with people from a different culture (W. G. Stephan & Stephan, 1984; W. G. Stephan, Stephan, & Gudykunst, 1999). Programmed learning, role-playing, experiential exercises, and face-to-face interaction also have the ability to provide information and experience that will lead to reduced anxiety.

Empathy can be evoked by learning about ethnocentrism, stereotyping, and prejudice, as well as by studying the history, religion, economics, politics, and values of other cultures and their people; and empathy is incompatible with prejudice (A. Smith, 1990). The experiential, intercultural training techniques, which are very involving and emotional, provide excellent opportunities for the creation of empathy. In these techniques, people learn how bound by their own culture they are, practice interacting with dissimilar others, and build their interaction skills. These engrossing, affective experiences create an ideal setting for evoking empathy for others (McGregor, 1993; A. Smith, 1990).

Similarities between cultures are also typically presented in didactic techniques. Because similarity is associated with liking, this latter type of information should increase liking for the group being studied (Byrne, 1971). Experiential exercises, such as role-playing and face-to-face contact that allows for overriding uniformity in hopes and desires to emerge, should also increase perceptions of similarity.

Some prejudiced attitudes originate in perceived symbolic threats; prejudice stems from people's beliefs that dissimilar others have different values and attitudes from their own (McConahay, 1986; Sears, 1988; W. G. Stephan & Stephan, 2000; W. G. Stephan, Stephan, &

Gudykunst, 1999). Information about overriding human values common to all groups of people should decrease symbolic racism.

The origin of some other prejudiced attitudes is realistic; these attitudes are developed through the perception that dissimilar others are competing for scarce resources with one's own group (Bobo, 1988; W. G. Stephan & Stephan, 2000; W. G. Stephan et al., 1999). Information regarding the exaggerated nature of people's beliefs regarding the scarcity of resources, as well as the creation of superordinate identities, should reduce the level of perceived realistic threats.

The attributional training techniques, such as the cultural sensitizers, are directed at correcting negative misattributions about other people's behaviors. Typically, the positive behavior of members of groups other than one's own is attributed to the situation, and the negative behavior of outgroup members is attributed to the individuals' characteristics and traits. Attributional training that focuses on culturally appropriate explanations for behaviors has the potential to eliminate the stereotyping and negative attitudes associated with incorrect negative attributions.

Experiential exercises—in which trainees learn and practice positive, appropriate behaviors and also determine which of their behaviors are unintentionally negative or inappropriate—lead to greater value-behavior consistency over time. These exercises increase self-regulation by allowing trainees to experience inappropriate affect, come to understand the inaccuracies of their affect, and consciously replace it with more appropriate affect.

Experiential exercises also allow trainers to model positive, appropriate behaviors for trainees, and reinforce positive, appropriate trainee behaviors. As a result, more and more trainees begin to model appropriate behaviors for one another and self-reinforce when they do well.

Problems and Recommendations

A primary goal of many intercultural training programs is to present group differences in a way that fosters understanding of, and respect for, cultural differences. One problem with difference training is that it runs the risk of creating overgeneralized stereotypes. All such training needs to clearly direct attention to within-group differences, both individual (some individuals in collectivist cultures pursue self-actualization) and group (some groups within a culture are more traditional than others). This caution holds regardless of the praiseworthiness of the characteristic.

Intergroup prejudice is clearly associated with intercultural ineffectiveness and maladjustment. A serious problem associated with intercultural and intergroup training is the reluctance of participants and trainers to address intergroup prejudices. However, these prejudices must be examined before long-term attitudinal and behavioral change can take place (Gudykunst et al., 1996). A number of researchers have suggested that a strong antiracism component is a necessary part of any intercultural training program (Barlow & Barlow, 1993; Gudykunst et al., 1996). Antiracism training is at least as important in intergroup contexts within a multicultural society.

Most intercultural training experts would agree on some of the components of successful programs. In general, the use of multiple techniques is more effective than the use of a single technique (Gudykunst et al., 1977; J. K. Harrison, 1992). Typically, trainers begin with low-risk cognitive techniques and then move to higher-risk affective and behavioral techniques (Bennett, 1986; Paige & Martin, 1996).

Many intercultural experts suggest that short-term training can have only limited success in changing cultural awareness and knowledge, altering attitudes about the individuals and their culture, and teaching new skills and behaviors (Gudykunst et al., 1996). Thus, long-term training is almost always more effective than short-term training. However, the question "Which technique is best?" is likely to have no general answer: The best technique is related to the goals of the intercultural or intergroup training as well as to the resources, time, and motivation of the trainees (B. F. Blake, Heslin, & Curtis, 1996). Intercultural and intergroup training should therefore be tailored to the exact needs of the trainees. For this reason, experts recommend that trainers conduct a needs assessment to fully understand whom they will be training and why, and the context of the intercultural or intergroup interactions (Brislin & Yoshida, 1994a).

Summary

Programs designed to help people learn about and adapt to other cultures constitute a valuable technique for improving intercultural relations that can also be used to improve intergroup relations within a multicultural society. Most training programs combine information regarding both cultural differences and similarities and include both experiential and didactic components. Intercultural training can be either culture specific or cultural general, although most culture-specific training also includes culture-general information. Many intercultural experts argue that intercultural training should be based on theory. Culture theories, such as those of individualism and collectivism and of intergroup anxiety, are among the theories used to explain problems of intercultural contact and to design intercultural training programs.

Numerous widely used intercultural training techniques exist, including lectures and discussions, language training, cultural sensitizers, critical incidents, and such experiential techniques as simulation games, role-playing, and cultural simulations. Reviews of the literature have found that intercultural training programs are generally successful in improving relationship skills and accuracy of intergroup perceptions. Lectures and discussions are effective means of conveying cultural information. A number of studies indicate that the culture-specific cultural sensitizers lead to improved understanding of another culture. Experiential techniques appear to be among the most powerful of intercultural training tools. However, much more research documenting the effectiveness of these techniques needs to be conducted.

Intercultural training programs may be effective because they reduce ignorance, decrease intergroup anxiety, create empathy, increase perceived similarity, decrease both symbolic prejudice and prejudice based on perceived realistic conflict, correct misattributions, reduce value-behavior discrepancies, increase self-regulation, and provide a setting in which positive behaviors can be modeled and reinforced.

Intercultural training programs are more effective if they avoid overgeneralized stereotypes, include a strong antiracism component, use multiple techniques, and employ long-term training.

COOPERATIVE LEARNING GROUPS

7

COOPERATIVE LEARNING IS widely used in educational settings as a means to improve intergroup relations and increase academic achievement. As early as 1981, over 25,000 U.S. teachers used some form of structured cooperative learning (Kohn, 1986). By the early 1990s, fully 79% of elementary school teachers and 62% of middle school teachers reported making some sustained use of cooperative learning (Puma, Jones, Rock, & Fernandez, 1993). In this introductory section, we first briefly describe cooperative learning and its target populations. Then, we discuss the goals and characteristics of cooperative learning techniques and focus on their origins.

Cooperative learning is typically used in educational settings, although it has also been used in professional training conducted in the workplace (Cavalier, Klein, & Cavalier, 1995). Cooperative learning usually consists of placing students in small learning groups in which the task and reward structure requires face-to-face interaction in a situation in which students are interdependent. That is, the students can only reach their individual goals through the success of the group. Typically, students from two or more ethnic groups, both sexes, and of varying academic abilities are brought together in groups of 4 to 6 to learn academic materials that have been tailored for these groups. Cooperation guides the within-group interactions. However, in some cooperative learning techniques, the small, cooperative groups compete with one another, whereas in other cooperative learning techniques, they do not. Cooperative techniques typically include pretraining of students—practice in cooperative techniques and team building—as well as training of teachers in their new roles as group facilitators.

Cooperative learning techniques have been used to integrate many different types of individuals into cohesive groups. These have most frequently included individuals of differing race and ethnicity, social class, nationality, and achievement, as well as special (emotionally or academically handicapped) and regular education students. Cooperative learning techniques have been employed most often in elementary and secondary school classes, in which they have been used to teach every type of subject matter. They have also been used in some college classes, such as math (Dubinsky, 1997; Quinn, 1997), accounting (A. Berry, 1997; Cottell & Millis, 1997), chemistry labs (M. E. Smith, Hinckley, & Volk, 1997), multiprofessional, role and teamwork courses for fifth-year students in medical-related majors (Parsell, Spalding, & Bligh, 1998), and introduction to computers (McInerney, McInerney, & Marsh, 1997), and have been used to supplement distance education courses (Boling & Robinson, 1999). Studies have shown positive results of cooperative learning techniques in North America, Europe, and Israel, as well as Australia (McInerney et al., 1997; I. Walker & Crogan, 1998), Japan (Araragi, 1983), and Africa (Okebukola, 1985; 1986).

In Chapter 1, we categorized cooperative learning programs as being an interactive-indirect technique (see Figure 1.1). It is an interactive technique because it consists of face-to-face interaction with outgroup members in an active-learning setting. It is an indirect technique because the focus of attention is on cooperative learning, not intergroup relations. Positive outcomes of intergroup relations are an intended but unmentioned result of this type of learning.

Later in this chapter, we review the research findings of the outcomes of cooperative learning in more detail. Here, we note that one reason for the popularity of cooperative learning techniques is that they lead to significant improvements in intergroup relations in classrooms diverse in race and ethnicity, nationality, and performance levels. In addition, cooperative learning techniques increase student achievement, especially the achievement of minority students and low-achieving students.

Cooperative learning stems from two types of social-psychological research. First, early research on cooperation demonstrated that small, cooperative learning groups performed better than competitive learning groups on measures of motivation, effective communication, friendliness, and productivity (Deutsch, 1949). Even in a study of sustained intergroup conflict, the introduction of superordinate goals—goals desired by all but only achievable through intergroup cooperation—led to a reduction of hostility and the creation of intergroup friendships (Sherif, Harvey, White, Hood, & Sherif, 1961). In these cooperative settings, the positive *goal interdependence* of groups— their joint dependence on one another to achieve their desired goals— was identified as the key causal factor in accomplishing positive interpersonal and achievement outcomes (Deutsch, 1962). Second, research conducted between the 1950s and today on the contact hypothesis has shown that equal status and cooperative, intimate contact among different types of people, which is positively sanctioned by those in authority, leads to improvements in intergroup relations (F. H. Allport et al., 1953; Pettigrew & Tropp, 2000; W. G. Stephan, 1987; W. G. Stephan & Stephan, 1996).

In the remainder of this chapter, we describe several popular cooperative learning programs, summarize the research on the outcomes of cooperative learning, and identify the psychological processes underlying cooperative learning. These include creating goal interdependence and positive contact; providing conditions in which expectations for performance are not based on status characteristics; emphasizing multiple identities and creating conditions for self-disclosure; creating subordinate groups; and reducing anxiety. We end with problems and recommendations for successful, cooperative learning programs.

Major Cooperative Learning Programs

We examine five popular and well-researched programs of cooperative learning: the Slavin techniques, the Johnsons' Learning Together technique, the Jigsaw Classrooms, Group Investigation, and Complex

TABLE 7.1   Dimensions of Cooperative Learning Techniques

Technique	Group Rewards	Team Competition	Task Specialization	Presentation of Material	Curriculum Provided	Group Activities
STAD	Yes	Sometimes	No	Teacher	No	Prepare for quizzes
TGT	Yes	Yes	No	Teacher	No	Prepare for quizzes
Learning together	Yes	No	Yes	Teacher	No	Practice, team building, debate
Jigsaw	No	No	Yes	Students	No	Students teach
Jigsaw II	Yes	No	Yes	Students	No	Students teach
Group investigation	No	No	Yes	Students	No	Group projects
Complex instruction	No	No	Yes	Within activities	Yes	Complete activities

Instruction. These techniques differ in the student reward structure (group vs. individual) based on whether student groups compete, whether task specialization exists within the groups, who does the actual teaching, whether curriculum materials are provided, and the content of the group activities (see Table 7.1). We briefly summarize the research findings on the individual techniques. Later in the chapter, we describe the findings for cooperative learning techniques as a whole.

The Slavin Techniques

Robert Slavin has introduced and researched a number of cooperative learning techniques at Johns Hopkins University. The best known of these is Student Teams-Achievement Divisions (STAD). In STAD, the teacher presents a lesson. Subsequently, students study worksheets in 4-member groups diverse with regard to ability, sex, and race or ethnicity (Slavin, 1978, 1990). The goal of the teams is to ensure that each team member has mastered the material. The team members discuss discrepancies in answers to questions on the worksheets, help one another with misunderstandings, devise problem-solving approaches, and quiz one another on the material they are studying. Then, students take individual tests, and the group receives a team score based on the degree to which the students improved over their own past records. Teams performing above a certain level earn certificates or other rewards. Thus, in order to earn team rewards, students must help one another learn the material. Groups may or may not compete with one another.

A second technique, Teams-Games-Tournament (TGT), is the same program as STAD but uses a grading system of academic-game tournaments (DeVries & Edwards, 1974; Slavin, 1990). Students from each team compete with students from other teams at the same level of past performance to try to contribute to their team scores. A third technique, Team-Assisted Individualization (TAI), consists of cooperative groups and individual instruction in elementary math (Slavin, 1984; Slavin, Leavey, & Madden, 1984). Another technique, Cooperative Integrated Reading and Composition (CIRC), includes cooperative groups and individual instruction in oral reading, reading comprehension, and integrated writing and language arts (Stevens, Madden, Slavin, & Farnish, 1987; Stevens & Slavin, 1995). The latter two techniques use specific instructional materials prepared by the creators of the techniques. In a typical STAD classroom, fifth graders might study spelling in teams of 4 (Slavin, 1995a). The day before, the teacher might have taught a lesson to the whole class on forming possessives. The students would then work in groups to practice this skill. In each group, students would work in pairs to complete a worksheet on forming possessives. They would have 30 minutes to practice before an individual quiz would be given. The pairs would confer about the answers and, when they had questions, ask the other pair in their team. After they had completed their worksheets, the pairs would check the worksheet answers and work on any items they did not answer correctly. Next, the students would move their desks apart and take a 10-minute exam, which they would complete individually. The exams would be scored by nonteammates and then returned to their owners. The teacher would recheck the exam scores, and at the end of the week, on the basis of multiple exams, name a "superteam" in spelling.

Most studies have shown that STAD, TGI, and TAI increase cross-racial friendships (DeVries, Edwards, & Slavin, 1978; Kagan, Zahn, Widaman, Schwarzwald, & Tyrell, 1985; S. Sharan et al., 1984; Slavin, 1977, 1979; Slavin & Oickle, 1981) and academic achievement (Okebukola, 1985, 1986; Sherman & Thomas, 1986; Slavin, 1977; Slavin et al., 1984) relative to students in traditional classes.

The Johnsons' Learning Together Technique

During the course of their careers in education, David and Roger Johnson (1975, 1994a) have developed and tested a cooperative learning technique called Circles of Learning, or Learning Together. Learning Together includes three types of cooperative learning procedures: formal cooperative learning, in which students work together for one class period for up to several weeks to complete specific assignments and master particular skills; informal cooperative learning, consisting of temporary ad hoc groups that work together for from a few minutes to as long as a class period to complete a goal; and cooperative base groups, consisting of long-term, diverse learning groups whose members provide social and academic support to one another. Learning Together groups consist of no more than six students. Instructional materials promote interdependence in a variety of ways (e.g., students must share materials and students might have access to only one part of the lesson). Complementary roles (e.g., recorder, reader, checker) are assigned to further ensure interdependence. Both group rewards and individual rewards may be given.

The Johnsons believe that for cooperative learning to be effective, it must include positive resource and reward interdependence, face-to-face positive interaction, individual accountability for one's own share of the work, and training in social skills and group processing. In their technique, teachers ensure that the group members assess their goal attainment and the effectiveness of their working relationships.

In an integrated use of the three types of cooperative learning employed in Learning Together, elementary school students might start their day in their *cooperative base groups* to welcome one another, complete a self-disclosure task, and check each member's homework (Johnson & Johnson, 1994a). The teacher might then give them a lesson on world interdependence, perhaps bringing out a series of objects (e.g., one might be a silk shirt with plastic buttons) and ask students to identify all the countries that contributed to each object's creation. *Informal cooperative learning* would be used when the teacher asks the students to turn to a person next to them and, in under 5 minutes, identify the seven continents and one product produced in each of them. *Formal cooperative learning* would be employed in the lesson through learning about global economic interdependence. The students would count off from one to three to form random triads. Each group would receive three objects. The teacher would assign the roles of an hypothesizer, who would make hypotheses about the number of products in each object and their origin; a reference guide, who would look up the hypothesized countries to determine their exports; and a recorder, who would keep track of the information. The roles would rotate after each object was discussed. All members of the group would have to agree with the answer before it could be recorded, and all members would have to be able to explain the answer. To achieve group points, each group would have to turn in a correctly completed report, and each group member would have to score 90% or better on an exam given the next day on world economic interdependence. If the report were correct, each group member would receive 15 points, and if all group members achieved 90% or more on the exam, each member would receive 5 bonus points.

In their recent work, the Johnsons have argued that the school needs to be turned into a cooperative community through the cooperative learning techniques we have discussed. In addition, they believe students also need to be trained in constructive conflict resolution and taught civic values. These three interventions together will produce positive intergroup relations (Johnson & Johnson, 2000). The Johnsons' techniques for training students in constructive conflict resolution is discussed in Chapter 8, Conflict Resolution Programs. They believe civic values are taught in the process of forming a cooperative community and learning constructive conflict resolution techniques.

Researchers have found positive intergroup relations outcomes from Learning Together (Cooper, Johnson, Johnson, & Wilderson, 1980; Johnson & Johnson, 1981), as well as increases in achievement, relative to traditional instruction (Humphreys, Johnson, & Johnson, 1982; Okebukola, 1986). However, many of the assessments of the technique involve short periods of time, and thus the results of these studies may not generalize well to classroom interventions of many months or years (Slavin, 1995a).

The Jigsaw Classroom

In the Jigsaw Classroom techniques, associated with Elliot Aronson and his colleagues (E. Aronson, Blaney, Stephan, Sikes, & Snapp, 1978; E. Aronson & Patnoe, 1997; E. Aronson & Thibodeau, 1992), students learn material in small groups selected at random or grouped by the teacher for diversity of race, sex, and achievement level. Each group has a student leader, selected by the teacher or rotated among group members, and a recorder. Two variants of the technique exist. In Jigsaw I, resource materials are divided into as many segments as there are students in the group. This division is initially made by the teacher but can later be done by students themselves. All students learn the assigned materials, practice them in "expert groups" consisting of students from other groups who have received the same assignment, and teach them to the other students in their group. Students are tested individually. In Jigsaw II, each student first reads the entire lesson; then students learn their individual pieces of the puzzle and teach them to the other students. Here, the assessment may be a combination of individual improvement over past scores and group scores, or it may be based on individual test scores and public recognition of team success.

In a sixth-grade social studies class using Jigsaw I, a topic might be the colonial period in the United States (E. Aronson & Patnoe, 1997). If the material is part of a larger learning unit, as in this example, each group might have one portion of the unit (e.g., religion in this period) to learn and then to pass on to other groups, or each group might study the same materials. At the beginning of the lesson, students first would get into their groups and spend 5 minutes reviewing the agenda for the period, focusing on what they had done thus far on the unit and what they must do that day, as well as on group processing issues (e.g., "Will we finish our unit on time? Is everyone listening?"). Next, the groups would summarize their progress on the unit for the other groups.

The group leaders would then divide up the subject matter among the group members (e.g., Puritanism, religious persecution) and pass out Jigsaw activity cards for each student's topic. These activity cards would contain information to be mastered (e.g., each student should be able to name two colonies in which the Puritan religion was found), resource materials available, and questions to be discussed by the group (e.g., "Do you think the colonists should have been forced to learn Puritanism at school and go to a Puritan church?"). After a period of time devoted to learning their piece of the puzzle, the students would then teach the other members of their group the information they had learned and would lead the discussion on their set of questions. After the end of the unit, students would be tested on material about the colonial period individually.

In this example, each group has different materials; every group studies a different aspect of the colonial period. If the groups had been studying the same materials (e.g., if each group were studying religion in the colonial period), students would have spent about one third of their time in expert groups in which students with the same assignment would have learned it and practiced teaching it to other students.

Most studies of Jigsaw classes have found greater increases in numbers of cross-ethnic friendships in Jigsaw than comparison classes, as well as increased liking for group mates and higher self-esteem (Blaney, Stephan, Rosenfield, Aronson, & Sikes, 1977; Ziegler, 1981). Several studies have found achievement gains of the Jigsaw technique over traditional classes (Okebukola, 1985; Matttingly & Van Sickle, 1991). Lucker, Rosenfield, Sikes, and Aronson (1977) have found increased academic performance among minority students in Jigsaw classrooms compared to minorities in traditional classes, and equal performance by White students.

Group Investigation

Group Investigation is a technique developed by researchers in Israel (S. Sharan & Hertz-Lazarowitz, 1980; Y. Sharan & Sharan, 1992). In Group Investigation, the emphasis is on student self-regulation of learning activities. A teacher first stimulates interest in a broad general problem. Group Investigation is then implemented in six stages: (a) the class selects subtopics and organizes into small groups based on individual students' interest in the subtopics; (b) groups plan their investigations cooperatively; (c) group members carry out their investigations and pool their findings to form conclusions; (d) groups plan their presentations; (e) groups make their presentations to the class; and (f) both teachers and students evaluate the group projects. Grades are based on individual performances on exams. The developers of Group Investigation consider its critical components to be the organization of learning as a process of inquiry, communication in small groups, interpretation of material at the interpersonal as well as individual level, and emotional involvement in the learning process (Y. Sharan & Sharan, 1992).

Group Investigation has been used in multiethnic classrooms in Israel composed of students of lower-class Middle Eastern background and middle-class Western backgrounds. Variants of this technique are also used in England, Australia, and the United States (Hertz-Lazarowitz & Zelniker, in press; Slavin, 1995a).

In a third-grade classroom, a Group Investigation project might concern what and how animals eat (Y. Sharan & Sharan, 1992). For this project, students might first visit a local zoo during feeding time. Students would be asked to determine what questions they wished to ask about feeding during the visit, and the teacher would summarize the students' individual questions into a few primary questions to be investigated (e.g., "What kinds of food do the animals of each species eat?"). Before the trip, students might be given a chart of the five classes of vertebrates. The children would pair off during the trip and fill in as many names and types of food as possible on the chart. Back in the classroom, the children would discuss the answers they obtained, and the teacher might add to the primary questions developed earlier (e.g., "How do animals get their food in the wild?").

Next, groups of 5 would form by numbering off. Each group would select a class of animals to study, and the group members would collect material at home to add to the reference materials in the classroom. Within the groups, each child would select one animal from the type of animals chosen by the group for individual study. Then, individually, the children would look up information on the animals they had selected and answer the primary questions for that animal. The following day, the group would put together the work of the individual members. They would create a summary of their findings and post it, along with their individual reports, for the other class members to read. Each group might then prepare a simulated television documentary about the animals they studied and design a quiz for the class about these animals. Next, the groups would present their documentary and administer their quiz to the class. Students would also be tested individually on the topic. Finally, the teacher would give each student a written evaluation of her or his individual work, and the class would discuss the experience of working in groups together.

S. Sharan and colleagues (1984) found much more positive interethnic attitudes between Jews of Middle Eastern and European backgrounds in Group Investigation classes than between similar students in traditional classes. S. Sharan and Shachar (1988) found great increases in achievement in Group Investigation classes studying geography and history, compared to traditional classes. Other researchers have also found significant academic gains (S. Sharan et al., 1984; Talmage, Pascarella, & Ford, 1984).

Complex Instruction

Elizabeth Cohen's work with cooperative groups has a theoretical focus that differs from most of the other cooperative learning researchers (Cohen, 1986, 1992, 1994; Cohen & Lotan, 1997). Her work is based on expectation states theory, which argues that characteristics such as sex and race or ethnicity reflect status, and that expectations for performance are based on these status characteristics (Berger, Rosenholtz, & Zelditch, 1980; Cohen, 1997). Furthermore, differential expectations are self-fulfilling and result in behavioral inequalities, such as lower rates of interaction and influence with peers for children with lower-status characteristics (e.g., ethnic minorities, low-achieving students). Her interest in cooperation is thus as a means to establish equity in diverse classrooms, and she believes cooperation alone is not sufficient to change expectations concerning competence.

In Cohen's technique, Complex Instruction, tasks are intellectually challenging even for the most advanced students. The focus is on the development of higher-order thinking skills. The teachers begin by giving a brief orientation to the overall topic to be covered. Their job is then to maximize student interaction in the small groups. The teacher delegates authority to the students to stay on task, keep their group mates on task, and produce individual and group products. There are 6 to 8 learning stations in each classroom, each with a different open-ended task. The groups rotate through every learning station. At each one, each student assumes a specific procedural role. For example, a materials manager gathers supplies, a resource manager gathers academic resources, and a facilitator makes certain that students understand the task, are involved in each activity and communicate with the teacher if necessary. In addition, a student-reporter presents the group's work to the class. The roles rotate so that each student has experience with every role. Students interact at each learning station as they engage in their roles and cooperatively work toward a group product, and at each station, they practice reading, writing, and calculating. Curricular materials are provided at each station. Grades are based on individual performances on exams covering the topic studied.

The study of social stratification and social barriers in the context of the Tokugawa Period in Japan provides an example of a Complex Instruction task for middle-school students in an integrated social studies and language arts class (Lotan, 1997). Students work at 1 of 7 learning stations where they investigate topics such as the housing patterns of Tokugawa, Japan, and their implications for social standing, and the legal codes of the Tokugawa Period and their implications for social stratification. In the course of passing through these stations, students build a three-dimensional map of a castle town, prepare a skit on law enforcement, analyze a graph showing the frequency of peasant uprisings, and play a game illustrating the rise of the merchant class, among other activities. At the end of each period, the reporter presents a summary to the class of the group's task and discussion, and then all the group members participate in the presentation of their work. The students complete individual reports as homework and are individually tested over major concepts during the following week.

Cohen (1984) argues that in other cooperative learning techniques, systematic inequities in participation among students lead to inequities in influence among peers and, most important, inequities in benefits to students of cooperative learning. She has shown that these status inequities are directly associated with both interaction patterns and learning gains, with lower-status students interacting less with others than higher-status students and making lower academic gains than higher-status students. Thus, in order to maximize the productivity of cooperative groups, she believes status relations within the groups must be modified. If the task involves simple learning, scripting interactions and requiring turn taking can treat status differentials. If, however, the task is an *ill-structured problem,* one with no single correct answer or clear set of procedures and which cannot be completed individually, differing expectations regarding competence based on status must be addressed.

Cohen and her colleagues have had success with two status interventions to counteract these problems (this work was reviewed by Cohen and Lotan, 1997). She calls the first the Multiple-Ability Treatment. In one version of this treatment, teachers give lower-status students a new status inconsistent with their general status, by informing all the students that the lower-status students will be good at the new task to be completed, and the higher-status students will not be as good at the task. In a second version of this treatment, teachers tell students that the new task requires many abilities, no one possesses high abilities in all the areas, and everyone possesses high ability in at least one of them.

The second status intervention is Assigning Competence to Low-Status Students. In this treatment, lower-status students can be pre-trained in necessary skills, or the teacher can merely look for instances in which lower-status students perform well and then give specific, favorable, and public evaluations of these students. If the task involves many different types of skills, at some point, all lower-status students should be able to exhibit a particular talent.

In one study, Cohen (1997) reports evaluations of year-long status interventions associated with Complex Instruction in elementary schools and middle schools. In 11 of 13 elementary school classrooms, the interventions were highly successful: No longer was there a significant association between student status and rate of task-related talk. Furthermore, the interventions boosted the participation rate of low-status students without lowering the participation of high-status students. However, the results were not as positive in the middle schools. In a sample of 58 middle school students, the teachers' rate of status treatments (e.g., pretraining, public praise of low-status students performing well) was unrelated to task-related talk for low-status students. Thus, the status interventions had no effect in the middle school setting. A number of explanations are possible. Without a pre-post design to measure the level of status problems prior to the treatment, it is unclear whether the treatment was ineffective, the teachers did not use the status interventions with the students the researchers defined as low in status, the classes were improving but only from severe to moderate status problems, or the classes had few status problems initially.

Cohen and her colleagues (Cohen et al., 1997) have summarized research conducted on Complex Instruction from 1982-1994 in elementary and middle schools using both standardized tests and tests designed to measure specific curricular content. The students were primarily working-class, White, Latino, and Southeast Asian students from the second through eighth grades. Students in Complex Instruction classes showed greater overall academic gains from pretest to posttest in comparison to students in regular classrooms. These gains included both factual knowledge and higher-order thinking skills. The elementary school children showed large gains in math computation and math concepts and application and significant gains in science concepts and vocabulary as well as ability to apply science information. The middle school students showed significant gains in knowledge of science, social studies, and math. In social studies, in which comparison classes existed, Complex Instruction students showed greater gains in higher-order thinking than did students in regular classes. In general, such gains take place only when teachers have adequate administrative support, students have appropriate curricular materials, and students spend enough time in the Complex Instruction classes to rotate through all the activities.

We turn now to an overall assessment of cooperative learning programs based on the research findings on the outcomes of a variety of cooperative learning techniques. We discuss both intergroup relations variables and measures of achievement. Then, we focus specifically on outcomes for racial and ethnic minorities.

Summary of Research Findings for Cooperative Learning Techniques

Intergroup Relations Measures

With respect to intergroup relations, the main measure of interest in studies of cooperative groups has been increased interracial friendships. In an analysis of 53 studies comparing cooperative and competitive conditions, liking and other measures of the quality of interpersonal relationships were more positive under cooperation than competition (Johnson & Johnson, 1989). In a review of their own studies, Johnson and Johnson (1992b, 2000) found not only that cooperation produced more cross-racial friendships in a class than competition or individualistic learning did but also that competition may reduce these friendships. In addition, they found increased cross-racial friendships even when the minority students had lower achievement levels. Moreover, they found that intellectual disagreements between minority and majority students can increase cross-racial friendships within cooperative groups and that these friendships extend to free time, school, and out-of-school situations.

Another review of studies of cooperative learning also found that cooperative learning generally had more positive effects on intergroup relations than traditional competitive or individual learning (Slavin, 1995a). Specifically, this review showed that all the major cooperative learning techniques lead to greater increases in interracial friendships than other types of classes. Slavin (1979) found that these increases in friendship choices were greatest for the creation of close friends, compared to more distant friends.

Other relevant intergroup relations measures have included empathy, liking for classmates and feeling liked by them, and liking for school. Bridgeman (1981) and Johnson, Johnson, Johnson, and Anderson (1976) found increased empathy, compared to regular classes. The data on liking classmates and feeling liked by them also generally support the superiority of cooperative over other types of instruction (Slavin, 1995a). The results on liking for school are mixed, possibly because students were responding to questions about school in general rather than to questions about particular learning techniques (Slavin, 1995a). When students were asked about liking for particular types of instruction, they rated cooperative learning higher than traditional classes (Humphreys et al., 1982; Johnson et al., 1976; Madden & Slavin, 1983).

Cooperative learning has also been employed to facilitate the mainstreaming of academically and emotionally handicapped students. In this context, the evidence indicates that cooperative learning has had generally positive effects in increasing friendship choices, reducing rejection, and increasing intergroup interactions during free time (Slavin & Stevens, 1991). In an analysis of over 60 studies including regular education and special education students, Johnson and Johnson (1989) also found greater interpersonal attraction in cooperative than in competitive or individualistic conditions. In addition, a review of studies of the use of cooperatively structured recreation groups involving groups of children with moderate to severe emotional or intellectual disabilities and nondisabled children showed that these techniques led to many more positive intergroup social interactions than either independent or competitive recreational play (Rynders et al., 1993).

Personality and Social Skills Measures

A number of studies have measured the effects of cooperative learning on self-esteem. In 11 of 15 studies reviewed by Slavin (1995a), increased self-esteem was found on at least one self-esteem measure relative to students in comparison classrooms. Slavin (1995a) also reported that several studies showed that cooperative groups increased internal locus of control. Increases in intrinsic motivation have also been found. Johnson and Johnson (1989) found that cooperation was associated with a number of other measures of psychological well-being, and competition was associated with measures of psychological distress.

Intergroup Relations Findings: A Summary

Overall, the findings from research on cooperative learning suggest that the consequences of cooperative learning include more positive feelings toward racial and ethnic outgroups; increased numbers of friends in general and friends from different racial and ethnic groups in particular; and interpersonal gains, such as enhanced liking and respect among students.

However, not all studies comparing cooperative learning to traditional classes or individualistic learning have shown positive interpersonal gains from cooperation. Slavin (1995a) found that some studies obtained mixed findings (DeVries et al., 1978; Slavin & Oickle, 1981) and others, no effects of cooperative learning (Lazarowitz, Baird, Hertz-Lazarowitz, & Jenkins, 1985; Sherman, 1988; Slavin, 1978). Overall, each of the cooperative learning techniques we have reviewed shows considerable success in improving intergroup relations, but each technique has been shown to be ineffective in some studies (Slavin, 1995a).

Many failures to show changes in liking have occurred in elementary school classrooms in which liking for all classmates and liking for school are extremely high in pretests, allowing for little posttest change (Slavin, 1995a). Other failures are likely to have been created by problems in implementing the technique. Like other intergroup training techniques, these programs are most prone to failure when they are forced on the unwilling. In particular, teachers need to be committed to the program. They must be willing to give up their sole authority in the classroom and able to tolerate some noise and disorder in the classroom as group members move around to prepare and practice materials.

Achievement Measures

Slavin (1995a) performed a meta-analysis of 99 studies that met stringent criteria for inclusion including length of cooperative treatment (4 weeks or longer) and equivalence of comparison classes. Overall, he found positive results: 64% of the studies showed greater gains for students in cooperative classes than students in other types of classes. He reported that the greatest effects occurred for his own techniques (STAT, TGT, TAI, and CIRC), and weaker effects occurred for the Learning Together and the Jigsaw techniques. However, most of the studies of Learning Together were omitted from this analysis because they lasted less than 4 weeks. In Slavin's analysis, the Jigsaw and Group Investigation techniques showed the most inconsistent results, and his own techniques employing within-group cooperation and between-group competition showed the most consistent results. By contrast, Johnson and Johnson's (1989) analysis showed their pure-cooperation technique to have stronger effects than other cooperative learning techniques, with the overwhelming majority of measures showing the superiority of all types of cooperative techniques over other methods of instruction. The difference in the conclusions reached on the basis of these two reviews appears to be due to the inclusion of different studies in the reviews along with differing inter-pretations of research findings, statistical standards and methods, and theoretical understandings of the data.

On a measure related to achievement, an analysis of 46 studies of the quality of problem solving in cooperative versus competitive groups found that the overall quality of problem solving was higher in the cooperative than the competitive groups (Qin, Johnson, & Johnson, 1995). Cooperative learning has also been shown to be generally supe-rior to other techniques when time spent on task, positive classroom behaviors, and the acceptance of norms supporting high achievement were measured (Slavin, 1995a).

Many of the studies of cooperative groups we have just reviewed were conducted in elementary schools. Two reviews of the effect of cooperative learning on secondary school students, one of 27 stud-ies and one of 75, also found higher achievement in cooperative groups than in competitive groups or individual instruction (Johnson, Johnson, & Smith, 1995; Newmann & Thompson, 1987).

The data thus strongly suggest that cooperative learning tech-niques are effective in increasing academic achievement levels. How-ever, the reviews of the effectiveness of cooperative achievement have been criticized on a variety of grounds (Slavin, 1995b; Vedder, 1985). Some researchers have included additional conditions favorable to learning when implementing the cooperative learning techniques, making it unclear which factors created the achievement benefits. In addition, some reviews have included laboratory tests of cooperative learning that may not be relevant to the actual classroom use of coop-erative groups. Furthermore, differences exist between the results re-ported in some review articles and in the original published studies. Finally, it is possible that the achievement tests used were not always highly reliable. Despite these criticisms, the overall achievement benefits of cooperative learning seem clear.

With respect to handicapped students, a review of studies (Slavin, 1995a) showed that mainstreamed, academically handicapped students performed at least as well and often better in cooperative learning classes than in traditional programs. In a 2-year study of over 1,000 academically handicapped, elementary school students, Stevens and Slavin (1995) found significantly higher achievement scores for academically handicapped students in cooperative learning programs than in traditional remedial programs. These gains were not obtained at the expense of the more academically talented students; gifted students in these cooperative programs also had significantly greater achievement scores than gifted students in the comparison schools.

A Focus on Racial and Ethnic Minorities

The effects of cooperative learning techniques on minority students are of special interest. There are several reasons that racial and ethnic minorities might particularly benefit from cooperative learning techniques. First, cooperative learning has usually been implemented under the same conditions that lead to improvements in intergroup relations (e.g., contact is characterized by equal status and is cooperative, personal, and positively sanctioned by those in authority). Second, these conditions are consistent with the cultural norms, values, and socialization practices of the major ethnic minorities in the United States (Grossman, 1995; Haynes & Gebreyesus, 1992; Kitano & Daniels, 1995; Malloy & Malloy, 1998). Among Blacks, Latinos, and Asian Americans, norms are generally more group oriented than individualistically oriented, and more emphasis is placed on cooperation than competition. Third, the traditional competitive classroom often demands individualistic values and competitive behaviors inconsistent with these minority cultural norms, values, and socialization practices.

Overall, cooperative learning techniques show especially positive effects for minority students, both in friendship formation and academic achievement (Haynes & Gebreyesus, 1992; Lampe, Rooze, & Tallent-Runnels, 1997). The academic gains of low achievers do not come at the expense of high-achieving students, who maintain their high levels of achievement (Cohen, 1994; Johnson & Johnson, 1989; Slavin, 1995a).

The research data are somewhat inconsistent, however. Blaney and colleagues (1977) found greater liking for school among African Americans and Whites in Jigsaw classes than in traditional classes but the reverse effect for Latinos. These researchers believe that many Latinos in these classes had low English skills and had been allowed to sit silently in traditional classes, whereas they were forced to participate in Jigsaw classes, causing some anxiety. In addition, all these children were the lone Latino individuals in their groups. Speculating that the anxiety created by this situation would be decreased if these children were in a setting in which the school population was at least 50% Spanish speaking (A. Aronson & Gonzales, 1988), researchers conducted two studies in such a situation. In both, the Latino children showed only positive effects in the Jigsaw classes; gains were found in self-esteem, prosocial behavior, and academic performance. In one, Latino students shifted their locus of control from external toward internal as the proportion of their members in the groups approached parity.

In summary, cooperative learning techniques have demonstrated intergroup and achievement benefits. Next, we turn to the psychological processes that may be responsible for the positive intergroup relations findings.

Psychological Processes Underlying Cooperative Learning

Thus far, the benefits of cooperative groups have been attributed to positive goal interdependence of individuals (Deutsch, 1962); equal status; cooperative, personal contact among different types of students that is also positively sanctioned by those in authority (F. H. Allport et al., 1953; W. G. Stephan, 1987); and conditions in which expectations for performance are not based on status characteristics (Berger et al., 1980). These are all active-cognitive processes (see Figure 2.3). In this section, we take a further look at the ways in which creating interdependence improves intergroup relations. Then, we examine other psychological processes that might help explain the success of cooperative learning techniques in promoting positive intergroup relations. These include two active-cognitive processes, counteracting expectancies and decategorization by emphasizing multiple identities; one passive-cognitive process, creating subordinate groups; and one passive-affective process, reducing anxiety.

Both theory and research have shown that interdependence, the basic relationship among individuals in cooperative groups, produces cognitive processes that undermine stereotypes (Fiske, 2000). Interdependence leads to attention to information about what individuals are like rather than to the group stereotype. Since people need to understand the individuals on whom they are dependent, they look for information to supplement the group stereotype. Furthermore, because most individuals do not exactly match the group stereotype, it is usually apparent that information about each individual is needed. Interdependence also directs attention to information that is inconsistent with stereotypes. Stereotype-consistent information provides nothing new, but stereotype-inconsistent information augments what is already "known." Likewise, interdependence produces personal rather than situational explanations regarding people's stereotype-inconsistent behaviors. This tendency to make personal attributions is enhanced by the need for information.

A variety of conditions integral to cooperative learning have the capacity to reduce stereotyping. People are most likely to acquire and process information that is inconsistent with their stereotypes if the inconsistent information occurs frequently, occurs among a variety of outgroup members, happens in many different situations, and arises when the stereotype holder is dependent on the outgroup members (Erber & Fiske, 1984; Johnston & Hewstone, 1992; Rothbart & John, 1985). Many cooperative groups provide just such an environment: Stereotype-inconsistent behaviors occur daily; many different classmates exhibit these behaviors; they occur in the course of completing a variety of tasks; and members of cooperative learning groups are usually interdependent in a number of ways. In addition, the positive nature of interactions in cooperative learning groups are associated with the disconfirmation of negative expectations (Desforges et al., 1991). The positive quality of the interaction is critical and can be enhanced by providing scripted learning materials that guide the interactions.

Positive attitudes toward outgroup members within cooperative groups are most likely to generalize to other outgroup members, and thereby undercut stereotyping, when the assignments to groups appear to be based on factors other than racial and ethnic categories (Harrington & Miller 1992; Miller & Harrington, 1990a). However, the group identities of the participants must ultimately be salient if the positive interpersonal effects resulting from intergroup contact are to generalize to outgroup members who are not a part of the training (Hewstone, 1996; Pettigrew, 1998). Attitudes also generalize better when students are switched from group to group or team to team after a period of time, so that students have examples of many different outgroup members from within the classroom (E. Aronson et al., 1978).

Social identity theory provides another explanation for the success of cooperative learning techniques. Social identity theorists believe that individuals attempt to maintain or enhance their levels of self-esteem by judging ingroups more favorably than outgroups (Tajfel, 1978, 1982; Tajfel & Turner, 1986). Researchers have shown that two processes that often exist in cooperative groups, the first of which is personalization, undercut this tendency toward ingroup favoritism. Brewer and Miller (Brewer & Miller, 1984; Miller & Brewer, 1986) have shown that intergroup relations can be improved by structuring interactions so that people are seen as individuals. One way to create an individual focus, or personalization, is to place individuals in cooperative groups that contain cross-cutting identities, so that group members are similar on some dimensions (e.g., sex, ability level) even though they may be dissimilar on other dimensions (e.g., race, academic interests). Cooperative groups often promote personalization because the groups are typically selected to be diverse on a variety of dimensions so that any one category is low in salience.

Personalization can also be achieved through self-disclosure (Miller & Harrington, 1990b). As individuals come to know one another better, the depth of their self-disclosure increases, and its basis changes. Initially, individuals' self-disclosures tend to be based on similarities of demographic characteristics, but as self-disclosures become more intimate, they tend to be based on similarities of personal characteristics. Many of the properties of cooperative groups, such as their duration, informality, openness of communication, and absence of a single group goal or formal group structure (Brewer & Miller, 1984), foster a climate in which self-disclosure can become more intimate.

The second way that ingroup favorability may be undercut in cooperative groups is through recategorization—the creation of a superordinate group that is salient, causing differences among group members to diminish in importance (Gaertner et al., 1990; Gaertner, Mann, Murrell, & Dovidio, 1989). If students bond in cooperative groups, then the importance of the differences between the individual group members should decrease in salience. Cooperative groups may be particularly likely to create feelings of oneness because they tend to be associated with increased rewards, such as academic achievement, heightened self-esteem, and making new friends.

Another psychological process that explains the success of cooperative learning groups in increasing intergroup attraction involves the concept of intergroup anxiety. Unfortunately, intergroup interaction initially tends to produce anxiety (C. W. Stephan, 1992; W. G. Stephan & Stephan, 1985). Individuals often fear face-to-face interaction with outgroup members for several reasons, including fears about not knowing how to act and fears of being disliked or rejected. The types of interaction typical of cooperative learning groups can reduce anxiety not only by lowering uncertainty about the behaviors of outgroup members but also by providing a base of positive interaction (Mackie et al., 1989).

We end this chapter by exploring problems regarding the use of cooperative learning groups and making recommendations for successful programs.

Problems and Recommendations

Cooperative learning theorists agree that merely putting students in small groups and asking them to work together does not ensure that either cooperation or learning will take place. All the cooperative learning theorists stress the necessity of training teachers to implement the techniques through instruction in cooperative learning strategies, giving feedback, and classroom management. Pretraining students in cooperation, helping, and teaching skills—including cognitive strategies that promote academic success—is also very important. Attention should to be paid to the creation of the feeling of "groupness." It is all too easy for groups to become simply a collection of individuals who work separately and then put their work together without any group interaction or feeling of interdependence. For this reason, all these techniques are structured so that face-to-face interaction must take place and the peer interaction facilitates productive study and learning.

Some parents may initially object to the introduction of cooperative techniques because they believe their children need to be prepared to survive in a competitive world. Most become less concerned when they are reminded that cooperative learning is only a small portion of the child's total educational experience and that people need to be able to cooperate as well as to compete in order to succeed. However, the school should allow children to join classes not engaged in cooperative learning if the parent or the child expresses sustained objections to the technique.

Cooperative learning techniques are not appropriate in all situations in which the goal is improved intergroup relations. Clearly, they cannot be used to improve intergroup relations in monocultural settings, and their effectiveness outside educational settings is just beginning to be documented. The techniques are typically not appropriate for children who are so young that they cannot read, work together cooperatively, and take responsibility for their own outcomes. They are initially labor intensive and sometimes expensive, requiring new classroom materials, teacher training, and student training. Perhaps most difficult, cooperative learning techniques require the courage to rethink the entire educational process and move from a teacher-centered focus to a student-centered focus.

Summary

Cooperative learning usually consists of placing students in small learning groups in which the task-and-reward structure require cooperative, face-to-face interaction in a situation in which students are interdependent. The Slavin techniques, the Johnsons' Learning Together technique, the Jigsaw Classrooms, Group Investigation, and Complex Instruction are highly successful programs of cooperative learning. These techniques vary on a number of dimensions including the student reward structure (group vs. individual), whether student groups compete, whether task specialization exists within the groups, who does the actual teaching, whether curriculum materials are provided, and the content of the group activities.

Overall, the findings from research on cooperative learning suggest that the consequences of cooperative learning include more positive feelings toward racial and ethnic outgroups, increases in numbers of friends in general and friends from different racial and ethnic groups in particular, and interpersonal gains, such as enhanced liking and respect among students. In addition, cooperative learning typically increases student achievement, especially the achievement of minority students and low-achieving students. Cooperative learning has particularly positive benefits for racial and ethnic minorities.

Researchers continue to identify the causal mechanisms that underlie the positive intergroup benefits of cooperative learning. These include positive goal interdependence; equal status; cooperative, personal contact among different types of students that is positively sanctioned by those in authority; conditions in which expectations for performance are not based on status characteristics; decategorization by emphasizing multiple identities and self-disclosure; creating subordinate groups; and reducing anxiety.

Finally, cooperative learning techniques are not appropriate in all situations in which the goal is improved intergroup relations. They cannot be used to improve intergroup relations in monocultural settings, and the techniques are typically not appropriate for extremely young children.

CONFLICT RESOLUTION PROGRAMS 8

MEDIATION, POSITIVE BARGAINING, third-party consultation, town meetings, and conflict containment are among the formal conflict resolution techniques that have been created to resolve conflicts in an effective and supportive way. These conflict resolution techniques are increasingly being used to settle many types of conflicts including school conflicts, divorce, legal cases, neighborhood disputes, public interest controversies, and industrial disputes.

Why are conflict resolution programs relevant to improving intergroup relations? Although people would label most conflict as interpersonal rather than intergroup, both types of conflict are common. Furthermore, because issues of race, ethnicity, nationality, and religion permeate cultures, they are often unarticulated elements of many seemingly interpersonal conflicts (Gadlin, 1994). Particularly in community-based conflicts, intergroup issues are often important elements in the conflict. In other conflict settings, intergroup relations may be central to the conflict, but the parties may be unwilling to admit this intergroup involvement initially. In some instances, intergroup relations issues may emerge as important in the conflict—to the surprise of the parties.

Successfully resolving intergroup conflict should improve intergroup relations because it can lessen individuals' and groups' negative feelings (stemming from the conflict) about outgroup members. In addition, the conditions under which these programs are implemented (e.g., equal status, cooperative, successful interactions) have been shown to improve intergroup relations. Furthermore, the consequences of the programs (e.g., increased understanding and respect for others, heightened feelings of self-esteem and self-efficacy, feelings of empathy, the rewards of success, and being viewed positively by important authorities) also have been shown to enhance intergroup relations.

The focus of this chapter is conflict resolution in educational, business, and community settings. The target populations are individuals actively involved in disputes, representing themselves, their organizations, or groups from their communities. We do not include settings unlikely to have intergroup relations implications (e.g., most legal mediation). We also exclude competitive conflict resolution strategies designed merely to maximize one's own outcomes (e.g., most business negotiations) and the process of arbitration, in which solutions are imposed on disputing parties. International conflict resolution is discussed in Chapter 5, because dialogue techniques play such a prominent role in international conflict resolution.

The major goal of conflict resolution programs is to end or attenuate the conflicts. Although the improvement of intergroup relations is typically not a central goal of these programs, to lessen or solve conflict occurring in schools and organizations, intergroup issues based on race, ethnicity, religion, and culture must often be addressed, and intergroup misunderstandings and misperceptions must be corrected. Community-based conflict resolution commonly has intergroup issues at its core. Ending the conflict entails solving the intergroup relations issues.

In Figure 1.1, we listed conflict resolution programs as active and indirect. Conflict resolution always involves interventions in which the participants play an active role. The programs are indirect because their goals are to end or lessen the conflict. Intergroup relations issues are not necessarily directly addressed, although in some conflicts they are. Most programs do not collect data on the effects of these programs on intergroup relations.

In this chapter, we first consider various types of conflict resolution programs employed in community, organizational, and educational settings. Then, we examine the research literature on the effectiveness of these conflict resolution approaches. Next, we explore psychological processes that might underlie the effectiveness of these programs. These processes are both active and passive and involve changes in both affect and cognitions (see Figure 2.3). They include increasing interdependence, creating conditions for positive inter-action, increasing participants' sense of empowerment, observing the norm of reciprocity, creating empathy, and increasing rewards re-ceived from others. Finally, we make suggestions for the design of suc-cessful conflict resolution programs, discuss problems, and focus on the special requirements of interethnic conflict resolution programs.

Types of Conflict Resolution Programs

Of the conflict settings we discuss, those based in the community are most likely to contain overt or covert intergroup elements. For this rea-son, we focus first on the conflict resolution programs most commonly used in community settings. Then, we explore the types of conflict res-olution programs employed in organizational settings. Finally, we examine conflict resolution programs based in the schools.

Community-Based Conflict Resolution Programs

We discuss four methods of conflict resolution commonly used in community settings: mediation, third-party consultation, town meet-ings, and conflict containment.

Mediation

Mediation consists of assisted discussions between conflicting parties involving the intervention of a neutral, third-party mediator in the negotiation (Burgess & Burgess, 1997). The mediator's role is to help the conflicting parties communicate with one another, analyze the conflict, and develop a mutually acceptable solution. The mediator has no decision-making authority; the conflicting parties reach their own decision aided by the mediator. Research indicates considerable user satisfaction with mediation and provides some evidence that agree-ments reached through mediation are less costly and longer lasting than agreements obtained through traditional dispute resolution methods (Kressel & Pruitt, 1989).

Mediation is commonly used to solve community conflicts. In one model of mediation, the disputants first agree to a set of ground rules and then make brief initial statements, which usually consist of demands or positions (Corder & Thompson, 2000). The mediator next asks questions of the disputants to help the disputants exchange information regarding the interests underlying their demands. This stage takes some time. Name calling and interrupting are not tolerated. When necessary, the mediator rephrases the disputants' statements into neutral terms. When all the interests have been identified, the disputants take a break while the mediator puts all the interests into a joint problem statement that includes each party's needs (e.g., "How can the Chinese American street vendors' rights to operate be protected at the same time that the Portuguese American business owners' concerns regarding the influence of these vendors on their businesses be respected?"). The disputants are then asked if the statement captures the problem to be solved. If it does, the disputants are asked to brainstorm as many creative solutions to the problem as they can, without evaluating any of them. In the final stage, the parties select the options that best fit the needs of both. Once an agreement is obtained, it is written up. Throughout the process, the mediator is a neutral processor of information provided by the disputants themselves.

Mediation is one of the conflict resolution techniques that has been specifically applied to intergroup relations issues. Community racial disputes were first mediated in the late 1960s. By 1971, dozens of centers had been established specifically to mediate conflicts between two or more racial or cultural groups within a community (Dukes, 1996; Schoene & DuPraw, 1994). One New York mediation center, the Black/Korean Mediation Project, provides an example of a center specializing in racial mediation. It was created after the Rodney King beating by police in Los Angeles had led to Black and Korean American intergroup violence (Schoene & DuPraw, 1994). The situation in Los Angeles exacerbated Black and Korean American tensions nationwide. In response to this increased intergroup hostility, two Korean American community organizations and three community dispute resolution centers obtained funding to train members of the Black and Korean American communities in mediation. They also conducted community outreach so that tensions between members of the two groups would be referred to the project.

Third-Party Consultation

Third-party consultation is commonly used in resolving community conflicts. Interactive Conflict Resolution (ICR) provides one model of third-party consultation used to resolve community conflicts (Fisher, 1972, 1997). ICR consists of small-group problem-solving discussions between unofficial representatives of parties engaged in long-standing conflicts. The conflicting parties may be typical members of their group or appointed, influential representatives of the group. A neutral, third-party team provides the consultation. This third-party team typically consists of a group of social scientist practitioners with expert knowledge of conflict processes and human relations skills.

The third party's role is facilitative and diagnostic. In addition, it is noncoercive, nonevaluative, and nondirective with respect to outcomes. The third party thus has low external control over the conflicting parties but high internal control over the discussion. The facilitators organize a series of informal discussions regarding the conflict. These discussions are intended to help establish trust and respect among the disputants, provide a neutral setting for discussions that allows for informal interaction, and encourage mutual motivation for problem solving. The third party's goal is to improve the openness and accuracy of communication, diagnose the conflict, and regulate the interaction among the participants. These goals are met through a set of specific behavioral tactics, such as summarizing each party's major points and stopping repetitive interactions. They are also met through a number of general procedures and exercises, such as allowing the parties to exchange perceptions of the other group.

An example of the use of third-party consultation in community disputes is provided by a case in Eugene, Oregon, where a number of disputes between the minority community and the city government were settled (Schoene & DuPraw, 1994). The consultant first interviewed key people in the community and the government to identify the issues, the stakeholders, and the agenda to be discussed. Then, the consultant moderated a 2-day collaborative discussion among the representatives of the two communities. One important result of this conversation was the creation of personal relationships among members of the two groups that served to make the resolution of subsequent problems much easier.

The Town Meeting

Another model of community conflict resolution is provided by the town meeting (Volpe, 1998). In a town meeting, individuals or groups from a community or organization come together to discuss controversial issues with the assistance of a facilitator in a safe, respectful context. Such meetings are not undertaken with the specific expectation of agreements, although agreements may occur on the basis of the interactions among the participants. Whereas most ordinary town meetings are one-time-only events, the use of town meetings for conflict resolution requires an ongoing series of meetings. Once the town meeting approach has become institutionalized, all members of the community know that concerns regarding relations among diverse groups can be incorporated as part of an ongoing process of communication among them. When town meetings are used for intergroup conflict resolution, the meetings may either have an open agenda, in which current problems can be raised, or they may have set agendas dealing with specific intergroup issues (e.g., "Do members of your group feel respect in our community?"). They are particularly useful as conflict resolution tools when community members have few opportunities to interact with one another in a group setting.

An instance of an ongoing set of town meetings with intergroup undertones takes place once a month during the school year at the John Jay College of Criminal Justice at the City University of New York. The meetings are open to all members of the academic community. Key administrators, leaders of the faculty senate, and student leaders are always present. Facilitators remind the audience about the ground rules, enforce time limits, and make certain all voices have an opportunity to be heard. When a theme meeting is held, resource experts may be invited. The town meetings were instituted at John Jay College in 1989 after a largely minority student takeover of the offices of the mostly White administration. The driving issue was a proposed tuition increase, but many other issues involving race and racial representation surfaced in the aftermath of the takeover. One of the agreements was a provision for a town meeting to air all the issues. This highly charged meeting was so successful in resolving the students' concerns that the students asked for regularly scheduled town meetings. After no meetings were held, the students again took over the campus, and the agreement to hold monthly town meetings was then implemented. The meetings have been held henceforth.

Conflict Containment

Glazer (1997) considers conflict containment to be a form of community conflict resolution. In conflict containment, mechanisms are developed by the conflicting parties themselves to find solutions to resolvable issues and to learn to contain unresolvable issues by bringing the parties together in a common effort. The goal of conflict containment is not to settle all long-standing issues among disputing parties but rather to develop channels of communication among the parties and keep them open through structured, continuing interaction to de-escalate conflict. In the process, members of the conflicting groups form personal ties and make mutual commitments to continued communication.

One such conflict containment took place in the Crown Heights neighborhood of Brooklyn (Glazer, 1997). After years of ethnic tensions between fundamentalist Jews and Black inhabitants of the neighborhood, riots erupted in 1991 as a result of an accident in which a car driven by a Jewish leader went out of control, killing a Guyanese immigrant child. A Crown Heights Coalition was created within days of the riot, headed by leaders on both sides. The coalition met frequently to discuss the causes of the riots and ultimately issued a report, thus resolving this specific conflict. The broader conflict between Jews and Blacks did not disappear, but it has been contained. The coalition meetings created friendships among its members that were based on shared community interests. Members of the coalition began to work together on other intergroup issues. New networks were formed, and intergroup community projects were initiated that involved other members of the conflicting ethnic groups, leading to the formation of more intergroup bonds.

Conflict Resolution Programs in Organizational Settings

We will discuss three methods of conflict resolution commonly used in organizational settings: mediation, positive bargaining, and

third-party consultation. As in community settings, intergroup relations issues often play a role in these conflicts.

Mediation

Mediation is used in resolving business and other organizational
disputes as well as in settling community conflict. It is often successful
in mediating bankruptcy, creditor-debtor, real estate, construction,
franchise, employment, environmental, insurance coverage, partner-
ship, product liability, regulatory, securities, patents, technology, and
trademark and unfair competition disputes (Picker, 1998). Mediation
in business settings typically consists of an initial conference involving
both parties, followed by separate sessions with each party. Sometimes
additional joint sessions occur, and at other times, mediators move between the parties, relaying perspectives and settlement proposals.

In disputes among employees, formal mediation using a neutral third party is preferable to using a manager as the third party
(Karambayya & Brett, 1994). Managers are rarely neutral parties to a
dispute among the individuals they supervise, because they have personal relations with their employees and may have a stake in the outcome of the dispute. Also, they rarely have training in mediation.

The now famous 1968 Memphis public-works employees strike
provides an example of a successful mediation of an organizational
dispute with strong racial overtones (Marshall & Van Adams, 1971).
The strike began over the working conditions of the largely Black sanitation workers in the White-run public-works administration. The
employees struck after an incident of discriminatory treatment within
the department, with the strikers' main goal being recognition of their
union by the city. Deep dissatisfaction already existed regarding the
White power structure's lack of response to the needs of the Black community. The strike received nationwide attention, and the events
associated with the strike ultimately resulted in riots and in the assas-
sination of Dr. Martin Luther King Jr.

Immediately after the workers struck, union leaders and the
mayor met for several informal negotiations, but the mayor refused to
consider granting the union's key demands. During this time, the
Black community marched in support of the strikers, picketed, and

boycotted White businesses. The city responded with hired strike-breakers and a show of police force. Next, a professional mediator was asked to intervene, and a memo of understanding was drawn up, but agreement could not be reached on its exact language. The following day, a march in support of the strikers led by Dr. King was disrupted by window breaking and looting, and Dr. King and his aides had to flee for safety. Charges of police brutality during the disturbance were later investigated and substantiated. Another meeting was set between city and union officials, but Dr. King was assassinated before it could take place. A U.S. undersecretary of labor and the original mediator then met with the union and city representatives. A nightlong meeting settled the major issue of recognition, with the remaining issues resolved after 10 additional days of mediated negotiations. Although the strike was ultimately successfully mediated, the initial resistance of the mayor and other city officials in earlier negotiations led to great personal, financial, and societal cost that could have been avoided.

Positive Bargaining Models

Traditional business negotiations, often called distributive bargaining, hard bargaining, or win-lose bargaining, emphasize achieving the best possible outcome for oneself, without respect for the other's outcomes or feelings. Many business negotiations today still follow this model. In contrast, a newer, positive model of business negotiation, called principled negotiation, integrative bargaining, or win-win bargaining, perceives the negotiators as problem solvers who can find a solution of mutual benefit to both parties (Fisher & Ury, 1983). This type of negotiation is based on objective criteria and logical reasoning rather than on narrow self-interest and is designed to promote positive interpersonal and intergroup relations (Fisher & Ury, 1983). In order to achieve such negotiations, both parties must be able to focus on the problem at hand as well as on restoring positive relations among the parties in the conflict. Each party must also focus on meeting the interests of both parties, not on maintaining a single position or demand. Finally, the parties need to devise options for mutual gain rather than focusing on one-sided solutions to the problem.

Many researchers have documented the need to move both parties in any organizational conflict from a high concern only for the self to a high concern for both the self and the other (D. R. S. Blake & Mouton, 1984; Pruitt & Carnevale, 1993; Rubin, Pruitt, & Kim, 1994), and attention has been focused on positive communication in negotiation as a way to facilitate this dual focus (Putnam & Roloff, 1992). One model of bargaining that incorporates dual concerns for the self and the other is added-value negotiating (Albrecht & Albrecht, 1993). In this model, the goal is to arrive at an agreement that cooperatively increases the value involved for both parties. In using this technique, parties are discouraged from taking positions; instead, they clarify their respective interests and search for options that will meet all of them. One focus is on empathy. Another is on the presentation of several offers to find the best one for both parties.

Although the mediation literature emphasizes the importance of equal status among participants in the conflict, in organizational and intergroup contexts, equal status cannot always be achieved. Fortunately, these positive bargaining models can also be used successfully in situations in which the conflicting parties are unequal in status. For example, when the problem involves an employee with a complaint about the company, taking the problem to the supervisor is often the first step in a prescribed grievance procedure. In such instances, the supervisor and the employee thereby become the negotiating parties. Supervisors and employees in such disputes would especially benefit from training in cooperation and open-mindedness (Tjosvold, Morishima, & Belsheim, 1999). This training is designed to help people adopt a cooperative strategy in solving organizational conflict and use an open, flexible discussion style that allows for the consideration of the others' views. Cooperation and consideration for the others helps to reduce the practical and psychological costs of filing a grievance (Olson-Buchanan, 1996).

Third-Party Consultation

Third-party consultation is commonly used in resolving all types of organizational conflict as well as in community conflicts. A variety of consulting models exist (French & Bell, 1990). Interactive Conflict

Resolution (ICR) provides one model of third-party consultation used to resolve conflicts in organizational settings (Fisher, 1972, 1997; Fisher & Keashly, 1990).

The third-party consultation model was used to resolve a series of staff-client conflicts between housing agency staff and public housing tenants. These conflicts had been created by two organizational problems: a combination of a traditional management style on the part of the staff and a lack of constructive tenant input (Fisher, 1976). At the time of the consultation, levels of mutual antagonism, blame, and ineffective communication were high. A public housing committee was formed including tenant, management, and policy representatives, as well as members of an impartial social-planning council and a team of third-party consultants who were associated with the planning council. In the course of three meetings, objectives were clarified and motivation to work together increased. Consequences of the meetings included the organization of one tenant housing association and the reconstitution of another, a survey of tenant concerns, and the establishment of a tenant newsletter. Subsequently, regular meetings were held between tenant representatives and agency personnel to deal quickly and directly with any problems.

School-Based Conflict Resolution Programs

School-based conflict resolution programs are becoming increasingly popular. By 1995, over 300,000 students had been trained in over 6,000 programs (Girard & Koch, 1995). While many types of school-based, conflict resolution programs exist (Johnson & Johnson, 1996), virtually all include some type of mediation.

Most school-based mediation programs involve peer mediation—student mediation of student problems. Peer mediation has the potential not only to end specific conflicts but also to teach children conflict resolution skills that they can use throughout their lives. For this reason, peer mediation is typically preferred to teacher or administrator mediation (T. S. Jones & Brickman, 1994). The large number of conflicts among schoolmates provides an impetus for school-based peer mediation programs. Children have more conflicts with their schoolmates than with any other group of people including siblings and parents.

Unfortunately, children generally rely on antisocial strategies (e.g., coercion, manipulation) to try to resolve them (T. S. Jones & Brickman, 1994).

Like other conflict resolution programs, school-based peer mediation programs are rarely designed with the improvement of intergroup relations as a primary goal. However, intergroup conflicts as well as interpersonal conflicts with intergroup components are commonly mediated. Some peer mediation training includes intergroup relations exercises in an effort to help students understand conflict that involves group differences (e.g., Myers & Filner, 1994; Schrumpf, Crawford, & Usadel, 1991).

Peer mediation programs differ on a variety of dimensions. First, they diverge in the proportion of students in a school that are trained. In some programs, only a select group of students is trained (e.g., students take an elective course or teachers select or recruit a group of students). In other programs, the whole student body undergoes training. Second, they vary in the purpose of the training. The training can be aimed at prevention, at education, or at reactions to ongoing conflicts. Third, these mediation programs may use differing approaches to training. Some programs are skills oriented and others are knowledge oriented.

One well-researched and widely used elementary through high school program is the Teaching Students to be Peacemakers Program (Johnson, 1970; Johnson & Johnson, 1995a, 1995b). The goal of this program is to train all students to positively negotiate their own conflicts and mediate schoolmates' conflicts. Significantly, one goal of this training is to improve intergroup relations. Training is repeated each year in this 12-year curriculum. In the beginning of the school year, 20 hours of training are given to students in 30-minute lessons over the course of several weeks. Subsequently, students receive at least two 30-minute lessons each week to refresh and refine their negotiation and mediation skills. Each student serves as a peer mediator for an equal amount of time so that all receive the benefits of mediating. This training program is accompanied by the creation of a cooperative climate in the school through the use of cooperative learning procedures.

At the primary school level, the initial lessons might include defining conflict and discussing why it should be studied, asking the individual students what conflict means to each of them, and asking each student to write down what they do in conflict situations (Johnson, Johnson, & Bartlett, 1990). Later, students might be asked to bring in newspaper or magazine articles about conflict or negotiation and to think about the presentation of conflict on television. They would ultimately be shown the steps involved in negotiation. The six negotiation steps are: (1) jointly defining the problem as mutual, small, and specific; (2) describing one's own feelings; (3) describing the reasons for one's own position; (4) reversing perspectives by presenting the other party's position; (5) inventing options for mutual benefit; and (6) reaching a wise decision. Next, the students practice the individual steps and then rehearse putting the steps together.

The same process would be repeated for mediation. Students would first learn the steps involved in mediation. The seven mediation steps are: (1) end hostilities; (2) ensure the disputants' commitment to the mediation; (3) facilitate the negotiations; (4) help the disputants present their views; (5) help the disputants reverse perspectives; (6) help the disputants invent options; and (7) formalize agreement. Again, the students would practice the steps and experience putting the steps together.

As a part of the Peacemakers Program, teachers also use structured academic controversies to increase students' reasoning and conflict skills. In structured academic controversies, students prepare scholarly positions on an academic issue, advocate their positions, and refute opposing positions. They then rebut their opponents, view the issue from both perspectives, and come to a consensus based on a synthesis of the two positions. The civil disobedience of individuals during the civil rights movement in the 1960s provides an example of a topic for a structured academic controversy (Avery, Johnson, Johnson, & Mitchell, 1999; Johnson & Johnson, 1994b). The question might be whether civil disobedience in a democracy is constructive or destructive. Students might be placed in cooperative groups of 4 students. Two students could be assigned to make the best case possible for the destructiveness of civil disobedience, and 2 assigned to make the best case possible for the constructiveness of civil disobedience.

The Johnsons believe that in order to improve intergroup relations, schools must not only provide training in constructive conflict resolution but also use cooperative learning techniques to create a cooperative community (Johnson & Johnson, 2000). In the process of providing constructive conflict resolution and creating a cooperative community, participants will also learn civic values. In Chapter 7, we discuss the Johnsons' techniques for training students in cooperative learning techniques.

Many other school-based conflict resolution programs exist. Some programs are offered by organizations committed to nonviolence, such as the Children's Creative Response to Conflict, established by Quaker teachers in New York City (Johnson & Johnson, 1995a). Other programs have been devised by groups trying to prevent nuclear war, such as the Educators for Social Responsibility in New York, who devised the Resolving Conflict Creatively program (Johnson & Johnson, 1995a). Neighborhood justice centers, established through Carter administration (1987-1990) financial support, provide another source of school-based programs. Some community mediation centers have formed alliances with school systems to promote school-based conflict resolution and peer mediation programs. The Community Board Program in San Francisco, which helped develop a conflict management curriculum for elementary schools (Johnson & Johnson, 1995b; Maxwell, 1990), provides an example of one such alliance.

School-based mediation need not be limited to students. Once students and professional staff have received training, mediation can be used to resolve staff-staff, staff-administration, staff-parent, and even staff-student conflicts (Lupton-Smith, Carruthers, Flythe, Goettee, & Modest, 1996).

Having explored various types of conflict resolution programs found in communities, organizations, and schools, we will now examine the existing data on the outcomes of these programs.

Summary of Research Findings on Conflict Resolution Programs

First, we consider the research on conflict resolution programs in community and organizational settings. Because little empirical data exist, we consider these two settings together. Next, we review the existing research on school-based peer mediation programs.

Research in Community and Organizational Settings

We consider research on mediation, negotiation, and the remaining conflict resolution techniques used in these settings.

Research on Mediation

Most of the research literature on mediation in community or organizational contexts is anecdotal, consists of case studies, or is based on laboratory simulations of mediation. Few studies have systematically examined the effects of the mediation of actual disputes. A review of the existing literature finds that mediation is more effective when conflict is moderate rather than intense, the parties are highly motivated to reach a settlement, and they are committed to mediation (Carnevale & Pruitt, 1992; Pruitt, 1998). Agreement is more likely, and the agreement is more likely to be a win-win agreement, when the parties have positive working relationships. Mutual dependence facilitates such relationships (Carnevale & Pruitt, 1992). Disagreements within the negotiating teams are associated with poor outcomes.

In a study of 73 actual community mediations, the use of joint problem solving was associated with the perception of improved relations with the other party (Pruitt, Peirce, McGillicuddy, Welton, & Castrianno, 1993). The perception that the mediation was fair and had aired all the problems was associated with the long-term success of the mediation, as measured by compliance with the agreement, the perception of improved relations between the parties, and the absence of new problems. Surprisingly, the extent to which the mediation solved the immediate problem was unrelated to the long-term success of the mediation.

Research on Negotiation

As with the research literature on mediation, few assessments have been published of the outcomes of negotiations conducted in

actual community or organizational settings. The negotiation literature is mostly composed of laboratory simulations. This literature
finds that negotiations lead to faster and more reliable agreements
when options provide equal outcomes for the parties involved or the
agreement is equidistant from their initial positions (Carnevale &
Pruitt, 1992; Pruitt, 1998). Higher initial demands and slowness in
reaching concessions make agreement less rapid and less likely. However, if agreements are ultimately reached, the party who makes higher
initial demands and is slower in making concessions is likely to obtain
larger outcomes (Carnevale & Pruitt, 1992; Pruitt, 1998). Other data
suggest that information exchange regarding each party's priorities or
the interests underlying their positions promotes the development of
win-win solutions (Carnevale & Pruitt, 1992). Finally, concern for the
other party's outcomes as well as for one's own is associated with
problem solving that leads to high joint benefits (Carnevale & Pruitt,
1992).

One team of researchers examined the outcomes of the actual
mediation of 68 employee complaints in a large sawmill (Tjosvold
et al., 1999). They found that supervisors and employees who believed
their interests were interdependent were more likely to consider one
another's views and to find an integrative solution to the problem,
compared to supervisors and employees who viewed their interests as
competitive or independent.

Research on Other Conflict Resolution Techniques in Community and Organizational Settings

A number of case studies of the Interactive Conflict Resolution
(ICR) technique applied to international conflict resolution have been
published (for a complete list, see Fisher, 1997). One well-controlled
community study of the ICR model took place in a small Canadian city
in a neighborhood with attractive private homes on one side of a long
street and public housing units on the other side (Fisher, 1997). Over
several years, conflict had escalated between the homeowners and
the public housing tenants. Relations between the groups were poor,
with stereotyping, discrimination, ineffective communication, and
low motivation to deal constructively with the problems evident in
parties on both sides. Two consultants employed the ICR model using

influential leaders from each group who met in several 3-hour discussions over 2 weeks. Compared to parallel, nondiscussion control groups, members of the ICR groups showed significantly more complex and positive attitudes. However, they did not demonstrate significantly more behavioral orientations to improve the situation.

The literature on the effects of town halls and conflict containment consists of case studies and anecdotal evidence, such as those we have reported. This literature tends to report benefits of the techniques. In the absence of systematic qualitative or quantitative measurements, however, the specific effects of these techniques and the reasons for them remain unknown.

In summary, the literature on the effects of community and organizational conflict resolution programs is largely descriptive or only anecdotal (Johnson & Johnson, 1996). Case studies are common. Many seemingly successful organizational and community-based conflict resolution programs are not currently being evaluated. To our knowledge, absolutely no intergroup relations data exist. The conflict resolution discipline needs more field research on the specific effects of the actual programs as well as on the causes of these outcomes. Most specifically, intergroup relations data are needed. Until research is conducted on the intergroup outcomes of conflict resolution programs, their utility in improving intergroup relations in community and organizational settings is unproven.

School-Based Peer Mediation Programs

Very little research has been conducted specifically on the mediation of interethnic conflicts in schools (Coleman & Deutsch, 1998). The studies assessing school-based dispute resolution or mediation programs focused on interethnic mediation usually report that participants are satisfied with these programs and find them useful (Lam, 1989).

The existing literature mostly consists of evaluations of general school-based conflict resolution and peer mediation programs. Reviews of that literature show that these programs are typically effective in teaching students integrative negotiation and mediation procedures and that trained students tend to use them to reach constructive solutions to conflict (Carruthers, Sweeney, Kmitta, & Harris, 1996; Johnson & Johnson, 1996; Lam, 1989).

Peer mediation appears to be successful among children as young as kindergarten age (Johnson & Johnson, 1996). However, children younger than 11 tend to reach only simple solutions (e.g., we will stay away from one another), whereas older children are able to make more complex integrative agreements that actually achieve resolution of the issue through joint problem solving. The data on these programs further show that agreements are reached in most instances and that these agreements tend to endure (Carruthers et al., 1996; Johnson & Johnson, 1996).

One large-scale program illustrates some of the benefits these programs can achieve (Deutsch, 1992). It was found that students in an alternative inner-city school who completed a mediation program were able to better manage their conflicts than were those who had not completed the program. In addition, they experienced increased social support and less victimization from others. These improvements led to increased self-esteem, feelings of personal control, more frequent feelings of positive well-being, and decreased anxiety and depression. The increases in self-esteem and sense of personal control were also associated with higher academic performance.

Reviews of the existing literature draw inconsistent conclusions regarding whether or not peer mediation programs reduce the dropout rate, suspension rate, number of violent incidents, and number of referrals to the principal (Carruthers et al., 1996; Johnson & Johnson, 1996). Disagreement also exists regarding whether or not the data suggest that peer mediation training increases self-esteem and increases academic achievement when conflict resolution training is integrated into academic units and is accompanied by cooperative learning teaching strategies (Carruthers et al., 1996; Johnson & Johnson, 1996; Stevahn, Johnson, Johnson, Green, & Laginski, 1997).

In addition, most of the consequences of the programs that researchers claim (e.g., lowered violence in schools) are not directly related to the training. The variables that mediate the relationships between the conflict resolution techniques and their specific outcomes need to be identified (Johnson & Johnson, 1996).

Even though some conflict resolution programs have improved intergroup relations as their ultimate goal, none of the peer mediation literature directly assesses intergroup relations outcomes. These outcomes very much need to be measured.

Next, we turn to an examination of the psychological processes that might underlie the potential for conflict resolution programs to improve intergroup relations.

Psychological Processes Underlying Conflict Resolution

The assessment of conflict resolution programs has focused on their success in resolving conflict rather than on the intergroup benefits of the techniques. Interestingly, each of the theoretical explanations given for the success of these programs could also be used to explain how they might improve intergroup relations. These include the active-cognitive processes of increasing interdependence, creating conditions for positive interaction, increasing participants' sense of empowerment, and observing the norm of reciprocity. They also encompass the passive-cognitive process of creating empathy and the active-affective process of increasing rewards received from others (see Figure 2.3).

The most frequently researched conflict resolution program, Teaching Students to Be Peacemakers (Johnson, 1970; Johnson & Johnson, 1995a, 1995b), employs social interdependence theory (Deutsch, 1949, 1973) and conflict strategies theory to explain its success (Johnson, 1991; Johnson & Johnson, 1997). According to interdependence theory, conflict exists in all relationships. The outcome of conflict is dependent on the way it is managed. Most people who have not been trained in conflict resolution and peer mediation techniques deal with conflict in a competitive manner (Johnson & Johnson, 1996). Working on conflicts in a cooperative manner, as conflict resolution and peer mediation programs teach students to do, predisposes individuals to try to achieve the goals of both parties. That is, this cooperative process promotes constructive and healthy resolutions of conflicts.

Conflict strategies theory argues that two concerns exist in conflict resolution settings: reaching one's goals and maintaining an appropriate relationship with the other person (Johnson & Johnson,

1997). The relative importance of these two goals determines what strategy people will use in resolving a conflict. The most complex and constructive strategy is integrative problem solving negotiation, which is capable of meeting both goals. Integrative problem solving is the type of strategy employed in conflict resolution and peer mediation programs. This type of problem solving involves processes known to improve intergroup relations, including empathy, concern for the other party, and cooperative interaction.

Third-party consultation specialists also believe that their technique and other conflict resolution techniques are effective because they create equal power and cooperative relationships within the intervention context (Coleman & Deutsch, 1998; Fisher & Keashly, 1990). The conditions of contact in these conflict resolution programs—cooperation, interdependence, equal status of participants—provide the type of contact that has been shown to promote positive intergroup relations (G. W. Allport, 1954; W. G. Stephan, 1987).

Bush and Folger's (1994) mediation model centers on transformative mediation, in which one outcome is empowerment as experienced in increased self-determination and self-respect. Another outcome is recognition of the other as evidenced by enhanced interpersonal communication and expressions of concern for the other. In transformative mediation, both the self and the other party become more a part of one another and become more caring and morally concerned. When obtained, empowerment and recognition should facilitate intergroup relations. Increased moral concern might also improve intergroup relations because high levels of moral thinking are incompatible with prejudice and discrimination.

Third-party consultation specialists believe that their technique is effective because the norm of reciprocity—the norm that people should help others who help them—facilitates mutual concessions (Fisher & Keashly, 1990). This norm highlights the cooperativeness and relatively fair exchange embedded in the process. Furthermore, face-to-face interaction helps break down rigid stereotypes, and information exchanges allow conflicting parties to discover both similarities and the reasons for their differences. The conflict resolution process should also reduce anxiety about interacting with the other party. All these processes have been associated with improved intergroup relations (Byrne, 1971; Rothbart & John, 1985; Schroeder,

Penner, Dovidio, & Piliavin, 1995; W. G. Stephan & Stephan, 1984; 1985).

Broome (1993) believes that conflict resolution programs are effective because they evoke relational empathy—empathy based on the creation of a shared understanding of the problem. This type of empathy results from the interaction among the parties in which a third culture is created that includes some aspects of each person's initial views on the issue. Empathy has been shown to be incompatible with prejudice (A. Smith, 1990). Della Noce (1999) argues that relational empathy arises only from transformative mediation and not from other models of mediation, but she presents no data to support her view.

Perhaps more than any of the other techniques reviewed in this book, learning conflict resolution skills and techniques has a positive impact on the way the learner is viewed by others, both within and outside the conflict situation. Many articles report that children use the conflict resolution skills learned in school to manage conflicts in the family and the community. This generalization leads to parental and community approval (Hall, 1999; Johnson & Johnson, 1996; Lindsay, 1998). Adults and children tend to apply conflict resolution skills to other arenas of life because the process of resolving a difficult conflict is itself rewarding (Fisher & Keashly, 1990). In addition, working cooperatively with the goal of maximizing everyone's outcomes promotes positive interactions within and among groups. Thus, the most basic mechanisms of reinforcement can be used to explain the benefits of conflict resolution programs.

In the next section, we mention some contraindicated conditions for conflict resolution training and discuss the ideal conditions for a conflict resolution program designed to improve intergroup relations.

Problems and Recommendations

A single course or workshop in conflict resolution is generally not enough to produce lasting effects (Coleman & Deutsch, 1998). People need repeated opportunities and encouragement to practice conflict resolution skills. In addition, according to Kressel and Pruitt (1989),

> Intensely conflicted disputes involving parties of widely disparate
> power, with low motivation to settle, fighting about matters of princi-
> ple, suffering from discord or ambivalence within their own camps,
> and negotiating over scarce resources are likely to defeat even the most
> adroit mediators. (p. 405)

Not all disputes are appropriate for mediation. For instance, disputes
that involve criminal violence should not be referred for mediation
within regular organizational settings (Lupton-Smith et al., 1996).

Conflict resolution programs should not be viewed as a panacea
for all conflicts. The atmosphere in most organizations is competitive
and authoritarian, which can undermine the effects of a cooperative,
egalitarian program such as peer mediation (Lindsay, 1998). Conflict
resolution programs will be more effective if they are only one part of
an overall concern with an organizational climate that includes such
elements as an emphasis on cooperation, moral behavior, and multicultural diversity (Bickmore, 1999; Johnson & Johnson, 1996; Sweeney
& Carruthers, 1996). An ideal program would include teaching negotiation techniques combined with peer mediation techniques. Conflict
resolution programs should be coordinated with other programs, such
as anger management training, and with additional conflict resolution programs in other settings (Lindsay, 1998; Sweeney & Carruthers,
1996).

The support of relevant authorities is critical to the success of
conflict resolution programs (Carruthers et al., 1996; T. S. Jones &
Brickman, 1994; Lupton-Smith et al., 1996). Before the program is
implemented, the entire population of the school, organization, or
community needs to be educated about mediation in general as well as
about the particular program to be used (Lupton-Smith et al., 1996). In
school settings, parents and community members should be informed
about the program. Total organizational training is ideal, but where
pockets of resistance exist, a partial training program may be preferable; conflict resolution programs cannot meet with success if they are
forced on unwilling participants (T. S. Jones & Brickman, 1994).

The peer mediators should be as diverse as possible (Day-Vines,
Day-Hairston, Carruthers, Wall, & Lupton-Smith, 1996). Preferably,
they should reflect the organizations' diversity with respect to race,
ethnicity, culture, sex, and ability levels. Oversampling from groups in

the numerical minority should be considered. It is not necessary for mediator and conflicting parties to be from the same group, and it may not always be advisable. However, individuals who do not see themselves represented in the pool of mediators are likely to conclude that the mediation services are not really intended for them and will not represent their interests well. Organizational members who are at risk or handicapped are often omitted from activities and leadership positions in organizations; every effort should be made to include them as mediators and participants.

Coleman and Deutsch (1998) have made a series of recommendations for an ideal conflict resolution program, based on interviews with mediators of interethnic disputes. Mediation should only occur if all the parties voluntarily agree (see also Carter, 1999). In addition, Coleman and Deutsch (1998) believe that the earlier in the dispute the resolution can begin, the better. The mediator and the procedures must be credible. If the conflict involves groups, a team of mediators, one from each of the disputing parties, is ideal. Peer mediators typically have high credibility. If hostility is high and widespread, premeetings with each group to clarify issues and options can be helpful.

In the last section, we will focus on additional issues that must be addressed when the conflict resolution involves individuals from more than one racial or ethnic group.

Interethnic Conflict Resolution: Special Concerns

Conflicts involving race and ethnicity have some unique features that should be considered in conflict resolution programs. Racial issues often pervade conflicts, whether they are at the center of the dispute, an unacknowledged part of a specific conflict, or part of a general societal backdrop of unequal power and respect (Gadlin, 1994). Moreover, racial issues are often embedded within issues of identity. For these reasons, a conflict with racial elements cannot be completely solved, because only the specific conflict needing resolution is likely to be addressed. Broader issues of inequality, oppression, and identity will

remain. Gadlin believes that broad issues of discrimination and prejudice need to be brought into the open as they relate to specific conflicts.
When racial and ethnic issues are addressed rather than denied, they
are less destructive, and implicit racism receives less support.

McCormick (1997) and Forester and Stitzel (1989) make an interesting argument that mediators have an obligation to confront injustice. They believe that in cases in which the parties have a large power
imbalance outside the mediation setting, as occurs with racial and ethnic power imbalances, mediator impartiality can reinforce these imbalances. In such instances, they feel that the less powerful party often
receives second-class justice. These authors suggest that the interests
of the less powerful party need explicit attention because they are typically downplayed or ignored in the larger society and, thus, in the
mediation setting. They further believe that mediator neutrality is
actually just a myth, because mediators must make hundreds of decisions that affect the outcome of the mediation and, therefore, never
remain neutral. These judgments include deciding whether or not to
reintroduce or forget bits of information, or revisit issues mentioned
but not addressed, and choosing what to ask or not ask. Even small
decisions make some final options more likely and others less likely.

Mediators need a variety of skills: They need to be able to form an
effective working relationship with each of the parties; establish a
cooperative, problem-solving attitude; develop a creative group
decision-making process; and have substantive knowledge about the
issues around which the conflict revolves (Coleman & Deutsch, 1998).
For interethnic conflict, the mediator needs additional skills (Coleman
& Deutsch, 1998). These include being attuned to the misunderstandings and miscommunications caused by cultural differences, recognizing the ethnocentrism characteristic of most groups, and knowing the
stereotypes the groups hold of one another. They must also understand the importance of ethnic membership with respect to self-
identity; the symbols, persons, and events essential to each group's
definition of itself; and the prior relations between the conflicting
groups (positive and negative).

McCormick (1997) suggests that in a culturally sensitive mediation
process, attention should, in addition, be paid to the differing goals
that individuals from different groups may have for the mediation.
Mediators need to share each group's assumptions about conflict and

the appropriate manner of handling conflicts. In addition, racial, ethnic, and cultural groups may have different views regarding both conflict and ways to respond to it (T. S. Jones & Brickman, 1994). Many individualists and collectivists interact differently in intergroup negotiations (Gelfand & Realo, 1999) and other types of dilemmas (Probst, Carnevale, & Triandis, 1999). For instance, cultural differences in the expression of needs and emotions can hamper interethnic mediation. Collectivists, such as many Asian Americans, Latinos, and Native Americans, often feel it is inappropriate to state individual needs or anger directly. Individualists, such as many European Americans, are socialized to state their needs directly and express felt emotion. Furthermore, Black communication styles are often more emotional and verbally confrontational than those of many other groups (Kochman, 1981; Labov, 1972). Because of their experience with discrimination, Blacks have reason to fear that racial discrimination may be a component of any conflict and question the motives of Whites in any dispute with them (M. N. Davidson & Greenhalgh, 1999; Friedman & Davidson, 1999).

At the same time, individuals should be considered just that, not representatives of their racial, ethnic, or cultural groups. Reliance on group stereotypes in negotiations may lead to inferences about the opposing party's ideas and behaviors that are overgeneralized and undermine the possibility of negotiation success (Craver, 1997; Berg-Cross & Zoppetti, 1991). Thus, mediators and conflicting parties should be aware of the norms of each disputing party but should be flexible enough to treat one another as individuals who might not personally conform to the norms of their group. At times, the issue of negative stereotyping of groups may need to be addressed directly to mitigate the effects of these beliefs (Craver, 1997).

It is possible that the standard neutral, third-party mediation model is not productive for all groups. For example, La Resche (1992) suggests that this type of mediation is not appropriate for traditional Korean Americans, who feel that conflict reflects shame and an inability to maintain positive relationships with others. A type of mediation takes place in the Korean American community, but it occurs through a respected intermediary who has an ongoing relationship with the individuals involved. In this circumstance, standard mediation by an outsider would be considered embarrassing and culturally inappropriate.

La Resche believes that conflict resolution centers should provide culturally acceptable alternatives to mediation, based on the cultural backgrounds of the individuals who seek help from them. For example, a culturally appropriate mediation model for Native people in Canada has been designed for individuals in urban areas who do not have access to traditional Native dispute resolution forums (Schoene & DuPraw, 1994). This model uses the Native people's medicine wheel to orient conflicting parties visually and spiritually to the mediation process and provide structure to discussions.

Even with culturally sensitive techniques, problems associated with paying special attention to the views of the less powerful groups, trying to bring unvoiced issues of race and discrimination into the conflict situation, and the consequences of institutional racism remain. Trying to level the playing field for disputants in conflict resolution settings affects only those particular outcomes. Disputants must return to their positions in a society stratified by race, sex, and class and to the conditions of unequal privilege and power that will continue to create other intergroup conflicts. The ultimate solution must be to rectify institutional racism and discrimination.

Summary

Formal conflict resolution programs are used to settle a wide variety of disputes. They are designed to resolve conflicts in a respectful, positive way. While the improvement of intergroup relations has not typically been a central goal of these programs, racial issues often pervade these conflicts. Community conflict resolution techniques include mediation, third-party consultation, town meetings, and conflict containment. Organizational conflict resolution programs include mediation, positive bargaining, and third-party consultation. Peer mediation is by far the most common form of school based conflict resolution programs.

Little research has been conducted on negotiations in actual community or business settings. The negotiation literature, mostly composed of laboratory studies, finds many benefits of positive negotiation. The literature on the effects of third-party consultation, town halls, and conflict containment is largely based on case studies and anecdotal evidence that reports benefits of the techniques. The existing literature on school-based peer mediation programs shows that these programs are typically effective in teaching students integrative negotiation and mediation procedures and that trained students tend to use them to reach constructive solutions to conflict. Overall, the data are sparse and largely descriptive. More research is needed on the specific effects of these programs and their causes.

These conflict resolution techniques may be successful because they increase interdependence, create conditions for positive interaction, increase participants' sense of empowerment, observe the norm of reciprocity, create empathy, and increase rewards received from others.

Successful conflict resolution programs should be voluntary, intervene early in the dispute, and have institutional support. In interethnic conflict resolution, broad issues of prejudice and discrimination need to be addressed, and every effort should be made to redress power imbalances. These programs must be sensitive to cultural differences regarding the meaning of conflict, the appropriate way to deal with conflict, the goals of the parties, and the expression of needs and emotions.

MORAL AND VALUES
EDUCATION PROGRAMS 9

L IKE THE CONFLICT RESOLUTION techniques described in the previous chapter, moral and values education programs are rarely designed specifically to improve intergroup relations. However, many of them have the potential to create positive changes in intergroup attitudes and behaviors. Most of these programs were designed to improve the level of moral functioning of young people so that they will think and act in accordance with principles of understanding, justice, and caring for others. Moral education programs are relevant to intergroup relations because these principles are incompatible with prejudice and intolerance. Significantly, higher levels of moral development are associated with lower levels of racial prejudice. For instance, F. H. Davidson and M. M. Davidson (1994) report data from fifth graders showing an inverse correlation between moral stage and racial prejudice. A longitudinal study following some of these fifth graders through high school found the same negative correlation between moral stage and prejudice in repeated tests in junior high school and high school (F. H. Davidson & M. M. Davidson, 1994). Higher levels of moral development are also associated with greater acceptance of outgroups (Battistich, Solomon, Kim, Watson, & Schaps, 1995).

The originators of most of the programs that we describe state that moral and values education programs should not indoctrinate, or specify the values that should be adopted (Power, Higgins, & Kohlberg, 1989; Purpel & Ryan, 1976; Simon, 1976). From their perspective, moral thought is possible only through learning basic intellectual skills, such as analysis, critical thinking, and reflection, which allow for independent, informed judgments. Another belief underlying many of these programs is that moral development and improved intergroup relations are facilitated by a moral, caring environment that reinforces the educational material.

Virtually all moral and values education programs take place in the schools. The programs are most commonly designed for elementary school students, but some focus on middle school and high school students. In Figure 1.1, we listed moral and values education programs as interactive-indirect programs. They are interactive because all these programs involve active student involvement. They are indirect because, as previously stated, most programs are designed to increase students' level of moral development rather than to improve intergroup relations.

Many moral and values education training programs use Kohlberg's stages of moral development as a theoretical foundation. Kohlberg (1969a, 1969b, 1984) postulated the existence of a sequence of six invariant, cross-culturally universal stages of moral development. They start with two preconventional stages (1 and 2), in which individuals infer morality on the basis of rewards and punishments. These stages are followed by two conventional stages (3 and 4), in which individuals assume that morality consists of conformity to social norms. In the two postconventional stages (5 and 6), individuals transcend particular systems of social norms and use universal principles of morality as standards. These stages are measured through the reasoning that people use in the answers they give to situations involving moral dilemmas (e.g., "Should a man steal a drug he can't afford to buy in order to save his wife's life?").

Kohlberg wished to increase levels of moral development without the use of moral indoctrination. To promote moral development, Kohlberg and his colleagues measured students' levels of moral development, presented students with moral dilemmas, and then introduced them to moral arguments one stage above the reasoning level of the students. Dozens of studies have demonstrated the effectiveness of this technique (Leming, 1981; Lockwood, 1978; Schlaefli, Rest, & Thoma, 1985). In one study, 64% of sixth graders advanced one full level after a 12-week intervention program consisting of discussions of moral dilemmas (Blatt & Kohlberg, 1975). These moral development interventions are more effective for older students. Short-term interventions are ineffective.

Kohlberg's stages have been criticized as pertaining only to the moral reasoning of males and for using a scoring system based on Western individualistic values (Gilligan, 1982; Shweder & Bourne, 1982). However, many moral development studies in non-Western, collectivist cultures (e.g., India, Korea) have supported Kohlberg's stage model (for a review of these studies, see Puka, 1994b). Partly in response to Gilligan's criticisms, Kohlberg changed his scoring schema in the mid-1980s so that caring orientations, said to be characteristic of women, were not scored lower than justice and equity orientations (Reed, 1997; for a review of this issue, see Puka, 1994a).

Next, we review nine approaches to moral and values education. We examine the available literature on these training programs' effectiveness in increasing level of moral development and improving intergroup relations. After this initial review of the programs, we discuss the psychological processes that might underlie these programs' ability to reduce prejudice and improve intergroup relations. These include cognitive processes of both an active and passive nature (Figure 2.3), such as implementing conditions for positive contact, changing attitudes and subjective norms, modeling and reinforcing positive behaviors, and counteracting expectancies. Finally, we critique the discipline of moral and values education and speculate about the characteristics of programs that would best improve intergroup relations.

Major Approaches to Moral and Values Education

We discuss nine approaches to moral and values education, all of which are interactive (Figure 2.3). Some of these programs are direct, but most are indirect. Moral and values education techniques vary on a number of dimensions including their primary goal, whether or not change in the whole community is attempted, and whether or not the approach includes values indoctrination. These program dimensions are listed in Table 9.1.

TABLE 9.1   Dimensions of Moral and Values Education Programs

Program	Primary Goal	Whole Community Change Attempted	Values Indoctrination
Caring communities	Intergroup relations	Yes	No
Facing History and Ourselves	Intergroup relations	No	No
Just Communities	Moral development	Yes	No
Berkeley model	Various prosocial behaviors	Yes	No
Moral discourse	Moral development	No	No
Personality development	Psychological development	No	No
Interpersonal sensitivity/ respect	Consideration for others	No	No
Values clarification	Value awareness	Sometimes	No
Character education	Instill values	No	Yes

We begin with the programs that are unusual in being direct, or are specifically designed to improve intergroup relations. These are the caring model and the Facing History and Ourselves curriculum. Then, we review the indirect programs, those designed to raise levels of moral reasoning. These include the Just Community approach based on Kohlberg's states of moral development and two programs strongly influenced by aspects of Kohlberg's work, the Berkeley model and moral discourse. Last, we consider other popular moral and values education programs that may have the potential to improve intergroup relations: those based on personality development, interpersonal sensitivity and respect, values clarification and education, and norm transmission or character education.

Caring Models of Antiprejudice

The idea of caring forms the basis of a series of programs that are specifically designed to reduce prejudice in the schools. They stem from the notion that antiprejudice and moral development programs can only be effective if the entire school atmosphere is one in which a caring and welcoming atmosphere for minority children exists. A system of overt caring experienced by and for every member of the academic community—teachers, aides, students, parents, janitors, secretaries, and administrators—is considered to be a requisite for increased moral development and decreased prejudice (F. H. Davidson & Davidson, 1994).

Educators create a caring environment through an antiprejudice curriculum, a school atmosphere based on concern and empathy, explicit moral education, and smaller school size. Caring is thought to be enhanced by a school's diversity. The caring model is based on the idea that warmth, fairness, and respect for all are as important in reaching the ultimate goal of decreasing prejudice as is specific moral learning.

Educators who use the caring approach tailor their antiprejudice treatments to the stage of moral development of the children. They assume that children will start school life with prejudice because they do not yet have the cognitive maturity to reason about and value respect for others. For those children, the focus is on positive social values and skills. Children at moral stage one are led to focus on pride in success, politeness, observing, caring, obeying, and contributing to those in need. For children at stage two, the emphasis is on learning to negotiate, broadening their other social skills and friendships, and recognizing similarity as well as diversity among others. Children at stage three learn about social stratification and human oppression, and they focus on rewarding caring acts in their educational community. Children at stage four are drawn into local human rights actions, and they study racism and classism.

The Comer schools, which implement the School Development Program, provide an example of a caring program in elementary schools (F. H. Davidson & Davidson, 1994). This program is centered on caring for the needs of the parents and children so that the children come to school ready and able to learn. The school provides a circle of support for families, to narrow the social and cultural gap between school and home. Parents must attend orientations before the school year begins, and teachers work to get all parents engaged in the school. In addition to the parents' program, a governance team consisting of representatives from the administration, teachers, parents, support staff, and students—and a mental health team—try to promote a positive, calm environment. The school climate is based on three principles: consensus, collaboration, and avoiding faultfinding. No verbal or physical fighting is allowed, and discipline is carried out in a positive, nonpunitive manner. Over 100 elementary schools have adopted the Comer program, and it is also used in some middle schools and high schools.

F. H. Davidson and M. M. Davidson (1994) argue that as children approach adolescence, different caring techniques are needed to foster moral growth and overcome prejudice. Shoreham–Wading River Middle School in Long Island, which employs small groups and an advising system, provides an example of a caring model for middle school students. The advising system is designed to give each child a close, caring relationship with an adult other than a parent. Each teacher has 10 advisees. The advising group starts the day together, eats lunch together every day, and goes on field trips together, among many other joint activities. Once a month, each student meets individually with the advisor. The school is divided into academic teams consisting of students from all three grades. Academic competition is discouraged, and students are taught through team teaching and cooperative learning techniques. The schools attempt to teach tolerance and respect through race and cultural awareness programs, as well as through the entire school system, which requires students to work together.

The Coalition of Essential Schools has caring programs appropriate for high school students' levels of cognitive development. One member school is Central Park East Secondary School in Spanish East Harlem, which emphasizes community service. Students are not allowed to fail; they may take incompletes and redo assignments as many times as they wish. Tenth- through 12th-grade students participate in a program consisting of internships in a career field, college classes, portfolios, and a major project. These schools also insist that parents take an active role in their children's educations. Because their student body is among the most disadvantaged in the United States, college attendance is stressed from the first day in school. Their high school graduation rate is in the high 90 percentiles as compared to the 50% graduation rate of other New York City public schools. Over 100 schools have adopted this system of education.

Retention, absenteeism, discipline, and self-esteem data show that caring communities have positive effects on students, and caring behaviors have been linked with higher stages of moral development (F. H. Davidson & Davidson, 1994). However, we know of no measures of level of moral development or racial attitudes or behaviors in the caring model. Although these programs seem likely to improve inter-group relations if the entire school atmosphere is the antithesis of prejudice and discrimination, direct measures are needed to document the effects these programs have on intergroup relations.

Facing History and Ourselves

Facing History and Ourselves is a multidisciplinary moral education program that employs a one-semester history course about Nazi Germany before and during World War II to help adolescents reflect critically on contemporary moral issues (Fine, 1993, 1995). Facing History and Ourselves was begun in 1976, and by the early 1990s, it was reaching about 500,000 students per year. The curriculum focuses on the Nazi rise to power and the Holocaust, and it takes students back and forth between this historical case study and reflection on the causes and consequences of present-day prejudice, intolerance, violence, and racism. That is, it moves between facing history and facing ourselves. The goals of the program are to foster perspective taking, critical thinking, and moral decision making among adolescent students. The program attempts to accomplish these goals by pointing out connections between anti-Semitism and contemporary racism, showing how easily one can become an oppressor, and helping students to recognize tendencies toward prejudice in themselves.

In the first week of the program, the class readings focus on universal value and identity questions, and students are asked to think about how values are formed, what social factors influence their beliefs, and how social conditions enable or constrain acting on their beliefs (Fine, 1991/1992, 1993, 1995). The class reads about the conflicting demands of loyalty, obedience, and social responsibility, and the competing desires both to fit in and to be unique.

Several weeks into the curriculum, students read about religious differences and discrimination based on religious beliefs and anti-Semitism. In the next-to-last week, they cover the period from the end

of World War II to the present. In one activity, the class sees a documentary film about an anti-Semitic teacher in Canada who taught students that the Holocaust was a hoax and that there is an international
Jewish conspiracy. The class then talks about the resulting beliefs of his
students. Next, the class studies Jewish history after World War II, discusses the creation and future of Israel, and analyzes other contemporary political conflicts. Later, they see a documentary about the Ku
Klux Klan, and talk about why democracies favor free speech.

Fine (1991/1992, 1993, 1995) has qualitatively documented the students' increased abilities to reflect critically on their own beliefs and
behaviors and on their responsibilities toward one another as a result
of the Facing History and Ourselves program. She notes that the
students make uneven and partial movements toward ideals in this
domain. However, she believes that the program provides an important step toward prejudice reduction through critical thinking. Fine
also writes that the program is very teacher and context dependent; its
success "is necessarily contingent on making changes in everything
around it" (Fine, 1991/1992, p. 49).

Schultz, Barr, and Selman (in press) found that eighth-grade students who participated in Facing History and Ourselves had significantly lower scores on the modern racism scale, as measured by
greater pretest to posttest differences, relative to the scores of students
in a control condition, who did not participate in Facing History and
Ourselves but whose teachers included issues of intergroup relations, prejudice, and racism in their teaching. These authors found no
significant increase of the Facing History and Ourselves students'
scores on a test of moral development, relative to students in the control condition.

Bardige (1981) assessed the journals kept by two classes of eighth-
grade students as they studied Facing History and Ourselves. She categorized the writings into 1 of 3 stages of moral development. Bardige
found that throughout the course, most entries remained of the
middle-interpretative type, in which students attempted to understand the intentions, motives, and thinking of the individuals studied.
However, Lieberman (1981) assessed complexity of moral reasoning
through an open-ended moral interview and found significant increases in complexity and level of moral reasoning relative to students
who were not studying the curriculum.

Kohlberg's Just Community Concept

A variety of events caused Kohlberg to believe that sustained increases in moral reasoning required a *moral atmosphere* (Power et al., 1989). The first was the use of moral dilemma interventions in a prison population, where he found that the prison environment did not support higher levels of moral reasoning. Another event was Kohlberg's discovery that one year after a successful moral development intervention, teachers had not continued the program on their own. A kibbutz visit in Israel also helped shape Kohlberg's ideas by showing him the importance of an environment that modeled the desired values and behaviors in all domains of everyday life.

These experiences led Kohlberg to try to turn school settings into moral communities. He believed that part of the hidden curriculum of traditional schools was teaching children to deal with authority and power. Kohlberg wanted to change this hidden curriculum to a "curriculum of justice." He attempted to do so through the creation of an educational democracy (which he labeled *a just community*) in which everyone has an equal voice in making rules and in which the validity of the rules is judged by their fairness to all interested parties. He believed that a school community based on these standards would increase the levels of moral development of those involved.

The Just Community approach was begun with three pilot school projects that had the following characteristics: (a) The school was governed by direct democracy; (b) weekly community meetings were held with each teacher and student member having one vote; (c) standing committees of students, teachers, and parents held minicommunity meetings to generate issues to be taken up in the community meetings; and (d) a social contract defined the rights and responsibilities of all members, with students and teachers having the same basic rights. In these schools, moral development training took place through open discussions focused on fairness and morality as well as through cognitive conflict stimulated by exposure to different points of view and higher-order reasoning. It was aided by participation in rule making, the exercise of power and responsibilities, and the development of a sense of community.

Cluster School in Cambridge was one of the pilot schools. Its program was based on the principles of open discussion, cognitive conflict, participatory democracy, and the development of a community governed by high moral reasoning. The two other pilot schools were Scarsdale Alternative High School (A School) in Westchester County, New York, and School-Within-a-School (SWS) in Brookline, Massachusetts, which had a greater emphasis on school democracy and less focus on moral development than the other two schools.

Several studies have shown that the Just Community approach can increase the level of moral development (Power et al., 1989). Moral development data were collected after 4 years at Cluster and SWS and after two years at A School. In all three schools, moral judgment scores were significantly higher at the end of this period for students in the program than for students in the traditional programs at these schools, and the students rated their schools higher in "moral culture." By the end of the first year, significant changes in the average level of moral development were found in Cluster and A Schools. By the third year, the average level of moral development was stage 3-4 in Cluster School. The school emphasizing democracy over moral development, SWS, showed no significant increases in the level of moral development across the 4-year period. Ethnographic data and transcripts of community meetings were also collected during Cluster School's first 4 years. They were analyzed to determine the moral level of the norms that developed at the school. Both types of data show that over the course of the 4 years, the average moral level of norms progressed from stage 2-3 to stage 4.

The Just Community approach has also been implemented in Germany (Oser, 1992c, 1992d), where Lind and Althof (1992) showed that in three Just Community schools, the level of moral development doubled, compared to natural increases in same-age students measured in another study. As mentioned early in our discussion, high levels of moral development have been linked with low levels of prejudice (F. H. Davidson & Davidson, 1994) and acceptance of outgroups (Battistich et al., 1995). Unfortunately, no direct measures of the effects of the Just Community on intergroup relations have been conducted.

The Just Community approach has been criticized for being time-consuming and complex and requiring a commitment to cognitive moral development as a primary goal of the schools (Hersh, Miller, &

Fielding, 1980). Many teachers find it difficult to wait months or years to see improvements in moral development, and they find such improvements difficult to assess. Also, both teachers and students have expressed some discomfort with a process that involves consistently inducing conflict through the presentation of opposing points of view.

The Berkeley Model

Like the Just Community approach, the Berkeley model is a program designed to promote the school as a community in which a climate of mutual respect and concern for others prevails (Battistich et al., 1995; Battistich, Solomon, Watson, Solomon, & Schaps, 1989; Solomon, Watson, Delucchi, Schaps, & Battistich, 1988). In the Berkeley model, this sense of community in the school setting is used to enhance children's cognitive problem-solving skills. These enhanced skills are designed to produce a number of prosocial behaviors, many of which are relevant to improved intergroup relations. For instance, one major goal of the training is for students to develop the ability to consider a problem situation from the other person's perspective as well as their own and arrive at a mutually acceptable solution.

The Berkeley program consists of five components, the first of which is a literature-based reading and language arts program centered on works that are intended to evoke empathy, interpersonal understanding, and a consideration of ethical issues. The program also includes a collaborative approach to learning and a classroom management and discipline system that attempts to optimize student autonomy and self-determination. The final components of the Berkeley model are active parental involvement and inclusive, noncompetitive, schoolwide activities. Teachers are trained in the implementation of the program through a combination of curriculum materials, workshops, and coaching.

An example of this type of program is provided by three elementary schools serving middle- to upper-middle-class students from a suburban California community (Battistich et al., 1989). Students in kindergarten through fourth grade participated in a longitudinal study of the effects of the program. Cooperative approaches to academic and nonacademic tasks were among the elements stressed in these particular classes. The students were encouraged to strive for fairness, consideration of others, and social responsibility. They were also provided with training to help them apply these values and skills in their social relations. A developmental discipline approach that promotes a culture of caring was also employed. Finally, students were encouraged to engage in helping activities.

In the study most relevant to intergroup relations, feeling a sense of community in the school setting was found to be associated with a variety of positive intrapersonal and interpersonal consequences including acceptance of outgroups (Battistich et al., 1995). Other evaluations of this program have shown that participants had significantly greater cognitive problem-solving skills (e.g., interpersonal sensitivity; consideration of others' needs; and use of prosocial, conflict resolution strategies) than nonparticipating students (Battistich et al., 1989). In another study, 12 elementary school classes participating in the program for 5 consecutive years were compared with 12 classes that did not participate. Significant differences in favor of program participants were found on measures of cooperative activities, activities promoting social understanding, and other prosocial behaviors (Solomon et al., 1988). Thus, indirect evidence suggests that the Berkeley model could reduce prejudice, but no direct measures of intergroup relations have been published.

Moral Discourse

The moral discourse technique is based on the belief that teaching moral discourse within the school context will raise students' levels of moral thought (Oser, 1985, 1992a). Moral discourse consists of interactive discussions about problems of justice. From the perspective of moral discourse educators, moral discourse is the common denominator of all moral learning. In their view, if moral discourse does not occur, moral development cannot take place.

The moral discourse approach begins with the presentation of a moral conflict generated from curriculum materials or classroom activities. The conflict is between two moral principles or between egoism and altruism. The teacher creates a roundtable discussion in which all people concerned with the issue are invited to participate. The discussions of needs, blame, solutions, and justifications are coordinated so that all participants listen to one another and together search for the best solutions. The discourse is intended to stimulate higher levels of moral judgments.

The teacher is the chair of the discussion and is also an engaged participant. An attempt is made to present every available argument, with the criterion for the final decision being rationality. The teacher expects every student to collaborate in an effort to construct a just solution, one that considers and balances the three moral dimensions of truthfulness, care, and justice. It is hoped that all class members will participate equally, and all are presumed to be equal. The method is based on the belief that moral judgments cannot be imposed by others but must be constructed by individuals themselves. For this reason, teachers try to avoid indoctrination.

One example of classroom-generated discourse is provided by a class of 9-year-olds in which a child with cerebral paralysis was the target of ridicule by class members (Oser, 1985). One day when the child was absent, the teacher asked the students to talk about a "serious problem" in the class. She told them about the disease and showed concern for the absent student's feelings when ridiculed, but she expressed no anger toward the students. A discussion ensued to which almost everyone contributed. No explicit formal decision resulted, but the children treated the student with cerebral paralysis differently when he returned.

Oser (1992b) believes that the discourse model both increases levels of moral development and reduces intergroup prejudice. He feels that putting moral discourse into practice is itself a form of overcoming prejudice. In one study of the moral discourse approach, groups of high school students discussed moral problems under one of three sets of directions: consider the consequences, intentions, and effects of the situation (stimulation of cognitive complexity instructions); use a set of rules of justice (moral discourse instructions); or employ guidelines as to how to conduct an orderly discussion (Oser, 1984). Only the use of a set of rules of justice significantly increased the average level of moral discussion. To our knowledge, no research documents the effects of the discourse approach on intergroup relations.

Personality Development Programs

The personality development approach is designed to stimulate personal psychological development in adolescents through classroom learning, experiential activities, and self-reflection (Mosher & Sprinthall, 1970; Mosher & Sullivan, 1976; Schlaefli et al., 1985). These programs attempt to promote personality and social development in general, with moral development as a major goal. A variety of activities (e.g., empathy training, children teaching younger children, communication skills training, cooperative simulation games, volunteer work) is combined with readings and classroom discussions of developmental psychology, such as Kohlberg's theory of moral development.

The personality development technique stems from the belief that adolescents have many difficulties in personal development, such as perceiving themselves and others accurately and with understanding and respect (Mosher & Sprinthall, 1970). In fact, because schools perpetuate or exacerbate social and educational differences among students and generate negative expectations for many categories of students (e.g., ethnic minorities), some of these difficulties appear to be induced by the schools.

In one personality development program, high school juniors and seniors take a course in individual and human development (Mosher & Sprinthall, 1970). The students study psychological principles of development and read literature relevant to this topic. All take part in an extensive set of laboratory activities. Each of the activities is directed toward learning tolerance, sympathy, and empathy, with the ultimate goal being self-acceptance and acceptance of others. In another personality development curriculum, high school students introduce themselves in detail, discuss and analyze moral dilemmas, learn counseling skills, and tutor younger students (Mosher & Sullivan, 1976).

A meta-analysis of research findings showed that personality development programs produced significant increases in levels of moral judgment compared with groups studying the humanities, social sciences, literature, and contemporary issues and with short-term interventions (e [experimental − control] = .25, −.7, and −.20, respectively) (Schlaefli et al., 1985). However, the meta-analysis showed moral dilemma interventions produced stronger effects on moral development than the personality development programs (*e* [experimental – control] = .32). Personality development training was more powerful with older students. Short-term treatments were ineffective. We know of no direct measures of prejudice reduction stemming from personality development programs.

Interpersonal Sensitivity and Respect Programs

McPhail and his colleagues have created a British moral education curriculum that focuses on interpersonal sensitivity and respect (McPhail, Ungoed-Thomas, & Chapman, 1972). The premise of this approach is that the schools have a responsibility to help students learn how to care for themselves and others, make positive choices, and display consideration for others. It uses two sets of curriculum materials, *Startline* (McPhail, Middleton, & Ingram, 1978) and *Lifeline* (McPhail et al., 1972). *Startline* is a program for children ages 8-13 that uses specific curriculum materials to help children learn to develop social skills, consider others' needs, and make positive social decisions (McPhail et al., 1978).

Lifeline is used with junior high school and high school students and employs discussions and role-playing (McPhail et al., 1972). It consists of three programs: "In Other People's Shoes," "Proving the Rule?" and "What Would You Have Done?"

"In Other People's Shoes" has three themes. The first theme is sensitivity, and it is designed to improve students' abilities to recognize their own and others' needs and feelings. The second theme, consequences, emphasizes improving one's ability to predict the consequences of one's actions. The third theme, points of view, focuses on learning to choose what to do in conflict situations after considering the needs of all persons involved. "Proving the Rule?" is interpersonally oriented and is designed to provide opportunities to work out solutions to common problems in social situations. The situations used concern conflicting social expectations, personal desire versus societal expectations, group membership, authority, and tradition. "What Would You Have Done?" encourages understanding of moral problems in a wider context. Students read about incidents in other cultures that are designed to allow students to consider the effect of cultural, social, and economic conditions on people's behaviors. The creators of the program believe that race relations are a significant part of moral education, and they have included race relations themes throughout their materials.

The interpersonal sensitivity and respect programs have been criticized for their lack of a clear theoretical base that would help guide teachers and direct the curriculum (Hersh et al., 1980). They have also been criticized for being more concerned with conventional moral responses than with autonomous higher-level thinking (Hersh et al., 1980). We have found no evaluations of this program, either of its efficacy in promoting moral behavior and thought or in promoting positive intergroup relations.

Values Clarification and Education Programs

Values clarification is designed to help students to become aware of their own values. A central concern of this approach is the personal and social consequences of one's values and their ongoing development. Values clarification experts perceive that young people today have many more choices available to them than did previous generations, and the conflict among these choices leads to bewilderment and confusion. They believe that values cannot be imposed on students, because every individual has a different set of values (Simon, Howe, & Kirschenbaum, 1972). Instead, they believe individuals must be helped to identify their own values. In this approach, all coherent sets of values are treated with equal respect.

According to Kirschenbaum (1977), several subprocesses are associated with values clarification. First, students must learn that one can make value choices from among various alternatives. Then, students must learn to thoughtfully consider the consequences of these alternatives so that they can freely choose their own values. Once they have chosen these values, students must learn to prize and cherish them, publicly affirm them, and act repeatedly and consistently on the basis of them. Values clarification approaches use questions and activities to help students move through these processes (Simon et al., 1972). The teachers share their own values but try not to impose them on the students. Many of the topics discussed do not concern moral values but, rather, preferences regarding lifestyles and personal interests.

In one approach, students are asked a question that helps them understand and define their values (Kirschenbaum, 1977). They may also participate in an interview in which the teacher publicly asks a series of questions or engages them in activities designed to assist them in exploring and clarifying a decision or choice that they must make. Students always have the right not to answer a question or to end the interview. Students learn the values clarification subprocesses (e.g., learning to make choices from among alternatives) and apply them to areas of confusion or conflict in their lives. The students learn traditional academic subjects at the same time that they learn the values clarification process, with the hope that they will relate the subject matter to their own values development. One of the activities commonly employed is values voting, in which students answer a set of questions to provide a public statement of their values and then discuss the values in groups. Next, the group members rank order answers to the questions and debate these ranks (Simon et al., 1972).

The values clarification approach has been criticized because it accepts whatever values emerge (Licona, 1991; Lockwood, 1976; Stewart, 1976). Thus, any set of values is seen as being as valid as any other set, and students could even come to agree on immoral beliefs (e.g., students could decide it is acceptable to discriminate against others). It has also been condemned for accepting conflicting values and not using the existence of conflict to search for moral consensus or promote moral universals. Outlawing discussion aimed at moral consensus is a constraint imposed in this technique in order to limit value conflict between students and their teachers and among students during the clarification process (Hersh et al., 1980). Thus, important issues of value conflict and moral justification cannot be discussed, and the values that remain to be discussed tend to be nonmoral, personal values. From the perspective of some critics, it is simultaneously morally relativistic and judgmental (Stewart, 1976). Another concern is that due to the power disparity between students and teachers, teachers' sharing of their own values with students may seem to be an imposition of values on the students. In addition, values clarification has been faulted for being superficial (Stewart, 1976).

Reviews of the values clarification literature show that claims of self-esteem, personal adjustment, and intergroup relations benefits have not been substantiated by the research (Leming, 1981; Lockwood,

1978). In one review of 21 studies, no significant differences were found in self-concept, self-actualization, thinking processes, or dogmatism as a result of participation in values clarification programs (Leming, 1981). Three unpublished studies claim improved classroom behaviors as a result of values clarification programs, but two are based on teachers' perceptions rather than on measurements of students' behaviors, and one is based only on behaviors observed during structured values clarification exercises. For this reason, a reviewer of these studies suggests that any claim of improved interpersonal relations in the classroom is unwarranted (Lockwood, 1978). We know of no data on prejudice reduction as an outcome of values clarification programs.

Some values education approaches do specifically promote the values of tolerance and interpersonal understanding. A popular Canadian technique, the values reflective approach, uses a set of workbooks to help students refine and assess their values in the light of fundamental human values (Beck, Boyd, & Sullivan, 1978; Beck, Hersh, & Sullivan, 1978). Banks's values inquiry model specifies a 9-step process in which students start by recognizing value problems, move through examining conflicting values and hypothesizing about the possible consequences of different values, and finally justifying these values morally (Banks & Banks, 1999). The intent is for students to recognize and select values that can be morally justified in terms of the principles of equality, justice, and human dignity. Additional units instruct students in decision making and citizen action, to help guide them in implementing their values. This process takes place in social science classrooms from elementary school through high school. Because both of these programs were designed to promote the selection and use of values consistent with basic moral principles, they seem more likely to improve intergroup relations than other values clarification approaches, but we know of no assessments of these programs.

Norm Transmission and Character Education Programs

Among the moral and values education programs, the norm transmission and character education programs alone attempt to impart a particular set of values. Dozens of these programs exist. They were initiated because numerous educators believe that many students do not receive effective socialization into the moral values of their society and that the schools provide a place in which lack of positive socialization can be remedied.

Many of the character education programs do not have improved intergroup relations as a goal and do not support multicultural education and understanding. For example, in M. Holmes's (1980) conceptual rationale for norm transmission and character education programs, multiculturalism is viewed as a form of "moral anarchy." Holmes believes in teaching the basic culture to which the vast majority of individuals within a society adhere. He feels that the educational system should work to preserve and enhance the fundamental values and the "most worthy" elements of a culture, and he states that schools should be deliberately used to produce outcomes consistent with the ideals of the larger society. Holmes writes in the context of Canadian society, but his ideas have been widely applied in the United States as well.

However, in one popular U.S. approach to character education, Licona (1991) argues that the public schools should teach such values as respect and responsibility but should also include many other prosocial elements. Some of these elements have the possibility of improving intergroup relations. For example, Licona urges that a democratic classroom environment be created in which students share in rule making, cooperative learning, and encouraging moral reflection. He also suggests that character education include teacher modeling of the values to be transmitted, the creation of a moral community in the classroom, and moral discipline.

Licona believes that a moral community can be created through such factors as fostering the process of getting to know and value other students and developing group cohesion. Moral discipline is enacted through the process of teachers and students together making classroom rules, and using enforcement of the rules to teach them, as in using nonpunitive questioning methods about why the rule is important. The class meeting is the major vehicle for the creation of a democratic classroom environment. In these regularly scheduled meetings, all teachers and students are invited to participate in the discussions. The topics include good-news meetings, compliment time, rule setting, feedback, discussion of moral ideas, problem solving, and expanding students' roles in decision making.

Licona argues that values can be taught through the addition of curriculum materials (e.g., teaching concern for animal rights) and also by the way the regular curriculum material is taught (e.g., teaching ethical values in American history, for example, by teaching justice through the study of the treatment of Native Americans, and of Blacks during slavery). In addition, moral reflection can be encouraged through discussions of Kohlberg's moral dilemmas and school problems. Licona suggests using a structured, rational, decision-making format to foster increased levels of moral reasoning. He also advocates the use of role-playing and the teaching of conflict resolution skills.

Character education programs are very popular. We have found no research data, however, on their ability to increase moral behaviors or positive intergroup relations. Licona's technique appears to show potential for improving intergroup relations, but many other character education programs appear to discourage intergroup understanding and appreciation.

We now turn to the evidence regarding the effects of moral and values development programs. Then, we discuss the psychological processes that might underlie positive intergroup or moral development results. Last, we critique the techniques for moral and values education and explore the conditions under which these programs would be most likely to improve intergroup relations.

Summary of Research Findings on Moral and Values Education

As we have seen, Facing History and Ourselves has shown decreased racism scores as a result of the program. The Berkeley program has also been found to increase sense of community, which has been associated with acceptance of outgroups. In addition, schools promoting caring behaviors, Facing History and Ourselves, the Just Community approach, the Berkeley program, moral discourse, and personality development programs have been shown in one or more studies to increase the level of moral reasoning. The empirical data have not shown support for benefits of values clarification programs. We have found no evaluations of interpersonal sensitivity and respect or norm transmission and character education programs.

Thus, most of the evidence suggesting that some moral and values education programs improve intergroup relations is indirect. More evidence shows increased levels of moral development as a result of these programs, but little enough of this type of data exists. In addition, the data on increased moral development rely too heavily on indirect evidence of moral development. Until more quantitative and qualitative studies of the intergroup relations aspects of most of these programs are published, we cannot conclude that they lead to improvements. In particular, programs that discourage multicultural understanding may, in fact, increase prejudice and discrimination.

Some moral education researchers themselves believe that the technique has yielded much advocacy for aims and methods of moral education but very little hard evidence regarding their merits (Emler, 1996; Mosher, 1980). Emler (1996) argues that in order to justify their time, effort, and expense, moral education programs should have a continued effect on moral conduct, but observes that "a clear causal link from moral reasoning to conduct . . . still awaits convincing demonstration" (p. 125). Emler (1996) also presents methodological concerns regarding the research data. He argues that researchers must pay attention to the size of the effects that moral education programs produce, not just to whether or not the programs produce statistically significant differences, and that research on moral education should measure the relative effects of differing programs. He cites a variety of measurement problems, including construct validity (the measure used does not actually assess level of moral reasoning), internal validity (alternative explanations for the research findings exist), and external validity (the research results may not generalize). Emler also notes that the reliability of some measures is low. For example, level of moral development is typically measured by the multiple-choice Defining Issues Test (DIT). However, students may be able to score high on the DIT moral dilemma items without, in fact, really understanding them (see also Schlaefli et al., 1985).

Finally, Emler (1996) argues that we must assess moral education inputs as well as moral education outcomes. He cites as an example the fact that few people are still involved in the Just Community programs because the cost of implementing them is too high for most school systems. Obviously, if moral educators advocate programs that are unlikely to be implemented, then levels of moral development will not increase because of them.

Psychological Processes Underlying Moral and Values Education

Moral and values education researchers believe their techniques produce high levels of moral reasoning, which are incompatible with prejudice and discrimination. In this section, we examine psychological processes that help explain how moral and values education training methods could promote positive intergroup relations. These include implementing conditions for positive face-to-face contact, which involve a series of passive-cognitive processes (see Figure 2.3). These training techniques may also draw on another passive-cognitive process, changing attitudes, and on subjective norms. In addition, they may employ three active-cognitive processes, modeling and reinforcing positive behaviors and counteracting expectancies.

The creation of moral communities could be successful in intergroup settings in part because they replicate the conditions under which face-to-face contact has been shown to reduce prejudice: The contact involves equal status and is cooperative and personal. It involves shared goals and is instituted by those in authority (F. H. Allport et al., 1953; W. G. Stephan, 1987). The creation of a superordinate group consisting of the entire educational community may also decrease prejudice and discrimination within the group (Gaertner et al., 1990; Gaertner, Mann, Murrell, & Dovidio, 1989). If all are members of the ingroup, then outgroup bias cannot exist (Tajfel, 1978, 1982; Tajfel & Turner, 1986). During the formation of a moral community, and through discussing group conflicts and resolving differences, numerous opportunities are provided for students to discover the underlying similarities in their values and beliefs (Byrne, 1971). Also, during these discussions, successful face-to-face interactions should lower anxiety about interacting with individuals different from oneself (C. W. Stephan, 1992; W. G. Stephan & Stephan, 1985).

In addition, in some of these programs, students engage in positive, prosocial, caring, nonprejudiced behaviors. As a result of these behaviors, negative stereotypes about outgroup members should be weakened (Brigham, 1971; W. G. Stephan & Stephan, 1996), and attitudes consistent with these nonprejudiced behaviors should be reinforced through the psychological demand for consistency among one's thoughts and values (Bodenhausen & Wyer, 1985; Stangor & McMillan, 1992). At the same time, the type of face-to-face interaction associated with this training should also lead to personalization of outgroup members. When outgroup members are viewed as individuals rather than as group members, the propensity to stereotype is further reduced (Brewer & Miller, 1984; Miller & Harrington, 1990b).

Moral education programs make much better use of the principles of social learning theory than most other techniques for improving intergroup relations (Bandura, 1982, 1986). In some of these programs, the entire community is asked to model positive, caring behaviors toward all others. Most of these programs explicitly reward a variety of prosocial behaviors and discipline students in a nonpunitive way that avoids the problems typically associated with the use of punishment.

Moral education programs are unique among techniques for improving intergroup relations in their emphasis on reason and values as guidelines for behavior. The theory of planned behavior suggests that our behavioral intentions are rationally calculated, based on attitudes, subjective norms, and perceived behavioral control (Ajzen, 1991; Fishbein & Ajzen, 1975). Moral education programs attempt to influence all these factors. Beliefs provide the basis for attitudes, and most of the moral education programs focus on acquiring positive, humanitarian beliefs. Subjective norms refer to our beliefs that important people and groups approve or disapprove of a behavior. The norms of nonprejudiced, caring behavior are openly taught and modeled in most of these programs. Finally, such programs aim to increase perceived behavioral control, helping students to believe they can choose positive over negative behaviors. Several studies have shown that moral norms have an important influence on beliefs, subjective norms, and perceived behavioral control (Gorsuch & Ortberg, 1983; Schwartz & Tessler, 1972).

Problems and Recommendations

Two moral education researchers have recently raised concerns regarding the current state of the discipline of moral education. Boyd (1996) argues that two serious deficiencies exist in moral education theory, the first of which is that the range of programs is so broad as to provide poor practical guidance to practitioners. As we have seen in this chapter, a variety of different types of moral education programs exists, and they derive from many theoretical sources. Boyd believes that moral education needs an integrated theory. He feels the discipline would benefit from a higher level of moral interaction among the practitioners themselves, with less competitiveness and more cooperation, to determine how each program contributes to a unified theoretical whole.

Boyd also believes the shared assumption that moral education should focus only on individuals and their interactions is flawed. He feels this individual level focus prevents moral education from addressing the most serious moral problems of our times, those pertaining to group relations. Boyd argues that the discipline of moral education does not acknowledge that individuals are defined and limited by their group identification or that groups are embedded in systematic power politics that individuals alone cannot change. He believes that the focus on individuals works against the recognition of structural oppression while absolving individuals when group relations issues are considered. Boyd feels that students learn that if they are not personally prejudiced, then they are exonerated. Social structures are not their fault or responsibility, so they do not need to think about helping to make structural changes. He thinks that moral education thus promotes an easy acceptance of group oppression, through its concentration on individual purity of thought. Boyd believes this view characterizes moral educators, who pass it on to their students.

Applebaum (1997) notes that moral education does not challenge Western standards and values that have been used to marginalize many people throughout the world. She feels moral educators need to acknowledge systems of domination and work to change them. Applebaum says moral educators must learn the difference between criticizing the dominance of a set of values and beliefs and criticizing the values and beliefs themselves. The values and norms of many dominant groups are generally positive and should be recognized as such. However, the imposition of those particular values and norms on all peoples is oppressive and furthers systems of inequality. She believes moral educators should teach students to recognize and work to change systems of oppression.

We believe this latter set of criticisms should be taken seriously. Currently, only some of the moral education programs include information on structural oppression. The programs designed specifically to improve intergroup relations, the caring model and Facing History and Ourselves, incorporate such learning. In addition, the remaining techniques designed to create a sense of community in the schools, the Just Community approach and the Berkeley model, also teach students about prejudice and power at the societal level as well as at the individual level, and they incorporate caring behaviors outside the immediate school setting. The remaining programs (moral discourse, personality development, interpersonal sensitivity and respect, values clarification, and norm transmission and character education) do not address structural issues.

Under what conditions is moral education most likely to improve intergroup relations? At present, little data directly link moral education programs with prejudice reduction. On the basis of the existing studies, several conclusions can be drawn regarding the types of moral education programs that are most likely to reduce prejudice (Oser, 1992a). First, educating to reduce prejudice should be theory driven. If educators do not know how and why the desired effects can be obtained, programs are unlikely to be successful. Social psychological theory can be employed to help shape prejudice reduction in the schools (see F. H. Davidson & Davidson, 1994, for an excellent resource). For example, an antiprejudice curriculum developed to deal specifically with issues of prejudice should be more effective than merely embracing cultural diversity (F. H. Davidson & Davidson, 1994). Second, moral education is likely to be most successful in settings informed by a high moral climate and in the absence of prejudice. The most successful programs are likely to be those in which a transformation of the entire educational community has been attempted. Finally, single, short-term interventions are less effective than multiple, long-term interventions.

Summary

Moral and values education programs are rarely designed to improve intergroup relations but typically are created to increase the level of moral functioning of students. Moral education programs are relevant to intergroup relations because the principles they hope to instill, such as understanding, justice, and caring for others, are incompatible with prejudice and intolerance. Kohlberg's stages of moral development provide the basis for several moral interventions.

In this chapter, nine major approaches to moral and values education were reviewed:

1. The idea of caring forms the basis of a series of programs that are specifically designed to reduce prejudice in the schools. The goal is for the entire school atmosphere to be a caring and welcoming one for minority children.

2. Facing History and Ourselves is a multidisciplinary, moral education program using a one-semester history course about Nazi Germany before and during World War II, which is designed to help adolescents reflect critically on contemporary moral issues.

3. In Kohlberg's Just Community approach, schools are governed by direct democracy, with the goal of creating a moral community.

4. The Berkeley model is also designed to promote the school as a community. The goal of this model is improved cognitive, problem-solving skills.

5. The moral discourse technique consists of an interactive discussion about problems of justice.

6. Personality development programs are designed to stimulate personal psychological development through classroom learning, experiential activities, and self-reflection.

7. Several moral education approaches focus on interpersonal sensitivity and respect.

8. Values clarification is designed to help people to become aware of their own values, develop them, and understand the personal and social consequences.

9. The norm transmission and character education approach attempts to inculcate specific values, such as respect, responsibility, honesty, tolerance, and compassion.

Facing History and Ourselves has been shown to reduce racism scores in one study. The Berkeley program has also been shown to lead to an increased sense of community, which has been associated with acceptance of outgroups. Caring behaviors, participation in Facing History and Ourselves, the Just Community and other programs based on Kohlberg's moral development stages, discussions guided by rules of justice, and personality development have been shown to increase levels of moral reasoning in one or more studies. Increased levels of moral development have been linked with reduced prejudice. Overall, data on the intergroup relations consequences of these programs are mostly indirect and almost nonexistent, and the data for increased levels of moral development as a result of these programs are scarce for most programs. The moral and values education area very much needs comparative evaluations showing the relative effectiveness of the programs in improving intergroup relations.

These programs have been criticized for their broad and incompatible range of approaches and goals and for a lack of unifying theory. The moral education programs have also been faulted for focusing on individuals and their interaction, to the exclusion of group relations and power structures in societies, although some programs contain a structural as well as an individual focus.

Moral and values education programs may have the potential to improve intergroup relations through their ability to implement conditions for positive contact, change attitudes and subjective norms, model and reinforce positive behaviors, and counteract expectancies.

It seems likely that they succeed best when based on theory and take place in a highly moral and unprejudiced climate. In addition, short-term programs are likely to be ineffective.

EVALUATING INTERGROUP RELATIONS PROGRAMS **10**

WE INCLUDE A CHAPTER on evaluation in this book on intergroup relations programs because we believe that evaluation can play an invaluable role in improving these programs. This chapter is designed primarily for practitioners, would-be practitioners, and students of intergroup relations, in the hope of demystifying the evaluation process. It will not transform readers into professional program evaluators, but it will provide a basic understanding of the range of evaluation techniques that are available and how they are used. Readers who are already well acquainted with program evaluation research techniques may still find the examples and special problems of intergroup relations programs of interest.

Throughout this book, we have stressed the need for more evaluations of programs designed to improve intergroup relations, both to establish the effects of intergroup relations programs and to understand why they occur. Evaluations make it possible to pinpoint the elements of a program that are most effective as well as to determine what aspects of the program need to be changed. When a program contains ineffective elements, leaving them in the program leads to wasting valuable time and resources. In addition, there are a host of other reasons to do evaluations. Information on the effectiveness of programs can be used to seek funding, justify expenditures, and disseminate the program more widely. As information on the effectiveness of different types of programs begins to accumulate, it becomes possible to compare programs and determine which ones are most effective in what contexts and for what populations. Furthermore, understanding why different techniques work can enable us to design better techniques in the future. Without systematic evaluations, it is impossible to make informed choices about such matters.

Fortunately, evaluating the effects of intergroup relations programs does not have to be difficult, and it does not necessarily require extensive resources, although both can be true. Outlined below are a series of different types of evaluations that range from the nonrigorous and informal to very rigorous and formal. All can be valuable.

Before presenting the various types of evaluations, we note that simply providing a thorough and detailed description of programs that are widely used makes a valuable contribution to the literature on intergroup relations programs. When writing this book, we often had a difficult time determining what exactly took place during these programs. Making such descriptions available in the literature would be invaluable to practitioners who are trying to select among different types of programs.

There are two basic approaches to evaluation research, qualitative and quantitative. Qualitative approaches consist of careful analyses of programs by participants, practitioners, or researchers who are attempting to understand what occurs during the programs, what effects the program has on participants, and why these effects occur. Quantitative approaches to program evaluation share some of the goals of qualitative approaches, but the techniques differ. Quantitative techniques rely heavily on systematic measurement instruments such as questionnaires. Those who use these techniques quantify the type and magnitude of effects produced by the programs and measure the variables thought to produce these effects. We will present qualitative techniques first and follow that with a discussion of quantitative techniques.

Qualitative Techniques

The five types of qualitative techniques we present vary in who makes observations about the program and how systematically these observations are performed.

Postprogram Surveys

One of the simplest types of evaluations of intergroup relations programs consists of asking participants to evaluate the programs after they end. Two basic questions that are often asked are, "What aspects of the program were most influential (effective)?" and "What aspects of the program were least influential (effective)?" Another commonly asked question is, "What did you learn from this program?" Participants can also be asked to discuss the impact of specific facets of the program. These are known as open-ended questions, and to be effective, they should be short, clear, and precise. They also must be suited to the age and sophistication of the participants. In general, these questions should be answered anonymously so that participants will feel comfortable providing negative as well as positive feedback. To encourage honest and open responding, it may be useful to indicate the purposes for which this information will be used (e.g., to improve the program).

In Chapter 4, we discussed a study by Adlerfer (1992) that examined a 3-day diversity training program at a large corporation. The participants were asked about their reactions after the program. Although most of them agreed that the program had helped race relations in the corporation, more Blacks than Whites thought the program was useful. Nearly 20% of the White males actually thought the program hurt race relations in the corporation. This type of information can be very important to trainers because it suggests that the program needs to be modified if it is to be effective for White participants.

The responses to these types of questions can provide valuable information about the aspects of the program that the participants feel are either beneficial or ineffective. However, self-reports of this nature are limited by the insight of the participants into what is effective and by their willingness to accurately report their feelings. In particular, they may be reluctant to report on the portions of the program that they did not like, for fear of hurting the presenters' feelings or being identified. Negative information is potentially the most useful because it can point to shortcomings in the program as it is currently implemented.

Additional questions can also be asked, especially to obtain information on specific aspects of the program that were presented. For instance, it is often useful to ask, "What aspects of the program should be changed?" Because these types of evaluations are so simple and inexpensive, they should be done routinely for all programs in an effort to improve the program. They do have an important drawback to which we want to draw some attention. These types of evaluations should not be taken as valid evidence of the actual effects of the program. Many types of training lead participants to feel good about themselves and the other people with whom they have gone through the training. These participants will report that the program had beneficial effects, and they will say favorable things about the program. Such positive comments, however, do not necessarily mean that they have changed their attitudes and behaviors in lasting ways.

Nonsystematic Observation

The presenters, the participants, and others who are affiliated with the program can be asked to analyze what they have observed during the program. This approach can yield insights into the strengths and weaknesses of the program. The observations of those who are most intimately involved in it are likely to be rich and detailed. They may have insights into what works and what does not that other approaches cannot yield. But their hopes and expectations can also bias presenters and participants. They may be too close to the programs and too vested in the outcomes to be objective in their observations.

Nonsystematic observations can also be done by neutral observers who may be less influenced by their preconceptions and less subject to bias. This technique is similar to the approach that ethnographers employ when observing other cultures. For instance, people with a background in anthropology, psychology, sociology, or education who are knowledgeable about intergroup or interpersonal behavior can observe a program and report on what they observe. On the one hand, their neutrality and background may enable them to see things that the presenters and participants may not. On the other hand, they are unlikely to be as knowledgeable about the program as the presenters and may miss nuances and subtleties that presenters would not. The reactions of both neutral and nonneutral observers are typically gathered as written statements or reports, but they could also be collected through interviews. Before doing this type of observation, the permission of the participants in the program must be obtained.

A good example of a nonsystematic observational study of an intergroup relations program is Fine's (1993) analysis of the Facing History and Ourselves curriculum. As the reader may recall from our earlier discussion of the program (Chapter 9), it employs an examination of the Holocaust to sensitize students to anti-Semitism and a host of related issues (Stoskopf & Strom, 1990). The curriculum is a one-semester, history-related course that guides students to use historical incidents to reflect on present-day problems of prejudice and racism. The curriculum materials also encourage students to analyze their own values and identities as they analyze the Holocaust. The concluding segments of the curriculum address students' responsibility for protecting civil liberties. Fine carefully observed a class in which this program was being implemented and took notes on what she saw and heard. Then, she analyzed what happened during the program and what effects the program had.

Here is a sample of a classroom dialogue that took place after students in a middle school heard a presentation by a Holocaust survivor.

Denise: Like Zezette said yesterday, no one should be treated like the Jews were treated. I think it's better to talk and teach people.

Frank: I agree you should talk, but personally I think if I went through what she went through, I would hate all Germans, 'cause they took it on themselves to follow Hilter.

Gregory: I personally don't think hitting back at all is the right answer. That's also my religious belief. The reason Zezette said what she said was, if you like get them back and it starts a fight, that's not going to make you like the person any better.

Jake: Why do you have to like the person any better? I'm not saying fighting is right, but if somebody does something to you, no matter who's right or wrong, you don't have to love everybody . . .

Andrea: What's the sense of talking to the other person and bringing yourself down to their standard. You know the other person's gonna want to fight you!

Gregory: Who cares! The other person can hit me.

Denise: Somebody's gonna hit you, you're gonna sit there? . . .

Gregory: My religion says you shouldn't hit back.
Alexandra: But what does your fist say? (Fine, 1993, pp. 784-785).

Fine (1993) comments that "Zezette's lecture . . . served as a window onto choices these students make on a daily basis" (p. 785). And, later, that "the passion behind these students' exchanges was also noteworthy, for here students typically disaffected from school were vitally engaged in the process of thinking" (Fine, 1993, p. 786). She believes the program

> Effectively facilitated a climate wherein students were able to recognize that there are a variety of viewpoints, identities, and interests in the world, all of which have some social grounding, and all of which must be understood if not necessarily accepted. (Fine, 1993, p. 786)

From her study we get a clear sense of why the curriculum is involving and potentially effective.

Focus Groups

Focus groups involve facilitated discussions. The interviewer could be the person who presented the program, although participants might be more willing to talk freely with a person who was not involved in presenting the program. The groups might consist of participants in the programs or a variety of program presenters. The participants would be asked to discuss their experiences with an emphasis on analyzing the strengths and weaknesses of the program. The interviewer is likely to have a list of topics to be addressed, but the sequence in which they are covered and the particular questions that are asked are left to the discretion of the interviewer. This allows the interviewers considerable freedom to explore the answers and probe for details.

Group discussions capitalize on the synergy of groups and often bring out issues that no individuals would have thought of on their own. These discussions may also tend to the extremes of positive or negative evaluations and may not provide a balanced assessment of what occurred during the program. Focus groups are most likely to be productive when the interviewers have a clear set of protocols to guide the discussion. Their effectiveness depends to a great extent on the interpersonal skills of the interviewer, who serves as a catalyst for the discussion. It is the interviewer who must create a climate in which participants feel free to express themselves without fear of disapproval and who provides warm support and encouragement (Judd, Smith, & Kidder, 1991).

Systematic Observation

Systematic observation typically involves the use of carefully structured coding schemes concerning what behaviors are to be observed. The initial goal is to categorize, itemize, and count behaviors (Judd et al., 1991). Coding systems have been developed for observing the behavior of people in groups, which can be applied to some types of intergroup relations programs, such as dialogue programs (e.g., Bales, 1998; Bales & Cohen, 1979; Hare & Hare, 1996; Polley, Hare, & Stone, 1988). For other types of programs, for instance, those that are more didactic, the investigators may have to develop their own coding schemas based on the goals of the programs and the processes by which they believe the program achieves these goals. For example, observers may focus on the type of information that is presented, the nature of the interaction among the participants (e.g., cooperative, competitive), the language the participants use, or the behavior of participants toward one another.

Systematic observation yields a record of what occurred during the program and can be used to establish changes in the patterns of behavior over the course of the program as well as to study other processes by which change may have occurred. An example of a coding scheme designed for use in evaluating social processes during intergroup relations programs is presented in Table 10.1. Using this coding scheme, an observer watching a program such as dialogue groups would record the frequency with which particular types of communications (e.g., positive emotional displays, question asking, and responding to questions) occurred. They would also record the characteristics of the context in which these communications occurred (e.g., one-on-one dialogues, small group, task-oriented interactions).

TABLE 10.1   A Coding Scheme for Social Process Features in Intergroup
Relations Programs

Communication Context:
    Group leader lectures, provides directions or guidance.
    Group leader facilitates discussion.
    Large-group, open discussion is dominated by one group (minority, majority).
    Large-group, open discussion involves multiple groups.
    Small-group interaction is task oriented.
    Small-group interaction is interpersonally oriented.
    One group member provides information, gives report, or lectures.

Nature of Communication:
    Individual provides positive self-disclosures (opinions, beliefs, feelings,
        experiences).
    Individual provides negative self-disclosures (opinions, beliefs, feelings,
        experiences).
    Remarks comprise praise, encouragement, acceptance, and agreement.
    Remarks comprise criticism, hostility, challenge, and disagreement.
    Behaviors are friendly.
    Behaviors are unfriendly.
    Emotional displays are positive.
    Emotional displays are negative.
    Questions are asked and responded to.
    Activities involve no interaction (reading, written exercises).

Another example of a way in which systematic observational techniques could be used to evaluate the effects of intergroup relations training can be found in a study by Hauserman, Walen, and Behling (1973). In this study, systematic observation was used to examine who sat next to whom in the cafeteria, as an indicator of voluntary intergroup contact. Using these types of coding schemes makes it possible to examine what types of communications characterize the program and to chart changes over time. They have the advantage of focusing on the actual behavior of the participants rather than on their self-reports. The disadvantages are that they are necessarily narrow in focus and they are very labor intensive. Systematic observational approaches are likely to be most effective if conducted by trained observers who are not actively involved in the presentation of the program.

Content Analyses

It is possible to record the participants during the presentation of the program and later analyze these audio or visual recordings. These analyses could include the same types of information that systematic observations yield, but it is also possible to do more fine-grained analyses, because the record is permanent and can be replayed. For instance, the language people use can be analyzed in great detail, as can interaction patterns among members of different groups.

Content analyses can also be applied to participants' responses to questions about the impact of the program on them. For example, Heppner and O'Brien (1994) did a content analysis of reactions of students to a 15-week, multicultural counseling course. The students were asked to respond to seven open-ended questions at the completion of each class. The responses to these questions were then categorized. It was found that 13% of the responses reflected an increase in interest in their own backgrounds, 15% of the responses indicated that the class prompted the students to think about their biases between class meetings, and 19% of the responses indicated that the students were concerned that their biases might hinder their counseling effectiveness. The students' responses seem to indicate that only for a limited proportion of the students was the class having the desired effect of causing them to think about their identities and biases and the effects these may have on their behavior. An advantage of doing content analyses of open-ended questions is that the respondents are allowed to use their own words and may express themselves freely. A disadvantage is that coding schemes must be devised for each of the questions.

Quantitative Techniques

In general, quantitative approaches are better than qualitative techniques at establishing what the effects of the program actually are, and they can provide more precise information on the exact processes that may be responsible for these effects. The designs that are used in quantitative studies vary from the simple to the complex. We will start with the simplest designs.

Pretest and Posttest

This design is typically used to assess the effects of programs when no control group is available. The intended effects of the program must be carefully considered before using this or any other type of quantitative analysis. What is expected to change as a result of the program? Is the program expected to influence attitudes (e.g., prejudice) or other cognitions (e.g., stereotypes), or is it more oriented toward feelings (e.g., self-esteem, anger, resentment) or behaviors (e.g., willingness to interact with outgroup members on an equal basis)? Is knowledge acquisition a goal of the program? Are the participants expected to think differently about their own group or their own identity after the training? Is the training expected to influence their perceptions of the place of their own group in a larger social schema (the school, the community, humankind)? Should they emerge with specific skills? Deciding what the specific goals of the program are and how to measure them is often a useful exercise by itself because it leads practitioners to consider whether or not the techniques they are proposing to use will achieve their goals.

To assess whether or not these goals have been achieved using this design, practitioners ask the participants the same questions at the pretest and at the posttest. For example, attitudes toward specific groups, knowledge, or skill levels might be measured at the pretest and posttest.

This design can provide information about whether or not the program had the desired effects, but it is subject to several limitations. It does not provide definitive knowledge about the effects because there is no control group. It is possible that the observed changes would have occurred even without the program (e.g., as children mature during the school year), or they might be due to external events that have nothing to do with the program (e.g., other programs in the school that are having a positive impact on intergroup relations). In addition, if there has been a substantial number of dropouts between the pretest and the posttest, the meaning of any differences that are obtained is questionable. For instance, it may be the case that only the participants who are favorably disposed toward outgroup members stay in the program. When their positive-attitude scores at the posttest are compared to the pretest scores of all participants, the program looks to be successful but only because the people with negative attitudes have dropped out of the program. Sometimes, these dropout problems can be so severe that no conclusions can be drawn about the program. For instance, in one study, only 6 of 32 participants in the treatment condition completed the program, and only 10 of the 27 participants completed the control program (Neville & Furlong, 1994).

Pretesting has the drawback of alerting the participants to what is being measured and what types of changes are anticipated. Participants may remember their responses on the pretest if the time interval between testing sessions is relatively short. Participants who are motivated to appear consistent may then respond to the posttest with answers that match their pretest responses. If the participants provide answers on the posttest that indicate the program produced positive changes, they may only be reporting what they think the presenters want them to say. In other words, they may simply be trying to be helpful by reporting positive changes that do not represent their real feelings.

A study by Lopez, Gurin, and Nagda (1998, Study 1) provides an example of a pretest and posttest design. Students in this study were enrolled in a one-semester college course on intergroup relations that centered on active learning exercises (role-playing, simulation games) and intergroup dialogues. The students' assessments of the role of social structural factors in causing poverty and racial inequality were measured at the beginning and the end of the course. The questionnaire included items such as, "The system prevents people of color from getting their fair share of the good things in life, such as better jobs and money." The participants in the course made significantly more causal attributions to structural causes for racial inequality and poverty after the course than they had before the course.

If a program is multifaceted, the pretest and posttest approach usually will not provide information on what specific aspects of the program were the most likely causes of the obtained effects. This problem can be remedied in all the quantitative approaches by adding questions about variables that might be responsible for the effects of the programs, such as degree of involvement, changes in self-esteem, identification with superordinate groups, empathy, and outgroup differentiation. In the study by Lopez and colleagues (1998, Study 2), at the posttest, the students completed questions about their involvement in the lectures and readings as well as their involvement in the active learning (experiential) exercises. Analyses of their responses revealed that the students who were most involved in the course changed their attributions to structural factors as causes of inequality the most. This result suggests that if the program leaders wanted the program to have a greater impact on attributions, they should devise ways to make it more involving for the participants.

Posttest Only With Control Group

In this design, the responses of the treatment group to the posttest are compared to those of a control group. Ideally, the control group is comparable to the treatment group in all respects except that they did not receive the treatment. If so, comparing the treatment and control groups provides information on the effectiveness of the program. The limitation is that if the treatment group and the control group are not completely comparable, any differences between the two groups at the posttest may be due to preexisting differences between the groups.

There is a solution to this problem. The solution is random assignment to conditions, which involves randomly assigning prospective participants to the treatment and control groups. If the sample is large enough, random assignment almost guarantees the equivalence of the two groups. However, random assignment to conditions often is not practical in intergroup relations programs that are tested in field settings. For example, students usually cannot be randomly assigned to teachers who are using cooperative groups or teachers who are not. Likewise, employers are reluctant to randomly assign employees to take diversity training or not to receive it—they would prefer to have all their employees trained. When random assignment is not possible, a particularly good control group consists of people who will be participating in the program in the future but who have not yet done so (see Dunnette & Motowildo, 1982). Other control groups that can provide useful comparisons would be composed of students in comparable classes who are not receiving the program, employees in other branches of the company, and college students in the same major as those in the treatment group. The most important dimensions of equivalence are racial or ethnic group composition, sex ratio, age, interests (e.g., major), level in the organization (e.g., all managers), and experience with the relevant outgroups.

Research indicates that receiving training of almost any kind can have positive effects on people because it makes them feel special and appreciated. This effect is called the Hawthorne effect, after the factory in which it was first discovered. To counteract Hawthorne effects, the control group could receive some type of training program other than intergroup relations training (e.g., computer skills training) so that both groups would be receiving some type of special treatment. This would make the control group similar to a placebo group in medical research. The control group would receive a treatment, but it would be a treatment not expected to affect intergroup relations.

A study by Gurin, Peng, Lopez, and Nagda (1999) examined the long-term effects of the same intergroup relations course examined in Lopez and colleagues (1998, Study 1). This study employed a posttest-with-control-group design. In this study, students who had taken this course in their freshman year were tested during their senior year to examine the long-term effects of taking the class. These students were then compared to seniors who had not taken the course during their college careers and who were matched to the treatment group in terms of gender, ethnicity, precollege state of residence, and college residence hall. One of the measures assessed racial or ethnic divisiveness with questions such as, "The current focus on multiculturalism in our schools undermines the common ties that bind the nation." The Black students who had taken the course reported that there was less racial divisiveness in American society than did the Black students who had not taken the course. On this measure, for the White students, there were no differences between those who had taken the course and those who had not. Although this pattern of results suggests that the course changed the beliefs of the Black students but not of the White students, it is possible that the differences for the Black students were due to what is called a selection problem. It may be that the Black students who took the course believed that there was less racial divisiveness in American society even before they took the course. That is, it is possible that Black students who were not alienated by racial divisiveness were more likely to take the course on intergroup relations than Blacks who were alienated. When measured at the posttest, these students still believed there was less divisiveness in American society than did Blacks in the matched control group. Thus, it is possible that the course did not change their attitudes.

Pretest and Posttest With Control Group

In this design, both the treatment group and the control group are tested before and after the program. If the results show that there are changes in the attitudes, feelings, or behaviors of the treatment group, but no changes occur in the control group, it suggests that the program is successful. In this design, it is also possible to establish whether or not the treatment group and the control group are equivalent before the program begins. If they are equivalent, it increases the chances that any observed differences between these two groups at the posttest are due to the program. Thus, this design eliminates most of the problems of the other quantitative designs. For instance, in a moral development program, the maturation of students' moral reasoning abilities could pose an alternative explanation for increases in moral reasoning if only a pretest and posttest design were used. The addition of a control group eliminates this problem because the control group should mature at the same rate as the treatment group. A disadvantage of this approach is that it requires more testing than the other designs and thus is more labor intensive.

In the best of all possible worlds, the participants are randomly assigned to the treatment and control groups, thus ensuring that they are equivalent. In practical terms, random assignment often is not possible, in which case the two groups should be made as comparable as possible, perhaps by using as a control group people who are waiting to participate in the program.

The importance of using this type of design can be seen in a study by Brooks and Kahn (1990) of a class for graduate students in counseling that was designed to teach students to be sensitive to sex differences and cultural issues. It employed lectures, discussions, roleplaying, and other experiential exercises. Students taking the class were compared to counseling students in other classes who had not yet taken the class. The students' behaviors were measured using the Robinson Behavioral Inventory (E. A. Robinson & Follingstad, 1985),

TABLE 10.2   Means for the Sex-Role Behavior Inventory

	Pretest	Posttest
Treatment Group	165.8	172.9
Control Group	186.6	191.2

NOTE: High numbers indicate positive changes in sex-role behaviors.
SOURCE: Adapted from Brooks & Kahn (1990).

which assesses sex-role behaviors. The means for the pretest and the posttest of the treatment group and the control group are presented in Table 10.2. Notice that if they had employed a pretest and posttest design, they would have concluded that the class was successful in changing behaviors because the scores increased from 165.8 to 172.9. If they had used a posttest with control group design, they would have concluded that the program was a failure because the posttest scores of the treatment group are lower (172.9) than the control group posttest scores (191.2). The use of the pretest and posttest design with a control group makes it possible to compare the change in the treatment group (+6.1) with the change in the control group (+4.6). The statistical analyses for this study indicated that the improvement in the treatment group was not significantly larger than the improvement in the control group. Thus, the most reasonable conclusion is that the program had no effect on sex-role behaviors beyond those produced by being in the counseling program for the same period of time. The point is that using any other design would have led to conclusions that were wrong.

Technically, this approach uses a longitudinal design—that is, measurements are made of the same group at two points in time. For intergroup relations programs, it is desirable to extend this approach by using additional posttests after a period of time has passed. These additional measures make it possible to assess the durability of the program effects and look for the emergence of changes that may take some time to occur (e.g., changes in actual levels of intergroup contact). If there is no control group, it can also be valuable to gather additional pretest information well before the program begins. This information makes it possible to examine changes that are occurring

TABLE 10.3   Changes Over Time in Attitudes Toward Ethnic Groups

Control Group	Experimental Group						
	Week 1	Week 3	Week 5	Week 7	Week 9	Week 11	Week 13
252	264	264	291	279	254	244	243

SOURCE: Adapted from Tansik & Driskill (1977).

naturally over time (e.g., the increasing cognitive and emotional maturation of children) to see if the program is producing changes that are larger than those that would be expected naturally.

Tansik and Driskill (1977) did a study that involved a series of posttests on a group of supervisors who had received intergroup relations training in the military. They asked the participants to evaluate five different racial and ethnic groups every 2 weeks for 12 weeks after the 20-hour training program ended (Table 10.3). The initial results indicated that the program had improved attitudes toward these racial and ethnic groups, but the changes were not significant. However, 5 weeks after the termination of the program, the difference between the trained group and a control group of untrained supervisors was significant. After the 5th week, a gradual decline in attitudes set in and by the 12th week, the trained group had somewhat less positive attitudes than the untrained group, but these differences were not significant. This study shows how important it is to assess changes over time. If only the initial attitude measure had been taken, it would have been concluded that the program was not successful. But in this case, the changes took some time to emerge. And then they were gradually lost, suggesting that ongoing institutional support may be necessary to sustain changes once they have taken place.

Mediational Analyses

In all the pretest and posttest designs, it is possible to do mediational analyses to examine the processes that are thought to be responsible for the improvements in intergroup relations brought about by the program. Throughout this book, we have suggested a wide variety of psychological processes that may be responsible for the success of intergroup relations programs. Many of these processes specify variables that could be measured, such as empathy, outgroup differentiation, knowledge about the outgroup, dissonance, guilt, intergroup anxiety, stereotypes, superordinate groups, levels of moral reasoning, and humanitarian values. By measuring these variables, it is possible to do mediational analyses that provide indications of the degree to which these psychological processes are operating to create changes (for a discussion of mediational analyses, see Kenny, Kashy, & Bolger, 1998).

The logic of the type of mediational analysis most relevant to intergroup relations programs is as follows. Assume that a given program is designed to change attitudes toward a particular outgroup by creating empathy for the members of that group. At the pretest, both attitudes and empathy toward this group would be measured. At the posttest, both empathy and attitudes toward this group would be measured again. For each participant, one would obtain a score for the change from pretest to posttest in attitudes and the change in empathy. Then, a correlation between these two types of changes would be obtained for all participants. If a positive correlation between changes in empathy and changes in attitudes exists, this result would suggest that the changes in empathy brought about by the program are responsible for the changes in attitudes that were found. However, because this conclusion is based on correlational evidence, it is only suggestive, because correlation does not prove causation. It is possible that it was changes in attitudes that brought about changes in empathy.

An example that illustrates such an analysis comes from a study of Facing History and Ourselves in multiethnic, eighth-grade classes (Schultz, Barr, & Selman, in press). In this study, it was found that the Facing History and Ourselves program reduced racism and that reductions in racism were related to reductions in fighting behavior. One interpretation of these results is that the program reduced racism and these reductions in racism led to decreases in fighting.

Statistical Analyses

All quantitative approaches require statistical analyses. If members of the research team lack this type of expertise, statistical assistance can sometimes be found in the institutional studies departments of large school districts. People with these skills are also available in a variety of departments on university campuses (sociology, psychology, educational psychology, statistics, math, etc.). In universities with graduate programs, professors or graduate students may be willing to provide their services on a consulting basis and not necessarily at great cost. The statisticians should be involved in the programs at the beginning so they can help formulate questions and data collection procedures.

Creating Measures

Quantitative approaches rely on the use of valid and reliable measures. A considerable number of measures meet these criteria, which have been used in the research we have reviewed and in other related studies (Table 10.4). A valid measure is one that cleanly assesses the variable it was designed to assess. A measure of racial prejudice would be valid if it effectively measured prejudice and was not contaminated by related concepts, such as stereotyping or general antagonism toward others. It should be correlated with other measures of the same concept, and it should be useful in predicting behaviors that are thought to be caused by prejudice, such as discrimination. A measure is reliable if it is free from measurement error. When the same people receive the same scores on repeated testing of a measure, or when all the items in a measure are highly correlated with one another, the measure can be said to be reliable.

Sometimes, it is necessary to create new measures to assess variables that are expected to be influenced by particular intergroup relations programs. To create a new measure is often better than to employ one that does not quite measure the variable that the program is expected to influence. Here are some rules of thumb to follow in creating measures. In creating new measures, it is essential to start with a very clear definition of the concept to be measured. Valid and reliable measures typically consist of multiple items. Single-item measures are notoriously unreliable and should not be used. Three items would be a minimum, but 5-10 would be better. The items in any measure should have multiple-response options, such as a seven-point scale running

TABLE 10.4   Measures of Variables Relevant to Evaluating Intergroup
Relations Programs

Racial Attitudes:
  Biernat, M., & Crandall, C. S. (1999). Racial attitudes. In J. P. Robinson, P. R.
  Shaver, & L. S. Wrightsman (Eds.), *Measures of political attitudes* (pp. 297-412).
  San Diego, CA: Academic Press.

Stereotypes:
  Stephan, W. G., Ageyev, V. S., Stephan, C. W., Abalakina, M., Stefanenko, T., &
  Coates-Shrider, L. (1993). Soviet and American stereotypes: A comparison of
  methods. *Social Psychology Quarterly, 56*(1), 54-64.
  Stephan, W. G., Ybarra, O., & Bachman, G. (1999). Prejudice toward immigrants.
  Journal of Applied Social Psychology, 29, 2221-2237.

Intergroup Anxiety:
  Stephan, W. G., Ybarra, O., & Bachman, G. (1999). Prejudice toward immigrants.
  Journal of Applied Social Psychology, 29, 2221-2237.

Empathy:
  Davis, M. H. (1994). *Empathy: A social psychological approach.* Madison, WI: Brown &
  Benchmark.
  Stiff, J. B., Dillard, J. P., Somera, L., Kim, H., & Sleight, C. (1988). Empathy, commu-
  nication, and prosocial behavior. *Communication Monographs, 55*, 198-213.

Measures That Can Be Used to Evaluate Multicultural Counseling Programs:
  D'Andrea, M., Daniels, J., & Heck, R. (1991). Evaluating the impact of multicultural
  counseling training. *Journal of Counseling and Development, 70*, 143-150.
  Pope-Davis, D. B., & Coleman, H. L. K. (1997). *Multicultural counseling competencies:
  Assessment, education and training, and supervision.* Thousand Oaks, CA: Sage.
  Sodowsky, G. R., Taffe, R. C., Gutkin, T. B., & Wise, S. L. (1994). Development of
  the Multicultural Counseling Inventory. *Journal of Counseling Psychology, 41*,
  137-148.

Group Identity:
  Fischer, A. R., Tokar, D. M., & Serna, G. S. (1998). Validity and construct contamina-
  tion of the Racial Identity Attitude Scale—Long Form. *Journal of Counseling Psychology, 45*(2), 212-224.
  Luhtanen, R., & Crocker, J. (1992). A collective self-esteem scale: Self-evaluation of
  one's own identity. *Personality and Social Psychology Bulletin, 18*, 302-318.
  Pope-Davis, D. B., Vandiver, B. J., & Stone, G. L. (1999). White racial identity attitude development: A psychometric examination of two instruments. *Journal of
  Counseling Psychology, 46*(1), 70-79.

Intergroup Contact:
  Phinney, J. S., Ferguson, D. L., & Tate, J. D. (1997). Intergroup attitudes among ethnic minority adolescents: A causal model. *Child Development, 68*(5), 955-969.

from "Disagree strongly" to "Agree strongly." Using fewer than five
response options can make a scale insensitive to change by providing
too little room in which change can manifest itself. However, sometimes scales with a limited number of response options are necessary,
as would be the case with young children.

To develop items, brainstorming, perhaps in a focus group, can be
useful. Items should be clearly worded and tap into only one idea.
Consider the following items that are the essence of simplicity. "On the
whole, I am satisfied with myself." "At times, I think I am no good at
all." These item are taken from Rosenberg's (1965) self-esteem scale.
Here is an item from a measure of authoritarianism (Altemeier, 1981):
"The facts on crime, sexual immorality, and the recent public disorders
show we have to crack down harder on deviant groups and trouble-
makers if we are going to save our moral standards and preserve law
and order." This item would be difficult to respond to if there have
been no recent public disorders, or if crime and sexual immorality are
not seen to be closely related to one another. Having a mixture of items
that are phrased positively and negatively is useful. These items can
then be scrambled in the questionnaire. Using balanced items counter-
acts any tendency that people might have to agree with all the items
they are asked. For instance, a scale measuring value differences between groups might include the following two items. "The family values of most (Native Americans) are not compatible with the values of
my ethnic group." "The moral values of most (Native Americans) are
very similar to the values of my ethnic group."

If at all possible, the new measures should be assessed for reliability and validity. Reliability can be assessed by testing the same group
of people twice, to see if the measure yields similar results on both
occasions, or by examining the correlations of the items within the
measure. Validity can be assessed by showing that the new measure is
positively correlated with established measures of similar constructs
and by showing that it is uncorrelated with measures of theoretically
unrelated constructs. Thus, a measure of intergroup attitudes should
correlate with other measures of intergroup attitudes, but it should not
correlate with measures of presumably unrelated constructs (e.g.,
social desirability, conscientiousness). Examples of a measure we developed to measure intergroup attitudes is presented in Table 10.5. For

TABLE 10.5   Measure of Intergroup Attitudes

My attitude toward group X is:

1.   A   B   C   D   E   F   G   H   I   J
   No hostility   Extreme
   at all   hostility

2.   A   B   C   D   E   F   G   H   I   J
   No admiration   Extreme
   at all   admiration

3.   A   B   C   D   E   F   G   H   I   J
   No dislike   Extreme
   at all   dislike

4.   A   B   C   D   E   F   G   H   I   J
   No aceptance   Extreme
   at all   acceptance

5.   A   B   C   D   E   F   G   H   I   J
   No superiority   Extreme
   at all   superiority

6.   A   B   C   D   E   F   G   H   I   J
   No affection   Extreme
   at all   affection

7.   A   B   C   D   E   F   G   H   I   J
   No disdain   Extreme
   at all   disdain

8.   A   B   C   D   E   F   G   H   I   J
   No approval   Extreme
   at all   approval

9.   A   B   C   D   E   F   G   H   I   J
   No hatred   Extreme
   at all   hatred

10.   A   B   C   D   E   F   G   H   I   J
   No sympathy   Extreme
   at all   sympathy

11.   A   B   C   D   E   F   G   H   I   J
   No rejection   Extreme
   at all   rejection

12.   A   B   C   D   E   F   G   H   I   J
   No warmth   Extreme
   at all   warmth

SOURCE: Stephan, Ybarra, & Bachman, 1999.

a more complete discussion of the development of measurement instruments, see Judd and McClelland (1998) and Krosnick (1999).

It is valuable to have collaborators and research assistants from the ethnic groups included in the study—not only to help create the questionnaire but also to administer it. Ensuring privacy and confidentiality is also important. If possible, it is best to have the respondents answer the questions when they are alone. Administering questionnaires in a group setting leads to increases in errors of measurement. Because the quality of the data collected will depend on the motivation of the respondents, they should be provided with compelling explanations for why they should answer the questions carefully and truthfully. Obtaining organizational support for the study can be crucial in collecting high-quality data. If the organization supports the evaluation effort, it means it is willing to allow participants to take the time to participate, and, typically, it means that participants will be more willing to take part in the study.

Unobtrusive Measures

Important data about the effects of intergroup relations programs can be obtained in ways that do not include the active involvement of the participants, that is, in ways that are unobtrusive. If the program is designed to reduce intergroup conflict in the schools, for instance, it would be possible to keep track of the number of interracial conflicts occurring before and after the program. If the program is designed to increase interaction among racial, ethnic, and religious groups, the composition of voluntary extracurricular organizations could be examined before and after the program. Teachers could track racial, ethnic, or religious slurs and teasing or bullying. Achievement scores before and after the program might also be examined. Improved intergroup relations might influence student absenteeism and retention rates, and these could be charted over time.

In work settings, information could also be gathered on absenteeism as well as on turnover and sick leave. Minority representation in recruiting, promotion, and in the various levels of the organization could also be charted. Salaries paid to women and minority groups could be compared with those paid to men and majority group members at the same level in the organization. These types of unobtrusively collected data have the advantage of not being influenced by the biases that can affect self-reports. If this type of information is gathered over time or across institutions, it can provide a valuable index of the effects of intergroup relations programs.

Comparative Studies

The need is growing to conduct studies that compare different techniques designed to be effective with the same populations, such as different multicultural education programs or different diversity training programs. These studies would make it possible to decide which programs are most effective for particular populations. Currrently, we can compare the studies that have been done of different programs, but these types of comparisons are beset by problems of noncomparability of measures, locations, and populations.

Publication

People who implement intergroup relations programs should be strongly encouraged not only to conduct evaluations of their programs but also to publish these evaluations. Forums exist for the publication of all these types of evaluations, from the least to the most formal. Different types of evaluations serve different purposes. When people are considering adopting a program, they need to know not only if it is effective but also what occurs during that program. Thus, thorough program descriptions serve a valuable function. Qualitative evaluations that include statements from participants are very useful in providing this type of information. Qualitative information on the aspects of the program that seem to be effective or ineffective can help prospective adopters to chose what elements of the program to present.

More formal quantitative analyses can provide information on the effects of the program and can be used to compare programs. Just as clinical trials are used to determine what drugs are the most effective in treating given diseases, for whom the drugs are most effective, and at what dosage—so, too, is it possible with systematic evaluations to select what programs to use for particular populations in specific contexts. The acquisition of knowledge is a cumulative and sometimes tedious process, but in its absence, intergroup relations trainers, educators, and facilitators may reinvent the same program, repeat the same mistakes, and not achieve maximal outcomes. In this case, if those in the field do not create a historical record of its failures along with its successes, others certainly will be doomed to repeat them.

Summary

This chapter was designed to provide practitioners and students of intergroup relations with an overview of techniques for evaluating intergroup relations programs. Two basic types of evaluation techniques are available: qualitative and quantitative. We reviewed five types of qualitative techniques. Postprogram surveys are used to determine what aspects of the program were perceived to be effective or ineffective. They can provide useful information but are limited by the participants' capacities to have insights into the program and by their reluctance to provide truthful critiques. Nonsystematic observations by neutral observers can provide useful information about what is occurring during the program and the processes that may be responsible for bringing about change. Their utility can be limited by any unintentional biases the observers may have. Focus groups of participants or trainers may yield insights into process variables that affect the outcomes of the program. They can capitalize on the synergy of groups, but their effectiveness depends on the skills of the interviewer. Systematic observation employing coding schemas can provide a precise record of specific types of events that occur during the program. They can be used to chart change and examine processes underlying changes. They are necessarily narrow in focus, and they are highly labor intensive. Content analyses can be used to examine records of spoken dialogues or written comments. They help to systematize people's behaviors for analytical purposes.

Quantitative techniques differ from qualitative techniques in that all of them require statistical analyses. The pretest and posttest design involves measuring relevant variables at the beginning and end of the program. It can be used to assess the effects of the program, but the lack of a control group means that it does not provide definitive evidence, because other factors could have created the changes (e.g., maturation or moral reasoning). The posttest with control group design can also provide evidence on the effects of the program but only if there is reason to believe that the treatment and control groups were equivalent before the program began. The best design is the pretest and posttest with control group design. This design eliminates most of the problems with the other designs. All these quantitative designs can be extended over time by gathering additional pretests or posttests. In both of the pretest and posttest designs, it is also possible to conduct mediational analyses if measures of process variables are obtained at the end of the program. These types of analyses make it possible to determine what processes (e.g., empathy, reductions in anxiety, the creation of superordinate groups) were responsible for the success of the program.

If measures are not currently available for variables of interest, they may have to be created. New measures should be developed in accord with accepted practices, to achieve maximal validity and reliability. They are likely to be most useful if they include multiple items, are carefully worded, and include multiple-response options.

Many programs can also be evaluated through the use of unobtrusive measures of variables that the programs are expected to affect (e.g., conflict in schools, turnover for jobs in the workplace).

We strongly encourage practitioners to publish the results of their evaluation efforts no matter what techniques they elect to employ. These published studies can be used to determine the effectiveness of intergroup relations programs and to improve them.

CONCLUSIONS

11

IN THIS CHAPTER, we present an overall assessment of the programs to improve intergroup relations that we have examined in this book. We first briefly describe the components of each program and summarize the research on their impact. Next, we assess the overall success of intergroup relations programs and critique both the nature of the research and the discipline as a whole. Afterwards, we discuss the psychological processes these programs evoke that could lead to improvements in intergroup relations. Then, we make recommendations for the design of effective programs to improve intergroup relations, and we consider a number of decisions that must be made in the creation of intergroup relations programs.

Programs to Improve Intergroup Relations

In addition to varying on the degree to which they are direct versus indirect and didactic versus interactive, the programs vary by setting, type of trainee, age of trainee, intent of the program, techniques used, and outcomes. All of the programs we have reviewed are unique in some respects, but they also all share certain features. We will briefly review the characteristics of each program and summarize what is known about the outcomes of these programs.

Multicultural Education Programs

Multicultural education programs have been used for the most part in primary and secondary schools. The goals of these programs are to increase knowledge about outgroup members and systems of inequality and to improve attitudes toward outgroups. These programs focus directly on intergroup relations by addressing differences among groups. The approach relies heavily on didactic techniques, but interactive techniques are sometimes employed. Typically, the students read about different ethnic groups and are taught about basic concepts in the field of intergroup relations such as prejudice, stereotypes, and racism. An implicit agenda of most of these programs is to increase students' identification with their racial, ethnic, religious, and cultural groups. Information about structural inequalities is usually included in the curriculum, and an attempt is often made to modify the structure and procedures of the school to reflect the egalitarian emphasis of the curriculum. These materials can be presented in either segregated or integrated settings. The psychological processes used to improve intergroup relations are largely passive and cognitive.

Hundreds, probably thousands, of these programs exist, but the literature consists of only around 30 studies assessing the outcomes of these programs. These studies cannot help but be nonrepresentative. Most of these studies of multicultural education have documented positive effects of these programs, but a small number of programs have shown no effects or negative effects. It is prudent to judge the effects of multicultural education programs as unproven.

Diversity Training Programs

Diversity training programs are used with adults in the workplace. Like multicultural education, this technique addresses intergroup relations directly. The goals of these programs are to increase awareness of differences among racial, ethnic, and cultural groups and to lead the participants to value these differences. In many organizations, diversity training is accompanied by an attempt to change the organizational structure and climate to reflect an emphasis on greater diversity. The focus is often on changing the attitudes and behaviors of members of the majority group. Diversity training programs usually include a strong didactic component along with some interactive elements, such as training in interaction skills or dialogue among groups. They tend to be rather brief. These programs appear to meet with greater resistance than most other intergroup relations programs. When they are successful, it is most likely to be due to the activation of passive, cognitive psychological processes, although some active processes may come into play.

Although diversity training is commonplace in the workplace, to date, only a handful of assessments of these programs have been published. Given their heavy usage, the lack of published evaluations of these programs is extremely worrisome. Although the data show some positive effects for this technique, as well as some negative effects in a small number of cases, no conclusions can be drawn regarding their effectiveness on the basis of such a small number of nonrepresentative studies.

Intergroup Dialogues

Intergroup dialogues take place in university settings as well as in communities and among conflicting nations. The goals of these dialogues range from solving a specific conflict to improving ongoing relations among groups with a history of negative relations. The technique is facilitated by trainers with members of two groups who participate in a series of face-to-face discussions and experiential exercises. The dialogues directly confront intergroup relations issues using a highly interactive approach. Conflict is often encouraged by being brought out into the open and discussed. In many respects, these programs maximize the conditions of intergroup contact. They rely on a wide variety of active, affectively oriented, psychological processes. It appears that these programs are more insight oriented than most other intergroup relations programs. In addition, the emphasis on social action in these programs is stronger than in most other programs.

Because this technique is relatively new, the data on the effects of intergroup dialogues are extremely limited. The handful of published studies suggests that this technique can be successful in improving intergroup attitudes. Behavioral measures are uncommon but also suggest improvements in intergroup relations. Thus, intergroup dialogues are promising techniques to improve intergroup relations, but as yet, their intergroup outcomes have not been fully substantiated.

Intercultural Training Programs

Intercultural training is a direct approach to improving relations between cultural groups that has typically been employed with adults and college students in work or educational settings. The goals of intercultural training are to provide information about interacting appropriately with members of other cultural groups and about understanding the behaviors and values of people from other cultures. The training is typically a mix of didactic and interactive techniques and tends to emphasize group differences more than group similarities. The training itself often involves only limited contact with members of the other group, but it is expected to prepare participants for high levels of contact. The psychological processes involved in bringing about changes in intercultural relations range across the active-passive and affective-cognitive dimensions.

Although some intercultural experts are critical of the quality of the research, most of the available data have shown them to be effective. The amount of evidence of their effects on intergroup relations varies by specific technique. Some techniques (e.g., the cultural sensitizer) are fairly well documented, but other highly praised techniques (e.g., most of the experiential techniques) have little verification of their effects.

Cooperative Learning Groups

Cooperative learning groups have been used predominantly in school systems, typically in primary and secondary schools. These techniques are designed to improve intergroup relations indirectly, through the use of intergroup contact. This goal is achieved through the introduction of small learning groups in which the task and reward structures require cooperative, face-to-face interaction in a situation in which the students are interdependent. A variety of cooperative learning techniques have been developed. The content of the programs does not involve intergroup relations; it includes traditional curricula taught in a new format. Similarly, the teachers' role is not to make intergroup relations interventions but to facilitate the groups. The psychological processes associated with these programs tend to be active and cognitively oriented.

Cooperative learning techniques are the best documented of the intergroup relations programs. They have been shown to improve intergroup relations by increasing empathy, cross-race friendships and helping, and liking for school and classmates. They frequently increase academic achievement, especially for minority students.

Conflict Resolution Training

Conflict resolution training techniques have also been used in schools as well as in organizations and communities. Mediation, negotiation, and third-party consultation provide examples of these techniques. The goal of these techniques is to lessen conflict or to resolve conflicts in a positive manner. These goals are achieved through teaching conflict resolution skills to contending parties or by placing contending parties in situations in which a third party helps to resolve the problem to the mutual benefit of the contending parties. The approach is intensely interactive. These techniques are not typically designed to impart intergroup relations skills or change intergroup attitudes. Thus, for the most part, these techniques improve intergroup relations indirectly by decreasing the level of conflict between groups. However, racial and other intergroup issues often pervade these conflicts. These techniques tend to involve cognitive psychological processes of both an active and passive nature.

Some of these techniques (e.g., peer mediation) have been shown to be successful in resolving conflicts. The effects of others have yet to be extensively documented. Virtually no information exists on their intergroup relations benefits.

Moral Education Programs

Moral education programs have been implemented primarily in school systems. The stated goal of most of these programs is to increase students' levels of moral reasoning. However, some have improving intergroup relations as a goal and others have the potential to indirectly improve intergroup relations by creating high levels of moral thought, which are incompatible with prejudice, and through their emphasis on justice and the creation of caring, egalitarian communities. The programs vary enormously, but many are implemented through the use of discussions of moral dilemmas and thus are cognitive in approach. The psychological processes involved in creating improvements in intergroup relations are primarily passive and cognitive.

Many moral education programs have been shown to increase levels of moral reasoning. Some moral education programs show great promise in improving intergroup relations, but their effects have not yet been fully documented. Other programs have been shown to be ineffective, and the effects of some programs have not been assessed.

Intergroup Relations Programs: Assessment and Critique

Any overall assessment of the effects of programs to improve intergroup relations must be mixed. On the positive side, all the programs we have considered in this book have some outcome data showing positive effects. Several programs (cooperative learning, intercultural relations training) have amassed considerable data showing their benefits. On the negative side, the great majority of these programs have not been sufficiently assessed. Beliefs in the benefits of these programs outweigh data supporting these beliefs. For most of the programs we have considered in this book, there are only a limited number of published studies on their effects, and in many cases, there are no measurements of their intergroup relations outcomes. When only a handful of studies has been published, the studies may not present a balanced picture of the outcomes of the program. It must be assumed that the studies that are actually published are more likely to report positive outcomes than are those that do not see print. In particular, studies showing that a program has no effects on intergroup relations are unlikely to be published.

Even positive findings are sometimes incomplete or difficult to interpret. Some beneficial consequences of the training are not directly related to goals of the training program (e.g., reduced absenteeism, increased intergroup helping or friendships, greater willingness to live in integrated neighborhoods) and thus go unmeasured. The mediating factors that link programs and outcomes have received too little investigation. Some programs are known to have specific effects, but what aspect of the program creates these effects and why remains unclear. For example, cooperation clearly leads to academic benefits, but researchers do not know what specific aspect of cooperation causes the benefits. The causes may include the ability to exercise higher cognitive functions in the groups (e.g., oral rehearsal and presentation), the opportunity to interact with students of greater ability levels, task clarity and task subdivision, or greater opportunities for feedback. In other instances, the effect is widely separated in time from the cause, and it seems certain that some third variable is mediating the effect. For example, some data show that peer mediation programs have resulted in lowered incidences of school violence. We need to understand the exact process by which this effect occurs.

In addition, methodological problems abound in these program assessments. Measurement quality is often low, relying on scales of uncertain reliability and validity. Problems exist with experimental design. For practical reasons, weak designs (e.g., pretest/posttest, with no control group) are often used and they yield data that are not convincing. The outcomes often include only the types of self-reports (e.g., did participants like the training; do they think it had positive effects) that are most susceptible to bias. Only infrequently are measures of behavioral outcomes obtained.

We mention these limitations of the studies that have been done— not to discourage people from doing evaluations but rather to encourage them to conduct evaluations that provide compelling evidence of the effects of their programs. We strongly believe that individuals involved in conducting intergroup relations training should always evaluate their programs. Even programs that seem to be effective on the basis of informal feedback from participants may in fact be promoting stereotypes or worsening intergroup relations for some participants. In the area of intergroup relations, the best of intentions do not guarantee positive outcomes.

Ideally, these evaluations would include both qualitative and quantitative data. Qualitative data should be gathered from the participants concerning their perceptions of the program and its components. These data have to be interpreted with due respect for their limitations (trainers should be skeptical of flattering findings), but they often provide useful information that can be obtained in no other way. Evaluations of program content by participants can be done on an ongoing basis as the program is presented, as well as at the end of the program. This information can be invaluable in making program improvements. It may also be worthwhile to gather more systematic qualitative data on the specific processes that are believed to bring about favorable changes in attitudes and behavior. For example, analyses of what was actually said by participants during the program may provide insights into the effects of the program and the causes of these effects.

The ideal quantitative analysis would be longitudinal, to determine if short-term gains endure over time. It would also use a control group, preferably with individuals randomly assigned to training and nontraining control groups. Only with the use of a control group can convincing data for the effects of the program be amassed. In addition, individuals planning to evaluate a program should carefully examine the measures used to assess the program. Program evaluators should make certain that their measures actually assess the concepts they are intended to measure and that they are as error free as possible. The measures should be carefully selected to assess the variables that are most likely to be influenced by the program and those that are most central to the goals of the program. The measures used should assess both attitudes and behaviors.

A serious criticism that has been made of many of the programs we have reviewed is that they do not address institutional racism, sexism, and other forms of institutional discrimination. They presume that by changing individual levels of prejudice, the levels of institutional discrimination will also change. Unfortunately, these programs exist in societies in which structural systems of oppression—racism, sexism, classism, homophobia, ableism, among others—are deeply embedded. Certainly, changing individual intergroup attitudes and values is important, but changing individual attitudes cannot change an entire social structure. Attention to oppression built into social structures should also be addressed in these programs.

All the popular techniques for improving intergroup relations could incorporate information regarding institutional discrimination and structural systems of oppression. They could also attempt to make structural changes in the institutions in which these programs are conducted. If the structure of societal institutions remains unchanged, it is unlikely that intergroup relations programs will have long-term, beneficial effects on relations between groups within these institutions. Both individuals and institutions must be free of prejudice and discrimination. In order for these goals to be accomplished, participants in intergroup relations programs should learn to recognize structural systems of inequality and oppression and to be equipped with the skills and motivation to change them.

In the next section, we will discuss the processes underlying the changes that occur during intergroup relations programs.

Psychological Processes Underlying Intergroup Relations Programs

In organizing our discussion of these programs, we have relied on two dimensions that can be used to distinguish them: didactic-interactive and direct-indirect. We recognize that few of these programs are exclusively at one end of either of these continua. For instance, most programs contain a mixture of didactic and interactive components. Nonetheless, most programs are composed primarily of one type of component. In the discussion that follows, we will examine the psychological processes that characterize programs that are predominantly interactive, and then we will consider the processes operative in programs that are predominantly didactic.

Psychological Processes in Interactive Programs

Most of the interactive programs (cooperative learning, dialogue groups, and, to a lesser extent, intercultural training) share a number of features that facilitate their success. Regardless of whether or not these programs are direct or indirect, they tend to emphasize active psychological processes of change. Most incorporate some intergroup contact. One of the common features of the contact that occurs in these programs is cooperative interactions among members of different groups. Cooperation makes individuals dependent on one another for success, and it provides them with a minisuperordinate group that includes all group members. Thus, individuals are no longer viewed as members of different groups but are seen as members of the same group, with a common goal (Dovidio, Kawakami, & Gaertner, 2000). In addition, displaying cooperative behaviors is inconsistent with the display of prejudice and discrimination. Furthermore, cooperative interaction brings about behavior changes that lead to positive attitude change. Inconsistencies between negative private attitudes and public cooperative behaviors displayed in training programs lead to discomfort that can be alleviated by bringing attitudes in line with nondiscriminatory behaviors.

Another common feature of the intergroup contact in most interactive programs is that it is equal status. Equal-status contact provides the conditions necessary for the formation of friendships and mutual respect and for a true exchange of information, so group stereotypes can be dispelled (Pettigrew & Tropp, 2000). Although equating participants in terms of status-related factors external to the situation (e.g., social class) may not be possible, creating equal-status interactions within the training situation is often possible, and most programs strive to do so.

Likewise, most interactive relations programs also strive to make the contact nonsuperficial and try to ensure that the contact occurs in a context that provides opportunities for informal interaction. These conditions further provide opportunities for friendship formation and can produce empathy and understanding. Self-disclosure is also a part of nonsuperficial contact, and it is linked with liking for those to whom people have self-disclosed. If these self-disclosures include information about experiences with prejudice and discrimination, it may lead to feelings of injustice, thus decreasing the tendency to blame the victims of injustice (W. G. Stephan & Finlay, 1999).

Nonsuperficial contact also provides information about the attitudes, beliefs, and behaviors of outgroup members. It dispels ignorance and thereby reduces stereotyping. This type of contact also lowers anxiety concerning intergroup interaction, because individuals learn how to interact with others who are different from them. Furthermore, in the course of interacting, people find similarities between groups as well as differences among the members of other groups.

Interactive intergroup relations programs go to some lengths to try to ensure that intergroup interactions are positive in nature and lead to success for the participants. Positive and successful interaction brings rewards to all the participants; furthermore, it increases liking for the individuals involved in the pleasant interaction. Success can also lead to increased self-esteem and self-efficacy, both of which are associated with positive intergroup attitudes. Feelings of self-efficacy also increase people's beliefs regarding their abilities to guide their behaviors in accordance with their intentions, which can lead to more effective self-regulation of stereotyping, prejudice, and discrimination.

In interactive intergroup relations programs, an attempt is typically made to promote interpersonal, rather than intergroup, interaction within the contact setting. That is, practitioners strive to have individuals relate to one another as individuals and not in terms of their group memberships. An interpersonal focus makes it likely that individuals will be judged on the basis of their own personal characteristics rather than on the stereotype of their particular group (Brewer & Miller, 1984). It also makes it easier for people to see that any given group includes a wide range of different types of individuals. Thus, when people are assigned to small groups, as they often are in many intergroup relations programs, the basis for these assignments should not be obviously tied to racial or ethnic group membership, for that leads people to think of one another in terms of their group memberships. However, if changes in attitudes, beliefs, and behaviors toward individual outgroup members are to generalize to the groups of which these individuals are members, some awareness of group membership needs to be maintained (Hewstone & Brown, 1986). In many intergroup relations programs, this awareness is created by having the individuals focus on group-level issues, as is done in dialogue groups. In this case, the participants relate to one another as individuals, but they are fully aware of one another's group affiliations.

In general, interactive programs try to create nonhostile, nonthreatening environments in order to avoid having the participants feel fearful or anxious. Although, in the interests of producing change, it can actually be useful for participants to feel some discomfort about their prior beliefs, feelings of threat are more likely to lead to prejudice than decrease it (W. G. Stephan & Stephan, 2000). This is a delicate issue because it is very likely that members of the majority group will feel threatened in intergroup relations programs: These programs often attempt to change their attitudes and behaviors as well as the systems that support the privileged position of their group. For these groups, change needs to be presented as a win-win proposition that fulfills values to which both majority and minority group members subscribe, such as justice, fairness, and equality. The guidelines for most trainers indicate that they should create norms for interaction within the training setting that increase the chances that members of all groups will feel that they will not come under personal attack and will be listened to with care.

The two remaining interactive programs, moral education and conflict resolution training, are the most indirect of the programs we have covered in this book. Neither was conceived as a program to improve intergroup relations although both programs have the potential to do so. Although moral education is more didactic than conflict resolution training, both also include interactive components. These programs, too, share certain features that can contribute to more positive relations between groups. For instance, both types of programs emphasize justice and fairness. Acquiring these values should reduce prejudice, stereotyping, and discrimination. Also, both programs reward prosocial behavior toward others.

However, these two programs differ in many respects and thus evoke different psychological change processes. In moral education programs, those in authority model justice, fairness, and caring—leading students to believe that important others support these values. A conscious attempt is made in such programs to change students' attitudes toward valuing moral behaviors. Thus, according to the theory of reasoned action, both the subjective norms in these schools and the students' attitudes toward moral behaviors should promote egalitarian, nondiscriminatory behavior (Fishbein & Ajzen, 1975). Caring schools and just communities create a superordinate group with which all the students can identify, and in mixed schools, this should help to erase the importance of group differences.

In contrast, conflict resolution training programs teach techniques that emphasize cooperative interdependence in resolving conflicts.

When the conflicts involve members of different groups, this cooperative interdependence should help to bring them together rather than divide them. These programs can improve intergroup relations by reducing intergroup conflict and helping students to get along better with one another. The techniques also teach students that conflicts need not be treated as a zero-sum game in which one side's gains are another side's losses. Instead, they focus on win-win solutions in which both sides benefit.

Psychological Processes in Didactic Programs

The direct, didactically oriented programs also share certain features that facilitate improvements in intergroup relations. As a rule, the psychological processes involved in bringing about change in these programs tend to be predominantly cognitive and passive, but creative trainers can also elicit active and affective processes.

The most didactically oriented programs (multicultural education and diversity training) provide participants with information on group differences in values, beliefs, norms, and behavior. This type of material makes the behavior of other groups more understandable and helps to prevent misunderstandings and conflicts based on misattributions. It can counteract stereotypes.

Often these programs include material designed to create cognitive and emotional empathy for outgroups. Reading about the experiences of members of other groups and role-playing being members of other groups provide insights into the nature and meaning of group differences. This can increase understanding for the other group and lead to valuing the other group and its members, thereby reducing prejudice (Batson et al., 1997). Members of the majority group, in particular, may come to see from a new perspective the injustices that members of minority groups have suffered, and this may undercut their tendencies to blame minority groups for the ills they suffer.

Information about other groups can also reduce uncertainty about how to interact with them and can attenuate feelings of anxiety as a consequence (Gudykunst, 1995). Information on group values, especially those that are shared in common across groups, can reduce feelings of threat due to misperceived differences in values (W. G. Stephan & Stephan, 2000). Accurate information on group differences can also counteract the tendency to exaggerate group differences and group conflict, and this too may reduce anxiety and prejudice toward other groups. Although most didactic programs have not attempted to do so, they could present information on the differences among the members of other groups that would counteract stereotypes of those groups. Similarly, although these types of programs do not usually attempt to do so, they could foster superordinate identities and present information on cross-cutting identities that would undermine intergroup prejudice and hostility.

Didactic programs are in a good position to emphasize the importance of the humanistic values of equality, fairness, justice, and compassion. These values could then be brought into contrast with the intergroup discrimination, prejudice, and stereotyping that is prevalent in all societies. If participants can be brought to realize that there are discrepancies between their own values and the attitudes, beliefs, and feelings they have toward outgroup members, the feeling of discomfort created by these discrepancies can be used as a basis for learning to regulate the expression of these thoughts and feelings (Grube, Mayton, & Ball-Rokeach, 1994; Monteith, 1993).

Recommendations for Intergroup Relations Programs

Long-term programs are more likely to have more beneficial effects than short-term programs. Any program must be of sufficient duration for the trainees to learn the material, practice the skills, become accustomed to new behaviors and ideas, and incorporate the material into their lives. Short-term programs are unlikely to achieve these goals.

In the Beginning

Before conducting a program, it may be valuable to conduct a cultural audit of the organization or setting in which the program will be introduced. Such an audit typically consists of an appraisal of the situational context and the needs of the people in this particular context. It might include an examination of what groups are present, the ratios of members from different groups, the power relations among groups, the prior history of relations among these groups, the current relations among these groups, the problems and conflicts existing among the groups, the perceived needs of each group, and an assessment of what types of interventions would be the most effective.

Program Contents

Intergroup relations programs should be theory driven. Good intentions are not a substitute for clearly conceptualized goals and means. Programs are unlikely to be well-designed and effective if a theoretical focus does not direct their planning, content, and implementation. When programs are based on a cohesive set of assumptions that detail the reasons that the program should be successful, it is possible to test the validity and utility of these assumptions and to make changes if they are not supported by research and practice.

Programs are more likely to be beneficial if they include a variety of tasks and situations so that trainees will be positively influenced by the program, whatever their interests, styles of learning, or capabilities. Programs are most effective when they transform the entire organization into a caring, inclusive, egalitarian one. In order to do so, the social climate should be one that supports social justice. Diverse program activities can change attitudes, teach needed interpersonal relations skills and moral reasoning, provide information that discredits stereotypes, and create empathy for other groups. The more actively involving the activities are, the more successful they will be in creating desired changes.

The techniques that are employed should be as interactive and involving as seems reasonable in the context. Techniques that rely primarily on didactic approaches and involve passive psychological processes can often be transformed into more interactive approaches involving active psychological processes. For example, the existence of cross-cutting identities in groups can be made apparent through interactive exchanges of information among small groups of participants.

If interactive exercises are to be employed, trainers, facilitators, and educators must be careful to establish clear guidelines for participation. Typical guidelines include the following: The participants should try to understand the position of people from other groups; they should adopt an analytical perspective, listen actively, behave in a civil manner (e.g., no interrupting), respect one another, be honest and open, suspend judgment, and disagree without attacking others; and they should treat the information exchanged as confidential. In general, trainers need to establish a safe climate in which participants can develop trust in one another. They can foster this climate by enforcing guidelines against abusive language, harmful diatribes, and personal blaming, as well as by being impartial and fair in their treatment of members of all groups.

Conducting Effective Programs

Ideally, the program should be voluntary, but evidence suggests that even involuntary contact with members of other groups can lead to improved intergroup relations (Pettigrew & Tropp, 2000). Programs should not blindside the participants. It is unlikely that intergroup relations programs can be successfully conducted with uniformed participants, unless the participants are very young.

If intergroup contact is a part of the program, attempts should be made to create equal-status interactions within the contact situation. If some participants are at a disadvantage because of the status characteristics they bring to the situation, interventions such as those employed in the Complex Instruction approach discussed in Chapter 7 (e.g., employing tasks requiring multiple competencies so that all group members are skilled on some of the relevant abilities) should be employed to counteract the status inequalities (Cohen, 1994). The ideal intergroup relations program also avoids ethnic or racial imbalances among the participants. At times, minority members in an organization receiving training should be oversampled to provide adequate representation of all groups. Participants should be seen as typical members of their groups, not as unusually skilled or accomplished, so that they are not simply dismissed as exceptional members of their groups. The normal range of differences existing within any group should be represented among the participants from each group so that group stereotypes will be undercut. It is also important that the ethnic or racial balance of program leaders, trainers, or facilitators be roughly equal to, or at least reflect the composition of, the individuals receiving the training. If trainees do not see people like themselves represented among the authority figures who are conducting the training, they may conclude that the training is unlikely to treat their group fairly.

The contact and the entire training program must be clearly supported by those in authority. Trainees should see positive, fair, egalitarian behaviors modeled throughout the course of the training so they can learn to imitate these behaviors. The support of authorities is particularly useful in facilitating imitation and in demonstrating that the subjective norms of the institution favor respect and caring.

Efforts should be made to assist participants to generalize what they have learned in intergroup relations programs to other settings. Often, participants can be asked to specifically address these issues during group discussions. Practicing skills during role-playing exercises can consolidate them. Also, providing participants with follow-up opportunities to discuss these issues after the training has been completed can assist participants in integrating into other settings what they have learned. If the training is not an ongoing part of the organization, changes in the organizational climate may be needed to support and strengthen the intergroup interventions that have been made. Real changes are most likely when organizations make long-term commitments to improving intergroup relations and provide enduring support for the people who have received the training.

Attention needs to be directed to the age of the trainees, to make certain that the program is appropriate to the social, emotional, and cognitive maturity of the participants. Developmental theories are useful in supplying information regarding the type of programs that can be effective at various age levels. Trainers must also be sensitive to the existence of different levels of racial and ethnic identity among the participants.

Issues for Trainers

First and foremost, trainers, educators, and facilitators should receive adequate training before offering any type of intergroup relations programs. Trainers need to be attuned to the misunderstandings and miscommunications caused by cultural differences, recognize the ethnocentrism characteristic of most groups, and be knowledgeable about the stereotypes that the groups hold of one another. They must also understand the importance of ethnic membership with respect to the symbols, persons, and events essential to each group's definition of itself and to the groups' communication styles. In addition, attention should be paid to the differing goals that individuals from different groups may have for the training.

Individuals should not be regarded as representatives for their racial, ethnic, or cultural groups, unless they wish to be. Thus, trainers must be aware of the values, norms, beliefs, and behaviors of different racial, ethnic, religious, and cultural groups, but they should treat members of these groups as individuals who may or may not personally fit the pattern of values and norms that characterize their group. Trainers must be particularly aware of any negative stereotypes they may possess of outgroups and avoid having these views affect their behavior.

Even with training techniques that are sensitive to group differences, problems associated with the treatment and views of the less powerful groups may remain. It may be important to try to bring unvoiced issues of race, ethnicity, religion, class, and gender into the discussions that occur during training. It may also be important to address the fact that after the training, the participants will be returning to societies that continue to be stratified by race, sex, and class, to the conditions of unequal privilege and power.

Next, we will consider a number of issues that must be addressed in any intergroup relations program.

Basic Design Issues

When designing intergroup relations programs, trainers, educators, and facilitators must make a series of basic decisions about the goals and nature of the program they will offer. The most important decision to be made is the selection of the intergroup relations technique. The types of trainees for whom the program is designed, the setting for the training, the problems to be addressed, and the desired outcomes of the program primarily determine this decision. Ways of assessing these outcomes should also be delineated before the program begins.

Another basic decision for many programs is how inclusive the program will be in terms of the groups to be discussed and the groups to be included as participants. In the simplest case, one group will be trained in the ways of another group, as often occurs in intercultural relations programs. More commonly, members of one group are trained to interact with members of several other groups, as is commonly done in diversity training programs. But even these programs must decide how inclusive the coverage of other groups will be. Will the groups to be covered include only racial and ethnic groups, or will sex, social class, sexual orientation, handicapped status, religion, age, or physical appearance (e.g., obesity) be included?

Other programs train a diverse set of participants to understand a wide range of other groups, as occurs in many multicultural education programs. This approach is obviously much more complicated than the less inclusive approaches, for trainers must take into consideration the differences among the groups to be trained. Of necessity, when more groups are covered, the coverage will be less extensive. If few groups are covered, the coverage can be more extensive, but the knowledge acquired may not generalize to the treatment of other outgroups.

A particularly difficult issue that confronts trainers is the degree to which the programs will emphasize group similarities or group differences. Emphasizing group differences means presenting information on values, norms, beliefs, and behaviors that can help people to avoid problems during intergroup interactions. This type of information can reduce conflicts, misunderstandings, and misattributions. However, information on group differences also runs the risk of creating divisions between groups, if the information is not presented in a non-evaluative manner that stresses the adaptive nature of the outgroups' beliefs and practices. Emphasizing group similarities can lead to a sense of common humanity but may gloss over differences that can create problems between groups. Most programs include a mixture of information on intergroup differences and similarities. Regardless of whether similarities or differences are emphasized, the range of differences among members of any given group should be stressed.

A related issue is the extent to which the program's goal is enhancing ingroup identities versus creating superordinate identities. Emphasizing similarities may enhance the chances that superordinate identities will emerge, but it may stifle identification with ethnic, racial, religious, and cultural ingroups. Emphasizing group differences may enhance ingroup identification at the risk of making it more difficult to create superordinate identities. Strengthening ingroup identities may be an important goal of programs designed for minority and other dispossessed groups, but it might lead to detrimental effects among majority group members, if their pride in group membership leads them to think that their dominant position is justified.

Another important decision concerns whether the approach to be adopted will be more didactic or more interactive in nature. Didactic approaches offer trainers control over the content of the program, and usually, more material can be covered. However, they may not be as involving as interactive approaches, and they are likely to be less effective in transmitting social skills than interactive approaches. On the other hand, interactive approaches are time-consuming. Most intergroup relations programs employ a mixture of techniques, but trainers must still decide which approach to emphasize, given the goals of the training and the groups to be trained.

A related decision that trainers must make is the degree to which they will emphasize changes in cognition, behaviors, or affect. This decision will probably be determined by the goals of the program. If cognitive changes in beliefs, attitudes, stereotypes, and knowledge of the other groups are considered to be of prime importance, didactic presentation styles may be called for. If changes in behaviors and the acquisitions of skills are of prime importance, interactive approaches may prove to be more effective. If the goal is to change the way that two or more groups feel about one another, techniques that emphasize interpersonal relations, self-disclosure, and positive interactions may be necessary. Thus, the goals of the program determine to some extent the techniques that should be employed.

These are real dilemmas with important consequences, and there are no simple solutions to them. The goals of the program, the setting, and the nature of the groups involved will all influence the choices that are made with respect to these issues.

Conclusion

Prejudice, stereotyping, and discrimination are deeply rooted in the history of American society and of most other countries around the world. They have defied all previous attempts to eliminate them, and they persist into the present day. Their causes are complex and multi-faceted. They are sustained through socialization, structural inequalities in society, the mass media, and the functions they serve in maintaining self-esteem and group dominance, in promoting personal and group gain, and in simplifying cognitive processing.

As our review of the programs presented in this book makes clear, social science has now provided a wealth of new tools with which to do battle against the age-old scourges of racism, sexism, classism, religious intolerance, ageism, ableism, homophobia, and a host of other types of discriminatory relations between groups. In the last quarter century, there has been a phenomenal proliferation of programs designed to improve intergroup relations: They reflect a renewed concern for social justice and a growing recognition that something must be done to address these issues that threaten to undermine American society as well as other societies around the globe.

The programs that have been developed are amazingly diversified. They rely on a wide array of approaches, varying from direct confrontation of the issues to indirect approaches that dismantle prejudice, stereotyping, and discrimination without ever directly addressing them. These programs can be used in a variety of domains of cultural life including schools, the workplace, the community, and recreational settings. There are programs suitable to all ages. Although many of these programs were developed in isolation from one another, umbrella organizations are forming to bring practitioners together to share ideas and techniques. A national movement to confront injustice through the use of intergroup relations programs now exists in the United States.

Most intergroup relations programs are targeted at changing the attitudes and behaviors of individuals in the hopes that by changing individuals, the society itself can be changed. But prejudice, stereotyping, and discrimination need to be attacked at the structural level as well as at the individual level. Changing social structures is more difficult than changing individuals, and some of the intergroup relations programs we have discussed have as one of their goals modifying the societies within which they are conducted.

Wide implementation of intergroup relations programs could play a valuable role in transforming intergroup relations. Individuals would start to be involved in intergroup relations programs at school and could later be involved in these programs in organizational settings and in their communities. The training in one domain of life would complement training in other domains. Individuals would benefit from the cumulative effects of childhood, adolescent, and adult training. Trained individuals would become less prejudiced as a result of a greater sense of interdependence with others, greater empathy for others, an inclusive sense of community, friendships with outgroup members, intergroup understanding and appreciation, and increased levels of moral reasoning. The need for stereotyping would be reduced, and stereotypes would be counteracted through intergroup contact and knowledge. People would learn to interact effectively with outgroup members and acquire the ability to resolve conflicts constructively. They would possess enhanced interpersonal relations skills along with increased feelings of self-esteem and self-efficacy. They would feel less threatened by outgroup members. In addition, they would also receive the rewards derived from being treated by others in an egalitarian, humane manner. At the same time, training would increase understanding of societal-level prejudice in all its forms and motivate people to fight for social justice. There would also be improvements in intragroup relations, moving the interactions of all people in the society more toward collaboration and cooperation. It is becoming possible to envision a future that fulfills Martin Luther King's dream that people be judged on the content of their character, not the color of their skin or any other social category.

To achieve this future, intergroup relations programs will need to be more widely disseminated. Their value to society needs to be presented to the public and to organizations that could adopt them. The people involved in promoting and implementing them need to be dedicated and committed because there will continue to be resistance to these programs, as there is to any kind of fundamental social change. And there is no doubt that eliminating prejudice, stereotyping, and discrimination would be a fundamental change in the way most societies function. More funding from philanthropic foundations will be needed for these programs. Additional funding is also needed for research to refine existing techniques and develop new ones. We have learned a great deal about these programs, but much is yet to be learned.

We urge you to become involved in programs to improve intergroup relations. Together we can work toward a better future.

RESOURCE LITERATURE

MULTICULTURAL EDUCATION

Banks, J. A. (1994). *An introduction to multicultural education* (3rd ed.). Boston: Allyn & Bacon.

Banks, J. A. (1997). *Educating citizens in a multicultural society.* New York: Teachers College Press.

Bowers, V., & Swanson, D. (1988). *More than meets the eye.* Vancouver, Canada: Pacific Educational Press.

Bowser, B. P., Auletta, G. S., & Jones, T. (1993). *Confronting diversity issues on campus.* Newbury Park, CA: Sage.

Burke, B. (1995). *Celebrate our similarities.* Huntington Beach, CA: Teacher Created Materials, Inc. (P.O. Box 1040, 92647)

Cech, M. (1991). *Globalchild: Multicultural resources for young children.* Menlo Park, CA: Addison-Wesley.

Derman-Sparks, L. (1995). *Anti-bias curriculum: Tools for empowering children.* Washington, DC: National Association for the Education of Young Children.

Diaz, C. E. (Ed.). (1992). *Multicultural education for the 21st century.* Washington, DC: National Education Association.

Hands across the campus. (1999). New York: American Jewish Committee. (165 East 56th Street, New York, New York 10002)

Hawley, W. D., & Jackson, A. W. (Eds.). (1995). *Toward a common destiny: Improving race and ethnic relations in America.* San Francisco: Jossey-Bass.

Jones, J. M. (1998). *The cultural psychology of African-Americans.* Boulder, CO: Westview.

Looking for America: Vol. 1. Promising school based practices in intergroup relations. Boston: National Coalition of Advocates for Students. (100 Boyston St., Suite 737, Boston, MA 02116)

Niedergang, M., & McCoy, M. L. (1994). *Can't we all just get along: A manual for discussion programs on racism and race relations* (2nd ed.). Pomfret, CT: Study Circles Resource Center.

Parker, W. M., Archer, J., & Scott, J. (1992). *Multicultural relations on campus.* Muncie, IN: Accelerated Development.

Rothenberg, P. S. (Ed.). (1997). *Race, class, and gender* (4th ed.). New York: St. Martin's.

Simon, K. T., et al. (1996). *Lessons on equal worth and dignity.* New York: United Nations Association of the United States of America. (485 Fifth Ave., 10017-6104)

Thomson, B. J. (1992). *Words can hurt you: Beginning a program of anti-bias education.* Reading, MA: Addison-Wesley.

DIVERSITY TRAINING

Hemphill, H., & Haines, R. (1997). *Discrimination, harassment, and the failure of diversity training.* Westport, CT: Quorum.

Henderson, G. (1994). *Cultural diversity in the workplace.* Westport, CT: Quorum.

Jackson, S. E. & Associates (Eds.). (1992). *Diversity in the workforce.* New York: Guilford.

Kincaid, T. M., & Horner, E. R. (1997, March/April). Designing, developing, and implementing diversity training: Guidelines for practitioners. *Educational Technology,* 19-26.

Prasad, P., Mills, A. J., Elmes, M., & Prasad, A. (Eds.). (1997). *Managing the organizational melting pot: Dilemmas for the workplace.* Thousand Oaks, CA: Sage.

Nile, L. N. (1994). *Developing diversity training for the workplace: A guide for trainers.* Washington, DC: National MultiCultural Institute.

DIALOGUE GROUPS

Adams, M., Bell, L. A., & Griffin, P. (1997). *Teaching for diversity and social justice.* New York: Routledge.

Fisher, R. J. (1990). *The social psychology of intergroup and international conflict resolution.* New York: Springer-Verlag.

Schoem, D., Frankel, L., Zuniga, X., & Lewis, E. A. (Eds.). (1993). *Multicultural teaching in the university.* Westport, CT: Praeger.

INTERCULTURAL RELATIONS

Brislin, R. W., & Yoshida, T. (1994). *Improving intercultural interaction: Modules for cross-cultural training programs.* Thousand Oaks, CA: Sage.

Cushner, K., & Brislin, R. (1996). *Intercultural interaction: A practical guide* (2nd ed.). Thousand Oaks, CA: Sage.

Fowler, S. M., & Mumford, M. G. (1995). *Intercultural sourcebook: Cross-cultural training methods* (Vol. 1). Yarmouth, ME: Intercultural Press.

Kohls, L. R., & Knight, J. M. (1994). *Developing intercultural awareness.* Yarmouth, ME: Intercultural Press.

Landis, D., & Bhagat, R. S. (1996). *Handbook of intercultural training.* Thousand Oaks, CA: Sage.

Seelye, H. N. (Ed.). (1996). *Experiential activities for intercultural learning.* Yarmouth, ME: Intercultural Press.

Seelye, H. N., & Wasilewski, H. (1996). *Between cultures: Developing self-identity in a world of diversity.* Yarmouth, ME: Intercultural Press.

COOPERATIVE LEARNING

Aronson, E., & Patnoe, S. (1997). *The Jigsaw classroom.* New York: Longman.

Cohen, E. G. (1992). *Restructuring the classroom: Conditions for productive small groups.* Madison: Wisconsin Center for Education Research.

Cohen, J. J., & Fish, M. C. (1993). *Handbook of school based interventions.* San Francisco: Jossey-Bass.

Johnson, D. W., Johnson, R., & Holubec, E. J. (1994). *Circles of learning: Cooperation in the classroom* (4th ed.). Edina, MN: Interaction.

Kagan, S. (1986). *Cooperative learning resources for teachers.* Riverside: University of California.

Sharan, Y., & Sharan, S. (1992). *Group investigation: Expanding cooperative learning.* New York: Teacher's College Press.

Slavin, R. E. (1991). *Student team learning: A practical guide to cooperative learning.* Washington, DC: National Education Association.

Slavin, R. E., Sharan, S., Kagan, S., Hertz-Lazarowitz, R., Webb, C., & Schmuck, R. (Eds.). (1985). *Learning to cooperate, cooperating to learn.* New York: Plenum.

CONFLICT RESOLUTION TRAINING

Blake, D. R. S., & Mouton, J. S. (1984). *Solving costly organizational conflicts.* San Francisco: Jossey-Bass.

Bush, R. A. B., & Folger, J. P. (1994). *The promise of mediation: Responding to conflict through empowerment and recognition.* San Francisco: Jossey Bass.

Johnson, D. W., & Johnson, R. (1995). *Teaching students to be peacemakers* (3rd ed.). Edina, MN: Interaction.

Johnson, D. W., & Johnson, R. (1995). *My mediation notebook* (3rd ed.). Edina, MN: Interaction.

Fisher, R., & Ury, W. (1983). *Getting to YES: Negotiating agreement without giving in.* New York: Penguin.

Fisher, R. J. (1972). Third party consultation: A method for the study and resolution of conflict. *Journal of Conflict Resolution, 16,* 67-94.

Girard, K., & Koch, S. J. (1995). *Conflict resolution in the schools: A manual for educators.* San Francisco: Jossey-Bass.

Myers, S., & Filner, B. (1994). *Mediation across cultures: A handbook about conflict and culture.* Amherst, MA: Amherst Educational Publishing.

Raviv, A., Oppenheimer, L., & Bar-Tal, D. (Eds.). (1999). *How children understand war and peace: A call for international peace education.* San Francisco: Jossey-Bass.

Schoene, L. P., Jr., & DuPraw, M. E. (1994). *Racing racial and cultural conflict: Tools for rebuilding community* (2nd ed.). Washington, DC: Program for Community Problem Solving.

MORAL EDUCATION

Banks, J. A., & Banks, C. A. M. (1999). Teaching strategies for the social sciences: Decision-making and citizen action (5th ed.). New York: Longman.

Davidson, F. H., & Davidson, M. M. (1994). *Changing childhood prejudice: The caring work of the schools.* Westport, CT: Greenwood.

Fine, M. (1995). *Habits of mind: Struggling over values in America's classrooms.* San Francisco: Jossey-Bass.

Oser, F. K. (1985). Moral education and values education: The discourse perspective. In M. C. Wittrock (Ed.), *Handbook of research on teaching* (3rd ed.). New York: Macmillan.

DATABANKS

Also search CD-ROMs, such as ERIC, PscyINFO, and FirstSearch, in the reference section of most university libraries for up-to-date materials on intergroup relations and related topics. Many of the materials on ERIC can be ordered from the ERIC Clearinghouse.

RESOURCE CENTERS

Center for Teaching Peace
4501 Van Ness St. NW
Washington, DC 20016

Educational Video Network
2688 19th St.
Huntsville, TX 77340

Educators for Social Responsibility
23 Garden St.
Cambridge, MA 02138

Facing History and Ourselves
25 Kennard Rd.
Brookline, MA 02146

Grace Cotrino Abrams Peace Education Foundation
3550 Biscayne Blvd., Suite 400
Miami, FL 33137

Human Rights Resource Center
615 B St.
San Rafael, CA 94901

National Association for Mediation in Education
425 Amity St.
Amherst, MA 01002

Southern Poverty Law Center
400 Washington Ave.
Montgomery, AL 36104

REACH Center
4464 Fremont Ave. N., Suite 800
Seattle, WA 98103

REFERENCES

Aboud, F. E., & Doyle, A. B. (1993). The early development of ethnic identity and attitudes. In M. E. Bernal & G. P. Knight (Eds.), *Ethnic identity: Formation and transmission among Hispanics and other minorities* (pp. 47-59). Albany, NY: SUNY Press.

Aboud, F. E., & Doyle, A. B. (1996). Does talk of race foster prejudice or tolerance in children? *Canadian Journal of Behavioral Science, 28*, 161-170.

Aboud, F. E., & Fenwick, V. (2000). Exploring and evaluating school-based interventions to reduce prejudice. *Journal of Social Issues, 55*(4), 767-786.

Abrams, D., & Hogg, M. A. (1990). *Social identity theory: Constructive and critical advances.* New York: Springer-Verlag.

Abu-Nimer, M. (1999). *Dialogue, conflict resolution, and change.* Albany: State University of New York Press.

Adlerfer, C. P. (1977). Improving organizational communication through long-term group intervention. *Journal of Applied Behavioral Science, 13*, 193-210.

Adlerfer, C. P. (1982). Problems of changing White males' behavior and beliefs concerning race relations. In P. Goodman & Associates (Eds.), *Change in organizations* (pp. 122-165). San Francisco: Jossey-Bass.

Adlerfer, C. P. (1992). Changing race relations embedded in organizations: Report on a long-term project with the XYZ corporation. In S. E. Jackson & Associates (Eds.), *Diversity in the workforce* (pp. 138-166). New York: Guilford.

Adorno, T. W., Frenkel-Brunswick, E., Levinson, D. J., & Sanford, R. N. (1950). *The authoritarian personality.* New York: Harper.

Ajzen, I. (1988). *Attitudes, personality, and behavior.* Chicago: Dorsey.

Ajzen, I. (1991). The theory of planned behavior. *Organizational Behavior and Human Decision Processes, 50*, 179-211.

Albrecht, K., & Albrecht, S. (1993). *Added value negotiating: The breakthrough method for building balanced deals.* Homewood, IL: Business One Irwin.

Allport, F. H., et al. (1953). The effects of segregation and the consequences of desegregation: A social science statement. *Minnesota Law Review, 37*, 429-440.

Allport, G. W. (1954). *The nature of prejudice.* Reading, MA: Addison-Wesley.

Altemeier, B. (1981). *Right-wing authoritarianism.* Winnipeg, Canada: University of Manitoba Press.

Amir, Y. (1976). The role of intergroup contact in change of prejudice and race relations. In P. Katz & D. A. Taylor (Eds.), *Towards the elimination of racism* (pp. 245-308). New York: Pergamon.

Applebaum, B. (1997). Good liberal intentions are not enough! Racism, intentions, and moral responsibility. *Journal of Moral Education, 26*, 409-421.

Araragi, C. (1983). The effect of Jigsaw learning method on children's academic performance and learning attitude. *Japanese Journal of Educational Psychology, 31*, 102-112.

Aronson, A., & Gonzales, A. (1988). Desegregation, Jigsaw, and the Mexican-American experience. In P. A. Katz & D. A. Taylor (Eds.), *Eliminating racism: Profiles in controversy* (pp. 301-314). New York: Plenum.

Aronson, E. (1997). The theory of cognitive dissonance: The evolution and vicissitudes of an idea. In E. Harmon-Jones & J. S. Mills (Eds.), *Cognitive dissonance theory: Revival with revisions and controversies* (p. 20-35). Oxford, UK: Blackwell.

Aronson, E., Blaney, N., Stephan, C., Sikes, J., & Snapp, M. (1978). *The Jigsaw classroom.* Beverly Hills, CA: Sage.

Aronson, E., & Patnoe, S. (1997). *The Jigsaw classroom.* New York: Longman.

Aronson, E., & Thibodeau, R. (1992). The Jigsaw classroom: A cooperative strategy for reducing prejudice. In J. Lynch, C. Modgil, & S. Modgil (Eds.), *Cultural diversity in the schools* (Vol. II, pp. 231-256). London: Falmer.

Astin, A. (1993, March/April). Diversity and multiculturalism on campus: How are students affected? *Change, 25*, 44-49.

Avery, P. G., Bird, K., Johnstone, S., Sullivan, J. L., & Thalhammer, K. (1992). Exploring political tolerance with adolescents. *Theory and Research in Social Education, 20*, 386-420.

Avery, P. G., Johnson, D. W., Johnson, R. T., & Mitchell, J. M. (1999). Teaching an understanding of war and peace through structured academic controversies. In A. Raviv, L. Oppenheimer, & D. Bar-Tal (Eds.), *How children understand war and peace: A call for international peace education* (pp. 260-280). San Francisco: Jossey-Bass.

Bales, R. F. (1998). *Social interaction systems theory and measurement.* Piscataway, NJ: Transaction.

Bales, R. F., & Cohen, S. P. (1979). *A system for the multiple level observation of groups.* New York: Fress.

Bandura, A. (1982). Self-efficacy: Mechanism in human agency. *American Psychologist, 37*, 122-147.

Bandura, A. (1986). *The social foundations of thought and action.* Englewood Cliffs, NJ: Prentice-Hall.

Banks, J. A. (1973). *Teaching ethnic studies: Concepts and strategies.* Washington, DC: National Council for the Social Studies.

Banks, J. A. (1988). *Multicultural education* (2nd ed.). Boston: Allyn & Bacon.

Banks, J. A. (1993). Multicultural education and its critics: Britain and the United States. *The New Era, 65*(3), 58-64.

Banks, J. A. (1997). *Educating citizens in a multicultural society.* New York: Teachers College Press.

Banks, J. A., & Banks, C. A. M. (1999). *Teaching strategies for the social sciences: Decision-making and citizen action* (5th ed.). New York: Longman.

Bardige, B. (1981, Summer). Facing History and Ourselves: Tracing development through analysis of student journals. *Moral Education Forum, 6*, 42-48.

Bargal, D., & Bar, H. (1992). A Lewinian approach to intergroup workshops for Arab-Palestinian and Jewish youth. *Journal of Social Issues, 48*, 139-154.

Bargal, D., & Bar, H. (1994). The encounter of social selves: Intergroup workshops for Arab and Israeli youth. *Social Work With Groups, 17*(3), 39-59.

Barlow, D. E., & Barlow, M. H. (1993, Fall-Winter). Cultural diversity training in criminal justice: A progressive or conservative reform? *Social Justice, 20,* 69-84.

Barnard, W. A., & Benn, M. S. (1988). Belief congruence and prejudice reduction in an interracial contact setting. *Journal of Social Psychology, 128*(1), 125-134.

Batson, C. D., Polycarpou, M. P., Harmon-Jones, E., Imhoff, H. J., Mitchener, E. C., Bednar, L. L., Klein, T. R., & Highberger, L. (1997). Empathy and attitudes: Can feeling for a member of a stigmatized group improve feelings toward the group? *Journal of Personality and Social Psychology, 72,* 105-118.

Battistich, V., Solomon, D., Kim, D., Watson, M., & Schaps, E. (1995). Schools as communities, poverty levels of student populations, and students' attitudes, motives, and performance: A multilevel analysis. *American Educational Research Journal, 32,* 627-658.

Battistich, V., Solomon, D., Watson, M., Solomon, J., & Schaps, E. (1989). Effects of an elementary school program to enhance prosocial behavior on children's cognitive-social problem-solving skills and strategies. *Journal of Applied Developmental Psychology, 10,* 147-169.

Beck, C., Boyd, D., & Sullivan, E. (1978). *The moral education project (Year 5).* Toronto, Canada: Ontario Institute for Studies in Education.

Beck, C., Hersh, R., & Sullivan, E. (1978). *The moral education project (Year 4).* Toronto, Canada: Ontario Institute for Studies in Education.

Bennett, M. J. (1986). A developmental approach to training for intercultural sensitivity. *International Journal of Intercultural Relations, 10,* 179-200.

Berg-Cross, L., & Zoppetti, L. (1991). Person-in-culture interview: Understanding culturally different students. *Journal of College Student Psychotherapy, 5,* 5-21.

Berger, J. B., Rosenholtz, S. J., & Zelditch, M., Jr. (1980). Status organizing processes. *Annual Review of Sociology, 6,* 479-508.

Berry, A. (1997). Encouraging group skills in accountancy students: An innovative approach. In D. A. Riordan, D. L. Street, & B. M. Roof (Eds.), *Group learning: Applications in higher education* (pp. 47-62). Harrisonburg, VA: Institute for Research in Higher Education, James Madison University.

Berry, J. W. (1993). Ethnic identity in plural societies. In M. E. Bernal & B. P. Knight (Eds.), *Ethnic identity: Formation and transmission among Hispanics and other minorities* (pp. 271-296). Albany: State University of New York Press.

Bhagat, R. S., & Prien, K. O. (1996). Cross-cultural training in organizational contexts. In D. Landis & R. S. Bhagat (Eds.), *Handbook of intercultural training* (2nd ed., pp. 216-230). Thousand Oaks, CA: Sage.

Bhawuk, D. P. S. (1990). Cross-cultural orientation programs. In R. W. Brislin (Ed.), *Applied cross-cultural psychology* (pp. 325-346). Newbury Park, CA: Sage.

Bhawuk, D. P. S. (1998). The role of culture theory in cross-cultural training: A multimethod study of culture-specific, culture-general, and culture theory-based assimilators. *Journal of Cross-Cultural Psychology, 29,* 630-655.

Bhawuk, D. P. S., & Triandis, H. C. (1996). The role of culture theory in the study of culture and intercultural training. In D. Landis & R. S. Bhagat (Eds.), *Handbook of intercultural training* (2nd ed., pp. 17-34). Thousand Oaks, CA: Sage.

Bickmore, K. (1999). Teaching conflict and conflict resolution in school: (Extra)-curricular considerations. In A. Raviv, D. Bar-Tal, & L. Oppenheimer (Eds.), *How children understand war and peace: A call for international peace education* (pp. 233-259). San Francisco: Jossey-Bass.

Black, J. S., & Mendenhall, M. (1990). Cross-cultural training effectiveness: A review and theoretical framework for future research. *Academy of Management Review, 15*, 113-136.

Blake, B. F., Heslin, R., & Curtis, S. C. (1996). Measuring impacts of cross-cultural training. In D. Landis & R. S. Bhagat (Eds.), *Handbook of intercultural training* (2nd ed., pp. 165-182). Thousand Oaks, CA: Sage.

Blake, D. R. S., & Mouton, J. S. (1984). *Solving costly organizational conflicts.* San Francisco: Jossey-Bass.

Blake, R. R., & Mouton, J. S. (1964). *The managerial grid.* Houston, TX: Gulf.

Blanchard, F. A., Adelman, L., & Cook, S. W. (1975). Effect of group success and failure upon interpersonal attraction in cooperating interracial groups. *Journal of Personality and Social Psychology, 31*, 1020-1030.

Blaney, N., Stephan, C., Rosenfield, D., Aronson, E., & Sikes, J. (1977). Interdependence in the classroom: A field study. *Journal of Educational Psychology, 69*, 121-128.

Blatt, M., & Kohlberg, L. (1975). The effects of classroom discussion programs upon children's level of moral development. *Journal of Moral Education, 4*, 129-141.

Blumberg, R. G., & Roye, W. J. (1980). *Interracial bonds.* New York: General Hall.

Bobo, L. (1988). Group conflict, prejudice, and the paradox of contemporary racial attitudes. In P. A. Katz & D. A. Taylor (Eds.), *Eliminating racism: Profiles in controversy* (pp. 85-116). New York: Plenum.

Bodenhausen, G. V., & Wyer, R. S., Jr. (1985). Effects of stereotypes on decision making and information processing strategies. *Journal of Personality and Social Psychology, 48*, 267-282.

Boling, N. C., & Robinson, D. H. (1999). Individual study, interactive multimedia, or cooperative learning: Which activity best supplements lecture-based distance education? *Journal of Educational Psychology, 91*, 169-174.

Bond, M. A., & Pyle, J. L. (1998). The ecology of diversity in organizational settings: Lessons from a case study. *Human Relations, 51*, 589-623.

Boyd, D. (1996). A question of adequate aims. *Journal of Moral Education, 25*, 21-29.

Bredemeir, M. E., Bernstein, G., & Oxman, W. (1982). Bafa Bafa and dogmatism/ethnocentrism: A study of attitude change through simulation gaming. *Simulation & Games, 13*, 413-436.

Brewer, M. B. (2000). Reducing prejudice through cross-categorization: Effects of multiple social identities. In S. Oskamp (Ed.), *Reducing prejudice and discrimination* (pp. 165-183). Mahwah, NJ: Lawrence Erlbaum.

Brewer, M. B., & Miller, N. (1984). Beyond the contact hypothesis: Theoretical perspectives on desegregation. In N. Miller & M. B. Brewer (Eds.), *Groups in contact: The psychology of desegregation* (pp. 281-302). New York: Academic Press.

Brewer, M. B., & Miller, N. (1988). Contact and cooperation: When do they work? In P. A. Katz & D. A. Taylor (Eds.), *Eliminating racism: Profiles in controversy* (pp. 315-326). New York: Plenum.

Bridgeman, D. (1981). Enhanced role taking through cooperative interdependence: A field study. *Child Development, 52*, 1231-1238.

Brief, A. P., Buttram, R. T., Reizenstein, R. M., Pugh, S. D., Callahan, J. D., McCline, R. L., & Vaslow, J. B. (1997). Beyond good intentions: The next steps toward racial equality in the American workplace. *Academy of Management Executive, 11*(4), 59-72.

Brigham, J. C. (1971). Ethnic stereotypes. *Psychological Bulletin, 76*, 15-38.

Brislin, R. W., Cushner, K., Cherrie, C., & Yong, M. (1986). *Intercultural interactions: A practical guide.* Beverly Hills, CA: Sage.

Brislin, R. W., Landis, D., & Brandt, M. E. (1983). Conceptualizations of intercultural behavior and training. In D. Landis & R. W. Brislin (Eds.), *Handbook of intercultural training* (Vol. 1). New York: Pergamon.

Brislin, R. W., & Pedersen, P. (1976). *Cross-cultural orientation programs.* New York: Gardner.

Brislin, R. W., & Yoshida, T. (Eds.). (1994a). *Intercultural communication training: An introduction.* Thousand Oaks, CA: Sage.

Brislin, R. W., & Yoshida, T. (Eds.). (1994b). *Improving intercultural interactions: Modules for cross-cultural training programs.* Thousand Oaks, CA: Sage.

Brooks, G. S., & Kahn, S. E. (1990, September). Evaluation of a course in gender and cultural issues. *Cultural Education and Supervision, 30,* 66-76.

Broome, B. J. (1993). Managing differences in conflict resolution: The role of relational empathy. In D. J. D. Sandole & H. van der Merwe (Eds.), *Conflict resolution theory and practice: Integration and application* (pp. 97-111). New York: Manchester University Press.

Brown, S. P., Parham, T. A., & Yonker, R. (1996). Influence of cross-cultural training course on racial identity attitudes of White women and men: Preliminary perspectives. *Journal of Counseling & Development, 74,* 510-516.

Brown v. Board of Education of Topeka, 347 U.S. 483 (1954).

Bruschke, J. C., Gartner, C., & Seiter, J. S. (1993). Student ethnocentrism, dogmatism and motivation: A study of BAFA BAFA. *Simulation & Gaming, 24,* 9-20.

Burgess, H., & Burgess, G. M. (1997). *The encyclopedia of conflict resolution.* Santa Barbara, CA: ABC-CLIO.

Burke, R. J. (1970). Methods for resolving superior-subordinate conflict: The constructive use of subordinate differences and disagreements. *Organizational Behavior and Human Performance, 5,* 393-411.

Burnstein, E., & McCrae, A. V. (1962). Some effects of shared threat and prejudice in racially mixed groups. *Journal of Abnormal and Social Psychology, 64,* 257-260.

Burstein, P. (1985). *Discrimination, jobs, and politics.* Chicago: University of Chicago Press.

Burton, J. W. (1974). Conflict resolution. *International Studies Quarterly, 16,* 41-52.

Bush, R. A. B., & Folger, J. P. (1994). *The promise of mediation: Responding to conflict through empowerment and recognition.* San Francisco: Jossey Bass.

Byington, K., Fischer, J., Walker, L., & Freedman, E. (1997). Evaluating the effectiveness of a multicultural counseling ethics and assessment training. *Journal of Applied Rehabilitation Counseling, 28*(4), 15-19.

Byrne, D. (1971). *The attraction paradigm.* New York: Academic Press.

Byrnes, D. H., & Kiger, G. (1990). The effect of a prejudice reduction simulation on attitude change. *Journal of Applied Social Psychology, 20,* 341-356.

Byrnes, D. H., & Kiger, G. (1992). Prejudice reduction simulations: Ethics, evaluations, and theory into practice. *Simulation & Gaming, 23,* 457-471.

Campbell, D. E. (1996). *Choosing democracy: A practical guide to multicultural education.* Upper Saddle River, NJ: Prentice-Hall.

Caproni, P., & Finley, J. A. (1997). When organizations do harm. In P. Prasad, A. J. Mills, M. Elmes, & A. Prasad (Eds.), *Managing the organizational melting pot: Dilemmas for the workplace* (pp. 255-284). Thousand Oaks, CA: Sage.

Carnevale, P. J., & Pruitt, D. G. (1992). Negotiation and mediation. *Annual Review of Psychology, 43,* 531-582.

Carruthers, W. L., Sweeney, B., Kmitta, D., & Harris, G. (1996). Conflict resolution: An examination of the research literature and a model for program evaluation. *School Counselor, 44,* 5-18.

Carter, S. (1999). The importance of party buy-in in designing organizational conflict management systems. *Mediation Quarterly, 17,* 61-66.

Caudron, S. (1993). Training can damage diversity efforts. *Personnel Journal, 72*(4), 51-62.

Cavalier, J. C., Klein, J. D., & Cavalier, F. J. (1995). Effects of cooperative learning on performance, attitude, and group behaviors in a technical team environment. *Educational Technology Research and Development, 43*(3), 61-71.

Civil Rights Act of 1964, Pub. L. No. 88-352; 42 U.S.C. § 2000 *et seq.*

Cohen, E. G. (1980). Design and redesign of the desegregated school: Problems of status, power, and conflict. In W. G. Stephan & J. Feagin (Eds.), *School Desegregation* (pp. 251-280). New York: Plenum.

Cohen, E. G. (1984). The desegregated school: Problems in status power and interethnic climate. In N. Miller & M. B. Brewer (Eds.), *Groups in contact: The psychology of desegregation* (pp. 77-96). New York: Academic Press.

Cohen, E. G. (1986). *Designing groupwork: Strategies for heterogeneous classrooms.* New York: Teachers College Press.

Cohen, E. G. (1992). *Restructuring the classroom: Conditions for productive small groups.* Madison: Wisconsin Center for Education Research.

Cohen, E. G. (1994). Restructuring the classroom: Conditions for productive small groups. *Review of Educational Research, 64,* 1-35.

Cohen, E. G. (1997). Understanding status problems: Sources and consequences. In E. G. Cohen & R. A. Lotan (Eds.), *Working for equity in heterogeneous classrooms: Sociological theory in practice* (pp. 61-76). New York: Teachers College Press.

Cohen, E. G., Bianchini, J. A., Cossey, R., Holthuis, N. C., Morphew, C. C., & Whitcomb, J. A. (1997). What did students learn? 1982-1994. In E. G. Cohen & R. A. Lotan (Eds.), *Working for equity in heterogeneous classrooms: Sociological theory in practice* (pp. 137-165). New York: Teachers College Press.

Cohen, E. G., & Lotan, R. A. (1997). Raising expectations for competence: The effectiveness of status interventions. In E. G. Cohen & R. A. Lotan (Eds.), *Working for equity in heterogeneous classrooms: Sociological theory in practice* (pp. 77-91). New York: Teachers College Press.

Cohen, E. G., & Roper, S. (1972). Modification of interracial interaction disability: An application of status characteristics theory. *American Sociological Review, 37,* 643-657.

Colca, C., Lowen, D., Colca, L., & Lord, S. A. (1982). Combating racism in the schools. *Social Work and Education, 21*(1), 5-15.

Coleman, P. T., & Deutsch, M. (1998). The mediation of interethnic conflict in schools. In E. Weiner (Ed.), *Handbook of interethnic coexistence* (pp. 447-463). New York: Continuum.

Commins, B., & Lockwood, J. (1978). The effects on intergroup relations of mixing Roman Catholics and Protestants: An experimental investigation. *European Journal of Social Psychology, 8,* 383-386.

Condon, J. C. (1997). *Good neighbors: Communicating with the Mexicans* (2nd ed.). Yarmouth, ME: Intercultural Press.

Cooper, L., Johnson, D., Johnson, R., & Wilderson, F. (1980). Effects of cooperative, competitive, and individualistic experiences on interpersonal attraction among heterogeneous peers. *Journal of Social Psychology, 111,* 243-252.

Corder, J., & Thompson, M. (2000). *Mediation manual.* Austin, TX: Corder/Thompson & Associates.

Cose, E. (1999, September 18). The good news about Black America. *Newsweek, 83*(23), 29-40.

Cottell, P. G., Jr., & Millis, B. J. (1997). Cooperative learning structures in the instruction of accounting. In D. A. Riordan, D. L. Street, & B. M. Roof (Eds.), *Group learning: Applications in higher education* (pp. 9-28). Harrisonburg, VA: Institute for Research in Higher Education, James Madison University.

Cox, T. (1993). *Cultural diversity in organizations.* San Francisco: Berrett-Koehler.

Craver, C. B. (1997). *Effective legal negotiation and settlement* (3rd ed.). Charlottesville, VA: Michie Law.

Crocker, J., Hannah, D. B., & Weber, R. (1983). Person memory and causal attributions. *Journal of Personality and Social Psychology, 44,* 55-66.

Cross, W. E., Jr. (1991). *Shades of Black: Diversity in African-American identity.* Philadelphia: Temple University Press.

Cross, W. E., Jr. (1995). Oppositional identity and African-American youth: Issues and prospects. In W. D. Hawley & A. W. Jackson (Eds.), *Toward a common destiny* (pp. 185-204). San Francisco: Jossey-Bass.

Cui, G., & Awa, J. E. (1992). Measuring intercultural effectiveness: An integrating approach. *International Journal of Intercultural Relations, 16,* 311-328.

Culbertson, F. M. (1957). Modification of an emotionally held attitude through role playing. *Journal of Abnormal and Social Psychology, 54,* 230-233.

Cushner, K. (1989). Assessing the impact of a culture-general assimilator in intercultural training. *International Journal of Intercultural Relations, 13,* 125-146.

Cushner, K., & Landis, D. (1996). The intercultural sensitizer. In D. Landis & R. S. Bhagat (Eds.), *Handbook of intercultural training* (2nd ed., pp. 185-202). Thousand Oaks, CA: Sage.

D'Andrea, M., Daniels, J., & Heck, R. (1991). Evaluating the impact of multicultural counseling training. *Journal of Counseling and Development, 70,* 143-150.

Darley, J. M., Fleming, J. H., Hilton, J. L., & Swann, W. B., Jr. (1986). *Dispelling negative expectancies: The impact of interaction goals and target characteristics on the expectation confirmation process.* Unpublished manuscript, Princeton University, Princeton, NJ.

Dass, P., & Parker, B. (1999). Strategies for managing human resource diversity: From resistance to learning. *Academy of Management Executive, 13*(2), 68-80.

Davidson, F. H., & Davidson, M. M. (1994). *Changing childhood prejudice: The caring work of the schools.* Westport, CT: Greenwood.

Davidson, M. N., & Greenhalgh, L. (1999). The role of emotion in negotiation: The impact of anger and race. In R. J. Bies, R. J. Lewicki, & B. H. Sheppard (Eds.), *Research on negotiations in organizations* (Vol. 7, pp. 3-26). Stamford, CT: JAI.

Davis, M. H. (1994). *Empathy: A social psychological approach.* Madison, WI: Brown & Benchmark.

Day-Vines, N. L., Day-Hairston, B. O., Carruthers, W. L., Wall, J. A., & Lupton-Smith, H. A. (1996). Conflict resolution: The value of diversity in the recruitment, selection, and training of peer mediators. *School Counselor, 43,* 392-410.

Della Noce, D. J. (1999). Seeing theory in practice: An analysis of empathy in mediation. *Negotiation Journal, 15,* 271-301.

Derlega, V. J., Metts, S., Petronio, S., & Margulis, S. T. (1993). *Self-disclosure.* Newbury Park, CA: Sage.

Desforges, D. M., Lord, C. G., Ramsey, S. L., Mason, J. A., VanLeeuven, M. D., West, S. C., & Lepper, M. R. (1991). Effects of structured cooperative contact on changing negative attitudes toward stigmatized social groups. *Journal of Personality and Social Psychology, 60,* 531-544.

Deutsch, M. (1949). A theory of cooperation and competition. *Human Relations, 2,* 129-152.

Deutsch, M. (1962). Cooperation and trust: Some theoretical notes. In M. R. Jones (Ed.), *Nebraska symposium on motivation* (Vol. 10, pp. 275-319). Lincoln, NE: University of Nebraska Press.

Deutsch, M. (1973). *The resolution of conflict.* New Haven, CT: Yale University Press.

Deutsch, M. (1992). *The effects of training in conflict resolution and cooperative learning in an alternative high school.* New York: Teachers College, Columbia University, International Center for Cooperation and Conflict Resolution.

Devine, P. (1989). Stereotypes and prejudice: Their automatic and controlled components. *Journal of Personality and Social Psychology, 56,* 5-18.

Devine, P. (1995). Prejudice and outgroup perception. In A. Tesser (Ed.), *Advanced social psychology* (pp. 467-524). New York: McGraw-Hill.

Devine, P. G., Evett, S. R., & Vasquez-Suson, K. A. (1996). Exploring the interpersonal dynamics of intergroup contact. In R. M. Sorrentino & E. T. Higgins (Eds.), *Handbook of motivation and cognition: The interpersonal context* 3 (pp. 423-464). New York: Guilford.

Devine, P. G., & Monteith, M. J. (1993). The role of discrepancy-associated affect in prejudice reduction. In D. M. Macke & D. L. Hamilton (Eds.), *Affect, cognition, and stereotyping: Interactive processes in intergroup perception* (pp. 317-344). San Diego, CA: Academic Press.

Devine, P. G., Monteith, M. J., Zuwerink, J. R., & Elliot, A. J. (1991). Prejudice with and without compunction. *Journal of Personality and Social Psychology, 60,* 817-830.

DeVries, D. L., & Edwards, K. J. (1974). Student teams and learning games: Their effects on cross-race and cross-sex interaction. *Journal of Educational Psychology, 66,* 741-749.

DeVries, D. L., Edwards, K. J., & Slavin, R. E. (1978). Biracial learning teams and race relations in the classroom: Four field experiments on Teams-Games-Tournaments. *Journal of Educational Psychology, 70,* 356-362.

Digh, P. (1998, October). The next challenge: Holding people accountable. *HR Magazine, 43,* 63-69.

Dominguez, C. (1992). The challenge of Workforce 2000. *The Bureaucrat, 21*(4), 15-19.

Doob, L. W. (1974). A Cyprus workshop: An exercise in intervention methodology. *Journal of Social Psychology, 84,* 161-178.

Dovidio, J. F., Kawakami, K., & Gaertner, S. L. (2000). Reducing contemporary prejudice: Combating explicit and implicit bias at the individual and intergroup level. In S. Oskamp (Ed.), *Reducing prejudice and discrimination* (pp. 137-163). Mahwah, NJ: Lawrence Erlbaum.

Dubinsky, E. (1997). *Readings in cooperative learning for undergraduate mathematics.* Washington, DC: Mathematical Association of America.

Dubois, P. M., & Hutson, J. J. (1997). *Intergroup dialogues across America.* Hadley, MA: Common Wealth Printing.

Duckett, J. (1992). *The social psychology of prejudice.* New York: Praeger.

Dukes, E. F. (1996). *Resolving public conflict: Transforming community and government.* Manchester, UK: Manchester University Press.

Dunn, T. P., & Wozniak, P. R. (1976). Simulation review. *Simulation & Games, 7,* 471-475.

Dunnette, M. D., & Motowildo, S. J. (1982). Estimating benefits and costs of antisexist training programs in organizations. In H. J. Bernardin (Ed.), *Women in the workplace* (pp. 156-182). New York: Praeger.

Earley, P. C. (1987). Intercultural training for managers: A comparison of documentary and interpersonal methods. *Academy of Management Journal, 30,* 685-698.

Elementary and Secondary Education Act of 1965, 20 U.S.C. § 2701 *et seq.*

Ellis, C., & Sonnenfield, J. A. (1994, Spring). Diverse approaches to managing diversity. *Human Resource Management, 33,* 79-109.

Emler, N. (1996). How can we decide whether moral education works? *Journal of Moral Education, 25,* 117-126.

Erber, R., & Fiske, S. T. (1984). Affective and semantic priming: Effects of mood on category accessibility and inference. *Journal of Experimental Social Psychology, 27,* 480-498.

Feagin, J. R., & Vera, H. (1995). *White racism.* New York: Routledge.

Fine, M. (1991/1992). Facing history and ourselves: Portrait of a classroom. *Educational Leadership, 49,* 44-49.

Fine, M. (1993). Collaborative innovations: Documentation of the Facing History and Ourselves program at an essential school. *Teachers College Record, 94,* 771-789.

Fine, M. (1995). *Habits of the mind: Struggling over values in America's classrooms.* San Francisco: Jossey-Bass.

Finlay, K. A., & Stephan, W. G. (2000). Reducing prejudice: The effects of empathy on intergroup attitudes. *Journal of Applied Social Psychology, 30*(8), 1720-1737.

Fishbein, M., & Ajzen, I. (1975). *Belief, attitude, intention, and behavior: An introduction to theory and research.* Reading, MA: Addison-Wesley.

Fisher, R., & Ury, W. (1983). *Getting to YES: Negotiating agreement without giving in.* New York: Penguin.

Fisher, R. J. (1972). Third party consultation: A method for the study and resolution of conflict. *Journal of Conflict Resolution, 16,* 67-94.

Fisher, R. J. (1976). Third-party consultation: A skill for professional psychologists in community practice. *Professional Psychology, 7,* 334-351.

Fisher, R. J. (1990). *The social psychology of intergroup and international conflict resolution.* New York: Springer-Verlag.

Fisher, R. J. (1997). *Interactive conflict resolution.* Syracuse, NY: Syracuse University Press.

Fisher, R. J., & Keashly, L. (1990). Third party consultation as a method of intergroup and international conflict resolution. In R. J. Fisher, *The social psychology of intergroup and international conflict resolution* (pp. 211-238). New York: Springer-Verlag.

Fiske, S. T. (2000). Interdependence and the reduction of prejudice. In S. Oskamp (Ed.), *Reducing prejudice and discrimination* (pp. 115-136). Thousand Oaks, CA: Sage.

Flynn, G., (1998). The harsh reality of diversity programs. *Workforce, 77,* 26-30.

Forester, J., & Stitzel, D. (1989). Beyond neutrality: The possibilities of activist mediation in public sector conflicts. *Negotiation Journal, 1,* 251-264.

Fowler, S. M. (1994). Two decades of using simulation games for cross-cultural training. *Simulation & Gaming, 25,* 464-476.

Frable, D. E. S., Blackstone, T., & Scherbaum, C. (1990). Marginal and mindful: Deviants in social interactions. *Journal of Personality and Social Psychology, 59,* 140-149.

Frady, M. (1968). *Wallace.* New York: Knopf.

French, W. L., & Bell, C. H., Jr. (1990). *Organization development: Behavioral science interventions for organizational improvement* (4th ed.). Englewood Cliffs, NJ: Prentice-Hall.

Friedman, R., & Davidson, M. N. (1999). The Black-White gap in perceptions of discrimination: Its causes and consequences. In R. J. Bies, R. J. Lewicki, & B. H. Sheppard (Eds.), *Research on negotiations in organizations* (Vol. 7, pp. 203-228). Stamford, CT: JAI.

Furnham, A., & Bochner, S. (1986). *Cultural shock: Psychological reactions to unfamiliar environments*. New York: Methuen.

Fyock, J., & Stangor, C. (1994). The role of memory biases in stereotype maintenance. *British Journal of Social Psychology, 33,* 331-343.

Gadlin, H. (1994). Conflict resolution, cultural differences, and the culture of racism. *Negotiation Journal, 10,* 33-47.

Gaertner, S. L., & Dovidio, J. F. (1986). The aversive form of racism. In J. F. Dovidio & S. L. Gaertner (Eds.), *Prejudice, discrimination, and racism* (pp. 61-90). Orlando, FL: Academic Press.

Gaertner, S. L., Dovidio, J. F., Nier, J. A., Ward, C. M., & Banker, B. S. (1999). Across cultural divides: The value of superordinate identity. In D. A. Prentice & D. T. Miller (Eds.), *Cultural divides: Understanding and overcoming group conflict* (pp. 173-212). New York: Russell Sage Foundation.

Gaertner, S. L., Mann, J., Dovidio, J. F., Murrell, A., & Pomare, M. (1990). How does cooperation reduce intergroup bias? *Journal of Personality and Social Psychology, 59,* 692-704.

Gaertner, S. L., Mann, J., Murrell, A., & Dovidio, J. F. (1989). Reducing intergroup bias: The benefits of recategorization. *Journal of Personality and Social Psychology, 57,* 239-249.

Gannon, M. J., & Poon, J. M. L. (1997). Effects of alternative instructional approaches on cross-cultural training outcomes. *International Journal of Intercultural Relations, 21,* 429-446.

Garcia, M. H. (1995). An anthropological approach to multicultural diversity training. *Journal of Applied Behavioral Science, 31,* 490-500.

Gardiner, G. S. (1972). Complexity training and prejudice reduction. *Journal of Applied Social Psychology, 2,* 326-342.

Garrow, D. J. (1978). *Protest at Selma: Martin Luther King Jr. and the voting rights act of 1965.* New Haven, CT: Yale University Press.

Gelfand, M. J., & Realo, A. (1999). Individualism-collectivism and accountability in intergroup negotiations. *Journal of Applied Psychology, 84,* 721-736.

Genet, D. (1999). *Hands across the campus.* New York: American Jewish Committee.

Gilligan, C. (1982). *In a different voice: Women's conceptions of the self and of morality.* Cambridge, MA: Harvard University Press.

Girard, K., & Koch, S. J. (1995). *Conflict resolution in the schools: A manual for educators.* San Francisco: Jossey-Bass.

Glazer, I. M. (1997). Beyond the competition of tears: Black-Jewish conflict containment in a New York neighborhood. In D. P. Fry & K. Bjorkqvist (Eds.), *Cultural variation in conflict resolution: Alternatives to violence* (pp. 137-213). Mahwah, NJ: Lawrence Erlbaum.

Glick, P., & Fiske, S. T. (1996). The ambivalent sexism inventory: Differentiating hostile and benevolent sexism. *Journal of Personality and Social Psychology, 70,* 491-512.

Goldman, A. (1992). Intercultural training of Japanese for U.S.-Japanese interorganizational communication. *International Journal of Intercultural Relations, 16,* 175-216.

Goldstein, D. L., & Smith, D. H. (1999). The analysis of the effects of experiential training on sojourners' cross-cultural adaptability. *International Journal of Intercultural Relations, 23*, 157-173.

Gonzales, A. (1979, August). *Classroom cooperation and ethnic balance*. Paper presented at the annual convention of the American Psychological Association, New York.

Gorsuch, R. L., & Ortberg, J. (1983). Moral obligation and attitudes: Their relation to behavioral intentions. *Journal of Personality and Social Psychology, 44*, 1025-1028.

Gottfredson, L. S. (1992). Dilemmas in developing diversity programs. In S. E. Jackson & Associates (Eds.), *Diversity in the workforce* (pp. 279-305). New York: Guilford.

Grant, C. A., & Grant, G. A. (1985). Staff development and education that is multicultural. *British Journal of In-Service Education, 12*, 6-18.

Gray, D. B., & Ashmore, R. D. (1975). Comparing the effects of informational, role-playing, and value-discrepant treatments of racial attitudes. *Journal of Applied Social Psychology, 5*, 262-281.

Greenbaum, P., & Greenbaum, S. (1983). Cultural differences, nonverbal regulation, and classroom interaction: Sociolinguistic interference in American Indian education. *Peabody Journal of Education, 61*(1), 16-33.

Greenwald, A. G., McGhee, D. E., & Schwartz, J. L. K. (1998). Measuring individual differences in implicit cognition: The implicit association test. *Journal of Personality and Social Psychology, 74*, 1464-1480.

Griesbach, A. (1999). *The psychological processes in dialogue groups and facilitator interventions*. Unpublished master's thesis, School for International Training, Brattleboro, VT.

Grossman, H. (1995). *Educating Hispanic students* (2nd ed.). Springfield, IL: Charles C Thomas.

Grube, J. W., Mayton, D. M., & Ball-Rokeach, S. J. (1994). Inducing change in values, attitudes, and behaviors: Belief system theory and the method of value self-confrontation. *Journal of Social Issues, 50*, 153-173.

Gudykunst, W. B. (1988). Uncertainty and anxiety. In Y. Y. Kim & W. B. Gudykunst (Eds.), *Theories in intercultural communication* (pp. 123-156). Newbury Park, CA: Sage.

Gudykunst, W. B. (1993). Toward a theory of interpersonal and intergroup communication: An anxiety/uncertainty management (AUM) perspective. In R. Wiseman & J. Koester (Eds.), *Intercultural communication competence* (pp. 33-71). Newbury Park, CA: Sage.

Gudykunst, W. B. (1995). Anxiety/uncertainty management (AUM) theory: Development and current status. In R. L. Wiseman (Ed.), *Intercultural communication theory* (pp. 8-51). Thousand Oaks, CA: Sage.

Gudykunst, W. B., Guzley, R. M., & Hammer, M. R. (1996). Designing intercultural training. In D. Landis & R. S. Bhagat (Eds.), *Handbook of intercultural training* (2nd ed., pp. 61-80). Thousand Oaks, CA: Sage.

Gudykunst, W. B., & Hammer, M. R. (1983). Basic training design: Approaches to intercultural training. In D. Landis & R. W. Brislin (Eds.), *Handbook of intercultural training* (Vol. 1, pp. 118-154). New York: Pergamon.

Gudykunst, W. B., Hammer, M. R, & Wiseman, R. I. (1977). An analysis of an integrated approach to cross-cultural training. *International Journal of Intercultural Relations, 1*, 99-110.

Gunsch, D. (1993, June). Games augment diversity training. *Personnel Journal, 6*, 78-88.

Gurin, P., Peng, T., Lopez, G., & Nagda, B. R. (1999). Context, identity, and intergroup relations. In D. Prentice & D. Miller (Eds.), *Cultural divides: The social psychology of intergroup contact* (pp. 133-170). New York: Russell Sage Foundation.

Hacker, A. (1992). *Two nations: Black and White separate, hostile, unequal.* New York: Scribner.

Hall, R. (1999). Learning conflict management through peer mediation. In A. Raviv, L. Oppenheimer, & D. Bar-Tal (Eds.), *How children understand war and peace: A call for international peace education* (pp. 281-298). San Francisco: Jossey-Bass.

Hallinan, M. T., & Teixeira, R. A. (1987). Students' interracial friendships: Individual characteristics, structural effects, and racial differences. *American Journal of Education, 95,* 563-583.

Hamilton, D. L., & Rose, T. (1980). Illusory correlation and the maintenance of stereotype beliefs. *Journal of Personality and Social Psychology, 39,* 832-845.

Hamilton, D. L., & Sherman, S. J. (1996). Perceiving persons and groups. *Psychological Review, 103,* 336-355.

Hammer, M. R., Gudykunst, W. B., & Wiseman, R. I. (1978). Dimensions of intercultural effectiveness. *International Journal of Intercultural Relations, 2,* 382-393.

Hanover, J. M. B., & Cellar, D. F. (1998). Environmental factors and the effectiveness of workforce diversity training. *Human Resource Development Quarterly, 9,* 105-124.

Harding, J., Kutner, B., Proshansky, N., & Chein, I. (1954). Prejudice and ethnic relations. In G. Lindzey (Ed.), *Handbook of social psychology* (Vol. II, pp. 1021-1061). Cambridge, MA: Addison-Wesley.

Hare, S. E., & Hare, A. P. (Eds.). (1996). *SYMLOG field theory: Organizational consultation, value differences, personality and social perception.* Westport, CT: Praeger.

Harrington, H. J., & Miller, N. (1992). Research and theory in intergroup relations: Issues of consensus and controversy. In J. Lynch, D. Modgil, & S. Modgil (Eds.), *Cultural diversity and the schools: Prejudice, polemic or progress?* (pp. 159-178). London: Falmer Press.

Harris, M. J., Milich, R., Corbitt, E. M., Hoover, D. W., & Brady, M. (1992). Self-fulfilling effects of stigmatizing information on children's social interactions. *Journal of Personality and Social Psychology, 63,* 41-50.

Harrison, J. K. (1992). Individual and combined effects of behavioral modeling and the cultural assimilator in cross-cultural management training. *Journal of Applied Psychology, 77,* 952-962.

Harrison, R., & Hopkins, R. L. (1967). The design of cross-cultural training: An alternative to the university model. *Journal of Applied Behavioral Sciences, 3,* 431-460.

Hauserman, N., Walen, S. R., & Behling, M. (1973). Reinforced racial integration in the first grade: A study of generalization. *Journal of Applied Behavioral Analysis, 6,* 193-200.

Haynes, N. M., & Gebreyesus, S. (1992). Cooperative learning: A case for African-American students. *School Psychology Review, 21,* 577-585.

Hemphill, H., & Haines, R. (1997). *Discrimination, harassment, and the failure of diversity training.* Westport, CT: Quorum.

Henderson, G. (1994). *Cultural diversity in the workplace.* Westport, CT: Quorum.

Hennington, M. (1981, Spring). Effect of intensive multicultural non-sexist instruction on secondary student teachers. *Educational Research Quarterly, 6,* 65-75.

Heppner, M. J., & O'Brien, K. M. (1994, September). Multicultural counselor training: Students' perceptions of helpful and hindering events. *Counseling Education and Supervision, 34,* 4-18.

Hertz-Lazarowitz, R., Kuppermintz, H., & Lang, J. (1998). Arab-Jewish coexistence: Beit Hagafen coexistence programs. In E. Weiner (Ed.), *The handbook of interethnic coexistence* (pp. 565-584). New York: Continuum.

Hertz-Lazarowitz, R., & Zelniker, T. (in press). Cooperative learning in Israel: Historical, cultural, and educational perspective. *International Journal of Research in Education.*

Hersh, R. H., Miller, J. P., & Fielding, G. D. (1980). *Models of moral education: An appraisal.* London: Longman.

Hewstone, M. (1996). Contact and categorization. In C. N. Macrae, C. Stangor, & M. Hewstone (Eds.), *Foundations of stereotypes and stereotyping* (pp. 323-368). New York: Guilford.

Hewstone, M., & Brown, R. (1986). Contact is not enough: An intergroup perspective on the contact hypothesis. In M. Hewstone & R. Brown (Eds.), *Contact and conflict in intergroup encounters* (pp. 1-44). Oxford, UK: Basil Blackwell.

Hewstone, M., Islam, M. R., & Judd, C. M. (1993). Models of crossed categorization and intergroup relations. *Journal of Personality and Social Psychology, 64,* 779-793.

Hilton, J. L., & von Hippel, W. (1996). Stereotypes. *Annual Review of Psychology, 47,* 237-271.

Hitt, M. A., & Keats, B. W. (1984). Empirical identification of the criteria for effective affirmative action programs. *Journal of Applied Behavioral Science, 20,* 203-222.

Hohn, R. L. (1973). Perceptual training and its effects on racial preferences in kindergarten children. *Psychological Reports, 32,* 435-441.

Hollister, L., Day, N. E., & Jesaitis, P. T. (1993, Winter). Diversity programs: Key to competitiveness or just another fad. *Organization Development Journal, 11*(4), 49-59.

Holmes, M. (1980). Forward to the basics: A radical conservative reconstruction. *Curriculum Inquiry, 10,* 383-418.

Holmes, H., & Guild, S. (1971). *Manual of teaching techniques for intercultural education.* Amherst: University of Massachusetts.

Howitt, D., & Owusu-Bempah, J. (1990). The pragmatics of institutional racism: Beyond words. *Human Relations, 43,* 885-899.

Hubbard, A. S. (1997). Face-to-face and at arm's length: Conflict norms and extra-group relations in grassroots dialogue groups. *Human Organization, 56,* 265-274.

Humphreys, B., Johnson, R., & Johnson, D. W. (1982). Effects of cooperative, competitive, and individualistic learning on students' achievement in science class. *Journal of Research in Science Teaching, 19,* 351-356.

Jackson, S. E. (1992). Stepping into the future: Guidelines for action. In S. E. Jackson & Associates (Eds.), *Diversity in the workforce* (pp. 319-339). New York: Guilford.

Jackson, M. W. (1979). An antipodean evaluation of simulation in teaching. *Simulation & Games, 10,* 99-138.

Jacob, B. A. (1995). Defining culture in a multicultural environment: An ethnography of Heritage High School. *American Journal of Education, 103,* 339-376.

Jacobs, R. L., & Baum, M. (1987). Simulation and games in training and development: Status and concerns about their use. *Simulation & Games, 18,* 385-394.

Johnson, D. W. (1970). *Social psychology of education.* Edina, MN: Interaction.

Johnson, D. W. (1991). *Human relations and your career* (3rd ed.). Englewood Cliffs, NJ: Prentice-Hall.

Johnson, D. W., & Johnson, F. (1997). *Joining together: Group theory and group skills* (6th ed.). Englewood Cliffs, NJ: Prentice-Hall.

Johnson, D. W., Johnson, R., & Maruyama, G. (1984). Goal interdependence and interpersonal attraction in heterogeneous classrooms. In N. Miller & M. B. Brewer (Eds.), *Groups in contact* (pp. 187-213). New York: Academic Press.

Johnson, D. W., & Johnson, R. T. (1975). *Learning together and alone*. Englewood Cliffs, NJ: Prentice-Hall.

Johnson, D. W., & Johnson, R. T. (1981). Effects of cooperative and individualistic learning experiences on interethnic interaction. *Journal of Educational Psychology, 73,* 444-449.

Johnson, D. W., & Johnson, R. T. (1989). *Cooperation and competition: Theory and research.* Edina, MN: Interaction.

Johnson, D. W., & Johnson, R. T. (1992a). Positive interdependence: Key to effective cooperation. In R. Hertz-Lazarowitz & N. Miller (Eds.), *Interaction in cooperative groups* (pp. 174-199). New York: Cambridge University Press.

Johnson, D. W., & Johnson, R. T. (1992b). Social interdependence and crossethnic relationships. In J. Lynch, C. Modgil, & S. Modgil (Eds.), *Cultural diversity in the schools* (Vol. II, pp. 179-190). London: Falmer.

Johnson, D. W., & Johnson, R. T. (1994a). Learning together. In S. Sharan (Ed.), *Handbook of cooperative learning methods* (pp. 51-65). Westport, CT: Greenwood.

Johnson, D. W., & Johnson, R. T. (1994b). Structuring academic controversy. In S. Sharan (Ed.), *Handbook of cooperative learning methods* (pp. 66-81). Westport, CT: Greenwood.

Johnson, D. W., & Johnson, R. T. (1995a). *My mediation notebook* (3rd ed.). Edina, MN: Interaction.

Johnson, D. W., & Johnson, R. T. (1995b). *Teaching students to be peacemakers* (3rd ed.). Edina, MN: Interaction.

Johnson, D. W., & Johnson, R. T. (1996). Conflict resolution and peer mediation programs in elementary and secondary schools: A review of the research. *Review of Educational Research, 66,* 459-506.

Johnson, D. W., & Johnson, R. T. (2000). The three Cs of reducing prejudice and discrimination. In S. Oskamp (Ed.), *Reducing prejudice and discrimination* (pp. 239-268). Hillsdale, NJ: Lawrence Erlbaum.

Johnson, D. W., Johnson, R. T., & Bartlett, J. K. (1990). *My mediation notebook.* Edina, MN: Interaction.

Johnson, D. W., Johnson, R. T., Johnson, J., & Anderson, D. (1976). The effects of cooperative vs. individualized instruction on student prosocial behavior, attitudes toward learning, and achievement. *Journal of Educational Psychology, 68,* 446-452.

Johnson, D. W., Johnson, R. T., & Smith, K. A. (1995). Cooperative learning and individual school achievement in secondary schools. In E. G. Cohen & R. A. Lotan (Eds.), *Working for equity in heterogeneous classrooms: Sociological theory in practice* (pp. 15-27). NY: Teachers College Press.

Johnston, L., & Hewstone, M. (1992). Cognitive models of stereotype change. *Journal of Experimental Social Psychology, 28,* 360-386.

Jones, J. M. (1997). *Prejudice and racism* (2nd ed.). New York: McGraw-Hill.

Jones, T. S., & Brickman, H. (1994). "Teach your children well." Recommendations for peer mediation programs. In J. P. Folger & T. S. Jones (Eds.), *New directions in mediation: Communication research and perspectives* (pp. 159-174). Thousand Oaks, CA: Sage.

Jost, J. T., & Banaji, M. R. (1993). The role of stereotyping in system-justification and the production of false consciousness. *British Journal of Social Psychology, 33,* 1-27.

Judd, C. M., & McClelland, G. H. (1998). Measurement. In D. T. Gilbert, S. T. Fiske, & G. Lindzey (Eds.), *Handbook of social psychology* (Vol. 1, 4th ed., pp. 181-232). New York: Random House.

Judd, C. M., Smith, E. R., & Kidder, L. H. (1991). *Research methods in social psychology*. Fort Worth, TX: Holt, Rinehart & Winston.

Kagan, S., Zahn, G. L., Widaman, K. F., Schwarzwald, J., & Tyrell, G. (1985). Classroom structural bias: Impact of cooperative and competitive classroom structure on cooperative and competitive individuals and groups. In R. E. Slavin, S. Sharan, S. Kagan, R. Hertz-Lazarowitz, C. Webb, & R. Schmuck (Eds.), *Learning to cooperate, cooperating to learn* (pp. 277-312). New York: Plenum.

Karambayya, R., & Brett, J. M. (1994). Managerial third parties: Intervention strategies, processes, and consequences. In J. P. Folger & T. S. Jones (Eds.), *New directions in mediation: Communication research and perspectives* (pp. 175-192). Thousand Oaks, CA: Sage.

Katz, I., Wackenhut, J., & Hass, R. G. (1986). Racial ambivalence, value duality, and behavior. In J. F. Dovidio & S. L. Gaertner (Eds.), *Prejudice, discrimination, and racism* (pp. 35-60). New York: Academic Press.

Katz, J. H. (1975). *White awareness: Handbook for anti-racism training*. Norman, OK: University of Oklahoma Press.

Katz, J. H., & Ivey, A. (1977). White awareness: The frontier of racism awareness training. *Personnel and Guidance Journal, 55,* 485-489.

Kealey, D. J., & Protheroe, D. R. (1996). The effectiveness of cross-cultural training for expatriates: An assessment of the literature on the issue. *International Journal of Intercultural Relations, 20,* 141-165.

Kehoe, J. W., & Rogers, W. T. (1978). The effects of principle testing discussions on student attitudes toward selected groups subjected to discrimination. *Canadian Journal of Education, 3,* 73-80.

Kelman, H. C. (1979). An interactional approach to conflict resolution and its application to Palestinian-Israeli relations. *International Interactions, 6,* 99-122.

Kelman, H. C. (1990). Applying a human needs perspective to the practice of conflict resolution: The Israeli-Palestinian case. In J. W. Burton (Ed.), *Conflict: Human needs theory* (pp. 283-297). New York: St. Martin's.

Kelman, H. C. (1997). Group processes in the resolution of international conflicts. *American Psychologist, 52,* 212-220.

Kelman, H. C. (1999). The interdependence of Israeli and Palestinian national identities: The role of the other in existential conflicts. *Journal of Social Issues, 55,* 581-600.

Kelman, H. C., & Cohen, S. P. (1976). The problem-solving workshop: A social psychological contribution to the resolution of international conflict. *Journal of Peace Research, 13,* 79-90.

Kelman, H. C., & Cohen, S. P. (1986). Resolution of international conflict: An interactional approach. In S. Worchel & W. G. Austin (Eds.), *Psychology of intergroup relations* (pp. 323-342). Chicago: Nelson Hall.

Kenny, D. A., Kashy, D. A., & Bolger, A. (1998). Data analysis in social psychology. In D. T. Gilbert, S. T. Fiske, & G. Lindzey (Eds.), *Handbook of social psychology* (Vol. 1, 4th ed., pp. 233-265). New York: Random House.

Kincaid, T. M., & Horner, E. R. (1997). Designing, developing, and implementing diversity training: Guidelines for practitioners. *Educational Technology, 7*(2), 19-26.

Kinder, D. R., & Sanders, L. M. (1996). *Divided by race: Racial attitudes and democratic ideals.* Chicago: University of Chicago Press.

Kirschenbaum, H. (1977). *Advanced value clarification.* La Jolla, CA: University Associates.

Kitano, H. H. L., & Daniels, R. (1995). *Asian Americans: Emerging minorities* (2nd ed.). Englewood Cliffs, NJ: Prentice-Hall.

Kluger, R. (1976). *Simple justice.* New York: Knopf.

Kochman, T. (1981). *Black and White styles in conflict.* Chicago: University of Chicago Press.

Kohlberg, L. (1969a). Stage and sequence: The cognitive-developmental approach to socialization. In T. Mischel (Ed.), *Cognitive development and epistemology* (pp. 151-235). New York: Academic Press.

Kohlberg, L. (1969b). Stage and sequence: The cognitive developmental approach to socialization. In D. A. Goslin (Ed.), *Handbook of socialization theory and research.* Chicago: Rand McNally.

Kohlberg, L. (1981). *Essays on moral development.* New York: Harper & Row.

Kohlberg, L. (1984). *Essays in moral development* (Vol. 2). The psychology of moral development. San Francisco: Harper & Row.

Kohn, A. (1986). *No contest.* Boston: Houghton Mifflin.

Kossek, E. E., & Zonia, S. C. (1993). Assessing diversity climate: A field study of reactions to employer efforts to promote diversity. *Journal of Organizational Behavior, 14,* 61-81.

Kressel, K., & Pruitt, D. G. (Eds.). (1989). *Mediation research.* San Francisco: Jossey-Bass.

Krosnick, J. (1999). Maximizing questionnaire quality. In J. P. Robinson, P. R. Shaver, & L. S. Wrightsman (Eds.), *Measures of political attitudes* (pp. 37-58). San Diego, CA: Academic Press.

Labov, W. (1972). Rules for ritual insults. In T. Kochman (Ed.), *Rappin' and stylin' out* (pp. 265-314). Urbana: University of Illinois Press.

Lam, J. A. (1989). *The impact of conflict resolution programs on schools: A review and synthesis of the evidence.* Amherst, MA: National Association for Mediation in Education.

Lampe, J. R., Rooze, G. E., & Tallent-Runnels, M. (1997). Effects of cooperative learning among Hispanic students in elementary social studies. *Journal of Educational Research, 89,* 187-191.

Landis, D., Brislin, R. W., & Hulgus, J. F. (1985). Attributional training versus contact in acculturative learning: A laboratory study. *Journal of Applied Social Psychology, 15,* 466-482.

Landis, D., Day, H. R., McGrew, P. L., Thomas, J. A., & Miller, A. B. (1976). Can a Black cultural assimilator increase racial understanding? *Journal of Social Issues, 32,* 169-183.

Langer, E. (1989). *Mindfulness.* Reading, MA: Addison-Wesley.

La Resche, D. (1992). Comparison of the American mediation process with a Korean-American harmony restoration process. *Mediation Quarterly, 9,* 323-339.

Layng, J. M. (1998). Uncovering the layers of diversity: A semiotic analysis of the corporate training video series "Valuing Diversity." *Semiotica, 119,* 251-267.

Lazarowitz, R., Baird, J. H., Hertz-Lazarowitz, R., & Jenkins, J. (1985). The effects of modified Jigsaw on achievement, classroom social climate, and self-esteem in high-school science classes. In R. E. Slavin, S. Sharan, S. Kagan, R. Hertz-Lazarowitz, C. Webb, & R. Schmuck (Eds.), *Learning to cooperate, cooperating to learn* (pp. 231-253). New York: Plenum.

Lefley, H. P. (1985). Impact of cross-cultural training on Black and White mental health professionals. *International Journal of Intercultural Relations, 9,* 305-318.

Leippe, M. R., & Eisenstadt, D. (1994). Generalization of dissonance reduction: Decreasing prejudice through induced compliance. *Journal of Personality and Social Psychology, 67,* 395-413.

Leming, J. S. (1981). Curricular effectiveness in moral/values education: A review of research. *Journal of Moral Education, 10,* 147-154.

Lerner, M. J. (1980). *Belief in a just world: A fundamental delusion.* New York: Plenum.

Lessing, E. E., & Clarke, C. C. (1976). An attempt to reduce ethnic prejudice and assess its correlates in a junior high school sample. *Educational Research Quarterly, 1*(3), 3-16.

LeVine, R. A., & Campbell, D. T. (1972). *Ethnocentrism: Theories of conflict, ethnic attitudes, and group behavior.* New York: John Wiley.

Levinson, D. J. (1954). The intergroup relations workshop: Its psychological aims and effects. *Journal of Psychology, 38,* 103-126.

Lewin, K. (1947). Group decision and social change. In H. Proshansky & B. Seidenberg (Eds.), *Basic studies in social psychology* (pp. 423-436). New York: Holt, Rinehart & Winston.

Licona, T. (1991). *Educating for character: How our schools can teach respect and responsibility.* New York: Bantam.

Lieberman, M. (1981, Summer). Facing history and ourselves: A project evaluation. *Moral Education Forum, 6,* 36-41.

Lind, G., & Althof, W. (1992, Summer). Does the Just Community experience make a difference? Measuring and evaluating the effect of the DES project. *Moral Education Forum, 17,* 19-28.

Lindsay, C. (1998). Conflict resolution and peer mediation in public schools: What works? *Mediation Quarterly, 16,* 85-99.

Lippitt, R. (1949). *Training in community relations: Research exploration toward new groups.* New York: Harper.

Litcher, J. H., & Johnson, D. W. (1969). Changes in attitudes toward Negroes of White elementary school students after use of multicultural readers. *Journal of Educational Psychology, 60,* 148-152.

Lockwood, A. L. (1976). A critical view of values clarification. In D. Purpel & K. Ryan (Eds.), *Moral education . . . It comes with the territory* (pp. 152-170). Berkeley, CA: McCutchan.

Lockwood, A. L. (1978). The effects of values clarification and moral development curricula on school-age subjects: A critical review of recent research. *Review of Educational Research, 48,* 325-364.

Lopez, G., Gurin, P., & Nagda, B. R. (1998). Education and understanding structural causes of group inequalities. *Political Psychology, 19,* 305-329.

Lotan, R. A. (1997). Complex Instruction: An overview. In E. G. Cohen & R. A. Lotan (Eds.), *Working for equity in heterogeneous classrooms: Sociological theory in practice* (pp. 15-27). New York: Teachers College Press.

Lucker, G. W., Rosenfield, D., Sikes, J., & Aronson, E. (1977). Performance in the interdependent classroom: A field study. *American Educational Research Journal, 13*(2), 115-123.

Lupton-Smith, H. S., Carruthers, W. L., Flythe, R., Goettee, E., & Modest, K. H. (1996). Conflict resolution as peer mediation: Programs for elementary, middle, and high school students. *School Counselor, 43,* 374-381.

Lynch, F. R. (1997). *The diversity machine: The drive to change the White male workplace.* New York: Free Press.

Mackie, D. M., Allison, S. T., Worth, L. T., & Asuncion, A. G. (1992). Social decision making processes: The generalization of outcome-biased counter-stereotypic inferences. *Journal of Experimental Social Psychology, 28*, 23-42.

Mackie, D. M., Hamilton, D. L., Schroth, H. A., Carlisle, C. J., Gersho, B. F., Menses, L. M., Nedler, B. F., & Reichel, L. D. (1989). The effects of induced mood on expectancy-based illusory correlations. *Journal of Experimental Social Psychology, 25*, 524-544.

Madden, N. A., & Slavin, R. E. (1983). Effects of cooperative learning on the social acceptance of mainstreamed academically handicapped students. *Journal of Special Education, 17*, 171-182.

Maier, M. (1997). We have to make a MANagement decision. In P. Prasad, A. J. Mills, M. Elmes, & A. Prasad (Eds.), *Managing the organizational melting pot: Dilemmas for the workplace* (pp. 226-254). Thousand Oaks, CA: Sage.

Malloy, C. E., & Malloy, W. W. (1998). Issues of culture in mathematics teaching and learning. *Urban Review, 30*, 245-257.

Marshall, F. R., & Van Adams, A. (1971). The Memphis public employees strike. In W. E. Chalmers & G. W. Cormick (Eds.), *Racial conflict and negotiations: Perspectives and first case studies* (pp. 71-107). Ann Arbor, MI: Institute of Labor and Industrial Relations, University of Michigan-Wayne State University.

Mattingly, R. M., & Van Sickle, R. L. (1991). Cooperative learning and achievement in social studies: Jigsaw II. *Social Education, 55*, 392-395.

Maxwell, J. P. (1990). Mediation in the schools: Self-regulation, self-esteem, and self-discipline. *Mediation Quarterly, 7*, 149-155.

McClendon, M. J. (1974). Interracial contact and the reduction of prejudice. *Sociological Focus, 7*, 47-65.

McConahay, J. G. (1986). Modern racism, ambivalence, and the modern racism scale. In J. F. Dovidio & S. L. Gaertner (Eds.), *Prejudice, discrimination, and racism* (pp. 91-125). Orlando, FL: Academic Press.

McCormick, M. A. (1997). Confronting social injustice as a mediator. *Mediation Quarterly, 14*, 293-307.

McCoy, M., Emigh, P., Leighninger, M., & Barratt, M. (1999). *Planning community-wide study circle programs.* Unpublished manuscript. Pomfret, CT: Study Circle Resource Center.

McInerney, V., McInerney, D. M., & Marsh, H. W. (1997). Effects of metacognitive strategy training within a cooperative group learning context on computer achievement and anxiety: An aptitude-treatment interaction study. *Journal of Educational Psychology, 89*, 686-695.

McGregor, J. (1993). Effectiveness of role-playing and antiracist teaching in reducing student prejudice. *Journal of Educational Research, 86*, 215-226.

McLaughlin, K. A., & Brilliant, K. J. (1997). *Healing the hate.* Newton, MA: Educational Development Center.

McPhail, P., Middleton, D., & Ingram, D. (1978). *Moral education in the middle years.* London: Longman.

McPhail, P., Ungoed-Thomas, J. R., & Chapman, H. (1972). *Moral education in the secondary schools.* London: Longman.

Milhouse, V. H. (1996). Intercultural communication education and training goals, content, and methods. *International Journal of Intercultural Relations, 20*, 69-95.

Miller, N., & Brewer, M. B. (1986). Categorization effects on ingroup and outgroup perception. In J. Dovidio & S. L. Gaertner (Eds.), *Prejudice, discrimination, and racism* (pp. 209-230). New York: Academic Press.

Miller, N., Brewer, M. B., & Edwards, K. (1985). Cooperative interaction in desegregated settings: A laboratory analogue. *Journal of Social Issues, 41,* 63-81.

Miller, N., & Davidson-Podgorny, G. (1987). Theoretical models of intergroup relations and the use of cooperative teams as an intervention for desegregated settings. In C. Hendrick (Ed.), *Group processes and intergroup relations* (Vol. 9, pp. 41-67). Newbury Park, CA: Sage.

Miller, N., & Harrington, H. J. (1990a). A model of category salience for intergroup relations: Empirical tests of the relevant variables. In P. J. D. Drenth, J. A. Sargeant, & R. J. Takens (Eds.), *European perspectives in psychology* (Vol. 3, pp. 205-220). New York: John Wiley.

Miller, N., & Harrington, H. J. (1990b). A situational identity perspective on cultural diversity and teamwork in the classroom. In S. Sharan (Ed.), *Cooperative learning: Theory and research* (pp. 39-76). New York: Praeger.

Miller, N., & Harrington, H. J. (1992). Social categorization and intergroup acceptance: Principles for the design and development of cooperative learning teams. In R. Hertz-Lazarowitz & N. Miller (Eds.), *Interaction in cooperative groups* (pp. 203-227). New York: Cambridge University Press.

Mitnick, L. L., & McGinnies, E. (1958). Influencing ethnocentrism in small discussion groups through a film communication. *Journal of Abnormal and Social Psychology, 36,* 82-90.

Monteith, M. J. (1993). Self-regulation of prejudiced responses: Implications for progress in prejudice-reduction efforts. *Journal of Personality and Social Psychology, 65,* 469-485.

Monteith, M. J., & Walters, G. L. (1998). Egalitarianism, moral obligation, and prejudice-related personal standards. *Personality and Social Psychology Bulletin, 24,* 186-199.

Monteith, M. J., Zuwerink, J. R., & Devine, P. G. (1994). Prejudice and prejudice reduction: Classic challenges, contemporary approaches. In P. G. Devine, D. L. Hamilton, & T. M Ostrom (Eds.), *Social cognition: Impact on social psychology* (pp. 324-346). San Diego, CA: Academic Press.

Mosher, R. L. (1980). Moral education: The next generation. In R. L. Mosher (Ed.), *Moral education: A first generation of research and development* (pp. 369-385). New York: Praeger.

Mosher, R. L., & Sprinthall, N. A. (1970). Psychological education in secondary schools: A program to promote individual and human development. *American Psychologist, 25,* 911-941.

Mosher, R. L., & Sullivan, P. (1976). A curriculum in moral education for adolescents. In D. Purpel & K. Ryan (Eds.), *Moral education . . . It comes with the territory* (pp. 55-67). Berkeley, CA: McCutchan.

Myers, S., & Filner, B. (1994). *Mediation across cultures: A handbook about conflict and culture.* Amherst, MA: Amherst Educational Publishing.

Myrdal, G. (1944). *The American dilemma: The Negro problem and modern democracy.* New York: Harper & Row.

Nagda, B. A., Spearmon, M. L., Holley, L. C., Harding, S., Balassone, M. L., Moise-Swanson, D., & deMello, S. (1999). Intergroup dialogues: An innovative approach to teaching about diversity and justice in social work programs. *Journal of Social Work Education, 35,* 433-449.

Nagda, B. A., Zuniga, X., & Sevig, T. (1995). Bridging differences through peer facilitated intergroup dialogues. In S. Hatcher (Ed.), *Peer programs on a college campus: Theory, training, and voices of the peers* (pp. 378-414). San Diego, CA: New Resources.

National Advisory Commission on Civil Disorders. (1968). *Report.* Washington, DC: Government Printing Office.

National Council for the Social Studies Task Force. (1992, September). Curriculum guidelines for multicultural education. *Social education, 56* (pp. 274-294). Washington, DC: National Council for the Social Studies.

Neiswand, G. H. (1986). Gaming simulations for enhancing international education. *Simulation & Games, 17,* 376-394.

Neuberg, S. L. (1996). Social motives and expectancy-tinged thoughts. In R. M. Sorrentino & E. T. Higgins (Eds.), *Handbook of social cognition* (Vol. 3, pp. 225-261). New York: Guilford.

Neville, H., & Furlong, M. (1994). The impact of participation in a cultural awareness program on the racial attitudes and social behaviors of first-year college students. *Journal of College Student Development, 35,* 371-377.

Newmann, F. M., & Thompson, J. (1987). *Effects of cooperative learning on achievement in secondary schools: A summary of research.* Madison, WI: University of Wisconsin, National Center on Effective Secondary Schools.

Nile, L. N. (1994). *Developing diversity training for the workplace: A guide for trainers.* Washington, DC: National MultiCultural Institute.

Oakes, P. J., Haslam, S. A., & Turner, J. C. (1994). *Stereotyping and social reality.* Cambridge, MA: Blackwell.

O'Brien, G. E., & Plooij, D. (1977). Comparison of programmed and prose culture training upon attitudes and knowledge. *Journal of Applied Psychology, 62,* 499-505.

Okebukola, P. A. (1985). The relative effectiveness of cooperativeness and competitive interaction techniques in strengthening students' performance in science classes. *Science Education, 69,* 501-509.

Okebukola, P. A. (1986). Impact of extended cooperative and competitive relationships on the performance of students in science. *Human Relations, 39,* 673-682.

Olson-Buchanan, J. B. (1996). Voicing discontent: What happens to the grievance filer after the grievance? *Journal of Applied Psychology, 81,* 52-63.

Ordovensky, G. A. (1992, July 7). Teachers: 87% White, 72% women. *U.S.A. Today,* 3.

Orfield. G., & Eaton, S. F. (1996). *Dismantling desegregation.* New York: New Press.

Oser, F. (1984). Cognitive stages of interaction in moral discourse. In W. M. Kurtines & J. L. Gewirtz (Eds.), *Morality, moral behavior, and moral development* (pp. 159-174). New York: John Wiley.

Oser, F. K. (1985). Moral education and values education: The discourse perspective. In M. C. Wittrock (Ed.), *Handbook of research on teaching* (3rd ed.). New York: Macmillan.

Oser, F. K. (1992a). Morality in professional action: A discourse approach for teaching. In F. K. Oser, A. Dick, & J.-L. Patry (Eds.), *Effective and responsible teaching: The new synthesis.* San Francisco: Jossey-Bass.

Oser, F. K. (1992b). Prejudice and moral education. In J. Lynch, C. Modgil, & S. Modgil (Eds.), *Cultural diversity and the schools* (Vol. 2, pp. 307-329). London: Falmer.

Oser, F. K. (1992c, Summer). Three paths toward a Just Community: Process and transformation. *Moral Education Forum, 17,* 35-36, 18.

Oser, F. K. (1992d). Three paths toward a Just Community: The German experience. *Moral Education Forum, 17,* 1-4.

Paige, R. M., & Martin, J. N. (1996). Ethics in intercultural training. In D. Landis & R. S. Bhagat (Eds.), *Handbook of intercultural training* (2nd ed., pp. 35-59). Thousand Oaks, CA: Sage.

Parker, W. M., Moore, M. A., & Neimeyer, G. J. (1998). Altering White racial identity and interracial comfort through multicultural training. *Journal of Counseling Development, 76,* 302-310.

Parsell, G., Spalding, R., & Bligh, J. (1998). Shared goals, shared learning: Evaluation of a multiprofessional course for undergraduate students. *Medical Education, 32,* 302-311.

Pascarella, E. T., Edison, M., Nora, A., Hagedorn, L. S., & Terenzini, P. T. (1996). Influences on students' openness to diversity and challenge in the first year of college. *Journal of Higher Education, 67,* 174-195.

Paskoff, S. M. (1996). Ending the diversity wars. *Training, 33*(8), 42-50.

Peak, H., & Morrison, H. W. (1958). The acceptance of information into attitude structure. *Journal of Abnormal and Social Psychology, 57,* 127-135.

Pettigrew, T. F. (1971). *Racially separate or together?* New York: McGraw-Hill.

Pettigrew, T. F. (1979a). Racial change and social policy. *Annals of the American Academy of Political and Social Science, 441,* 114-131.

Pettigrew, T. F. (1979b). The ultimate attribution error: Extending Allport's cognitive analysis of prejudice. *Personality and Social Psychology Bulletin, 5,* 461-476.

Pettigrew, T. F. (1986). The intergroup contact hypothesis reconsidered. In M. Hewstone & R. Brown (Eds.), *Contact and conflict in intergroup encounters* (pp. 169-195). London: Basil Blackwell.

Pettigrew, T. F. (1998). Intergroup contact theory. *Annual Review of Psychology, 49,* 65-85.

Pettigrew, T. F., & Tropp, L. R. (2000). Does intergroup contact reduce prejudice: Recent meta-analytic findings. In S. Oskamp (Ed.), *Reducing prejudice and discrimination* (pp. 93-114). Mahwah, NJ: Lawrence Erlbaum.

Picker, B. G. (1998). *Mediation practice guide: A handbook for resolving business disputes.* Bethesda, MD: Pike & Fischer.

Plummer, D. L. (1998). Approaching diversity training in the year 2000. *Counseling Psychology Journal: Practice and Research, 50,* 181-189.

Polley, R. B., Hare, A. P., & Stone, P. (Eds.). (1988). *The SYMLOG practitioner: Applications of small group research.* New York: Praeger.

Ponterotto, J. G. (1996). Multicultural counseling in the twenty-first century. *Counseling Psychologist, 24*(2), 259-268.

Ponterotto, J. G., & Pedersen, P. (1993). *Preventing prejudice.* Newbury Park, CA: Sage.

Power, F. C., Higgins, A., & Kohlberg, L. (1989). *Lawrence Kohlberg's approach to moral education.* New York: Columbia University Press.

Prasad, P. (1997). The Protestant ethic and the myths of the frontier. In P. Prasad, A. J. Mills, M. Elmes, & A. Prasad (Eds.), *Managing the organizational melting pot: Dilemmas for the workplace* (pp. 129-147). Thousand Oaks, CA: Sage.

Probst, T. M., Carnevale, P. J., & Triandis, H. C. (1999). Cultural values in intergroup and single-group social dilemmas. *Organizational Behavior and Human Decision Processes, 77,* 171-191.

Pruegger, V. J., & Rogers, T. B. (1994). Cross-cultural sensitivity training: Methods and assessment. *International Journal of Intercultural Relations, 18,* 369-387.

Pruitt, D. (1998). Social conflict. In D. T. Gilbert, S. T. Fiske, & G. Lindzey (Eds.), *The handbook of social psychology* (Vol. 2, 4th ed., pp. 470-503). Boston: McGraw-Hill.

Pruitt, D. G., & Carnevale, P. J. (1993). *Negotiation in social conflict.* Pacific Grove, CA: Brooks/Cole.

Pruitt, D. G., Peirce, R. S., McGillicuddy, N. B., Welton, G. L., & Castrianno, L. N. (1993). Long-term success in mediation. *Law and Human Behavior, 17,* 313-330.

Puka, B. (Ed.). (1994a). *Caring voices and women's moral frames.* New York: Garland.

Puka, B. (Ed.). (1994b). *New research in moral development.* New York: Garland.

Puma, M. J., Jones, C. C., Rock, D., & Fernandez, R. (1993). *Prospects: The congressionally mandated study of educational growth and opportunity,* interim report (cited in Slavin, 1996). Bethesda, MD: Abt Associates.

Purpel, D., & Ryan, K. (1976). Moral education in the classroom: Some instructional issues. In D. Purpel & K. Ryan (Eds.), *Moral education . . . It comes with the territory* (pp. 55-67). Berkeley, CA: McCutchan.

Putnam, L. L., & Roloff, M. E. (1992). *Communication and negotiation.* Newbury Park, CA: Sage.

Qin, Z., Johnson, D. W., & Johnson, R. T. (1995). Cooperative versus competitive efforts and problem solving. *Review of Educational Research, 65,* 129-143.

Quinn, R. J. (1997). Effects of mathematics methods courses on the mathematical attitudes and content knowledge of preservice teachers. *Journal of Educational Research, 91,* 108-113.

Reed, D. R. C. (1997). *Following Kohlberg: Liberalism and the practice of democratic community.* Notre Dame, IN: University of Notre Dame Press.

Richards, H. C., & Gamache, R. (1979). Belief polarity: A useful construct for studies of prejudice. *Educational and Psychological Measurement, 39,* 791-801.

Riche, M. F. (2000). America's diversity and growth: Signposts for the 21st century. *Population Bulletin, 55*(2), 1-43.

Robinson, B., & Bradley, L. J. (1997). Multicultural training for undergraduates: Developing knowledge and awareness. *Journal of Multicultural Counseling and Development, 25,* 281-289.

Robinson, E. A., & Follingstad, D. R. (1985). Development and validation of a behavioral sex-role inventory. *Sex Roles, 13,* 691-713.

Rokeach, M. (1971). Long-range experimental modification of values, attitudes and behavior. *American Psychologist, 26,* 453-459.

Rokeach, M., Smith, P. W., & Evans, R. I. (1960). Two kinds of prejudice or one. In M. Rokeach (Ed.), *The open and closed mind* (pp. 132-168). New York: Basic Books.

Rosenberg, M. (1965). *Society and the adolescent self-image.* Princeton, NJ: Princeton University Press.

Rosenfield, D., Stephan, W. G., & Lucker, G. W. (1981). Attraction to competent and incompetent members of cooperative and competitive groups. *Journal of Applied Social Psychology, 11,* 416-433.

Rothbart, M., & John, O. P. (1985). Social categorization and behavioral episodes: A cognitive analysis and the effects of intergroup contact. *Journal of Social Issues, 41,* 81-104.

Rothbart, M., & Lewis, S. (1988). Inferring category attributes from exemplar attributes: Geometric shapes and social categories. *Journal of Personality and Social Psychology, 55,* 157-178.

Rubin, J. Z., Pruitt, D. G., & Kim, S. H. (1994). *Social conflict: Escalation, stalemate, and settlement* (2nd ed.). New York: Random House.

Rynders, J. E., Schleien, S. J., Meyer, L. H., Vandercook, T. L., Mustonen, T., Colond, J. S., & Olson, K. (1993). Improving integration outcomes for children with and without severe disabilities through cooperatively structured recreation activities: A synthesis of research. *Journal of Special Education, 26,* 386-407.

Rynes, S., & Rosen, B. (1995). A field survey of factors affecting the adoption and perceived success of diversity training. *Personnel Psychology, 48,* 247-270.

Salisbury, M. (2000). America 2000: A map of the mix. *Newsweek, 136*(12), 48.

Schaller, M., Asp, C. H., Rosell, M. C., & Heim, S. J. (1996). Training in statistical reasoning inhibits the formation of erroneous group stereotypes. *Personality and Social Psychology Bulletin, 22,* 829-844.

Schaller, M., & O'Brien, M. (1992). "Intuitive analysis of covariance" and group stereotype formation. *Personality and Social Psychology Bulletin, 18,* 776-785.

Schlaefli, A., Rest, J. R., & Thoma, S. J. (1985). Does moral education improve moral judgment? A meta-analysis of intervention studies using the Defining Issues Test. *Review of Educational Research, 55,* 319-352.

Schoem, D., & Stevenson, M. (1990). Teaching ethnic identity and intergroup relations: The case of Black-Jewish dialogue. *Teachers College Record, 91,* 579-593.

Schoene, L. P., Jr., & DuPraw, M. E. (1994). *Racing racial and cultural conflict: Tools for rebuilding community* (2nd ed.). Washington, DC: Program for Community Problem Solving.

Schroeder, D. A., Penner, L. A., Dovidio, J. F., & Piliavin, J. A. (1995). *The psychology of helping and altruism: Problems and puzzles.* New York: McGraw-Hill.

Schrumpf, F., Crawford, D., & Usadel, H. C. (1991). *Peer mediation: Conflict resolution in schools.* Champaign, IL: Research Press.

Shultz, L. H., Barr, D. J., & Selman, R. L. (in press). The value of a developmental approach to evaluating character development programs: An outcome study of Facing History and Ourselves. *Journal of Moral Education.*

Schuman, H., Steeh, C., & Bobo, L. (1985). *Racial attitudes in America.* Cambridge, MA: Harvard University Press.

Schwartz, S. H., & Tessler, R. C. (1972). A test of a model for reducing measured attitude-behavior inconsistencies. *Journal of Personality and Social Psychology, 24,* 225-236.

Sears, D. O. (1988). Symbolic racism. In P. A. Katz & D. A. Taylor (Eds.), *Eliminating racism: Profiles in controversy* (pp. 53-84). New York: Plenum.

Sears, D. O., & Huddy, L. (1990). On the origins of political disunity among women. In L. A. Tilly & P. Gurin (Eds.), *Women, politics, and change* (pp. 249-277). New York: Russell Sage.

Sessa, W. I. (1992). Managing diversity at the Xerox Corporation: Balanced workforce goals and caucus groups. In S. E. Jackson & Associates (Eds.), *Diversity in the workforce* (pp. 37-64). New York: Guilford.

Sharan, S., & Hertz-Lazarowitz, R. (1980). A group investigation method of cooperative learning in the classroom. In S. Sharan, P. Hare, C. Webb, & R. Hertz-Lazarowitz (Eds.), *Cooperation in education* (pp. 14-46). Provo, UT: Brigham Young University Press.

Sharan, S., Kussell, P., Hertz-Lazarowitz, R., Bejarano, Y., Raviv, S., & Sharan, Y. (1984). *Cooperative learning in the classroom: Research in desegregated schools.* Hillsdale, NJ: Lawrence Erlbaum.

Sharan, S., & Shachar, C. (1988). *Language and learning in the cooperative classroom.* New York: Springer-Verlag.

Sharan, Y., & Sharan, S. (1992). *Group Investigation: Expanding cooperative learning.* New York: Teacher's College Press.

Sheeran, P., & Orbell, S. (1999). Implementation intentions and repeated behaviors: Augmenting the predictive validity of the theory of reasoned action. *European Journal of Social Psychology, 29,* 349-369.

Sherif, M. (1966). *Group conflict and cooperation.* London: Routledge & Kegan Paul.

Sherif, M., Harvey, O. J., White, B. J., Hood, W. E., & Sherif, C. W. (1961). *Intergroup conflict and cooperation: The Robbers Cave experiment.* Norman: Institute of Group Relations, University of Oklahoma.

Sherman, L. W. (1988). A comparative study of cooperative and competitive achievement in two secondary biology classrooms: The group investigation model versus an individually competitive goal structure. *Journal of Research in Science Teaching, 26,* 35-64.

Sherman, L. W., & Thomas, M. (1986). Mathematics achievement in cooperative versus individualistic goal-structured high school classrooms. *Journal of Educational Research, 79,* 169-172.

Shweder, R. A., & Bourne, E. J. (1982). Does the concept of the person vary cross-culturally? In A. J. Marsella & G. M. White (Eds.), *Cultural conceptions of mental health and therapy.* Norwell, MA: Kluwer.

Sidanius, J. (1993). The psychology of group conflict and the dynamics of oppression: A social dominance perspective. In S. Iyengar & W. J. McGuire (Eds.), *Explorations in political psychology* (pp. 183-219). Durham, NC: Duke University Press.

Sidanius, J., & Pratto, F. (1999). *Social dominance: An intergroup theory of social hierarchy and oppression.* Cambridge, UK: Cambridge University Press.

Simon, S. B. (1976). Values clarification vs. indoctrination. In D. Purpel & K. Ryan (Eds.), *Moral education . . . It comes with the territory* (pp. 126-135). Berkeley, CA: McCutchan.

Simon, S. B., Howe, L. W., & Kirschenbaum, H. (1972). *Values clarification: A handbook of practical strategies for teachers and students* (rev. ed.). New York: A & W Visual Library.

Slavin, R. E. (1977). Classroom reward structure: An analytic and practical review. *Review of Educational Research, 47,* 633-650.

Slavin, R. E. (1978). Student teams and comparisons among equals: Effects on academic performance and student attitudes. *Journal of Educational Psychology, 70,* 532-538.

Slavin, R. E. (1979). Effects of biracial learning teams on cross-racial friendships. *Journal of Educational Psychology, 71,* 381-387.

Slavin, R. E. (1984). Team assisted individualized instruction: Cooperative learning and individualized instruction in the mainstreamed classroom. *Remedial and Special Education, 5,* 33-42.

Slavin, R. E. (1985). Cooperative learning: Applying contact theory in desegregated schools. *Journal of Social Issues, 41,* 45-62.

Slavin, R. E. (1990). *Cooperative learning: Theory, research, and practice.* Englewood Cliffs, NJ: Prentice-Hall.

Slavin, R. E. (1992). Cooperative learning: Applying contact theory in desegregated schools. In J. Lynch, D. Modgil, & S. Modgil (Eds.), *Cultural diversity and the schools: Prejudice, polemic or progress?* (pp. 333-348). London: Falmer.

Slavin, R. E. (1995a). *Cooperative learning: Theory, research, and practice* (2nd ed.). Boston: Allyn & Bacon.

Slavin, R. E. (1995b). When and why does cooperative learning increase achievement? Theoretical and empirical perspectives. In R. Hertz-Lazarowitz & N. Miller (Eds.), *Interaction in cooperative groups* (pp. 145-173). New York: Cambridge University Press.

Slavin, R. E. (1996). Research on cooperative learning and achievement: What we know, what we need to know. *Contemporary Educational Psychology, 21*(1), 43-69.

Slavin, R. E., Leavey, M., & Madden, N. A. (1984). Combining cooperative learning and individualized instruction: Effects on student mathematics achievement, attitudes, and behaviors. *Elementary School Journal, 84,* 409-422.

Slavin, R. E., & Oickle, E. (1981). Effects of cooperative learning teams on student achievement and race relations: Treatment by race interactions. *Sociology of Education, 54,* 174-180.

Slavin, R. E., & Stevens, R. J. (1991). Cooperative learning and mainstreaming. In J. W. Lloyd, N. N. Singh, & A. C. Repp (Eds.), *The regular education initiative: Alternative perspectives on concepts, issues, and models* (pp. 177-191). Sycamore, IL: Sycamore.

Sleeter, C. E. (1995). An analysis of critiques of multicultural education. In J. A. Banks & C. A. McGee Banks (Eds.), *Handbook of research on multicultural education* (pp. 81-93). Boston: Allyn & Bacon.

Sleeter, C. E., & Grant, C. A. (1987). Race, class, gender and disability in current textbooks. In M. W. Apple & L. K. Christian-Smith (Eds.), *The politics of the textbook.* New York: Routledge.

Smith, A. (1990). Social influence and antiprejudice training programs. In J. Edwards, R. S. Tisdale, L. Heath, & E. J. Posavic (Eds.), *Social influence processes and intervention* (pp. 183-196). New York: Plenum.

Smith, M. E., Hinckley, C. C., & Volk, G. L. (1997). Cooperative learning in the undergraduate laboratory. In D. A. Riordan, D. L. Street, & B. M. Roof (Eds.), *Group learning: Applications in higher education* (pp. 109-116). Harrisonburg, VA: Institute for Research in Higher Education, James Madison University.

Smith, P. C., & Warrior, R. A. (1996). *Like a hurricane.* New York: New Press.

Snyder, M. (1984). When belief creates reality. In L. Berkowitz (Ed.), *Advances in experimental social psychology* (Vol. 18, pp. 247-305). Orlando, FL: Academic Press.

Snyder, M. (1992). Motivational foundations of behavioral confirmation. In M. Zanna (Ed.), *Advances in experimental social psychology* (Vol. 25, pp. 67-114). Orlando, FL: Academic Press.

Snyder, M., & Swann, W. B. (1978). Hypothesis-testing in social interaction. *Journal of Personality and Social Psychology, 36,* 1202-1212.

Snyder, M., Tanke, E., D., & Berscheid, E. (1977). Social perception and interpersonal behavior: On the self-fulfilling nature of social stereotypes. *Journal of Personality and Social Psychology, 35,* 656-666.

Solomon, D., Watson, M. S., Delucchi, K. L., Schaps, E., & Battistich, V. (1988). Enhancing children's prosocial behavior in the classroom. *American Educational Research Journal, 25,* 527-554.

Sorcher, M., & Spence, R. (1982). The interface project: Behavior modeling as social technology in South Africa. *Personnel Psychology, 35,* 557-581.

St. John, N. H. (1975). *School desegregation: Outcomes for children.* New York: John Wiley.

Stangor, C., & McMillan, D. (1992). Memory for expectancy-congruent and expectancy-incongruent information: A review of the social and social developmental literatures. *Psychological Bulletin, 111,* 42-61.

Stephan, C. W. (1992). Intergroup anxiety and intergroup interaction. In J. Lynch, D. Modgil, & S. Modgil (Eds.), *Cultural diversity and the schools: Prejudice, polemic or progress?* (pp. 145-158). London: Falmer.

Stephan C. W., & Stephan, W. G. (1992). Reducing intercultural anxiety through intercultural contact. *International Journal of Intercultural Relations, 16,* 89-106.

Stephan, W. G. (1978). School desegregation: An evaluation of predictions made in Brown vs. the Board of Education. *Psychological Bulletin, 85,* 217-238.

Stephan, W. G. (1980). A brief historical overview of school desegregation. In W. Stephan & J. Feagin (Eds.), *Desegregation: Past, present and future* (pp. 3-24). New York: Plenum.

Stephan, W. G. (1985). Intergroup relations. In G. Lindzey & E. Aronson (Eds.), *Handbook of social psychology* (Vol. III, pp. 599-658). New York: Addison-Wesley.

Stephan, W. G. (1986). The effects of school desegregation: An evaluation 30 years after "Brown." In M. Saks & L. Saxe (Eds.), *Advances in applied social psychology* (pp. 181-206). New York: Lawrence Erlbaum.

Stephan, W. G. (1987). The contact hypothesis in intergroup relations. In C. Hendrick (Ed.), *Group processes and intergroup relations* (pp. 13-40). Beverly Hills: Sage.

Stephan, W. G. (1991). School desegregation: Short-term and long-term effects. In H. J. Knopke, R. J. Norrell, & R. W. Rogers (Eds.), *Opening doors: Perspective on race relations in contemporary America* (pp. 100-118). Tuscaloosa: University of Alabama Press.

Stephan, W. G., Diaz-Loving, R., & Duran, A. (2000). Integrated threat theory and intercultural attitudes: Mexico and the U.S. *Journal of Cross-Cultural Psychology, 32,* 221-231.

Stephan, W. G., & Finlay, K. A. (2000). The role of empathy in improving intergroup relations. *Journal of Social Issues, 55,* 729-744.

Stephan, W. G., & Rosenfield, D. (1978). The effects of desegregation on racial attitudes. *Journal of Personality and Social Psychology, 36,* 795-804.

Stephan, W. G., & Stephan, C. W. (1984). The role of ignorance in intergroup relations. In N. Miller & M. B. Brewer (Eds.), *Groups in contact: The psychology of desegregation* (pp. 229-257). New York: Academic Press.

Stephan, W. G., & Stephan, C. W. (1985). Intergroup anxiety. *Journal of Social Issues, 41,* 157-175.

Stephan, W. G., & Stephan, C. W. (1989). Antecedents of intergroup anxiety in Asian-Americans and Hispanic-Americans. *International Journal of Intercultural Relations, 13,* 203-216.

Stephan, W. G., & Stephan, C. W. (1996). *Intergroup relations.* Boulder, CO: Westview.

Stephan, W. G., & Stephan, C. W. (2000). An integrated threat theory of prejudice. In S. Oskamp (Ed.), *Reducing prejudice and discrimination* (pp. 225-246). Hillsdale, NJ: Lawrence Erlbaum.

Stephan, W. G., Stephan, C. W., & Gudykunst, W. B. (1999). Anxiety in intergroup relations: A comparison of anxiety/uncertainty management theory and integrated threat theory. *International Journal of Intercultural Relations, 23,* 613-628.

Stephan, W. G., Ybarra, O., & Bachman, G. (1999). Prejudice toward immigrants: An integrated threat theory. *Journal of Applied Social Psychology, 29,* 2221-2237.

Stephan, W. G., Ybarra, O., Martinez, C. M., Schwarzwald, J., & Tur-Kaspa, M. (1998). Immigrants to Spain and Israel: An integrated theory analysis. *Journal of Cross-Cultural Psychology, 29,* 559-576.

Stevahn, L., Johnson, D. W., Johnson, R., Green, K., & Laginski, A. (1997). Effects of conflict resolution training integrated into English literature. *Journal of Social Psychology, 137,* 302-316.

Stevens, R. J., Madden, N., Slavin, R. E., & Farnish, A. (1987). Cooperative integrated reading and composition: Two field experiments. *Reading Research Quarterly, 22,* 433-454.

Stevens, R. J., & Slavin, R. E. (1995). The cooperative elementary schools: Effects on students' achievement, attitudes, and social relations. *American Educational Research Journal, 32*, 321-351.

Stewart, J. S. (1976). Problems and contradictions of values clarification. In D. Purpel & K. Ryan (Eds.), *Moral education . . . It comes with the territory* (pp. 126-151). Berkeley, CA: McCutchan.

Storti, C. (1994). *Cross-cultural dialogues: 74 brief encounters with cultural difference.* Yarmouth, ME: Intercultural Press.

Stoskopf, A. L., & Strom, M. (1990). *Choosing to participate: A critical examination of citizenship in American history.* Brookline, MA: Facing History and Ourselves National Foundation.

Stroh, L. K., Brett, J. M., & Reilly, A. H. (1992). All the right stuff: A comparison of female and male managers' career progression. *Journal of Applied Psychology, 77*, 251-260.

Sumner, W. G. (1906). *Folkways.* Boston: Ginn.

Swann, W. B., Jr., & Ely, R. J. (1984). A battle of wills: Self-verification versus behavioral confirmation. *Journal of Personality and Social Psychology, 46*, 1287-1302.

Sweeney, B., & Carruthers, W. L. (1996). Conflict resolution: History, philosophy, theory, and educational applications. *School Counselor, 43*, 325-344.

Swim, J. K., Aiken, K. J., Hall, W. S., & Hunter, B. A. (1995). Sexism and racism: Old-fashioned and modern prejudices. *Journal of Personality and Social Psychology, 68*, 199-214.

Tajfel, H. (Ed.). (1978). *Differentiation between social groups: Studies in the social psychology of intergroup relations.* London: Academic Press.

Tajfel, H. (1981). *Human groups and social categories: Studies in social psychology.* Cambridge, UK: Cambridge University Press.

Tajfel, H. (1982). *Social identity and intergroup relations.* Cambridge, UK: Cambridge University Press.

Tajfel, H., & Turner, J. C. (1986). *The social identity theory of intergroup behavior.* In S. Worchel & W. G. Austin (Eds.), *Psychology of intergroup relations* (2nd ed., pp. 33-47). Chicago: Nelson-Hall.

Talmage, H., Pascarella, E. T., & Ford, S. (1984). The influence of cooperative learning strategies on teacher practices, student perceptions of the learning environment, and academic achievement. *American Educational Research Journal, 21*, 163-179.

Tan, D. L., Morris, L., & Romero, J. (1996, September). Changes in attitudes after diversity training. *Training and Development, 50*, 54-55.

Tansik, D. A., & Driskell, J. D. (1977). Temporal persistence of attitudes induced through required training. *Group and Organization Studies, 2*, 310-323.

Thiagarajan, S., & Steinwachs, B. (1990). *Barnga: A simulation game on cultural clashes.* Yarmouth, ME: Intercultural Press.

Thomas, M. B., Moore, H. B., & Sams, C. (1980). Counselor renewal workshop in sex equality. *Counsellor Education and Supervision, 20*, 56-61.

Tjosvold, D., Morishima, M., & Belsheim, J. A. (1999). Complaint handling on the shop floor: Cooperative relationships and open-minded strategies. *International Journal of Conflict Management, 10*, 45-68.

Tougas, F., Brown, R., Beaton, A. M., & Joly, S. (1995). Neosexism: Plus ça change, plus c'est pareil. *Personality and Social Psychology Bulletin, 21*, 842-849.

Trafimow, D. (1998). Attitudinal and normative processes in health behaviors. *Psychology and Health, 13*, 307-317.

Triandis, H. C. (1972). *The analysis of subjective culture.* New York: John Wiley.

Triandis, H. C. (1994). *Culture and social behavior.* New York: McGraw Hill.

Triandis, H. C. (1995). *Individualism and collectivism.* Boulder, CO: Westview.

Trifonovitch, G. J. (1977). On cross-cultural techniques. In R. W. Brislin (Ed.), *Culture learning: Concepts, applications, and research* (pp. 213-222). Honolulu, HI: East-West Center.

Vanbeselaere, N. (1991). The different effects of simple and crossed categorizations: A result of the category differentiation process or of differential category salience? *European Review of Social Psychology* (Vol. 2, pp. 247-278). Chichester, UK: Wiley.

Van Soest, D. (1996). Impact of social work education on student attitudes and behavior concerning oppression. *Journal of Social Work Education, 32,* 191-202.

Vedder, P. H. (1985). *Cooperative learning: A study on processes and effects of cooperation between primary school children.* Groningen, Netherlands: University of Groningen.

Verma, G. K., & Bagley, C. (1973). Changing racial attitudes in adolescents. *International Journal of Psychology, 8,* 55-58.

Verma, G. K., & Bagley, C. (1979). Measured changes in racial attitudes following the use of three different teaching methods. In G. K. Verma & C. Bagley (Eds.), *Race, education, and identity* (pp. 133-142). New York: St. Martin's.

Volkan, V. D. (1998). The tree model: Psychological dialogues and the promotion of coexistence. In E. Weiner (Ed.), *Handbook of interethnic coexistence* (pp. 343-358). New York: Continuum.

Volpe, M. R. (1998). Using town meetings to foster peaceful coexistence. In E. Weiner (Ed.), *Handbook of interethnic coexistence* (pp. 382-397). New York: Continuum.

Voting Rights Act of 1965, 42 U.S.C. § 1857c-10.

Vrij, A., Van Schie, E., & Cherryman, J. (1996). Reducing ethnic prejudice through public communication programs: A social-psychological perspective. *Journal of Psychology, 130,* 413-420.

Wade, P., & Bernstein, B. (1991). Cultural sensitivity training and counselor's race: Effects on Black female clients. *Journal of Counseling Psychology, 38,* 9-15.

Wah, L. (1999). Diversity at Allstate: A competitive weapon. *Management Review, 88(7),* 24-30.

Walker, B. A., & Hanson, W. C. (1992). Valuing differences at Digital Equipment Corporation. In S. E. Jackson & Associates (Eds.), *Diversity in the workforce* (pp. 119-137). New York: Guilford.

Walker, I., & Crogan, M. (1998). Academic performance, prejudice, and the Jigsaw classroom: New pieces to the puzzle. *Journal of Community and Applied Social Psychology, 8,* 381-393.

Wang, V. O. (1998). Curriculum evaluation and assessment of multicultural genetic counseling. *Journal of Genetic Counseling, 7,* 87-111.

Washington, V. (1981). Impact of antiracism/multicultural education training on elementary teachers' attitudes and classroom behavior. *Elementary School Journal, 81,* 186-192.

Watson, G. (1947). *Action for unity.* New York: Harper.

Weber, R., & Crocker, J. (1983). Cognitive processing in the revision of stereotypic beliefs. *Journal of Personality and Social Psychology, 45,* 961-977.

Weeks, W. W., Pedersen, P. B., & Brislin, R. W. (1982). *A manual of structured experiences for cross-cultural learning.* Yarmouth, ME: Intercultural Press.

Weigel, R. H., Wiser, P. L., & Cook, S. W. (1975). The impact of cooperative learning experiences on cross-ethnic relations and helping. *Journal of Social Issues, 31,* 219-244.

Weiner, M. J., & Wright, F. E. (1973). Effects of undergoing arbitrary discrimination upon subsequent attitudes toward a minority group. *Journal of Applied Social Psychology, 3*, 94-102.

Weldon, D., Carston, D., Rissman, A., Slobodin, L., & Triandis, H. C. (1975). A laboratory test of effects of culture assimilator training. *Journal of Personality and Social Psychology, 32*, 300-310.

White, M. B. (1999). Organization 2005: New strategies at P&G. *Diversity Factor, 8*(1), 16-20.

Williams, A., & Giles, H. (1992). Prejudice reduction simulations: Social cognition, intergroup theory, and ethics. *Simulation & Gaming, 24*, 472-484.

Williams, J. (1987). *Eyes on the prize.* New York: Penguin.

Williams, R. M., Jr. (1947). *The reduction of intergroup tensions.* New York: Social Science Research Council.

Williams, R. M., Jr. (1977). *Mutual accommodation: Ethnic conflict and cooperation.* Minneapolis: University of Minnesota Press.

Wilson, J. J. (1973). *Power, race relations, and privilege: Race relations in theoretical and sociohistorical perspective.* New York: Free Press.

Wittig, M., & Molina, L. (2000). Moderators and mediators of prejudice reduction in multicultural education. In S. Oskamp (Ed.), *Reducing prejudice and discrimination.* Mahwah, NJ: Lawrence Erlbaum.

Worchel, S. (1986). The role of cooperation in reducing intergroup conflict. In S. Worchel & W. G. Austin (Eds.), *Psychology of intergroup relations* (pp. 228-304). Chicago: Nelson-Hall.

Word, C., Zanna, M. P., & Cooper, J. (1974). The nonverbal mediation of self-fulfilling prophecies in interracial interaction. *Journal of Experimental Social Psychology, 10*, 109-120.

Wright, P., Ferris, S. P., Hiller, J. S., & Kroll, M. (1995). Competitiveness through management of diversity: Effects on stock price valuation. *Academy of Management Journal, 38*, 272-287.

Yawkey, T. D. (1973). Attitudes toward Black Americans held by rural and urban White early childhood subjects based upon multi-ethnic social studies materials. *Journal of Negro Education, 42*, 164-169.

Yawkey, T. D., & Blackwell, J. (1974). Attitudes of 4 year old urban Black children toward themselves and Whites based upon multi-ethnic social studies materials and experiences. *Journal of Educational Research, 67*, 373-377.

Ziegler, S. (1981). The effectiveness of cooperative learning teams for increasing cross-ethnic friendship: Additional evidence. *Human Organization, 40*, 264-268.

Zuniga, X., Scalera, C. V., Nagda, B., & Sevig, T. D. (1997). *Exploring and bridging race/ethnic differences: Developing intergroup dialogue competencies in a co-learning environment.* Unpublished manuscript, University of Michigan at Ann Arbor.

Zuniga, X., & Sevig, T. D. (1997). Bridging the "us/them" divide through intergroup dialogue and peer leadership. *Diversity Factor, 6*(2), 23-28.

Zuniga, X., Nagda, B., Sevig, T. D., Vasquez, C. M., & Dey, E. L. (1998). *Tearing down the walls: Peer facilitated intergroup dialogue processes and experiences.* Unpublished manuscript. Ann Arbor: University of Michigan.

Zuwerink, J., Devine, P. G., & Monteith, M. J. (1996). Prejudice toward Blacks: With and without compunction. *Basic and Applied Social Psychology, 18*, 131-150.

AUTHOR INDEX

Aboud, F. E., 56, 59, 68
Abrams, D., 28
Abu-Nimer, M., 122, 124
Adelman, L., 23
Adlerfer, C. P., 15, 24, 86, 88, 239
Adorno, T. W., 4, 25
Aiken, K. J., 26
Ajzen, I., 40, 91, 121, 231, 274
Albrecht, K., 190
Albrecht, S., 190
Allison, S. T., 39
Allport, F. H., 157, 174, 230
Allport, G. W., 4, 5, 20, 25, 66, 92, 117, 200
Altemeier, B., 256
Althof, W., 218
Amir, Y., 23
Anderson, D., 169, 170
Applebaum, B., 233
Araragi, C., 156
Aronson, A., 174
Aronson, E., 14, 22, 24, 33, 118, 162, 163, 174, 176
Ashmore, R. D., 33, 59, 65, 67
Asp, C. H., 37, 39
Astin, A., 58
Asuncion, A. G., 39

Avery, P. G., 56, 63, 193

Bachman, G., 136, 151, 257
Bagley, C., 56, 63
Baird, J. H., 171
Balassone, M. L., 104
Bales, R. F., 243
Ball-Rokeach, S. J., 30, 276
Banaji, M. R., 35
Bandura, A., 32, 231
Banker, B. S., 65, 120
Banks, C. A. M., 226
Banks, J. A., 13, 49, 50, 51, 226
Bar, H., 112, 113, 114, 124, 125
Bardige, B., 216
Bargal, D., 112, 113, 114, 124, 125
Barlow, D. E., 153
Barlow, M. H., 153
Barnard, W. A., 59
Barr, D. J., 216, 253
Barratt, M., 108, 122
Bartlett, J. K., 193
Batson, C. D., 33, 34, 65, 275
Battistich, V., 209, 218, 219, 220
Baum, M., 145
Beaton, A. M., 26

Beck, C., 226
Bednar, L. L., 33, 34, 65, 275
Behling, M., 32, 244
Bejarano, Y., 160, 165
Bell, C. H., Jr., 190
Belsheim, J. A., 190, 196
Benn, M. S., 59
Bennett, M. J., 153
Berg-Cross, L., 205
Berger, J. B., 165, 174
Bernstein, B., 60, 149
Bernstein, G., 146
Berry, A., 156
Berry, J. W., 68
Bersheid, E., 36
Bhagat, R. S., 130
Bhawuk, D. P. S., 134, 135, 141, 143,
    149
Bianchini, J. A., 165, 168
Bickmore, K., 202
Bird, K., 56, 63
Black, J. S., 149
Blackstone, T., 131
Blackwell, J., 56
Blake, B. F., 153
Blake, D. R. S., 15, 109
Blake, R. R., 190
Blanchard, F. A., 23
Blaney, N., 14, 22, 24, 162, 163, 174,
    176
Blatt, M., 210
Bligh, J., 156
Blumberg, R. G., 24, 67
Bobo, L., 10, 152
Bochner, S., 143
Bodenhausen, G. V., 37, 231
Bolger, A., 253
Boling, N. C., 156
Bond, M. A., 12, 75, 94
Bourne, E. J., 211
Boyd, D., 226, 232
Bradley, L. J., 58
Brady, M., 36
Brandt, M. E., 149

Bredemeir, M. E., 146
Brett, J. M., 75, 188
Brewer, M. B., 23, 31, 176, 177, 231,
    273
Brickman, H., 191, 192, 202, 205
Bridgeman, D., 169
Brief, A. P., 92
Brigham, J. C., 231
Brilliant, K. J., 52
Brislin, R. W., 14, 130, 131, 132, 139,
    141, 142, 143, 144, 146, 147, 148,
    149, 153
Brooks, G. S., 57, 250, 251
Broome, B. J., 201
Brown, R., 21, 26, 273
Brown, S. P., 55, 57
Brown v. Board of Education of Topeka,
    4, 5, 6, 53
Bruschke, J. C., 145, 146
Burgess, G. M., 183
Burgess, H., 183
Burke, R. J., 15
Burnstein, E., 23
Burstein, P., 7, 8, 9
Burton, J. W., 14, 110
Bush, R. A. B., 200
Buttram, R. T., 92
Byington, K., 55, 57
Byrne, D., 30, 68, 151, 201, 230
Byrnes, D. H., 59, 60

Callahan, J. D., 92
Campbell, D. E., 72
Campbell, D. T., 28, 36
Caproni, P., 1
Carlisle, C. J., 177
Carnevale, P. J., 190, 195, 196, 205
Carruthers, W. L., 194, 198, 202
Carston, D., 143, 144, 149
Carter, S., 203
Castrianno, L. N., 195
Cavalier, F. J., 155
Cavalier, J. C., 155

Cellar, D. F., 87, 88
Chapman, H., 223
Chein, I., 4, 25
Cherrie, C., 141
Cherryman, J., 60
Civil Rights Act of 1964, 7
Clarke, C. C., 56
Cohen, E. G., 23, 24, 39, 165, 166, 167, 168, 174, 278
Cohen, S. P., 1, 110, 111, 112, 243
Colca, C., 56
Colca, L., 56
Coleman, P. T., 197, 200, 201, 203, 204
Colond, J. S., 170
Commins, B., 31, 38
Condon, J. C., 135
Cook, S. W., 14, 23
Cooper, J., 36
Cooper, L., 161
Corbitt, E. M., 36
Corder, J., 184
Cose, E., 12
Cossey, R., 165, 168
Cottell, P. G., Jr., 156
Cox, T., 76, 78, 79, 96
Craver, C. B., 205
Crawford, D., 192
Crocker, J., 39
Crogan, M., 156
Cross, W. E., Jr., 5, 69
Culbertson, F. M., 59
Curtis, S.C., 153
Cushner, K., 140, 141, 143, 149

D'Andrea, M., 57
Daniels, J., 57
Daniels, R., 135, 141, 173
Darley, J. M., 39
Dass, P., 80
Davidson, F. H., 209, 213, 214, 215, 218, 233, 234
Davidson, M. M., 205, 209, 213, 214, 215, 218, 233, 234

Davidson-Podgorny, G., 23
Davis, M. H., 119
Day, H. R., 13, 35, 143, 144
Day, N. E., 80, 94
Day-Hairston, B. O., 202
Day-Vines, N. L., 202
Della Noce, D. J., 201
Delucchi, K. L., 219, 220
deMello, S., 104
Derlega, V. J., 117
Desforges, D. M., 120, 175
Deutsch, M., 157, 174, 197, 198, 199, 200, 201, 203, 204
Devine, P., 37, 65
Devine, P. G., 26, 27, 37, 39, 119, 131
DeVries, D. L., 14, 159, 160, 171
Dey, E. L., 107, 122
Diaz-Loving, R., 136
Digh, P., 78
Dominguez, C., 75
Doob, L. W., 14, 110
Dovidio, J. F., 27, 31, 38, 65, 120, 177, 201, 230, 272
Doyle, A. B., 59, 68
Driskell, J. D., 14, 85, 88, 252
Dubinsky, E., 156
Dubois, P. M., 103, 108
Duckett, J., 25
Dukes, E. F., 184
Dunn, T. P., 145
Dunnette, M. D., 86, 88, 248
DuPraw, M. E., 184, 185, 206
Duran, A., 136

Earley, P. C., 149
Eaton, S. F., 9
Edison, M., 58
Edwards, K. J., 14, 23, 159, 160, 171
Eisenstadt, D., 33, 59
Elliot, A. J., 27, 37
Ellis, C., 76, 87, 88, 96
Ely, R. J., 39
Emigh, P., 108, 122

Emler, N., 229
Erber, R., 175
Evans, R. I., 30
Evett, S. R., 131

Farnish, A., 159
Feagin, J. R., 131
Fenwick, V., 56
Fernandez, R., 155
Ferris, S. P., 76
Fielding, G. D., 219, 224, 225
Filner, B., 192
Fine, M., 215, 216, 241, 242
Finlay, K., 33, 34, 272
Finlay, K. A., 65, 119
Finley, J. A., 1
Fischer, J., 55, 57
Fishbein, M., 40, 91, 121, 231, 274
Fisher, R. J., 15, 109, 185, 189, 191,
    196, 200, 201
Fiske, S. T., 26, 175
Fleming, J. H., 39
Flynn, G., 75
Flythe, R., 194, 202
Folger, J. P., 200
Follingstad, D. R., 250
Ford, S., 165
Forester, J., 204
Fowler, S. M., 145
Frable, D. E. S., 131
Frady, M., 7
Freedman, E., 55, 57
French, W. L., 190
Frenkel-Brunswik, E., 4, 25
Friedman, R., 205
Furlong, M., 58, 247
Furnham, A., 143
Fyock, J., 37

Gadlin, H., 181, 203, 204
Gaertner, S. L., 27, 31, 38, 65, 120, 177,
    230, 272

Gamache, R., 58
Gannon, M. J., 149
Garcia, M. H., 82
Gardiner, G. S., 59
Garrow, D. J., 8
Gartner, C., 145, 146
Gebreyesus, S., 135, 141, 173
Gelfand, M. J., 205
Genet, D., 52
Gersho, B. F., 177
Giles, H., 60
Gilligan, C., 211
Girard, K., 191
Glazer, I. M., 187
Glick, P., 26
Goettee, E., 194, 202
Goldman, A., 147, 149
Goldstein, D. L. 144
Gonzales, A., 23, 174
Gorsuch, R. L., 232
Gottfredson, L. S., 79, 81, 97
Grant, C. A., 48, 55, 58, 72
Grant, G. A., 55, 58
Gray, D. B., 33, 59, 65, 67
Green, K., 198
Greenbaum, P., 147
Greenbaum, S., 147
Greenhalgh, L., 205
Greenwald, A. G., 11
Griesbach, A., 122, 123
Grossman, H., 135, 141, 173
Grube, J. W., 30, 276
Gudykunst, W. B., 44, 120, 132, 133,
    134, 135, 136, 137, 144, 147, 149,
    150, 151, 152, 153, 275
Guild, S., 143
Gunsch, D., 81
Gurin, P., 114, 115, 247, 248, 249
Guzley, R. M., 132, 133, 134, 136,
    137, 150, 153

Hacker, A., 11
Hagedorn, L. S., 58

Haines, R., 84, 97
Hall, R., 201
Hall, W. S., 26
Hallinan, M. T., 24, 67
Hamilton, D. L., 35, 37, 177
Hammer, M. R., 44, 132, 133, 134, 136, 137, 144, 147, 149, 150, 153
Hannah, D. B., 39
Hanover, J. M. B., 87, 88
Hanson, W. C., 81
Harding, J., 4, 25
Harding, S., 104
Hare, A. P., 243
Hare, S. E., 243
Harmon-Jones, E., 33, 34, 65, 275
Harrington, H. J., 23, 120, 176, 231
Harris, G., 198, 202
Harris, M. J., 36
Harrison, J. K., 147, 153
Harrison, R., 133
Harvey, O. J., 31, 157
Haslam, S. A., 35, 36
Hass, R. G., 26, 30
Hauserman, N., 32, 244
Haynes, N. M., 135, 141, 173
Heck, R., 57
Heim, S. J., 37, 39
Hemphill, H., 84, 97
Henderson, G., 77, 97
Hennington, M., 58
Heppner, M. J., 245
Hersh, R. H., 218, 224, 225, 226
Hertz-Lazarowitz, R., 114, 160, 163, 164, 165, 171
Heslin, R., 153
Hewstone, M., 21, 23, 31, 38, 175, 176, 273
Higgins, A., 209, 217, 218
Highberger, L., 33, 34, 65, 275
Hiller, J. S., 76
Hilton, J. L., 35, 39
Hinckley, C. C., 156
Hitt, M. A., 92
Hogg, M. A., 28

Hohn, R. L., 59
Holley, L. C., 104
Hollister, L., 80, 94
Holmes, H., 143
Holmes, M., 227
Holthuis, N. C., 165, 168
Hood, W. E., 31, 157
Hoover, D. W., 36
Hopkins, R. L., 133
Horner, E. R., 96
Howe, L. W., 224, 225
Howitt, D., 75
Hubbard, A. S., 110, 111
Huddy, L., 26
Hulgus, J. F., 143, 144, 147, 149
Humphreys, B., 162, 170
Hunter, B. A., 26
Hutson, J. J., 103, 108

Imhoff, H. J., 33, 34, 65, 275
Ingram, D., 223
Islam, M. R., 31, 38
Ivey, A., 58

Jackson, M.W., 145
Jackson, S. E., 96
Jacob, B. A., 54
Jacobs, R. L., 145
Jenkins, J., 171
Jesaitis, P. T., 80, 94
John, O. P., 39, 40, 69, 175, 201
Johnson, D. W., 14, 15, 23, 56, 160, 161, 162, 169, 170, 171, 172, 174, 191, 192, 193, 194, 197, 198, 199, 200. 201, 202
Johnson, F., 199, 200
Johnson, J., 169, 170
Johnson, R. T., 14, 15, 23, 160, 161, 162, 169, 170, 171, 172, 174, 191, 192, 193, 194, 197, 198, 199, 201, 202
Johnston, L., 175

Johnstone, S., 56, 63
Joly, S., 26
Jones, C. C., 155
Jones, J. M., 11, 12
Jones, T. S., 191, 192, 202, 205
Jost, J. T., 35
Judd, C. M., 31, 38, 158, 243

Kagan, S., 160
Kahn, S. E., 57, 250, 251
Karambayya, R., 188
Kashy, D. A., 253
Katz, I., 26, 30
Katz, J. H., 13, 58
Kawakami, K., 38, 65, 272
Kealey, D. J., 149, 150
Keashly, L., 191, 200, 201
Keats, B. W., 92
Kehoe, J. W., 59
Kelman, H. C., 1, 14, 110, 111, 112, 122
Kenny, D. A., 253
Kidder, L. H., 243
Kiger, G., 59, 60
Kim, D., 209, 218, 219, 220
Kim, S. H., 190
Kincaid, T. M., 96
Kinder, D. R., 10, 12
Kirschenbaum, H., 224, 225
Kitano, H. H. L., 135, 141, 173
Klein, J. D., 155
Klein, T. R., 33, 34, 65, 275
Kluger, R., 5
Kmitta, D., 198, 202
Koch, S. J., 191
Kochman, T., 205
Kohlberg, L., 15, 209, 210, 217, 218, 234
Kohn, A., 155
Kossek, E. E., 93
Kressel, K., 183, 201
Kroll, M., 76
Krosnick, J., 258

Kuppermintz, H., 114
Kussell, P., 160, 165
Kutner, B., 4, 25

Labov, W., 205
Laginski, A., 198
Lam, J. A., 197, 198
Lampe, J. R., 173
Landis, D., 13, 35, 140, 143, 144, 147, 149
Lang, J., 114
Langer, E., 40
La Resche, D., 205, 206
Layng, J. M., 89
Lazarowitz, R., 171
Leavey, M., 159, 160
Lefley, H. P., 57
Leighninger, M., 108, 122
Leippe, M. R., 33, 59
Leming, J. S., 210, 225, 226
Lepper, M. R., 120, 175
Lerner, M.J., 66
Lessing, E. E., 56
LeVine, R. A., 28, 36
Levinson, D. J., 4, 25, 109
Lewin, K., 121
Lewis, S., 39
Licona, T., 225, 227, 228
Lieberman, M., 216
Lind, G., 218
Lindsay, C., 76, 95, 96, 201, 202
Lippett, R., 109
Litcher, J. H., 56
Lockwood, A. L., 210, 225, 226
Lockwood, J., 31, 38
Lopez, G., 114, 115, 247, 248, 249
Lord, C. G., 120, 175
Lord, S. A., 56
Lotan, R. A., 23, 165, 166, 167
Lowen, D., 56
Lucker, G. W., 23, 163
Lupton-Smith, H. A., 202
Lupton-Smith, H. S., 194, 202

Lynch, F. R., 99

Mackie, D. M., 39, 177
Madden, N. A., 159, 160, 170
Maier, M., 98
Malloy, C. E., 135, 141, 173
Malloy, W. W., 135, 141, 173
Mann, J., 31, 177, 230
Margulis, S. T., 118
Marsh, H. W., 156
Marshall, F. R., 188
Martin, J. N., 133, 148, 153
Martinez, C. M., 136
Maruyama, G., 23
Mason, J. A., 120, 175
Mattingly, R. M., 163
Maxwell, J. P., 194
Mayton, D. M., 30, 276
McClelland, G. H., 258
McClendon, M. J., 23
McCline, R. L., 92
McConahay, J. G., 151
McCormick, M. A., 204
McCoy, M., 108, 122
McCrae, A. V., 23
McGhee, D. E., 11
McGillicuddy, N. B., 195
McGinnies, E., 59
McGregor, J., 67, 149, 151
McGrew, P. L., 14, 35, 143, 144
McInerney, D. M., 156
McInerney, V., 156
McLaughlin, K. A., 52
McMillan, D., 37, 231
McPhail, P., 223
McPhail, R., 223
Mendenhall, M., 149
Menses, L. M., 177
Metts, S., 118
Meyer, L. H., 170
Middleton, D., 223
Milhouse, V. H., 133
Milich, R., 36

Miller, A. B., 14, 35, 143, 144
Miller, J. P., 218, 224, 225
Miller, N., 23, 31, 120, 176, 177, 231,
    273
Millis, B. J., 156
Mitchell, J. M., 193
Mitchener, E. C., 33, 34, 65, 275
Mitnick, L. L., 59
Modest, K. H., 194, 202
Moise-Swanson, D., 104
Molina, L., 56
Monteith, M. J., 26, 27, 30, 37, 39,
    118, 119, 276
Moore, H. B., 145
Moore, M. A., 57
Morishima, M., 190, 196
Morphew, C. C., 165, 168
Morris, L., 87, 88
Morrison, H. W., 60
Mosher, R. L., 222, 229
Motowildo, S. J., 86, 88, 248
Mouton, J. S., 15, 109, 190
Murrell, A., 31, 177, 230
Mustonen, T., 170
Myers, S., 192
Myrdal, G., 26

Nagda, B. A., 104, 105, 106, 107, 108,
    122
Nagda, B. R., 114, 115, 247, 248, 249
National Advisory Commission on
    Civil Disorders, 8
National Council for the Social
    Studies Task Force, 48
Nedler, B. F., 177
Neimeyer, G. J., 57
Neiswand, G. H., 145
Neuberg, S. L., 39
Neville, H., 58, 247
Newmann, F. M., 172
Nier, J. A., 65, 120
Nile, L. N., 83
Nora, A., 58

Oakes, P. J., 35, 36
O'Brien, G. E., 143, 144, 149
O'Brien, K. M., 245
O'Brien, M., 37
Oickle, E., 160, 171
Okebukola, P. A., 156, 160, 162, 163
Olson, K., 170
Olson-Buchanan, J. B., 190
Orbell, S., 121
Ordovensky, G. A., 71
Orfield, G., 9
Ortberg, J., 232
Oser, F. K., 218, 220, 221, 233
Owusu-Bempah, J., 75
Oxman, W., 146

Paige, R. M., 133, 148, 153
Parham, T. A., 55, 57
Parker, B., 80
Parker, W. M., 57
Parsell, G., 156
Pascarella, E. T., 58, 165
Paskoff, S. M., 91, 95
Patnoe, S., 162
Peak, H., 59
Pedersen, P., 14, 69, 70, 139, 141, 142, 146, 148
Peirce, R. S., 195
Peng, T., 115, 249
Penner, L. A., 201
Petronio, S., 118
Pettigrew, T. F., 4, 10, 11, 20, 21, 23, 24, 34, 157, 176, 272, 278
Picker, B. G., 188
Piliavin, J. A., 201
Plooij, D., 143, 144, 149
Plummer, D. L., 81, 99
Polley, R. B., 243
Polycarpou, M. P., 33, 34, 65, 275
Pomare, M., 31, 177
Ponterotto, J. G., 69, 70
Poon, J. M. L., 149
Power, F. C., 209, 217, 218

Pratto, F., 26, 28
Prien, K. O., 130
Probst, T. M., 205
Proshansky, N., 4, 25
Protheroe, D. R., 149, 150
Pruegger, V. J., 145, 149
Pruitt, D. G., 183, 190, 195, 196, 201
Pugh, S. D., 92
Puka, B., 211
Puma, M. J., 155
Purpel, D., 209
Putnam, L. L., 190
Pyle, J. L., 12, 75, 94

Qin, Z., 172
Quinn, R. J., 156

Ramsey, S. L., 120, 175
Raviv, S., 160, 165
Realo, A., 205
Reed, D. R. C., 211
Reichel, L. D., 177
Reilly, A. H., 75
Reizenstein, R. M., 92
Rest, J. R., 210, 222, 229
Richards, H. C., 58
Riche, M. F., 12
Rissman, A., 143, 144, 149
Robinson, B., 58
Robinson, D. H., 156
Robinson, E. A., 250
Rogers, T. B., 145, 149
Rogers, W. T., 59
Rokeach, M., 30, 60
Roloff, M. E., 190
Romero, J., 87, 88
Rooze, G. E., 173
Roper, S., 39
Rose, T., 37
Rosell, M. C., 37, 39
Rosen, B., 88, 96, 97, 99
Rosenberg, M., 256

Rosenfield, D., 14, 23, 24, 163, 174
Rosenholtz, S. J., 165, 174
Rothbart, M., 39, 40, 69, 175, 201
Roye, W. J., 24, 67
Rubin, J. Z., 190
Ryan, K., 209
Rynders, J. E., 170
Rynes, S., 88, 96, 97, 99

Salisbury, M., 12
Sams, C., 145
Sanders, L. M., 10, 12
Sanford, R. N., 4, 25
Scalera, C. V., 106, 108
Schaller, M., 37, 39
Schaps, E., 209, 218, 219, 220
Scherbaum, C., 131
Schlaefli, A., 210, 222, 229
Schleien, S. J., 170
Schoem, D., 115
Schoene, L. P., Jr., 184, 185, 206
Schroeder, D. A., 201
Schroth, H. A., 177
Schrumpf, F., 192
Schultz, L. H., 216, 253
Schuman, G., 10
Schwartz, J. L. K., 11
Schwartz, S. H., 232
Schwarzwald, J., 136, 160
Sears, D. O., 26, 27, 151
Seiter, J. S., 145, 146
Selman, R. L., 216, 253
Sessa, W. I., 84
Sevig, T. D., 104, 105, 106, 107, 108, 115, 116, 122
Shachar, C., 165
Sharan, S., 160, 163, 164, 165
Sharan, Y., 160, 163, 164, 165
Sheeran, P., 121
Sherif, C. W., 31, 157
Sherif, M., 15, 28, 31, 157
Sherman, L. W., 160, 171
Sherman, S. J., 35

Shweder, R. A., 211
Sidanius, J., 26, 28
Sikes, J., 14, 22, 24, 162, 163, 174, 176
Simon, S. B., 209, 224, 225
Slavin, R. E., 14, 23, 24,159, 160, 162, 164, 169, 170, 171, 172, 173, 174
Sleeter, C. E., 48, 49, 50, 72
Slobodin, L., 143, 144, 149
Smith, A., 151, 201
Smith, D. H., 144
Smith, E. R., 243
Smith, K. A., 172
Smith, M. E., 156
Smith, P. C., 8
Smith, P. W., 30
Snapp, M., 14, 22, 24, 162, 176
Snyder, M., 36
Solomon, D., 209, 218, 219, 220
Sonnenfield, J. A., 76, 87, 88, 96
Sorcher, M., 85, 88
Spalding, R., 156
Spearmon, M. L., 104
Spence, R., 85, 88
Sprinthall, N. A., 222
St. John, N. H., 9
Stangor, C., 37, 231
Steeh, C., 10
Steinwachs, B., 145
Stephan, C., 14, 22, 24, 162, 163, 174, 176
Stephan, C. W., xiii, 9, 20, 24, 28, 64, 67, 69, 117, 135, 136, 150, 151, 152, 157, 177, 201, 231, 274, 275
Stephan, W. G., xiii, 9, 20, 23, 24, 25, 28, 33, 34, 64, 65, 67, 69, 117, 119, 135, 136, 150, 151, 152, 157, 174, 177, 200, 201, 230, 231, 257, 272, 274, 275
Stevahn, L., 198
Stevens, R. J., 159, 170, 173
Stevenson, M., 115
Stewart, J. S., 225
Stitzel, D., 204
Stone, P., 243

Storti, C., 138, 146
Stoskopf, A. L., 241
Stroh, L. K., 75
Strom, M., 241
Sullivan, E., 226
Sullivan, J. L., 56, 63
Sullivan, P., 222
Sumner, W. G., 29
Swann, W. B., 36
Swann, W. B., Jr., 39
Sweeney, B., 198, 202
Swim, J. K., 26

Tajfel, H., 28, 68, 176, 230
Tallent-Runnels, M., 173
Talmage, H., 165
Tan, D. L., 87, 88
Tanke, E. D., 36
Tansik, D. A., 14, 85, 88, 252
Teixeira, R. A., 24, 67
Terenzini, P. T., 58
Tessler, R. C., 232
Thalhammer, K., 56, 63
Thiagarajan, S., 145
Thibodeau, R., 162
Thoma, S. J., 210, 222, 229
Thomas, J. A., 14, 35, 143, 144
Thomas, M., 160
Thomas, M. B., 145
Thompson, J., 172
Thompson, M., 184
Tjosvold, D., 190, 196
Tougas, F., 26
Trafimow, D., 121
Triandis, H. C., 134, 135, 140, 143, 144, 149, 205
Trifonovitch, G. J., 148
Tropp, L. R., 157, 272, 278
Tur-Kaspa. M., 136
Turner, J. C., 28, 35, 36, 176, 230
Tyrell, G., 160

Ungoed-Thomas, J. R., 223
Ury, W., 189
Usadel, H. C., 192

Van Adams, A., 188
Vanbeselaere, N., 31, 38
Vandercook, T. L., 170
VanLeeuven, M. D., 120, 175
Van Schie, E., 60
Van Sickle, R. L., 163
Van Soest, D., 57
Vaslow, J. B., 92
Vasquez, C. M., 107, 122
Vasquez-Suson, K. A., 131
Vedder, P. H., 172
Vera, H., 131
Verma, G. K., 56, 63
Volk, G. L., 156
Volkan, V. D., 122, 124
Volpe, M. R., 186
von Hippel, W., 35
Vrij, A., 60

Wackenhut, J., 26, 30
Wade, P., 60, 149
Wah, L., 79
Walen, S. R., 32, 244
Walker, B. A., 81
Walker, I., 156
Walker, L., 55, 57
Wall, J. A., 202
Walters, G. L., 118
Wang, V. O., 57
Ward, C. M., 65, 120
Warrior, R. A., 8
Washington, V., 55, 58
Watson, G., 4
Watson, M., 209, 218, 219, 220
Weber, R., 39
Weeks, W. W., 146
Weigel, R. H., 14, 23
Weiner, M. J., 34, 60

Weldon, D., 143, 144, 149
Welton, G. L., 195
West, S. C., 120, 175
Whitcomb, J. A., 165, 168
White, B. J., 31, 157
White, M. B., 80
Widaman, K. F., 160
Wilderson, F., 161
Williams, A., 60
Williams, J., 6
Williams, R. M., Jr., 4, 24
Wilson, J. J., 11
Wiseman, R. I., 44, 133, 144, 147, 149, 153
Wiser, P. L., 14, 23
Wittig, M., 56
Worchel, S., 23
Word, C., 36
Worth, L. T., 39
Wozniak, P. R., 145
Wright, F. E., 34, 60
Wright, P., 76

Wyer, R. S., Jr., 37, 231

Yawkey, T. D., 56
Ybarra, O., 136, 151, 257
Yong, M., 141
Yonker, R., 55, 57
Yoshida, T., 130, 131, 132, 139, 144, 153

Zahn, G. L., 160
Zanna, M. P., 36
Zelditch, M., Jr., 165, 174
Zelniker, T., 164
Ziegler, S., 163
Zonia, S. C., 93
Zoppetti, L., 205
Zuniga, X., 104, 105, 106, 107, 108, 115, 116, 122
Zuwerink, J. R., 27, 37, 39, 119

SUBJECT INDEX

Accordion problem, dialogue groups and, 123-124
Added-value negotiating, 190
Affirmative action, 8, 65, 78
  plans, 8
Allstate Insurance company, 79
Ambivalence-amplification theory, 26, 29, 44
American Jewish Committee, 52
Antiprejudice, caring models of, 212-215
Antiracism training, 153
Anxiety and uncertainty management theory (AUM), 120-121
Anxiety reduction, 103, 117, 120-121, 127, 150, 151
Aversive-racism theory, 26, 27, 29, 44

BAFA BAFA, 145, 146
Bargaining models, 189
Bargaining models, positive, 181, 189-190, 206
  in organizational settings, 187, 189-190

See also Added-value negotiating; Integrative bargaining; Principled negotiation; Win-win bargaining
Barnga, 145
Berkeley Model, 212, 219-220, 228, 233, 234, 235
  components, 219
  example, 219-220
Black children, racial identification of, 4-5
Blacks:
  educational level, 11
  income, 11
  increased political participation, 11
  living conditions, 11
  occupations, 11
Blue-eyes/brown-eyes simulation, 60, 66
BostonBank Corporation, 78
Brown v. Board of Education of Topeka, 4-6, 7
Busing, school desegregation and, 9

Caring, 212

school diversity and, 213
See also Antiprejudice, caring
    models of; Caring communities;
    Coalition of Essential Schools;
    School Development Program
Caring communities, 212-215, 233,
    234, 235
Character education programs, 212,
    226-228, 229, 233, 235
Chavez, Cesar, 7
Children's Creative Response to
    Conflict, 194
Civil disobedience, 193
Civil Rights Act (1964), 7
Civil Rights movement, 4, 193
    intergroup relations progress and,
    11, 17
    protests/demonstrations, 6-9
Clark, Kenneth, 4, 5
Coalition of Essential Schools, 214
    Central Park East Secondary
    School, 214
Cognitive empathy, 33
    creating, 43
Comer schools, 213-214. *See also*
    School Development Program
Community Board Program (San
    Francisco), 194
Complex Instruction, 157-158, 165-
    168, 179, 278
    Assignment Competence to Low-
    Status Students, 167
    expectation states theory and, 165
    focus, 165
    Multiple-Ability Treatment, 167
    research on, 168
    status interventions, 167
Compunction theory, 26, 27, 29, 44
Conflict containment, 181, 206, 207
    community-based, 183, 187
    goal of, 187
    research on, 197
Conflict resolution, 18

problems/recommendations, 201-
    203
underlying psychological
    processes, 199-201
See also Interethnic conflict
    resolution
Conflict resolution programs, 181-
    194
    community-based, 183-187
    in organizational settings, 187-191
    major goal, 182
    school-based, 191-194
    See also Conflict containment;
        Conflict resolution techniques;
        Mediation; Positive bargaining
        models; Third-party
        consultation; Town meetings
Conflict resolution programs,
    research findings on, 194-199
    research on Interactive Conflict
        Resolution (ICR), 196-197
    research on mediation, 195
    research on negotiation, 195-196
Conflict resolution techniques, 181,
    267
    goal, 267
    See also Conflict containment;
        Mediation; Positive bargaining;
        Third-party consultation; Town
        meetings
Conflict resolution training, 10, 16,
    17, 80, 100, 267
Conflict strategies theory, 199-200
Contact:
    in intergroup relations, 20-24
    to improve intergroup relations,
    22-24
Contact hypothesis, 4, 66
    version of, 5
Contact theorists, 4
Contact theory, 13, 20, 24. *See also*
    Contact theory, revised
Contact theory, revised, 20-22, 44
    causal model of, 21

mediating factors, 20, 21
person factors, 20, 21, 22, 24
situational factors, 20, 21, 22, 23-24
societal factors, 20-21, 22, 22-23
See also Prejudice reduction
   processes; Personalization;
   Recategorization
Content analyses, 245, 260
Cooperative learning, 155-157
   formal, 161
   informal, 161
   outcomes, 179
   research base, 157
   underlying psychological
      processes, 157
   See also Cooperative learning
      groups; Cooperative learning
      programs; Cooperative learning
      techniques
Cooperative learning groups, 10, 155,
   178, 266-267
Cooperative learning programs, 156,
   157-168, 268
   as interactive-indirect, 156
   See also Complex Instruction;
      Cooperative learning techniques;
      Jigsaw Classrooms; Group
      Investigation; Learning Together
      technique, Johnsons'; Slavin
      techniques
Cooperative learning techniques, 14,
   16, 17, 18, 155-156, 177-178, 266-
   267
   dimensions, 158
   effectiveness, 156, 172-173, 174
   popularity, 156
   pretraining students in, 178
   problems/recommendations, 177-
   178
   training teachers in, 177-178
   See also Cooperative learning
      techniques, research findings for
Cooperative learning techniques,
   research findings for, 169-174

achievement measures, 171-173
intergroup relations findings, 170-
   171
intergroup relations measures,
   169-170
personality and social-skills
   measures, 170
racial/ethnic minority focus, 173-
   174
Corning Glass, 76
Counterstereotypical behaviors, 69
Critical incidents, 137, 143-144, 154
   effectiveness, 144
Crown Heights incident, 187
Cultural audit, 95-96, 101, 276-277
   IBM's, 96
Cultural sensitizer, 34-35, 137, 140-
   143, 152, 154, 266
   criticism of, 143
   example of culture-specific, 141-
   142
   purpose of, 140
   Thai American, 141-142
   types, 140-141
Culture theory, 134-135, 151, 154

Defining Issues Test (DIT), 229
Delgado, Maria, 72-73
Dialogue:
   versus debate, 105
Dialogue facilitators, 104, 105, 122,
   127
Dialogue groups, 103, 127
   action-oriented, 126
   community versus educational,
   108
   confidentiality in, 105
   duration, 125
   participant ages, 125-126
   participants, 104, 108, 126
   participation guidelines, 125, 127
   problems/recommendations, 121-
   126

research on effectiveness of, 114-
117, 127
setting, 125, 127
size, 104, 127
social action and, 121, 127
underlying psychological
processes, 117-121
See also Intergroup dialogues;
Problem-solving workshops;
Psychological processes,
intergroup dialogues and; Study
circles
Didactic programs:
psychological processes in, 275-276
See also Diversity training
programs; Multicultural
education programs
Didactic techniques, 14, 16, 17, 63-64,
73, 81, 150, 151
discussions, 14, 47, 73, 81, 92, 100
lectures, 14, 81, 100
readings, 14, 73, 104
See also Diversity training;
Intergroup dialogues;
Multicultural education
programs
Digital Equipment Corporation, 81
Direct techniques, 16, 17
Discrimination, 2, 13, 17, 19, 26, 40-
42, 44, 45, 271, 283, 285
attitudes toward, 10
causal model of, 19
changing, 41-42
prejudice and, 40
subtle, 75
See also Prejudice; Stereotypes;
Stereotyping; Theory of
reasoned action
Dissonance, 33, 103, 117, 118, 127
Dissonance theorists, 118
Dissonance theory, 33, 90
Diversity, managing, 75, 77-80, 84,
100, 101
processes related to, 90-91
ultimate goal, 78
Diversity, valuing, 78, 80-84, 100, 101

goal, 80
most widely used technique for,
92
processes related to, 91-92
Diversity trainers, 94-95, 97-99, 101
Diversity training, 44, 100-101
in military, 10
issues, 97-99
underlying psychological
processes, 90-93
See also Diversity training
programs
Diversity training programs, 13-14,
17-18, 80-81, 92, 100-101, 264-
265
evaluating, 93, 99-100, 101
focus, 264
goals, 80-81, 264
Hemphill and Haines skills
training program, 84, 97
in military, 13
in workplace, 14, 17-18, 75-84
multicultural, diversity
competence approach, 82
National MultiCultural Institute
program, 83
planning, 93, 95-97
pragmatically based, 83-84, 100
problems/recommendations, 93-
100
research on effectiveness of, 85-89,
101
resistance to, 93-95
theory-based, 82, 100
training issues, 93, 97-99
types, 82-84
Diversity training workshops, 95

Echo phenomenon, 122-123
Educators for Social Responsibility,
194
Effort justification, 118
Egalitarianism, 30
Elementary and Secondary
Education Act (1965), 7

Elliot, Jane, 60
Emotional empathy, 33-34
Empathy, 103, 117, 119, 127
    cognitive, 33
    creating, 29, 33-34, 45, 150, 151,
        199, 207
    creating cognitive, 43
    creating emotional, 43
    emotional, 33-34
    evoking, 151
    evoking relational, 201
Equal Employment Opportunity
    Commission (EEOC), 12, 75
    affirmative action guidelines, 8
    lawsuits, 75
Equal-status conditions, 22-23, 174,
    179, 272, 278
Ethnic-identity development, 70, 74
Ethnocentrism, 28-29, 68, 151, 280
    reducing, 30
Evaluation, intergroup relations
        program:
    comparative studies, 259
    of intergroup attitudes, 257
    publication of, 259-260, 261
    reasons for, 237-238
    See also Evaluation, intergroup
        relations program; Evaluation
        research techniques; Measures,
        evaluation
Evaluation research techniques, 238,
    260
    creating measures, 254-258
    qualitative, 238-245, 259, 260, 269-
        270
    quantitative, 238, 245-254, 259, 260,
        270
    quantitative versus qualitative,
        245, 261
    See also Content analyses; Focus
        groups; Measures; Mediational
        analyses; Nonsystematic
        observation; Postprogram
        surveys; Posttest only with
        control group; Pretest/Posttest
        design; Pretest/Posttest with

control group; Statistical
    analyses; Systematic
    observation
Expectancy-confirming information,
    37
Expectancy-disconfirming
    information, 37, 39
Experiential techniques, 14, 44, 47,
    81, 144-148, 151, 152, 266
    celebratory activities, 73
    cultural simulations, 144, 147-148
    face-to-face interaction, 151, 179
    in multicultural education
        programs, 47, 73
    role-playing, 14, 44, 47, 67, 81, 92,
        100, 104, 144, 146-147, 151, 279
    simulation games, 14, 44, 47, 73,
        81, 92, 100, 104, 144, 145-146
    videos/movies, 73, 81, 92, 100

Facing History and Ourselves, 212,
    215-216, 228, 233, 234, 235, 253
    nonsystematic observational
        study of, 241-242
Focus groups, 242-243, 260

Group-conflict theory, 44
Group Investigation, 157, 158, 163-
    165, 172, 179
    implementation stages, 163-164

Hate crimes, 11
Hate groups, 11
Hewlett-Packard, 97

IBM, 96
Illusory correlation, 37
Immigration, 12-13
Indirect techniques, 16, 17
Integrated-threat theory, 27, 28, 29,
    44
Integrative bargaining, 189

Integrative problem-solving
    negotiation, 200
Interactive Conflict Resolution (ICR),
    185, 190-191
    research on, 196-197
Interactive programs:
    psychological processes in, 271-275
    See also Conflict resolution training
    programs; Cooperative learning
    programs; Dialogue groups;
    Intercultural training; Moral and
    values education programs
Interactive techniques, 16, 17. *See also*
    specific interactive techniques
Intercultural training programs, 14,
    16, 17, 18, 129-133, 266, 268
    culture-general, 132, 133, 154
    culture-specific, 132, 133, 154
    designing, 133-137
    effectiveness, 133-134, 154, 266
    first, 10
    goals, 152-153, 266
    individualism-collectivism and,
    135
    long-term versus short-term, 153
    Peace Corps and, 14
    See also Intercultural training
    techniques
Intercultural training techniques,
    137-148, 154
    critical incidents, 137, 143-144, 154
    cultural sensitizers, 137, 140-143,
    154
    cultural simulations, 137, 144, 147-
    148, 154
    didactic, 132-133
    experiential techniques, 132, 133,
    137, 139, 144-148, 154
    language training, 137, 139, 154
    lectures and discussions, 137-139,
    154
    research finding on, 149-150
    role-playing, 137, 144, 146-147, 154,
    279

    simulation games, 137, 144, 145-
    146, 154
Interethnic conflict resolution, 203-
    206, 207
Intergroup anxiety, 135-137, 177
Intergroup communication,
    Gudykunst's model of, 136
Intergroup conflict resolution
    techniques, 15
Intergroup contact:
    processes, 103
    variables affecting, 22
Intergroup dialogue program,
    University of Michigan, 105-
    108, 114-116
    goals, 106
    stages, 106-108
Intergroup dialogues, 14, 16, 17, 18,
    44, 67, 103, 265-266
    definition, 103
    goals, 265
    in community settings, 108-109,
    116, 127
    in educational settings, 104-108,
    116, 127
    limited data, 265
    types, 104-113
    See also Dialogue groups;
    Dialogue groups, research on
    effectiveness of
Intergroup relations, 2
Intergroup relations in United
    States, historical overview of, 3-
    13, 17
    1970s, 7-9
    1960s, 7, 8
    post-World War II era, 3-6
Intergroup relations programs, 16,
    17, 19, 44-45, 283-285
    assessment, 263-271
    conceptualizing, 16-17
    conducting effective, 278-279
    contents, 277-278
    design issues, 280-282

evaluating, 15
funding for, 285
recommendations for, 276-280
underlying psychological
    processes, 42-44, 271-276
*See also specific intergroup relations
    programs*; Contact; Contact
    theory, revised; Discriminatory
    behavior; Prejudice; Stereotypes;
    Trainers, intergroup relations
Intergroup relations techniques, 13,
    34-35. *See also specific intergroup
    relations techniques*
Intergroup relations theory, 13
International relations problem-
    solving workshops, 10, 109-114
Interpersonal sensitivity/respect
    programs, 212, 223-224, 229, 233
    criticism of, 224
    curriculum materials, 223
    premise, 223

Jigsaw Classrooms, 157, 158, 162-163,
    171, 179
    cross-ethnic friendships in, 163
    Jigsaw I, 158, 162
    Jigsaw II, 158, 162
    minority students and, 163, 174
Johns Hopkins University, Slavin
    cooperative learning techniques
    and, 158
Just Communities program, 212, 217-
    219, 228, 230. *See also* Just
    community concept, Kohlberg's;
    Just Community schools; Just
    Learning communities
Just Community concept, Kohlberg's,
    217-219, 233, 234, 235
    pilot-school projects, 217-218
    See also Just Community schools;
    Just Communities program; Just
    Learning schools
Just Community schools, 15, 217

Just learning communities, 18

Kennedy, John F., 8
King, Martin Luther, Jr., 6, 8, 188,
    189, 284
King, Rodney, 1, 184

Language instruction, 80
Learning Together technique,
    Johnsons', 157, 158, 160-162,
    171, 179, 193-194
    Circles of Learning, 160
    cooperative base groups, 160-161
    cooperative learning procedures,
    160

Measures, evaluation:
    creating, 254, 256, 258, 261
    of intergroup attitudes, 257
    relevant to intergroup relations
        program evaluations, 255
    reliable, 254, 256
    unobtrusive, 258-259, 261
    valid, 254, 256
Mediation, 18, 181, 203, 206, 267
    Black/Korean Mediation Project,
    184
    community-based, 183-184
    in organizational settings, 187,
    188-189
    in school-based conflict resolution
        programs, 191
    research on, 195, 207
    See also Peer mediation;
        Transformative mediation
Mediational analyses, 252-253
    example, 253
Mediators, 204-205
Memory biases, 37
Memphis sanitation strike of 1968,
    188-189

Mentoring programs, 80, 100
  Proctor and Gamble, 80
Minority groups:
  cooperative learning groups and,
    173-174, 179
  poverty among, 12
  social progress of, 11
Misattributions, correcting, 29, 34-35,
    39-40, 43, 45, 150, 152
Montgomery bus boycott, 6
Moral and values education
    programs, 10, 15, 16, 17, 18, 209-
    211, 234-236, 267-268
  in school settings, 210
  major approaches to, 211-228, 234-
    235
  problems/recommendations, 232-
    234
  research findings on, 228-230
  underlying psychological
    processes, 211, 230-232
  See also Berkeley Model; Caring
    communities; Character
    education programs; Facing
    History and Ourselves;
    Interpersonal sensitivity/respect
    programs; Just Communities
    program; Moral discourse
    technique; Personality
    development programs; Values
    clarification programs
Moral atmosphere, 217
Moral community, 227
Moral development:
  acceptance of outgroups and, 209
  racial prejudice and, 209, 235
Moral development/reasoning
    stages, Kohlberg's, 15, 210-211,
    212, 222, 234, 235
  criticism of, 211
Moral discipline, 227
Moral discourse technique, 212, 220-
    221, 228, 233, 234, 235
Moral reflection, 228

Moral thought, 209-210
Motorola, 78
Multicultural education, 10, 18, 47-
    48, 73-74, 227
  conservative critics of, 49-50
  content/techniques, 51-54
  controversy, 47, 49-51
  goals, 48-49, 70
  liberal critics of, 50
  proponents of, 50-51
  teachers' role, 71-72, 73-74
  See also Multicultural education
    programs, studies on effects of;
    Multicultural education
    programs
Multicultural education programs,
    13, 17, 73-74, 264
  didactic, 47
  direct approach, 47
  geographic locations of, 49
  goals, 49, 264
  Hands Across the Campus, 52-53
  implementation of, 73-74
  interactive exercises, 47
  problems/recommendations, 68-
    73
  underlying psychological
    processes, 63-68
  values based on, 48
  variety of, 51-54
Multicultural education programs,
    studies on effects of, 55-63
  long-term, 55-59
  outcomes of long-term versus
    short-term, 56, 61
  overall evaluation, 61-63
  short-term, 55, 56, 59-61, 73
Multiculturalism, 227

National Association for the
    Advancement of Colored
    People (NAACP), 60
Native Americans, 7-8

Negative intergroup contact, 19, 44.
See also Contact; Contact theory
Negotiation, 267
research on, 195-196
Neighborhood justice centers, 194
Nonsystematic observation, 240-242,
260
of Facing History and Ourselves
curriculum, 241-242

Outgroups, 2, 18, 29, 36, 45, 68, 181
differentiating, 40, 43, 45
humanizing, 117, 119-120, 127
misattributing behavior of, 34
moral development and
acceptance of, 209
positive attitudes toward, 176

Parks, Rosa, 6
Peacemakers Program, 192-193
goal, 192
research on, 199
structured academic controversies
in, 193
Peer mediation, 191-192, 206, 267
effectiveness of, 198
Peer mediation programs, 192-193,
269
research on school-based, 197-199,
207
See also Peacemakers Program
Peer mediators, 202, 203
Personality development programs,
212, 222-223, 228, 233, 235
research findings, 222-223
Personalization, 21
Postprogram surveys, 239-240, 260
basic questions, 239
drawback, 240
Posttest only with control group, 248-
250, 261
Hawthorne effect and, 249

limitation, 248
Prejudice, 2, 13, 17, 19, 20, 24, 25-35,
44, 151, 271, 283
attitudes toward, 10
covert, 11
changing nature of, 11
definition, 25
early theories, 25-26
intergroup, 153
moral development and, 209, 235
studies, 4
See also specific theories of prejudice
Prejudice, theories of; Prejudice
reduction processes
Prejudice, theories of, 26-29, 44. *See
also specific theories of prejudice*
Prejudice reduction, *Hands Across
the Campus* curriculum and, 52-
53
Prejudice reduction processes, 29-35,
45
correcting misattributions, 29, 34-
35, 45
creating empathy, 29, 33-34, 45
creating superordinate groups, 21,
29, 31, 45
emphasizing multiple identities,
21, 29, 31-32, 45
increasing perceptions of
similarity among groups, 29, 30,
45
making value-behavior
discrepancies explicit, 29, 30, 45
modifying associations between
cognitions and affect, 29, 32, 45
reducing threat, 29, 30, 45
reinforcing and modeling positive
behaviors, 29, 32, 45
using dissonance to create
attitude change, 29, 33, 45
Pretest/Posttest design, 246-248, 261
example, 247
limitations, 246-247

Pretest/Posttest with control group,
        250-252, 261
    disadvantage, 250
    example, 250-251
Principled negotiation, 189
Problem-solving workshops, 18, 109-
        113, 116
    facilitators, 110, 111
    international conflicts and, 10, 110-
        114
    Israeli-Palestinian examples, 111-
        113, 114, 124
    location of, 110
    participants, 110
    size, 110
Pro-white bias, 11
Psychological processes, conflict
        resolution and, 199-201
    creating conditions for positive
        interaction, 199, 207
    creating empathy, 199, 207
    increasing interdependence, 199,
        207
    increasing participants' sense of
        empowerment, 199, 207
    increasing rewards received from
        others, 199, 207
    observing norm of reciprocity, 199,
        207
Psychological processes, cooperative
        learning and, 157, 174-177, 179,
        267
    anxiety reduction, 157, 175, 177,
        179
    creating conditions for self-
        disclosure, 157, 176-177, 272
    creating goal interdependence/
        positive contact, 157, 174, 175,
        179
    creating subordinate groups, 157,
        175, 177, 179
    emphasizing multiple identities,
        157, 175, 179
    equal status, 174, 179, 272, 278

    providing conditions in which
        performance expectations are
        not status-based, 157, 174, 179
Psychological processes, diversity
        training and, 90-93
    managing diversity, 90-91
    valuing diversity, 91-92
Psychological processes,
        intercultural training and, 150-
        152
    anxiety reduction, 150, 151
    correcting misattributions, 150,
        152
    creating empathy, 150, 151
    decreasing perceived symbolic
        and realistic threats, 150, 151-
        152
    increasing perceived similarities,
        150, 151
    increasing self-regulation, 150
    modeling and reinforcing positive
        behaviors, 150
    reducing cultural ignorance, 150,
        151
    reducing value-behavior
        discrepancies, 150, 152
Psychological processes, intergroup
        dialogues and, 117-121
    anxiety reduction, 103, 117, 120-
        121, 127
    changing attitudes/subjective
        norms, 117, 127
    creating superordinate groups,
        117, 120, 127
    creating value-behavior
        discrepancies, 117
    dissonance, 103, 117, 118, 127
    egalitarianism/fairness, 118-119
    empathy, 103, 117, 119, 127
    humanizing outgroups, 117, 119-
        120, 127
    intergroup contact, 117
    self-disclosure, 103, 117-118, 127,
        272
Psychological processes, intergroup
        relations and, 42-44

changing attitudes/subjective norms, 43
correcting misattributions, 43
counteractive expectancies, 43
creating cognitive empathy, 43
creating emotional empathy, 43
creating superordinate groups, 43
differentiating outgroup, 43
emphasizing multiple identities, 43
increasing perceptions of similarity, 43
modeling positive intergroup behaviors, 43
reducing threat, 43
Psychological processes, moral and values education and, 211, 230-232
changing attitudes/subjective norms, 211
counteracting expectancies, 211
implementing conditions for positive contact, 211
modeling/reinforcing positive behaviors, 211
Psychological processes, multicultural education and, 63-68
in integrated settings, 66-68
in segregated settings, 64-66

Racism, newer theories of, 26
Realistic group conflict theory, 27, 28, 29
Recategorization, 21
Resolving Conflict Creatively program, 194
Robinson, Jackie, 6
Robinson Behavioral Inventory, 250

School Development Program, 213-214
Segregation:
housing, 11
school, 6, 11

Self-fulfilling prophecies, 39
Shoney, 76
Shoreham-Wading River Middle School (Long Island), 214
Slavin, Robert, 158
Slavin techniques, 157, 158-160, 179
Cooperative Integrated Reading and Composition (CIRC), 159, 171
Student Teams-Achievement Divisions (STAD), 158-159, 160, 171
Team-Assisted Individualization (TAI), 159, 160, 171
Teams-Games-Tournament (TGT), 158, 159, 160, 171
Social-compunction theory, 37
Social-dominance theory, 27, 28, 29, 44
Social-identity theorists, 44-45
Social-identity theory, 27, 28-29, 30
cooperative learning techniques and, 176
Social-interdependence theory, 199
Social-learning theory, 32, 231
Social psychological theory, 233
Society for Human Resource Management, 78
Statistical analyses, 253-254, 261
Stereotypes, 19, 35-40, 45, 93
activation/maintenance, 37-38
creating overgeneralized, 153
definition, 35-36
functions, 36
negative, 35, 36, 39, 120, 205, 231
origins, 36
undermining, 175
Stereotyping, 13, 17, 35, 44, 69, 151, 283, 284
reducing, 175
See also Stereotypes
Stereotyping reduction processes, 38-40, 272
correcting misattributions, 39-40, 45

counteracting expectancies, 38, 39, 45

creating superordinate groups/ emphasizing multiple identities, 38, 45

differentiating outgroup, 40, 45

using self-regulation, 38, 39, 45

Study circles, 108-109

Study Circles Resource Center (SCRC), 108, 109

Subjective culture, 140

Subtyping, 40

stereotype preservation and, 38

Superordinate groups, creating, 21, 29, 31, 38, 43, 45, 117, 120, 127

Symbolic racism, 152

Symbolic-racism theory, 26, 27, 29, 44

Systematic observation, 243-244, 260

advantages, 244

coding schema, 243-244

disadvantages, 244

Texaco, 76

Theory of planned behavior, 231

Theory of reasoned action, 40-41, 45, 91, 274

Third-party consultation, 181, 206, 267

community-based, 183, 185

in organizational settings, 188, 190-191

See also Interactive Conflict Resolution (ICR)

Threat:

decreasing perceived symbolic and realistic, 150, 151-152

reducing, 29, 30, 43, 45

See also Integrated-threat theory

Town meetings, 181, 186-187, 206-207

community-based, 183

research on, 197

Trainers, intergroup relations:

issues for, 279-280

Transformative mediation, 200

Truman, Harry S., 6

U.S. population, changes in racial/ ethnic composition of, 12

Ultimate attribution error, 34

United Farmworkers (UFW) grape boycott, 7

University of Alabama, integration of, 7

Value-behavior discrepancies:

creating, 117

making explicit, 29, 30, 45

reducing, 150, 152

Values clarification/education programs, 212, 224-226, 229, 233, 235

criticism of, 225

research on, 225-226

Values clarification subprocesses, 224

Values inquiry model, Banks's, 226

Values reflective approach, 226

Victim blame, 66

Voice of America, 76

Voting Rights Act (1964), 7

Wallace, George, 7

Watts Riots, 8

Web sites, hate group, 11

Win-win bargaining, 189

Workplace discrimination complaints, 75

Wounded Knee siege, 8

Xerox Corporation:

diversity training program, 84

ABOUT THE AUTHORS

Cookie White Stephan is currently Professor of Sociology at New Mexico State University. She has also taught at the University of Texas at Austin. She received her PhD in psychology from the University of Minnesota in 1971. Her major research focus is intergroup relations. Currently, much of her research tests a model of the causes of prejudice, including prejudice directed toward the major minority groups in the United States, Whites, immigrants to the United States, and citizens of other cultures. She also researches the ethnic identity of mixed-heritage people, attachment theory, and the cultural expression of emotion. She is author of many articles and four other books in sociology and psychology, including *Intergroup Relations* (1996, with W. G. Stephan).

Walter G. Stephan is currently Professor of Psychology at New Mexico State University. He received his PhD in psychology from the University of Minnesota in 1971. He has taught at the University of Texas at Austin and has published numerous articles on attribution processes, cognition and affect, intergroup relations, and intercultural relations. He coauthored a textbook in social psychology and coedited two other books. His most recent book is *Reducing Prejudice and Stereotyping in Schools* (1999). In 1996, he won the Klineberg award for intercultural relations, which is given by Division 9 of the American Psychological Association.